SOONER CENTURY

100 GLORIOUS YEARS OF OKLAHOMA FOOTBALL

Authored by J. Brent Clark

1895　　1995

Quality Sports Publications

The intrepid university football squad
of 1896 went undefeated, posting
two wins over Norman High School.

SOONER CENTURY

Cover and dustjacket designed by
Mick McCay

All photographs compliments of:
OU Athletic Department
OU Western History Collection
The Daily Oklahoman
The Norman Transcript
Ned Hockman
Lisa Hall
Cathy Davis
J. Brent Clark

For information write:

Quality Sports Publications
#24 Buysse Drive
Coal Valley, Illinois 61240
(309) 234-5016
(800) 464-1116

Duane Brown, Project Director
Melinda Brown, Designer
Susan Smith, Editor

Printed in the U.S.A.
by
Richardson Printing Co.
Kansas City, Missouri

ISBN 1-885758-04-9

Contents

To: *Patrick and Peter*

"WE KNOW WE BELONG TO THE LAND
AND THE LAND WE BELONG TO IS GRAND!"

– FROM *OKLAHOMA!*
WORDS AND MUSIC BY
RICHARD RODGERS & OSCAR HAMMERSTEIN

Acknowledgements

A book like *Sooner Century* is written from the heart. And not just the author's heart. All manner of folks ultimately look deep into their own hearts in order to contribute. Through their memories, through their colorful expressions, through revelations of their cherished hopes, a treasured written and pictorial record is shaped. In addition, there are those who have the vision to see the historic value of such a project. These individuals provide financial support and moral support. They are all, in the end, indispensable to the production of such a book.

Sooner Century is, then, a product of dozens of individuals who heard about it and somehow contributed

to it. Leon Cross, Port G. Robertson and Harold Keith have, for decades, supported anything which benefits the University of Oklahoma and its athletic teams. It's no surprise, then, that they devoted their time and energies to the fashioning of *Sooner Century*. Mr. Keith's prior writings, including *Oklahoma Kick-Off* and *Forty-Seven Straight* were marvelous resources. From these books I have borrowed, with deepest respect. Former OU President George L. Cross contributed mightily to *Sooner Century* by virtue of his outstanding work, *Presidents Can't Punt*.

The wonderful photographs which are such an

important part of *Sooner Century* were meticulously accumulated under the able supervision of Ned Hockman, a true legend in the field of sports photography. Freelance photographers Lisa Hall and Cathy Davis cheerfully shared their work and proved that Sooner pride is, indeed, infectious. At the OU Western History Collection, curator John Lovett was an invaluable asset. At *Sooner Magazine*, editor Carol Burr was a tremendous help. David Lanier, sports editor, *Norman Transcript*, was great to work with as well.

Financial support for *Sooner Century* was made available by The Touchdown Club of Oklahoma and *The Daily Oklahoman*. Rick Knapp, executive director of The Touchdown Club, had the perseverance to support *Sooner Century* over many months. For that, I am extremely grateful. Other Touchdown Club members who were critical to the success of the project were John E. "Buddy" Leake, Tony Calvert, Greg Mahaffey, Henry Browne, Jr., Henry Browne, Sr., G.T. Blankenship, Jim Everest, Tom Dulaney, Gordon Brown, Richard Norville, Ed Cook, Charlie Coe, Boots Hall, Mickey Imel, Dee Replogle, Jr., Phil Kidd, Jr., D.L. Rippeto and Jakie Sandefer.

At *The Daily Oklahoman*, *Sooner Century* was first recognized as a viable publication endeavor by Edmund O. Martin, general manager. For weeks and weeks on end, Dick Dugan, marketing services manager, provided encouragement, guidance and assistance. The project was heartily embraced by Ed Kelley, managing editor. Carol Campbell, library manager, and her entire library staff later opened files, and doors, in a genuine desire to help make *Sooner Century* a splendid success.

University of Oklahoma President David L. Boren gave generously of his time and talents to prepare a foreword for *Sooner Century* and to embrace the book on behalf of the university. In addition, OU chief legal counsel Fred Gipson and assistant legal counsel Larry Naifeh are commended for shepherding *Sooner Century* along on its way to fruition. At the University of Oklahoma Foundation, executive director Ron D. Burton assisted in making the publication of *Sooner Century* an official, and significant, university achievement.

Within the OU Athletic Department, athletic director Donnie Duncan not only prepared his own foreword, but also led a group of dedicated individuals who honored me with their trust and confidence. Assistant athletic director John Underwood, licensing director

Danny Davis, sports information director Mike Prusinski and assistant SIDs Larry McAlister and Dustin Strait assisted immeasurably, as did Mike Treps. Secretary Betty Klima was always there to pitch in as well and to do so with limitless patience and joy. Special thanks go to assistant SID Debbie Copp for showing me the way on more than one occasion. Warmest of thanks goes to assistant athletic director Don Jimerson for hanging in there with *Sooner Century* all the way.

An old and valued friend, Paul Massad, director of OU Alumni Relations, went out of his way to insure that *Sooner Century* received the attention he believed it deserved.

There are several people, who by specific acts of professionalism and kindness, made *Sooner Century* a true team effort. Berry Tramel contributed editorially to the project, adding his valuable insights as well as his remarkable writing skills. Cathy Bark labored long to locate the resources needed to produce an exemplary book. Lindy Robinson performed outstanding work at the word processor over many months and many drafts.

I am, of course, indebted to Duane Brown and Melinda Brown at Quality Sports Publications. They gave encouragement. They believed in the project. In short, they shared the dream of producing the finest collegiate football history ever written.

There are others who cannot be overlooked. Dozens of Oklahoma Sooner faithful, too numerous to name here, sent me photos and letters. Much of what was submitted has made its way into these pages. To all of them, I offer my profound thanks. Steve and Susy Calonkey opened their Norman home to me many evenings, not because of *Sooner Century*, but just because that is the kind of friends they are. Bobbie and Orville Rose are fine folks who have always believed there were great things in store for me and helped me believe it myself. Personal, and special, thanks to my dad, J. Neal Clark, who has literally seen it all at Owen Field and allowed me to share it with him. And finally, gratitude is extended to my wife, Margee for her unflagging support and for the inspiration provided by the two finest young men I know, Patrick and Peter Clark.

J. Brent Clark
August 1995

Description of this and preceding pages: (1) Roy "Soupy" Smoot, 1920, & Cale Gundy, 1993; (2 & 3) 1896 team photo; (6) Billy Vessels, Heisman Trophy winner 1952; (7) Steve Owens, Heisman Trophy winner 1969: (8) Billy Sims, Heisman Trophy winner 1978; (9) OU fan with flag, (10) Bennie Owen, coach 1905-26; (11) Bud Wilkinson, coach 1947-63; (12) Barry Switzer, coach 1973-88; (13) University of Oklahoma; (14) Stadium as seen from the Oklahoma Memorial Union clock tower in 1936; (16) Another appearance by the Sooner Schooner; and (18) OU vs KU 1991.

Foreword

Dear Sooner Fan,

I vividly recall a sign on the wall in the University of Oklahoma football offices in 1973 when I joined the OU staff. It stated, "OU's winning tradition will never be entrusted to the timid or the weak." Millions who have watched, supported, or been a part of the Sooners realize that this never has and never will be the case. I believe this is because OU football reflects and represents much of the fabric, will, work ethic and great pride of the state, university and people of Oklahoma.

Six National Championships, 3 Heisman Trophy winners, 122 All-Americans, winning streaks of 47 (the longest in NCAA history) and 31 are the results of a commitment to excellence spanning a century. In 1995, as we remember and celebrate one hundred years of OU football, *SOONER CENTURY: 100 Glorious Years of Oklahoma Football* brings to life memories of thrilling moments, legendary people, the highest achievements and all the other ingredients that are Sooner Football. The stories in this book are about and belong to each person who in the past 100 years has represented, supported or loved the Sooners.

Best regards,

Donnie Duncan
Director of Athletics

Early day broadcasts of Oklahoma football games via Western Union on the Main Street of Norman, which was partially blocked to traffic for the games. The announcer is behind the podium and a makeshift diagram of a field is at second floor level to indicate the progress of the ball up and down the field.

Foreword

August 1995

Football at the University of Oklahoma has been a long and treasured tradition since before the turn of the century. Throughout the past 100 years, OU football has come to mean much not only to our University but to the entire state of Oklahoma.

By this book, *Sooner Century: 100 Glorious Years of Oklahoma Football,* we are reminded of how OU football developed into the institution we know today.

The history of football at this university is full of remarkable people, including Vernon Parrington, one of the first football coaches at OU. In many ways, he embodied the best traits of the scholar-athlete. An outstanding athlete and mentor to young players, he was also a great teacher and educator. During his academic career, he was awarded the Pulitzer Prize for his great work in literary and intellectual history, *Main Currents of Political Thought.*

The story of Bennie Owen, for whom the Oklahoma Memorial Stadium is named, is also important for us to remember. He has been called OU's first authentic legend. In spite of his own physical handicaps, he built a national football power through hard work, character, and instilling excitement for the game in his players.

Coach Bud Wilkinson brought OU football into the modern era of college sports with a string of continuous victories and national championships that will be long remembered by sports fans in the entire country. In many ways, he also set the national standard for coaching, as his advice went beyond the game. He inspired his players to perform their best not only in football but also in life, no matter what the outcome.

Many other coaches throughout OU football history, including Luster, Tatum, Switzer, Gibbs, and Schnellenberger, the assistant coaches, trainers, academic counselors, and sports information officers – along with exceptional talent, tenacity and high standards – all helped make Sooner football what it is today. Oklahoma's football players today are recognized as outstanding athletes and students with one of the highest graduation rates in our conference and region.

Beyond the stories of the great moments and legendary figures in Sooner football told in the following pages, one idea seems to transcend all others: football at the University of Oklahoma has always been a source of great pride and rallying spirit for all Oklahomans. For young men throughout the state, its standards of training, discipline and competition have represented goals to be achieved, and for fans, it has served as a point of pride when other hardships weighed down upon us. Football has held a unique place in the history of the University of Oklahoma, and this book reminds us of that special heritage and of why football brings us all together.

Sincerely,

David L. Boren
13th President of the University of Oklahoma

The Old-Style Game

Chapter One

A coming of morning in Norman, Oklahoma Territory, early September, 1897. A distant rumble and a faint vibration of steel rails harken the approach of a steam locomotive. The engine belches fire and groans to a halt at the prairie station.

A train steward steps down on the platform and deposits a small, worn leather bag out of harm's way. The bag bulges with only a few personal items – the rest, books.

Presently, a bespectacled, trim young man appears out of the train doorway, then gingerly steps to the ground. Vernon Lewis Parrington has arrived on an overnight coach from Emporia College, Kansas, to take up his post as instructor in English literature at the University of Oklahoma.

Parrington wrote some years later for the university yearbook, *The Mistletoe,* about his arrival. "I had never been in Oklahoma, and as I got off the train that September day, what lay before my eyes was disheartening. The afternoon became insufferably hot and dry. A fierce wind that was blowing from the southwest in great dust clouds – that I have gotten better acquainted with since – greeted me inhospitably. I asked the way to the university and set out along the plank walk that the heat had drawn the nails half out of. My mind was busy with the weather, the ugliness of the new little town, the bareness of the streets and yards. As I came on to the campus I stopped – *this* was the university! The word had always meant – well, something very different to me. A single small red brick building – ugly in its lines and with a wart atop – a sort of misshapen cross between a cupola and a dome – stood in a grove of tiny elms."

This young English instructor would, years later, win a Pulitzer Prize for his work in English literature. But his arrival in Norman that warm September day in 1897 marked the true arrival of college football to the Oklahoma Territory and its university.

Parrington had been exposed to the crude, primitive, yet developing game of football while studying at Harvard. The old-style game had little resemblance to the modern game. The earliest footballs were very nearly round in shape and were fashioned from the bladders of slaughtered hogs. These hog bladders were inflated by blowing air through a quill. Even today, the football is often referred to as a "pigskin." The first intercollegiate game was played between Princeton and Rutgers in the fall of 1869, almost twenty years before V.L. Parrington arrived at the University of Oklahoma. The game itself was an outgrowth of class fights which were prevalent whenever and wherever college matriculators gathered. The old-style game reflected the dual influences of rugby and soccer. Typically, 25 players to a side removed their jackets, rolled up their sleeves, and laid siege to the opposition. Slugging, shoving, kicking and boiling tempers were common. The object was to navigate through the sweating, heaving massed opposition and kick the hog bladder between goal posts set 25 feet apart at either end of a 140-yard-long field. The first team to score six goals was declared the winner. Rutgers won that first game, 6-4. The unstructured free-for-all which was undertaken that fall day eventually gave way to refinement. Football teams sprouted on many Eastern college campuses. Harvard and Yale had an already-established rivalry in the sports of rowing and baseball and so it was inevitable that they would seek to earn the added respect of their respective rivals on some verdant meadow. In 1875, representatives of the two schools met in Springfield, Massachusetts, to organize a football game. Yale representatives favored soccer rules while Harvard representatives proposed rugby-style rules. Harvard's preference

A relaxed V.L. Parrington contemplates the value of literature and perhaps, football, in his university quarters, 1897.

dominated the negotiations, a development which would greatly impact the future of modern football. Running with the ball, the scrum, lateral passing, tackling, and fifteen players to a side proved advantageous to Harvard, which won the first Harvard-Yale game, 4-0. Moreover, the Harvard success prompted other college teams to embrace the Harvard rules. American football was taking on a new look.

The Game Takes Shape

Innovation and experimentation influenced the old-style game for the next several seasons. A convention of school representatives convened, again in Springfield, Massachusetts, in October 1880, to consider new wrinkles and modifications and to attempt to standardize the rules of the exciting and expanding game. Yale's Walter Camp spoke up. He proposed that a team have undisputed possession of the ball in a so-called "scrimmage." A team would then be able to design and execute plays, improvise and introduce tactics. Football would become a miniature war game. While Walter Camp would conceive of many more rules for the conduct of a football game, it was the concept of a line of scrimmage and the resulting system of downs that altered football for all time.

Despite the evolution of the rules of the game, roughness and toughness were considered necessary, if not desirable, parts of the game, just as they are today. The old-style game was criticized as too violent, however. As early as 1884, a Harvard faculty committee investigated the game and reported brutal fist fights and routine bloodletting as endemic to the contests. Casualties were increased from the use of the notorious flying wedge in which players interlocked their arms to move down the field in a phalanx. It was not unusual for the ball carrier to be catapulted by his teammates through the opposing defense.

The popularity of the college game

Smartly attired faculty and students pose in front of the first university building, 1895.

continued to grow. While the seat of power in the college game remained in the East, the game was gaining attention on the campus of the University of Chicago. A young man named Amos Alonzo Stagg had played for Walter Camp at Yale. By 1892, Stagg was fielding football teams in Chicago which were noted for creativity and tactical superiority. Meanwhile, an itinerant young West Virginian named Fielding Yost had made his way to Nebraska, then to Lawrence, Kansas, where he was employed as football coach in 1899. Yost came in contact with a student named Bennie Owen, who had come to Kansas University in 1897 to study Pharmacy and Latin. Owen was fascinated by the game of football, although he weighed a mere 126 pounds. It was Fielding Yost's institution of speed and cunning which permitted Owen to quarterback an all-victorious team in '99, and to embrace college football as a life-long interest. Yost taught Owen and other students of the game to use the stiff-arm, the sidestep and the change of pace. Yost required gatling-gun pace while on the offense and, thus, earned the nickname "Hurry Up." Yost moved on to the University of Michigan, where he became a coaching legend. Bennie Owen would earn his own coaching credentials in his own time and on his own terms.

A clear eye allowed young Benjamin Gilbert Owen to become a visionary regarding the game of football, 1905.

Let's Get Up a Football Team!

But the old-style game, a kind of controlled chaos, is what young V.L. Parrington had observed while at Harvard and that is the game he introduced to a few brave souls in Norman, Oklahoma, in the fall of 1897. Actually, the first football team representing the University of Oklahoma was organized in September 1895, by a handsome, confident lad with compelling gray eyes. His name was John A. Harts. Harts fancied himself an athlete with more than a smattering of bravado. He'd played football on a college team in Winfield, Kansas, and as a school boy growing up north of Wichita. Harts was undoubtedly aware from newspaper accounts that the first organized football game in Oklahoma Territory had taken place a year before, in November

1894, between Oklahoma High School (later Oklahoma City Central High) and a rowdy group of townies billing themselves as the "Terrors." The Terrors had taken a terrible beating in that game.

In any event, when Harts' fellow students brought out an old Spalding football on a golden fall afternoon in Norman, they discovered Jack Harts the athlete. It came as no surprise, then, that the long-haired, brazen young man thereafter declared from his seat in Bud Risinger's barber shop, "Let's get up a football team!" Harts became the team's first captain and coach. Few of the students attending the university in the fall of 1895 had ever seen a football game, since the Oklahoma Territory had only a mere handful of high schools. Of the 148 students registered at the university that fall, 121 were taking high school work. The game of football was a curiosity only, but the glib tongue of Jack Harts ensured a representative attendance at the one and only university game of the season of 1895. Harts himself, in an over-abundance of enthusiasm, had suffered a knee injury in practice and could only hobble along on the sidelines, yelling instructions and encouragement. A North-South gridiron had been laid out on a field of low prairie grass just north of the lone university building. The site is, today, slightly north and west of Holmberg Hall. A single strand of wire fence was strung around the playing rectangle. Team members Joe Merkle and Jap Clapam volunteered teams of horses to haul wagons full of dirt to fill the field's buffalo wallows. On the eve of the contest, Harts discovered he was still two players short of a full team. At the last minute, the resourceful Harts enlisted the barber, Bud Risinger, and Fred

Horse-drawn carriages and horseless carriages surround the playing field at the fairgrounds in Arkansas City, Kansas, as Oklahoma battles a local team comprised of rail hands in the fall of 1898.

Perry, a 26-year-old married man who drove Norman's street sprinkling wagon. Risinger and Perry, representative of Oklahoma pioneers, could not resist Harts' exhortations and leapt into the fray. Neither, of course, was enrolled in the university.

The opponent was from Oklahoma City and was composed of high school students, a few college students from the Methodist College there, and a couple of town toughs. Most importantly, the visiting team had played a game or two prior. The victors drubbed Harts' valiant men, 34-0. The university's first football team, in its first game, neither scored a point nor made a first down. The disconsolate university players trudged back to Risinger's barber shop where they washed up, dressed their wounds, and discussed the merits and demerits of football. "I went out home and climbed in bed," Jap Clapam remembered. "I was too sore to do the chores, but I sure slept good. I was feeling kind of blue, but I had liked the rough physical contact."

That fall day in 1895, Grover Cleveland resided in the White House. Commercial pasteurization of milk had just begun, and a company called Sears Roebuck had opened a mail-order business which was destined to change the way rural America bought its dry goods. Then, however, as now, good folks enjoyed a spirited contest and prepared themselves for the football glories to come. Jack Harts, the university's first coach and team captain, yearned for greater challenges. Yielding to the siren call of high adventure, he left Norman for the Arctic, where he prospected for gold.

University students formed a team of sorts in the fall of 1896, but it was an informal undertaking at best. There was no coach. Two games with Norman High School were arranged, with the university winning both. In the second 1896 game, played west of the campus, the thinly padded players had to, on occasion, jump a frozen road that was rutted so deeply and so firmly by November frost that tumbling to the ground would have been life-threatening.

The 1896 census revealed that the Oklahoma Territory had 275,000 inhabitants; the neighboring Indian Territory, far fewer. Football would have to grow alongside the territory itself. Rural free mail delivery began that year. Book matches became popular. Former baseball star Billy Sunday began his career as an evangelist, conducting 300 revivals and being heard by over 100 million people over the next 40 years.

Jack Harts is credited with introducing the game of football to his university classmates and Norman town folk, 1895.

Parrington Arrives

To the extent that interest in the university's football fortunes had dipped in 1896, that interest was rekindled with the arrival of V.L. Parrington in September 1897. A year earlier, a serious-minded young man, Columbus C. Roberts, had arrived in Norman from distant Grant County, intent upon obtaining an education. "Lum," as he was known to his friends, intended to finance his way through the university with funds obtained from a loan on his frontier farm. Lum Roberts was 26 when he arrived on the campus, mature enough, it was said, to temper the young football hotbloods who surrounded him, yet young and strong enough to produce on the playing field. Roberts was, in fact, elected team captain four consecutive years, 1897-1900. This was a notable milestone in itself.

In more contemporary times, the family of C.C. "Lum" Roberts has provided large quantities of historic university memorabilia to the OU Western History Collection. While the early university football teams were peopled by raw-boned, boot-shod, shy young fellows, their coach was a well-groomed, genteel, eccentric bachelor. Parrington wore matching tweeds, well-pressed and elegant. He chain-smoked his own hand-rolled cigarettes, much to the consternation of Norman's church folk. Parrington believed that football contributed to the well-rounding of the college man, and so he enthusiastically accepted university President David Ross Boyd's assignment as football coach.

In quiet street corner conversations along Norman's Main Street, townspeople whispered that the university football team was going to have a Harvard man as coach. Everyone knew that the game of football had been shaped at that venerable old institution back in Boston. The Katzenjammer Kids cartoons were arousing interest in the local newspaper. Gentlemen Jim Corbett had won the heavyweight boxing title in the first boxing match to be photographed with moving pictures. Under president Boyd's able leadership, the university's revenue for the year was a paltry $23,000.

Parrington's football material was eager but without much understanding of the developing game of football. There were never more than 15 members on the team. Equipment in those days was virtually nonexistent. Each man was responsible for finding his own. What there was, was homemade. Crude leather cleats were nailed to heavy brogans. There were no athletic supporters, which created an additional whimsical element of risk. Not a single man had a helmet, until team member Joe Merkle engaged a pioneer Norman harnessmaker to build him one out of harness leather. The other players simply allowed their hair to grow out so as to afford some minimal protection. Pants were, more often than not, constructed of moleskin, an ancient fabric made of strong cotton fustian. The fabric itself was expected to soften the sting of flying elbows and thrusting knees.

Parrington's debut as the university's first legitimate football coach took place in Norman on Thanksgiving afternoon, 1897, once again against the old Oklahoma City crew which shut out the university in '95. Football remained a game of brute force. There was no forward pass. Five yards gained in three downs resulted in a first down. There was no finesse, no deception. Players simply crouched low in their stances, grunting in their lunges forward against their adversaries. To his credit, Parrington employed the cross-blocking techniques he'd seen at Harvard. The disciplined university team controlled the line of scrimmage. With touchdowns counting four points, the university coasted to a 16-0 victory. All through the second half, enthusiastic varsity rooters scaled the fence encircling the field in order to embrace the varsity players. President Boyd found himself in the midst of the jubilation, alternating between presidential rectitude and momentary ecstasy. Parrington's scrappers played only one more game in '97, two other games having to be canceled because of snow.

On December 31, the university team played its first college game of all time and also took its first trip away from Norman. The game was against Kingfisher College in Guthrie, at Guthrie's fairgrounds, not far from the Oklahoma territorial capitol. The contest was commenced by the crack of a .45 caliber revolver. Midway through the second half, the Logan County sheriff, who had never seen a football game, arrived on the scene and mistook the game for a drunken brawl. With gun drawn, he ran on the field and stopped play. Only President Boyd's remonstration with the sheriff allowed the resumption of play. The varsity defeated Kingfisher 17-8 and V.L. Parrington had completed the first year of his coaching tenure undefeated.

Enrollment on campus was on the rise, with 359 registered. The town of Norman was growing ever closer to the campus. President Boyd had planted beautiful trees along the campus drives. The *Umpire* student paper reported with pride, "The ivy on the north side of the university has reached the second story window." Prospects for the future at the University of Oklahoma seemed limitless.

Arkansas City, Kansas, was, in the fall of 1898, a freight terminus for the Santa Fe railroad. As such, the town attracted youthful, rock-hard rail hands who had come to Arkansas City seeking work in the rail yards of the town. Football was their off-hours entertainment. In fact, the town had supported a local football team for several years. V.L. Parrington arranged a game for his varsity team to be played in Arkansas City. Parrington's team in '98 was principally made up of new recruits, including Tom Tribbey of Burnett, Oklahoma. Tribbey weighed in at 230 pounds and complemented his size with strength and speed. John Hefley, an experienced guard from the previous year's team, had taken a position teaching at a one-room school southwest of Moore. Hefley's affection for football was such that, while he couldn't come to practice, he always came in on the day of the game, riding his bicycle, or driving a buggy pulled by a pair of ponies. The varsity found the town abuzz when they stepped off the train in Arkansas City. Mule-drawn carts transported players and spectators to the fairgrounds for the game. Preparation for the game had included burning off a portion of the tall buffalo grass. The resultant soot soon covered the game's combatants from head to toe. Parrington's troops were in superior physical condition, which proved to be the deciding factor. The Merkle brothers, Fred and Joe, led the way for the varsity. Joe Merkle scored the game's only touchdown on the team's favorite play, the tackle-around. The final score was 5-0 in favor of the varsity.

Substitutions in the old-style games were rare, because under the rules of the day, once a player was withdrawn, he could not re-enter the game. Additionally, early-day players took fierce pride in being able to play an entire game. To do otherwise was thought to compromise one's manhood. Bumps and bruises, breaks and sprains, lost teeth and split lips were accepted as part of the game's grand design.

After the Arkansas City game, the varsity players were introduced to the first custom-built bathtub they had ever seen. The victors delighted in jumping into the porcelain wonder two at a time to wash away the soot and grime.

The next day, when the triumphant varsity emerged from the train at the Norman depot, an old gentleman stood pensively next to his horse-drawn wagon which was filled with fresh straw. The old gentleman was John Merkle, father of the Merkle brothers. The old man had feared the worst for his boys, and had prepared a way to transport their broken bodies home. The Merkle boys had played the game brilliantly and without serious injury. They rode home with their dad on the buckboard, smiling broadly.

The first college game of all time at Norman was played Thanksgiving afternoon against Fort Worth University. A bone-chilling southeast wind greeted both teams. The start of the game was delayed until spectators from Oklahoma City and Purcell could arrive. The varsity had made great strides since the season opener. The team's crushing power was evidenced early despite the best efforts of the lighter Fort Worth team. After scoring a solo touchdown in the first half, the varsity quickly demoralized the visitors early in the second half. The varsity prevailed 24-0, in what proved to be the final game of the season.

Crimson Cloth and Rousing Cheers

While football was inexorably gaining in popularity, oratorical contests were far more significant to the student body in general. Guthrie's Brooks Opera House hosted the finest oratorical teams from the Oklahoma Territory for a spirited, annual competition. Noisy partisans from the four corners of the territory roused the crowds with clever yells. Partisans from the university proudly contributed the following:

"Hi! Rickety! Hoop-te-do!
Boomer! Sooner! Oklahoma U!"

A committee of faculty members appointed by President Boyd selected crimson and cream as the university colors. Students found pieces of crimson cloth to sew to their jacket lapels. Pride in the University of Oklahoma competitive successes was developing signs of permanence.

The Spanish-American War had erupted in 1898. News reports of Teddy Roosevelt's Rough Riders and his charge up San Juan Hill in Cuba spurred a nationalistic frenzy. Roosevelt's victories and the resultant end to the war brought Cuba its independence. Closer to home, it brought Parrington's football team its first nickname, the Rough Riders.

There were no rules of eligibility in the old-style game, although a fair inference was that a university's football team should be composed of mostly enrolled students. The Oklahoma Territory was, as the turn of the century approached, a special place where folks pitched in to help. It was a day when a football team's coach might play as well as coach if the need arose. Clyde Bogle was representative of the football players of his day. A Norman native, he would arise at 4 o'clock in the morning, milk his dairy cows for his own dairy, ride into the campus on horseback to attend classes, practice football, then ride his horse home for the evening milking. There were not many academic prospects in the fall of '99, for the demands on frontier youth were formidable just in trying to put food on the family table.

The Oklahoma Rough Riders were gaining followers nonetheless. On October 20, the Kingfisher College team from Guthrie visited Norman. Parrington introduced a Harvard maneuver, which was dubbed the "tackle back" alignment. The formation was little more than a designed battering ram with the tackle moving off the line of scrimmage, then being fed the ball by the quarterback and then being pushed from behind by the entire backfield. Kicking, slugging, hair-pulling, spitting, biting and poking were expected. The varsity dominated the game, winning 39-6.

The best player the varsity attracted to the old-style game showed up on campus that November. His name was Fred Roberts, a 185-pound farm boy and a cousin of Lum Roberts. Roberts was muscular and powerful with bronze hide, all a result of his years laboring in the farm fields. Roberts demonstrated his talents on the practice field, utilizing a sledge hammer stiff-arm and amazing nimbleness. He was the first Oklahoma player ever to cut back to the open field while running with the ball. Some two weeks after the Kingfisher game, the Rough Riders met the University of Arkansas at Shawnee. The game was played in a drizzle, and despite the cold and muddy conditions, the play was especially spirited. Fred Roberts impressed players and spectators alike with his running skills. The Rough Riders wore down the Arkansas squad and eventually prevailed, 11-5.

The season finale was against the town rascals from Arkansas City, Kansas, who traveled to Norman on Thanksgiving afternoon. The Railroaders from the north had improved dramatically from the year before, adding both talented players and innovative plays. The Railroaders surprised the varsity in building a 17-5 lead before Fred Roberts broke free for a stunning 70-yard touchdown run. Bill Owen, a defensive halfback for Arkansas City, recalled Roberts' run. "The Norman crowd, which had broken out on the edge of the field, made a lane for him. They were hitting me in the seat of the pants with their umbrellas as I tried to hem him in along the sidelines. I left my feet and dove for him, but only touched his heel. He was a wildcat, fast and good." The game ended with Arkansas City winning, 17-11. It was the varsity's first defeat in four years and the first ever defeat for Coach Parrington. The disappointed Oklahoma team ended its season, but spirits were hoisted high by the announcement of a scheduled game in 1900 against the University of Texas.

Fans and the merely curious were all handed yell cards at the gate on game days, courtesy of The Sooner Rooters, 1910.

The life expectancy of American males in 1900 was 48 years and for females, 51 years. Football, by necessity, was merely a pleasant diversion from the harsh realities of life on the prairies of Oklahoma Territory. William McKinley was reelected President with the grandly popular Theodore Roosevelt his vice president. Carrie Nation preached the virtues of abstinence from alcohol. L. Frank Baum, an unsuccessful writer, published an obscure volume called *The Wizard of Oz.*

The University of Oklahoma Rough Riders of 1900 were the first to play against the University of Texas.

The Red River Rivalry Begins

Fred Roberts had been lured away from Norman to play at Washburn University in Topeka, Kansas, by that school's first head football coach, Bennie Owen. Fred Merkle had retired from football. His brother Joe had married and begun farming. These losses were harmful to the prospects of the Rough Riders of double-ought. The prospect, however, of the first ever football game against the University of Texas generated intense interest across the Oklahoma campus. Parrington's charges boarded a chair car at the Norman train depot for the 400-mile, overnight journey to Austin. Clyde Bogle brought along a milk can full of his own dairy's sweet milk. Teammate Harve Short picked a sack of apples from his family's orchard. The team arrived in Austin fatigued, yet full of fight. The Texans, however, had been playing organized football two years longer than had the Oklahomans.

Seasoning and rest proved decisive for the Texans, as they triumphed, 28-2. A series rivalry of profound significance to the history of collegiate football, however, had begun. A week later, a team from Chilocco Indian School visited Norman. The Rough Riders rebounded from their stinging loss to Texas by shutting out the visitors 27-0. Varsity player John Hefley's opponent across the line played the entire game wearing a broad-brimmed western hat. The aggressive play by Hefley including grabbing the opponent's hat by the brim with both hands and pulling it down over the fellow's eyes, impairing his vision and neutralizing his play.

A team comprised of soldiers from Oklahoma's military outpost, Fort Reno, visited Norman on October 24, wearing blue army uniforms. The out-classed soldiers were whipped 79-0. When the Rough Riders traveled to Guthrie to play Kingfisher College two weeks later, defense prevailed as the game ended in a 0-0 tie. Oklahoma hadn't been blanked in five years. The final game of the season was played in Arkansas City against the revenge-minded Railroaders. The town toughs from Arkansas City were no match for the varsity on this day, as Oklahoma won 10-0 and completed its season by shutting out its last four opponents.

A new indoor game invented by a young gym teacher from Springfield, Massachusetts, named Dr. James Naismith was introduced on the Norman campus in 1900, although basketball would not appear as a varsity sport until 1906. The first class fight on the Norman campus took place, featuring a tug-of-war between college enrollees and students of the preparatory school. An infectious school spirit was manifesting itself across the Oklahoma campus of 393 students.

President Boyd assigned the serious-minded V.L. Parrington additional teaching responsibilities in the fall of 1901. As a result, Parrington reluctantly relinquished his post as football coach. Parrington's contributions to football fortunes had been tremendous, not only for his instruction in cross-blocking, bruising power plays and tackle-arounds, but also for his personal example of courtesy and gentlemanly conduct towards opponents and officials. He pro-moted game publicity, student support and fellowship with opponents. The scholarly Parrington, for which Parrington Oval on the Norman campus is named, laid a significant portion of the foundation for the giant strides in Oklahoma football which were to come.

Oklahoma's competitive concerns fomented by the departure of Coach Parrington and three men out of the '00 backfield were laid to rest when Fred Roberts was persuaded to return to the campus as player/coach. Like the two previous varsity coaches, Roberts had no coaching experience at all. Roberts did however, command respect from all with whom he came in contact. Most of the 1900 squad returned, including the old war horse, John Hefley, who had graduated but couldn't stay away from the gridiron.

It was an exciting time to reside in the Southwest. Oil was discovered at Spindletop, Texas, a true harbinger of the vast oil industry which would soon dominate the whole of the region. President McKinley was killed by an assassin's bullet in Buffalo, New York, with the old Rough Rider, Teddy Roosevelt, assuming the presidency. U.S. citizenship was granted to the noble members of the Five Civilized Tribes.

The Oklahoma team rode to Austin in Pullman cars for the first time. Most of the team members found it difficult to sleep despite having the luxury of sleeping berths with crisp white linens on them. One team member, Alex Clements, recalled, "We used horse collars for shoulder pads that year and nearly everybody wore shin guards." The two teams squared off on October 19, offering vastly different styles of play. Oklahoma plowed through the Longhorn line, while Texas backs skirted the ends, often employing a fake. Despite Fred Roberts' outstanding running, the Longhorns prevailed, 12-6.

The varsity sought to offset the expense of traveling to Austin by scheduling a game against Baylor at Waco on the return trip, a mere two days later. Despite the considerable fatigue incurred at Austin, Oklahoma rose to the occasion and walloped the lighter Baylor squad by the score of 17-0. The Baylor team had never witnessed a football player of the caliber of Fred Roberts. His savage play led to several penalties which were more a tribute to Roberts' enthusiasm than a punishment for bad behavior. Following the squad's return to Norman, they made short work of Fairmont College of Wichita, Kansas, by a tally of 42-0 and disposed of old rival Kingfisher College 28-6.

Mark McMahan, a disciple of the Texas style of play, coached the university to winning seasons in 1902-1903.

A return game with Texas loomed large as Thanksgiving Day approached. It was the first time the Longhorns had every played a football game in Oklahoma Territory. An estimated 1,200 spectators turned out on a perfectly golden autumn afternoon to witness the battle. Many in the crowd were transplanted Texans who had migrated to the territory for the Land Run of '89.

Texas employed an efficient and potent strategy in the game, a product of a longer, tougher schedule and advanced techniques. Three fumbles in the second half doomed the Oklahoma squad, which surrendered by a score of 11-0. It was clear that in order to compete with the leading teams in the Southwest, a full-time coach would be required. Fred Roberts had decided somewhat earlier to return to farming. More change for Oklahoma football was in the offing.

In some quarters, it was believed Fred Roberts would, at the eleventh hour, throw down his farm tools and return for more gridiron glory. It didn't happen, so the varsity team played the first three games of the 1902 season without a coach. Enrollment on the Norman campus had grown to 465, resulting in several new players being added to the squad. Few had any experience playing football. When it was learned that one newcomer had played center for Kendall College in Muskogee, he was selected varsity center before a single practice. "You're it," he was told. "The man we were counting on is at Anadarko putting up hay." In the season's first game against a motley crew of boys from Guthrie, the varsity prevailed 62-0. However, a week later in Austin, the Longhorns took the Oklahoma team to school by a count of 22-6.

A week later, the varsity met a group of ex-college players billed as the Texas and Pacific Railroad team. The game was notable for it was the first time an Oklahoma team had ever played at the State Fair of Texas. One member of the Dallas team was Mark McMahan, a disciple of the Texas style of play. The Dallas team defeated its guests from Oklahoma by a count of 11-6. After the game, McMahan visited the Oklahoma team's hotel and asked for the job of coaching the squad. McMahan was hired on the spot for $250 to coach the team for the balance of the season. The new coach quickly energized the Oklahoma football program. He immediately expanded the schedule to nine games, recruited new playing talent, and set out to put the program on sound financial footing. Under McMahan's leadership, the squad rebounded to win five of its remaining six games. By tutoring the team in primitive, yet effective deception, the varsity dispatched Arkansas 28-0. The game was particularly nasty, with one fist fight breaking out and recurrences of slugging. Hostility remained long after the final gun.

Oklahoma's first game of all time in Oklahoma City was played October 29 against a pick-up team calling itself the Oklahoma City Athletic Club. Downtown's Colcord Park boasted a permanent grandstand and reserved carriage parking. The Oklahoma team disposed of its opponent, 30-0. Against Kingfisher College in Norman, McMahan's charges prevailed 15-0. The next game had been eagerly anticipated for weeks. In fact, some of McMahan's more creative plays had been kept under wraps for this next game, to be played in Columbia, Missouri, against the Missouri Tigers. Just before the team was to board the train to Columbia, the mother of star player Chester Reeds refused to let him go. To compensate for the loss, the team called upon old reliable Fred Roberts, who agreed to finish his farm chores early and join the squad en route to Columbia. Despite late heroics by Roberts, Missouri dealt the Oklahoma team a setback by a score of 22-5. Two days later, against Emporia State, in Emporia, Kansas, the varsity limped to a 6-5 victory behind the aggressive play of Roberts and Coach McMahan himself. Back in Norman, McMahan was forced to confess to President Boyd that he had played in the game under the name of Chester Reeds, and that non-student Fred Roberts played as well. While there were no rules of eligibility in place, President Boyd was reflecting the growing sentiment that varsity teams should be composed only of enrolled students. The season finale with Kingfisher College in Norman ended in a Rough Rider victory, 17-0. Only enrolled students played for the varsity in that contest.

Campus life was rapidly changing. Fraternity men wooed sorority girls long after dusk along tree-lined walks. Students fished in the South Canadian and gathered persimmons along its banks. The typical student was changing too. More were coming to campus expecting to matriculate all the way through to a degree. Fourteen degrees would be issued the following year. At the conclusion of the football season in 1902, the first post-season football game was held at the Tournament of Roses in California, with Michigan defeating Stanford, 49-0. In January 1903, the university suffered a grievous loss when the lone

Rudimentary equipment such as shoulder padding and shin guards are in evidence in this photograph of the Rough Riders of 1902.

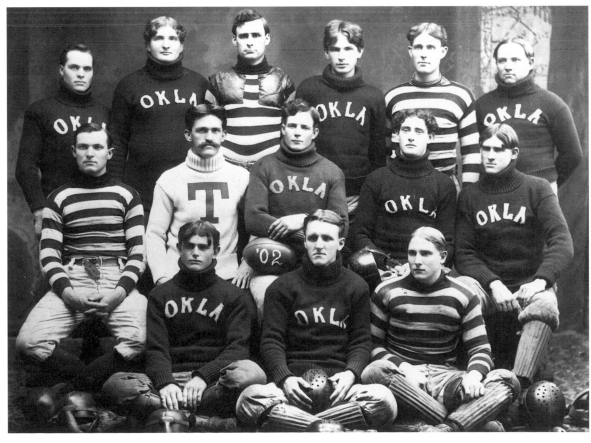

campus building was destroyed by fire. Some of President Boyd's records were saved along with a few precious educational tools such as microscopes. In large part, however, Oklahoma's trappings of its prairie heritage drifted away that evening in billows of lazy, black smoke.

Coach McMahan was as desirous of winning as his coaching predecessors, but he had also set his sights on increasing revenues for the young football program. With that in mind, he arranged a backbreaking schedule of twelve games for the fall of 1903, all played within two months and only two of which were to be played in Norman. It seemed that a financial guarantee from a distant host was the quickest way to ensure positive cash flow. McMahan's 1903 Rough Riders, therefore, spent most of October and November riding on the hard, wooden seats of passenger trains. The varsity defeated the Chilocco Indian team, 38-5 in the opener, in which Chester Reeds scored four touchdowns. A week later, against Kingfisher College, the varsity was held to a 0-0 tie. But against Texas at Austin, the Rough Riders rose up and tied the

The indomitable spirit of Oklahoma survived the fiery destruction of the lone university building, January 1903.

Longhorns 6-6 before meeting the Texas Aggies two days later in Bryan. In that contest, the Rough Riders prevailed 6-0. When the team returned to Norman from the Texas adventure, it was met by a vociferous gaggle of students and townspeople in what constituted the first celebration following a football trip.

The varsity defeated Fairmont College in Oklahoma City's Colcord Park 11-5, then tied Emporia 6-6 in the mud at Norman. The next game was of special import, as it was the first game played against the Kansas Jayhawkers. The Rough Riders boarded the train in Norman at 4:00 a.m. and traveled 14 hours before arriving in Lawrence the following evening.

It was not unheard of in those days for scoundrels to seek to affect the resolve of football teams in order to wager successfully on the outcome of a contest. Coach McMahan religiously subscribed to a healthy training regime, even going so far as to prohibit coffee drinking among his charges. On the eve of the Kansas game, he yielded to the wishes of a couple of players desiring coffee with dinner. The rest of the squad joined the coach in drinking milk. All but the coffee drinkers almost immediately suffered abdominal distress. Someone had adulterated the milk with a drug, causing diarrhea. Weak and suffering from dehydration, the varsity lost to the Jayhawkers, 17-5. On

November 20, the Texas Longhorns visited Colcord Park in Oklahoma City, where they defeated the varsity 11-5, thereafter declaring themselves "Champions of the South." The rigors of the schedule were beginning to take their toll on the Rough Riders. Two days after losing to Texas, the resolute Oklahoma squad boarded a train for Fayetteville, Arkansas. The trip was a disaster. First, there were problems with the train schedule. There was a playing field consisting of uneven frozen muddy terrain punctured by sharp rocks every few feet. Log fires were built around the sidelines to warm the spectators who stood alongside players in a freezing rain. The Rough Riders met a savage group of Razorbacks supported by a vocal, rowdy group of supporters. Officials looked the other way as holding, slugging and biting ensued. In the end, Arkansas won 12-0 and McMahon was denied payment of his financial guarantee by the Arkansas management. Finally, rocks from the playing field rained down on the Rough Riders as they left the field in dejection.

A mere two days later, Oklahoma met the Rolla Miners in Joplin, Missouri. Bloodied but unbowed, the varsity rallied to win 12-6. On Thanksgiving Day, a team from Bethany College, in Lindsborg, Kansas, met the Rough Riders at Colcord Park in Oklahoma City. The Terrible Swedes from Lindsborg were coached by young Bennie Owen. The Swedes played clean football. Moreover, they dazzled the Rough Riders with their innovative tactics. Time and time again, the visitors demonstrated their excellent conditioning, superb execution and sportsmanship. After jumping ahead 12-0, Bethany held on to win 12-10. The final game of the season was against a town team from Lawton. The cocky bunch in Lawton had virtually destroyed

Coach McMahan's distinctive handle-bar moustache reflects the frontier culture among his university football charges of 1903.

a series of town teams leading up to the Oklahoma game. The Rough Riders were battle-weary to be sure. However, with the addition of Fred Roberts, who agreed to play one more game, the Rough Riders were formidable indeed. To the astonishment of everybody present, the varsity struck for four first half touchdowns and led 22-0. Fred Roberts flung his

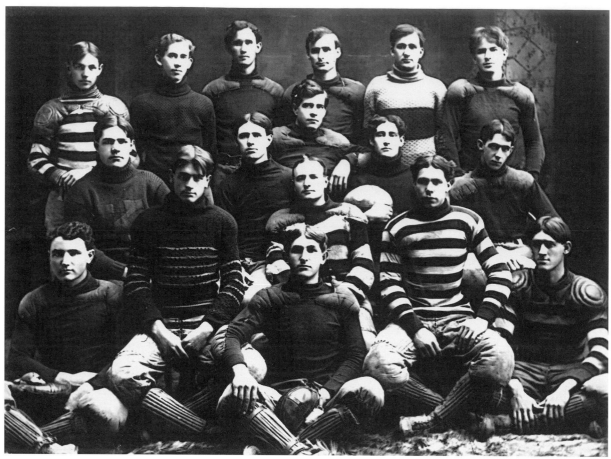

"Buck" Ewing's Rough Riders of 1904 defeated the Oklahoma A & M Aggies 75-0 in the legendary game at Cottonwood Creek.

aging body all over the field, seemingly aware that this was his final exit from organized football. The final score was 27-5. The long season came to an end as Fred Roberts and Coach Mark McMahan earned their respective places in the glorious annals of Oklahoma football.

1904 was a year of note for a variety of reasons. Teddy Roosevelt was elected President. Cy Young pitched the first perfect game in professional baseball history, and a woman was arrested in New York for smoking a cigarette while riding in an open automobile. University President David Ross Boyd had delegated to Dr. Hall, the physical culture instructor, the duties of athletic director in the absence of V.L. Parrington who was studying abroad. It therefore fell to Hall to select a replacement for Mark McMahan as football coach. McMahan had determined to give up coaching and practice law in Durant. Hall selected an acquaintance of his from the University of Chicago Medical School, Fred Ewing. Ewing, it seemed, was steeped in modern football, having played at Knox College in Galesburg, Illinois. Ewing, known as Buck, was dismayed by what he observed the first day of practice. All the key men from '03 had departed. Many of those reporting appeared frail and undernourished. One husky student, Frank Long, was recruited to play even though he had never even seen a football. Ewing did his best to round his charges into shape, utilizing a new tactic, the Minnesota Shift. In the season opener, Kingfisher College visited Norman and, for the third time in five years, managed a scoreless tie. Ewing's Rough Riders traveled to Pauls Valley to play a town team, emerging victorious 33-0. Against Kansas at Oklahoma City, the skillful Jayhawkers triumphed 16-0. A Lawton town team was dispatched 6-0 the following week, setting up one of the most colorful games in Oklahoma football history. On November 5, Oklahoma met Oklahoma A&M College of Stillwater at a neutral site in Guthrie. The game was played at Old Island Park in south Guthrie, hard by the banks of the rain-swollen Cottonwood Creek.

The Legendary Game at Cottonwood Creek

In the old-style game, there were no out-of-bounds on the ends of the playing field. The ball could be retrieved wherever it landed by one team or the other. On a sub-freezing afternoon, Oklahoma and Oklahoma A&M set about to play a football game for the first time. A gale force north wind erupted, enough to cause the formation of ice crystals on tree limbs and creek banks. Early in the game, Aggie fullback B.O. Callahan retreated to punt. Hurrying the swing of his leg, he punted the ball almost straight up, where it was caught by the stiff north wind, sweeping the ball back over Callahan's head. Players from both teams tracked the ball in its retreat until it came to earth along a foot path, where it bounded up again, then descended into the icy creek waters, bobbing like a fisherman's cork. Spectators huffed along behind to observe the spectacle of players from both teams leaping into the seven feet deep, swirling creek waters in frenzied search of the ball. Some suddenly remembered they could not swim and quickly retreated to the bank. Ed Cook, an Oklahoma team member who could swim like a fish, reached the pigskin first. Cook clutched the ball to his chest, swam ashore and touched the ball down in the sand for an Oklahoma touchdown. The university went on to win the game 75-0. Every man on the Oklahoma team scored a touchdown that day. The game itself became a treasured part of Oklahoma football lore and perhaps served as a harbinger for future oddities in games played against the Oklahoma A&M Aggies.

A week later, Oklahoma played the Texas Longhorns at the State Fair of Texas in Dallas, the first game of the interstate rivalry ever played there. As a reflection of Buck Ewing's raw football talent, Texas won the game by a score of 40-10. At Norman the following week, Oklahoma manhandled the Oklahoma Military Institute of Oklahoma City, 71-4. Bennie Owen's Terrible Swedes of Bethany College met Oklahoma at Sportsman's Park in Oklahoma City on Thanksgiving afternoon. Once again, Owen's charges played brilliantly, demonstrating refinements in the game that were foreign to the Rough Riders. Bethany won the game 36-9.

The '04 season came to a close. Buck Ewing was not invited to return as coach. He had in fact, insisted on strict compliance with informal eligibility standards. He had placed a priority on physical conditioning and medical care for his players.

Football was changing dramatically, as were the teams and individuals involved in it. Teams of the nation's southlands were beginning to attract attention. For example, John Heisman had produced a marvelous team at Georgia Tech. Eastern football was losing its grip on domination of the sport it had created. Stagg at Chicago was building a dynasty. Coach Eddie Cochems at St. Louis University was experimenting with a novel tactic – the forward pass. And in tiny Lindsborg, Kansas, a coaching genius named Bennie Owen was packing his belongings for a journey south.

The Bennie Owen Era

Thousands were lined up along the border. Most were on horseback. Others sat high on the wooden seats of covered wagons. Still others rode mules, while a few fidgeted nervously astride rickety bicycles. It has been called the "greatest horse race in history." On September 16, 1893, over six million Oklahoma acres were claimed within a matter of hours. The opening of the Cherokee Strip represented the chance of a lifetime for the hardy settlers gathered along the Kansas border. Land stretching 150 miles east and west and 58 miles from north to south was available to the claimants whose swift transportation could match the fervor of their dreams. Like so much of Oklahoma's rich heritage, there had never in the world been anything quite like this.

A little nubbin of a boy had been born in Chicago in 1874, and had moved with his parents to St. Louis at the age of 12. Baseball was the only game of any importance in those days and St. Louis boasted the famous St. Louis Browns of the old American Association. Little Benjamin Gilbert Owen rarely missed a game. He delighted in seeing the Brown manager, Charlie Comiskey, take charge of his players in dealing out thrashings to the best teams in the country. The competition kindled yearnings in the boy which would never be extinguished. After graduating from St. Louis Clay High School in 1891, Bennie accompanied his parents on the next move, this time to a wheat farm in Sumner County, Kansas, some 12 miles west of Arkansas City, not far from the border of the Oklahoma Territory. Bennie labored hard on the family farm, but found time to attend classes at Hendershot Academy and apprentice to an old country doctor. Bennie, it seems, had determined to become a doctor. In addition, Bennie and his father, George, organized baseball games among the strapping farm boys of the area. By the late summer of 1893, the baseball games were occasionally disrupted by all manner of strangers seeking directions to the border for the great Land Run. Some wished to locate a prospective claim. Others wished to train their horses for the demanding all-out race to come. A few men were intent on laying low in the lush greenery of the Cherokee Strip in order to stake an early, and illegal, claim. These rascals were called "Sooners." Young Bennie had often ridden his black mare, Beauty, into the eerily beautiful Oklahoma frontier in pursuit of jack rabbits. At the age of 17, he was too young to stake a legal claim but that didn't prevent him from making the run. Bennie was astride Beauty and at the ready when, at high noon, the soldiers' rifles cracked. The Great Land Run was on. The thunder of hoofs, the clanging of pots and the slapping of

reins upon hindquarters complemented the swift beating of hearts. Four miles into the Strip, Bennie pulled up and stood astride Beauty in awe of the spectacle – no doubt with a certain longing.

Owen Learns the Game

Meanwhile, back in Arkansas City, the influx of strangers led to the introduction of the game of football. Bennie embraced the sport immediately. In the fall of 1897, Bennie enrolled at the University of Kansas in Lawrence, aiming to learn something about pharmacy and Latin. These subjects would enable him to pursue his dream of a medical career. Although Bennie weighed only 126 pounds, he was drawn to the football practice fields where for the next two years, he broadened his understanding of the game. While at Kansas, he played quarterback on the offense, even though his erstwhile desire was to tackle on the defense. In the fall of 1899, Fielding "Hurry Up" Yost came to Lawrence from Nebraska to become the new football coach. Owen was Yost's quarterback on an all-victorious Kansas squad. Yost was one of football's foremost early-day innovators. While the old-style game had always suggested the application of brute force, Yost preferred speed and finesse. Yost introduced a tactic of rapid play-calling in order to disorient and exhaust the opposition, thus earning his nickname. Bennie Owen was all the while paying close attention. It was not in Owen's nature to join the roguish behavior exhibited by many players of his day. He was reserved and well-behaved in the heat of battle, exhibiting qualities which would serve him well in future years. After three years at Kansas, Owen was without sufficient funds to pursue a medical career, so when he was offered a position as football coach at Topeka's Washburn College, he jumped at the chance.

During the football season of 1900, Owen coached and played quarterback for his Washburn team which won six of eight games. His best player was Fred Roberts, Oklahoma's star halfback from the year before. "Hurry Up" Yost, meanwhile, had moved on to coach at Michigan. Yost, apparently a fine judge of character and coaching talent, brought Owen in to be his assistant in the fall of 1901. Michigan most probably had the best team in the nation that fall. Owen, however, had heard that Bethany College in Lindsborg, Kansas, was looking for a football coach. Big Swedish immigrant boys from the surrounding area flocked to Lindsborg to play for the new energetic young coach. Owen freely experimented with new concepts in the game of football, becoming one of the nation's leading coaches in this regard. It was a labor performed in obscurity, however. The eastern establishment, led by Walter Camp at Yale, had probably not yet heard of Bennie Owen. But it would. During Owen's three-year tenure at Bethany, his winning percentage was an astonishing .916. Moreover, clean play was the signature of Owen teams there, as it was throughout his coaching career.

In the spring of 1905, the junior class at the University of Oklahoma issued its first university yearbook which it called "The Mistletoe." That first effort contained pictures of students and faculty and a whole section devoted

"When Bennie told me to go in, my first reaction was to look around for a weapon. I wanted a club or a shotgun after what I'd been seeing. But I quickly forgot all that and ran right out into the middle of the roughest football game of my life."

– Clarence Reeds
OU Fullback, 1905

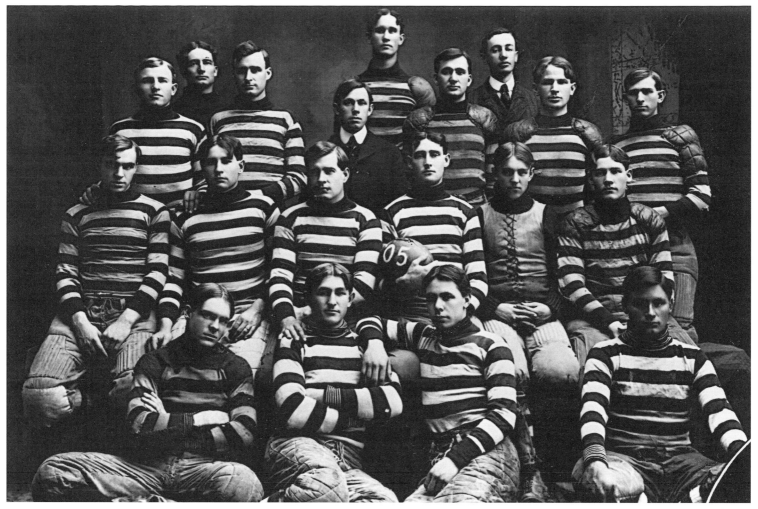

to clever statements about campus personalities. Enrollment in the fall of '05 reached 600. Many among these were preparatory school students. The annual income of the university reached $60,000. A year before, a new cement sidewalk had replaced the boardwalk along University Boulevard that for years had provided passage from the main street of Norman to the campus. Foot traffic and bicycles clogged the promenade. The university catalog spoke of a large athletic field containing a quarter-mile track, a football gridiron, and a baseball diamond. At the side of the football field was a wooden grandstand seating five hundred spectators. The field, later named Boyd Field, lay north and west of the current old Field House, where the University of Oklahoma Press building is now located.

Oklahoma was in search of a new football coach. Finding a good one under the circumstances might have proven difficult. The university's athletic association was in debt. Prior coaches McMahan and Ewing were still owed portions of their salaries. Obtaining the most promising young coach in the Midwest to lead the football program seemed a distant hope. Bennie Owen, however, remembered galloping across the Oklahoma Territory's Cherokee Strip back in 1893, too young to stake a claim. By the fall of 1905, Owen was about to stake a claim not only for himself, but for the coming national prominence of Oklahoma football. Owen accepted the opportunity to coach football at the university under a three-month contract for $900. He found lots of enthusiasm but little else to portend gridiron success. His first squad was composed of light young men lacking in experience. Owen often waxed

Simplicity and a sense of order are evoked, looking south from present day Boyd Street toward the administration building at center which was later destroyed by fire. The frame structure at far left was used for physical education classes, 1906.

nostalgic about the big Swedish boys he had coached at Bethany. One new-comer to the squad, Key Wolf, was an Indian lad of Chickasaw and Scottish descent. Wolf was a veteran of rough-and-tumble Indian tribal games but never American football. With that background, Wolf became an important cog in the Owen wheel of success. In the first game of the season, Owen's team, which was called the "Boomers" for the first time, defeated Central Normal of Edmond 28-0 in a lackluster performance, at least by Owen's stan-dards. A more formidable team from the Haskell Indian Institute visited Boyd Field next. In a game noted for its brawling and foul tactics, the Boomers emerged victorious, 18-12. The University erupted with unprecedented enthusiasm. Coach Owen observed the spectacle with conflicting emotions of glee and embarrassment. Oklahoma's lightweights had fought furiously, only occasionally losing their composure.

Boomer Sooner!

As evidence of the intense interest in football at the University, a stu-dent, Arthur M. Alden, son of a Norman jeweler, took pen in hand to write the lyrics to "Boomer Sooner." Alden freely borrowed from Yale's "Boola Boola" and North Carolina's "I'm a Tarheel Born," to create the University's fight song. About the same time, the athletic association appointed a yell leader and established a megaphone section in the Boyd Field grandstand.

Owen next led his team to Lawrence, Kansas. The Jayhawkers inflict-ed a licking on the Boomers, 34-0, in a game which raised Owen's competitive hackles. Meanwhile, finances continued to burden the Oklahoma football program. As a consequence, Owen scheduled three football games in five days. The Boomers followed the Kansas defeat with a victory over the Kansas City Medics at Kansas City, 33-0; then a loss to Washburn in Topeka two days later by a count of 9-6. The arduous road trip netted a tidy $408 profit for the athletic association.

A short week later, Oklahoma met the Texas Longhorns in Oklahoma City, defeating the Horns 2-0, the University's first victory of all-time over Texas. The most difficult portion of the schedule was over. Kingfisher College was dispatched 55-0 at Kingfisher and Central Normal was manhandled 58-0 a week later. In the season closer, Owen found solace for the long season with a 29-0 victory over the Bethany College Swedes. The game, played in Oklahoma City, set an all-time attendance record for a football game in Oklahoma City. Gate receipts totaled $1,126.50. The University's athletic association had cleared over $900 for the season. Old debts were paid off. "The Great Train Robbery" was playing at an Oklahoma City movie house. Admission to the movie was five cents and Owen had Oklahoma football on the right track.

Teddy Roosevelt had heard enough. Nobody enjoyed a good hard-nosed sporting competition any more than the President. But several college football players had died on the gridiron in 1905, with hundreds more suffering severe injuries. Moreover, the eastern press had seized upon the health scandal of the day, in the person of Typhoid Mary, to whip the general populace into a frenzy. Something had to be done about Typhoid Mary *and* the

Owen's Boomers of '06 welcomed sweeping rule changes in college football, including the legalization of the forward pass.

violence in college football. Roosevelt delivered an ultimatum. Reform the game or it would be banned by presidential edict. The President's sentiments were not shared in all quarters, however. Many of the active players and coaches liked the old-style game and cautioned against tampering with its rough nature. A national rules committee issued a new code in the spring of 1906. Most of the rules changes were directed at ending excessive brutality.

However, in altering the rules of the game, revolutionary changes in strategy resulted. For example, perhaps the most significant change was the legalization of the forward pass. Seven men were required on the line of scrimmage. Ten yards were required to be covered for a first down instead of five. Team

Thin layers of quilted felt were sewn into canvas jackets (pictured) to soften the blows of blocking and tackling incurred by these 1907 University squad men.

members in Norman reacted predictably. They didn't see how it would be possible to make ten yards in three downs. Bennie Owen, the visionary, saw things differently. "Taken all together, I believe the new rules will add a good deal to the game," he said. Owen's Boomers dispatched Central Normal 12-0 in the season opener with few surprises in the style of play. The following week, the varsity overcame Kingfisher College 11-6. The new rules were causing play to be tentative on both sides of the line. A little band of 14 Boomers traveled next to Stillwater to dispatch the Aggies 23-0. The Aggies hadn't quite gotten over the loss at Guthrie's Cottonwood Creek two years earlier. Against Kansas at Lawrence, the Boomers, weary from an all-night train ride, lost to the Jayhawkers 20-4. Against Texas at Oklahoma City two weeks later, Owen's light bodies were dealt a stinging defeat, 10-9. The close score and the quality of play was so good, however, that a bonfire celebration greeted the Boomers' return to campus. At Edmond the following week, the Boomers triumphed over Central Normal, 17-0. A Sulphur town team was thrashed 48-0 as the Boomers prepped for a Thanksgiving Day clash with Washburn. Incessant rains in Topeka yielded a muddy field and a 0-0 tie. Owen's football budget was so depleted that he scheduled a late-season game against a Pawhuska town team comprised almost exclusively of Indians. Eight-hundred Native Americans attended the contest which was followed by a tribal stomp dance. An attractive financial guarantee, however, was afforded the Boomers. After all, the Osage oil boom was under way. The young Indians were almost too much for the varsity. Owen himself was forced to play quarterback in the second half. At age 31, he'd finally played his last college football as the Boomers limped home with a 0-0 tie. The rules changes of 1906 had altered the game forever. In Norman also, major changes loomed on the horizon like thunder clouds.

A vigorous and highly partisan campaign was waged over the long hot summer of 1907 to determine by public vote whether Oklahoma should seek statehood. On September 17, 1907, the voters approved a new state constitution and on November 16, President Roosevelt issued a proclamation admitting the new state of Oklahoma to the union. Partisan debate had suggested that the University would be reorganized with the coming of statehood. President David Ross Boyd had served brilliantly for 16 years, but politics was about to overtake him. Governor Haskell purged the University of President Boyd and a substantial part of the faculty, including Vernon L. Parrington. In spite of the general unrest on campus, the enrollment totaled 790. All but nine of the state's 75 counties of the new state were represented in the student body. Seven Texans attended the university. Many miles away on New York's Broadway, Florenz Ziegfeld produced a saucy stage show called "The Follies" and all over the nation, Mother's Day was celebrated for the first time.

New material for Owen's football team ran largely to backs. One young man, Charley Wantland of Purcell, reported to the first practice carrying his football helmet. Noting that no one else was wearing one, he discreetly hid his in the hedge surrounding Boyd Field and joined the head-banging fearlessly while bare-headed. Owen believed in conditioning, not protective equipment. His Oklahoma teams were known for disdaining all manner of protection. A thin layer of quilted felt was sewn into the canvas jackets of the men to soften the blows of blocking and tackling. There were a few shin guards among the players, but no leather helmets. In support of his policies, Owen never had a player seriously injured in 27 years of coaching.

Owen Loses a Limb

Three days before the first game, on October 16, Owen and his hunting companion, druggist John Barbour, went quail hunting south of Adkins Ford, near where the I-35 South Canadian River Bridge exists today. After a successful day of hunting, the two men loaded up their dogs and weapons for the return to Norman in Barbour's horse-drawn wagon. The dogs' feet were full of burrs. In the resulting commotion, Owen's gun accidentally discharged. Shotgun pellets entered Owen's right arm, severing an artery below the shoulder. Medical treatment could not restore circulation and the arm was amputated. Visitors to Owen's bedside found him far more concerned about the upcoming football season than the loss of his arm. Within days he was back on the practice field and within weeks, he was hunting quail once again, swinging his light 20-gauge Browning automatic into position with one arm. The first two games of the year were walk-overs for the Boomers by the scores of 32-0 against Kingfisher College and 43-0 against the Chilocco Indians at Arkansas City.

However, Owen experienced his only loss in Norman of the first seven years of his regime against Kansas. The final score was 15-0. The game attracted a large crowd, thus ensuring a hefty, welcomed profit for the athletic association. Football, it seemed, was becoming central to the Norman community as well as the University itself. Against Epworth University of Oklahoma City in a game played at Colcord Park, varsity captain and quarterback, Bill Cross, was obligated to take charge. "The field was full of sand burrs. So was the ball. Nobody wanted to handle it. That was one game I had all the indirect passes I wanted." Three games in seven days faced the Boomers. They swamped Oklahoma A&M at Norman on Saturday, 67-0. They then traveled to College Station, Texas, for a Monday game against Texas A&M. The Texas Aggies were a dominating group led by "Choc" Kelly. The final score was 19-0 in favor of A&M. A varsity player had one of his teeth driven through his lower lip. He didn't miss a play. Against Texas the following Saturday, Owen issued one of his rare verbal protestations to the referee, only to learn that the official was coach at the nearby Texas School for the Deaf and couldn't hear a thing. Texas won the game 29-10. On Thanksgiving Day, the Boomers lost to a powerful Washburn team 12-0. The general misfortune of the year came to a close for all but Owen. He had to accept an I.O.U. from the athletic association for $175 of his yearly salary.

Some say the duo of Ralph Campbell and Willard Douglas represented, in the fall of 1908, the finest pair of tackles in the history of Oklahoma football. Campbell, a farm lad from Wellston, weighed 195 pounds and could run the 100-yard dash in 10.2 seconds. He was a seasoned veteran of the gridiron, having played three seasons at Central Normal before enrolling at Oklahoma. Willard Douglas was a squatty, 175-pounder from the wheat-farming community of Nash. Both men devastated opponents with Owen's ingenious deviation from the old tackle-around play. Owen introduced deception to the play. After several fast scoots around end by lighter men, Owen

The squad of '08 became known as the "Sooners." As a precursor to gridiron glories to come, these Sooners defeated the Texas Longhorns 50-0 and were champions of the old Southwest Conference.

had the quarterback fake the hand-off and slip the ball to Campbell or Douglas rumbling the opposite direction. Other team leaders were 200-pound captain Key Wolf, Porter English, and halfback Fred Capshaw. Artie Reeds of the famous Reeds clan got to play in only one game before being felled by the scourge of typhoid fever.

The squad of '08, like all Owen teams, rounded into fine physical condition, scrimmaging everyday, rain or shine. "Coach would let us rest for short spurts, then drive us again," halfback Charley Wantland recalled. Owen introduced brush blocking, a new technique designed to capitalize on speed and quickness. For the first time, Owen's football team was known as the "Sooners." In the season opener against Central Normal, the Sooner line quickly asserted itself and with that, the Sooners won 51-5. Against the Oklahoma A&M Aggies of Stillwater, Owen's charges dominated, 18-0, while incurring several injuries. Against Kingfisher College a week later, a limping Sooner squad emerged victorious, 51-0. The 1908 Kansas team was arguably that school's best of all time. The game was to be played in Lawrence. At the Sooner's send-off in Norman, new University president A. Grant Evans, a

Muskogee minister, read his poem, "When Key Wolf Gets the Ball." Evans, a scholarly introvert, loved football. The KU-OU game of '08 was as fiercely fought as any in the long history of the series. Oklahoma attacked furiously. They threatened to score five times in the first half, only to be rebuffed by the powerful Kansas eleven. In the second half, injuries began to mount on both sides. In the end, Kansas won 11-0, with the teams earning enormous respect for the other. In the first Oklahoma-Kansas State game of all time, the Sooners managed to win decisively, 33-4. "We skinned them way yonder!" Roy Campbell remembered years later. In the first home game of the season, the varsity entertained the Arkansas Razorbacks. A pep club known as the "Sooner Rooters" had their own seating section at Boyd Field. The wily visitors gave the Sooners a tussle before yielding 27-5. This was the first game against Arkansas since the 1903 Oklahoma team had been pelted with stones in Fayetteville. Against Epworth University of Oklahoma City, the biggest challenge was the sand burrs. Ball carriers braced themselves from falling down in order to avoid the painful burrs. "It took me two years to get all the sand burrs out of my back," Charley Wantland recalled. Oklahoma triumphed 24-0. Frigid temperatures greeted the Sooners' guests, the Texas Longhorns, on November 13, 1908. Six hundred fans huddled under blankets, turning shoulders to the knifing north wind. As was the norm for the day, the game was played on Friday, so local merchants could close up shop and attend the game, then re-open Saturday for Trades Day. Oklahoma had beaten Texas just once in ten years, and that by the margin of a safety in '05. In this game, however, Oklahoma overwhelmed the Horns in every department. Side-stepping, vicious blocking and clever deception carried the Sooners to a smashing 50-0 triumph. One normally taciturn university professor bolted onto the field and led a snake dance followed by 300 delirious fans. Risking pneumonia in the icy conditions, the fans concluded by tossing their hats over the south goal post. It was the most decisive defeat, save one, Texas had suffered since beginning football play in 1893. Oklahoma tackles Campbell and Douglas had rushed for 401 yards between them, averaging 11.1 yards per carry. A wild student celebration followed the contest which concluded with a bonfire on Norman's Main Street. Against Fairmont College in a game played in Wichita on a stiflingly hot day, the Sooners prevailed 12-4 in an unexpectedly tough contest. In the final game of the season against Washburn in Topeka, the Sooners were stymied by falling rain and a muddy field. The final was a tie, 6-6. Bennie Owen inherited the responsibilities of athletic director from the departed V.L. Parrington. The team of '08 had lost but one game. William Howard Taft was elected President and Henry Ford turned out 19,000 Model T automobiles at $850 each. Out on the plains, the Sooners were earning a reputation as football giants.

The last vestiges of the old-style game faded away in the fall of 1909. An increased emphasis on scholarship was felt across campus. Fifty-nine men reported for practice on the first day, despite the school's compliance with a new rule prohibiting the participation of first-year students. Boyd Field featured two new improvements – a ticket booth and a water sprinkler. Owen had set about to finance his athletic department with a vigorous ten-game

Cotton wagons clog Norman's Main Street in the days following statehood. Meanwhile, the Sooners were earning a reputation as football giants of the plains.

schedule, with only one major opponent, Washburn, visiting Norman. The Sooners efficiently dispatched Central Normal 55-0 and Kingfisher College 46-5, before losing to a tough Kansas team, 11-0. A surprisingly tough team from Alva, the Northwest Normal School, battled the Sooners before succumbing, 23-2. A week later, the Sooners traveled to Fayetteville to once again meet the Arkansas Razorbacks in what had become a fierce rivalry. Predictably, piles of rocks were at the ready along the sidelines of the craggy Fayetteville field. Two Razorback alumni were appointed game officials, despite Coach Owen's protests. Two Oklahoma touchdowns were called back by the officials. In the third quarter, a drunken spectator stumbled out of the

This well-groomed football squad of 1909 represented the "cream" of fifty-nine men who reported for fall practice.

crowd, and standing on the Arkansas goal line, drew two six-shooters. Firing two shots into the ground, he yelled, "That Oklahoma bunch won't cross this goal, I'll see to that!" The final score was Arkansas 21, Oklahoma 5. An indignant Owen told his hosts, "We'll never play Arkansas another football game as long as you have this kind of set-up." True to Owen's words, the two teams did not meet again for five years. The Sooners took out their frustration the following week at home against Washburn, destroying the Ichabods 42-8. Within the following six days, Oklahoma was to play three games. Oklahoma triumphed 11-5 at Sportsman's Park in Oklahoma City against St. Louis, then left Monday by train for Dallas and a game against the Texas Aggies. In a closely-fought game played on the site of the Texas State Fair, the Aggies won 14-8. Only two days after the Texas A&M game, and after an exhausting train ride to Austin, the Sooners stumbled badly, losing to the Texas Longhorns, 30-0. A road-weary varsity squad then defeated Epworth University at Oklahoma City's Colcord Park, 12-11. The hard-fought season was finally over. The athletic association netted $811.77, outside of the coach's salary.

Bennie the Innovator

Of the United States population of 92 million in 1910, fewer than half had completed grade school. Four percent had graduated from college. College football was sparking interest, however, any time and any place college students gathered. Coach Bob Zuppke at Illinois was a great innovator, devising, for example, the flea-flicker. Nowhere in America, however, was there a more skilled and creative football mind than Bennie Owen of Oklahoma. The major rules changes of 1910 provided opportunity for Owen to capitalize on his tremendous coaching talents. Games were divided into four quarters; forward passes were limited to 20 yards; ball carriers were permitted to advance the ball anywhere along the line of scrimmage. With the advent of this last

The 1910 Sooner squad utilized Owen's brainchild, the "direct pass," with devastating offensive results.

Above: Speed and deception were as important talents to these 1910 Sooners as they are to the Sooners of today.

Right: The Sooner yearbook featured a player roster and game results of the 1910 season. Game accounts, feature stories and player interviews were, as yet, unheard of.

FOOTBALL

The 1910 Varsity Foot Ball Team

Benjamin Gilbert Owen . . . . Head Coach
Harry Hughes . . . . Assistant Coach

THOMPSON (Captain)
Age 25 years, weighs 169 pounds. Captain of the Sooners during the season of 1910. He has played a star game for four years at center. Is an excellent general, and gets into the game with his whole spirit. He is conceded to play the "headiest" game of any man on the team.

James Rogers . . . . Left End
James Nairn . . . . Left Tackle
Earl Coots . . . . Left Tackle
Sam Burton . . . . Left Guard
Roger Berry . . . . Left Guard
Weaver Holland . . . . Left Guard
John C. Thompson . . . . Center
Clarence McReynolds . . . . Center
Homer Brown . . . . Right Guard
Harry Price . . . . Right Tackle
Sabert Hott . . . . Right Tackle
Glenn Clark . . . . Right End
Hubert Ambrister . . . . Quarter Back
Earle Radcliffe . . . . Quarter Back
Fred Capshaw . . . . R. Half Back
Mort Wood . . . . L. Half Back
Roy A. Morter . . . . L. Half Back
Claude Reeds . . . . Full Back
John Harley . . . . Full Back
Robert Wood . . . . Full Back

The Score

Oklahoma		Opponents
66	. . . . . . Kingfisher	0
79	. . . . . . Edmond	0
12	. . . . . . Stillwater	0
0	. . . . . . Missouri	26
0	. . . . . . Kansas	2
3	. . . . . . Texas	0
160		28

rule, Owen conceived the "direct pass." This simple offensive maneuver was, for years thereafter, devastating to defenses. With the direct pass, the ball was snapped directly from the center to one of several potential ball carriers in the backfield. Venerable old Walter Camp, holding forth at Yale, may not have heard of Bennie Owen, for his writings credit others with developing the direct pass. Oklahoma was still isolated from the distant eastern football establishment.

Owen's men of 1910 were lamentably light. The direct pass, then, was as much a creature of necessity as anything else. One varsity newcomer was Sabert Hott. Hott weighed only 157 pounds, but the tenacious lineman played with his nose almost on the ground, with his feet spread widely beneath him. He was virtually immoveable. A tall, round-shouldered freshman, tough as horse hide, came out for football. His name was Claude Reeds. Reeds was almost six feet tall and weighed in at 168 pounds. Reeds set about to learn the game of football. Within a couple of years, he would dominate the sport he had come to love. The direct pass was unveiled against Kingfisher College in the opening game. The Sooners won easily, 66-0. Against Central College of Edmond, the direct pass attack improved, with the Sooners winning 79-0. One week later in Norman, the Sooners' attack was held in relative check by the Oklahoma A&M Aggies, although the Sooners won 12-0. Against Missouri at Joplin, Oklahoma followed the strict prohibition against freshman participation. With Claude Reeds on the sideline, Missouri defeated the Sooners 26-0. Before 2,000 fans at Colcord Park in Oklahoma City, the Sooners lost a disputed contest 2-0 to the Kansas Jayhawkers. At Austin six days later, freshmen were permitted to play by mutual agreement. Punting was a crucial part of the college game, as teams were allocated three downs to make ten yards. Field position was paramount. In this closely fought contest, Claude Reeds retreated to punt from deep in his own end zone. The Texas crowd chanted for a blocked kick. Reeds' punt exploded off his foot. The spiraling ball rose overhead and amazingly, traveled seventy-five yards on the fly. From there, the ball bounded toward the Texas goal. Deep in his own end zone, the Texas returner managed to field the ball. Reeds' punt had traveled 107 yards, the longest ever booted by a Sooner player. His penchant for heroics had been exposed in a most spectacular way. Riding the resulting wave of emotion, the Sooners defeated Texas 3-0. Epworth University eagerly lobbied for a game against the Sooners. Needing extra money for equipment, Owen agreed. The game ended in a 3-3 tie, evidencing the varsity's weariness following the mon-

OU's first All-American – Claude Reeds dominated college football in the southwest with his running and kicking, 1910-1913.

strous win over Texas. That November, Lee Cruce was elected governor, replacing Charles Haskell. Julien C. Monnett conducted law classes at the University for the first time. More changes were on the way.

"You Have Shown the Oklahoma Spirit"

Norman's Main Street was paved. Town was growing closer to campus, although there were still expansive sections of open country. The first undefeated, untied team in Sooner history was taking shape over at Boyd Field. Coach Owen was blessed with just the type of talent required to excel in his system. "Six-Shooter Bill" Moss passed through the area, driving a herd of cattle. Liking what he saw, he decided to stay in Norman, study law and play a little football. The forward wall of '11 was light, fast and aggressive. In the backfield was, of course, Claude Reeds. He was an absolute artist at blocking. His punting was coming along, and he ran like the wind. The Sooners ran roughshod over Kingfisher College in the opener, 104-0. The score was a record for the state and the southwest. Oklahoma dispatched

Oklahoma Christian University of Enid 62-0 in the next contest, and followed up with a 22-0 win over the Oklahoma A&M Aggies. The Sooners of 1911 typified the best of football teams of the era. Play was marked by hard, swift, deceptive running. Washburn University was overtaken by the Sooner running attack by the score of 37-0. Up until Oklahoma's 1911 contest with Missouri in Columbia, the team labored in humble obscurity. The team rode day coaches, played in shabby uniforms and endured hostile crowds and biased officials. The Sooners wore the same uniforms in games that they practiced in – dilapidated tan duck pants and shredded red cotton jerseys stitched together precariously with cotton thread. But against Mizzou, Oklahoma came into its own with Owen's new end sweep off the direct pass. Also, Sabe Hott emerged as a first-class signal stealer. OU triumphed 14-6. The news of the victory reached Barbour's Drug Store in Norman by telegraph, setting off pandemonium. It was Oklahoma's first victory of all time over Missouri. Owen kept the team in Columbia in advance of the next game against Kansas at McCook Field in Lawrence. Everyone in the Midwest had by now heard of Owen and his modest little team of speedsters. Playing with resolve, the Sooners escaped with a victory, 3-0. Governor Cruce telegraphed Owen. "The people of

"The people of Oklahoma rejoice over your well-earned victory. You have shown the Oklahoma spirit."

– OKLAHOMA GOVERNOR, LEE CRUCE
BY TELEGRAPH TO OU COACH
BENNIE OWEN, 1911

At Lawrence, Kansas, on November 11, 1911, Owen's Sooners shut out the Jayhawkers, 3-0, prompting Oklahoma Governor Lee Cruce to praise the victory by telegram to the squad.

Oklahoma rejoice over your well-earned victory. You have shown the Oklahoma spirit." The Sooners dispatched a game squad from Alva Normal, 34-6, with Owen frequently substituting. The season ended with a game in Austin against the Longhorns. Four thousand fans turned up to witness the blood-letting. Texas controlled the action early, only to see the Sooners take

O.U. 3 - Texas O.

Claude Reeds punted the pigskin 107 yards, an all-time record, in the Sooners' 3-0 victory over the Texas Longhorns in Austin, 1910.

charge to win 6-3. *The Daily Oklahoman* editorialized, "Who can Oklahoma play next? All southwestern teams are outclassed. The bigger the foe the better. We fear none of them." The Oklahoma football dynasty had been given birth.

Young Jim Thorpe of Prague, Oklahoma, shocked the world by winning both the pentathlon and decathlon at the 1912 summer Olympic games in Sweden. Accordingly, Thorpe became known as "the world's greatest athlete." Woodrow Wilson was elected President and 1,500 people were led to watery graves as the Titanic luxury liner sank after striking an iceberg. Bennie Owen found his athletic department budget in need of a cash infusion in the fall of 1912. Accordingly, the Sooners were woefully over-scheduled. On the positive side, the national football rules committee finished its major overhaul of American football. The value of a touchdown was increased from five to six points; the field was shortened to 100 yards, and the limitations on the forward pass were repealed. A green freshman named Forrest "Spot" Geyer, began tossing the ball around in practice, honing his skills. Speed remained Owen's obsession. He didn't like equipment slowing down his troops. There were no hip pads. There were no helmets. "Bennie's system was never to admit an injury, therefore eliminating the need for a trainer," quarterback Charley Orr recalled. Kingfisher College was punished 40-0 in the opener. The following week, Central Normal was trailing 87-0 when the visitors wisely left to catch an early train back to Edmond. Oklahoma traveled to Dallas for the game against Texas at the State Fair. Six thousand spectators filled the wooden stands at Gaston Field as Oklahoma won for the third straight year, this time 21-6. Missouri shocked the Sooners in Norman the following week, 14-0. Claude Reeds sat out most of the game with a hip injury. Without him, Oklahoma generated very little offense. OU escaped Kansas 6-5 the following week, before losing to a fine Texas A&M team in Houston, 28-6. Owen won respect, however, as he complimented the Aggie opponents, thus building on the already fine tradition of Oklahoma sportsmanship. Oklahoma dispatched Oklahoma A&M 16-0, before traveling to Lincoln, Nebraska, for a game against the powerhouse Cornhuskers. Nebraska had already built a national reputation in football, painstakingly developing state pride in its home-grown youth – players plucked from the families of large-framed, muscular Scandinavian and Slavic settlers of the region. Back in Norman, loyal Sooner follower and druggist, John Barbour, arranged with Western Union to supply a play-by-play account which would be read through a megaphone from the window of an upstairs office over the drugstore. Nebraska demon-

Crowds gather in front of Barbour's Drug Store, Norman, to hear the delayed play-by-play of Sooner games received over Western Union telegraph lines and relayed enthusiastically through a megaphone, 1912.

There was no finer passer in all the land than All-American Forrest "Spot" Geyer during his playing days of 1913-1915.

strated its tremendous strength from the outset. Oklahoma countered with the magnificent running and punting of Claude Reeds. Nebraska mauled the lighter Oklahoma men, even while the crowd marveled at Oklahoma's speed, deception and blocking. In the end, Nebraska staved off a courageous Sooner effort, 13-9. A full year before Rockne's Notre Dame would defeat Army, effectively using the forward pass, out on the western prairie, Oklahoma was successfully slinging the ball down the gridiron, thereby terrorizing heavier opponents such as the Nebraska Cornhuskers. Five days later at Denver's Broadway Park on Thanksgiving afternoon, Oklahoma met Colorado. The Sooners sped to a 12-0 led, after which time the altitude visibly sapped the strength out of them. Colorado won the game 14-12. The University's athletic association reflected a balance of $62.79. The season had therefore, been deemed a success.

Some members of the Oklahoma legislature were openly opposed to college athletics. Others thought Bennie Owen's annual salary of $3,500 was far too high. One rather predictable eventuality was legislative meddling in all University affairs. Fortunately, new University president Stratton D. Brooks was amazingly adept at dealing with inquiring minds. Under Brooks' able leadership, the University shed its image of a territorial hodgepodge and began its ascent into a large, prestigious institution of higher learning. Bennie Owen ran his athletic department with dedication and grace. Financial stability was achieved by the institution of a new five-dollar student enterprise ticket, giving access for students to all athletic events and other extra-curricular activities. Boyd Street, running in front of the campus, was paved with brick. An electric interurban was extended to Norman from Oklahoma City. Free city mail delivery was set up. Old Sabe Hott showed up on campus with a glass eye. He'd lost his real one when a rail spike he was driving with a sledge hammer splintered and flew into his eye. He couldn't stay away from football, however. Hott's glass eye was left in his locker, while his gaping eye socket was covered over with white gauze. Hott played in three football games during the season. Certainly no man who ever played at Oklahoma loved the game more. Sabe was joined in Norman by his two younger brothers, Oliver and Willis. Playing along the line of scrimmage with such fury and pure spirit, the brothers became known as "The Terrible Hotts."

Reeds, Geyer Lead the Way

"Spot" Geyer was perfecting his passing skills in practice in the golden afternoons of September 1913. The Sooners began the season thumping three in-state rivals, Kingfisher College, Central Normal and Northwestern of Alva, by a combined score of 258-0. At Missouri, however, the Sooners were stunned to be told by game officials that Claude Reeds was ineligible to play. Reeds had played a few games in 1910 by agreement but had not played in games against Missouri Valley Conference teams. Missouri officials were adamant. Reeds could not play.

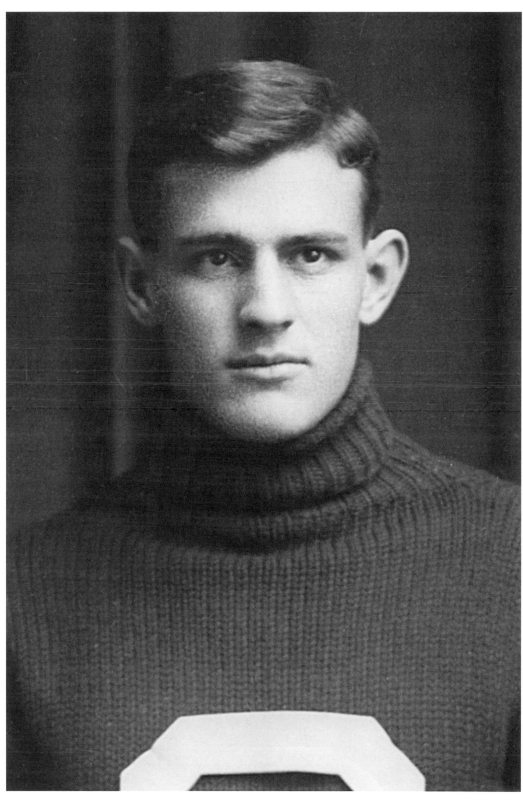

Of 1913 All-American Claude Reeds, Coach Owen said, "the harder the game, the harder Claude played."

Into Reeds' fullback spot went Geyer, who immediately went to work. His passes flew straight and true. When time ran out, Geyer had led the Sooners to the Missouri 16-yard line, poised to score the winning touchdown. However, the Tigers managed to escape, 20-17. Against Kansas, Reeds' eligibility had been resolved by the Missouri Valley Conference. The Oklahoma full-back played one of his finest games ever. Oklahoma played brilliantly against a quality opponent, winning 21-7. At Houston, Oklahoma lined up against Texas. A tough Longhorn squad defeated the Sooners 14-6, the first victory over Oklahoma in four years. At Stillwater the following week, Claude Reeds plowed through ankle-deep mud to score the game's only touchdown as the Sooners won 7-0. Against Colorado at Oklahoma City on Thanksgiving afternoon, both teams were presented with a Fair Park gridiron sodden with heavy, black mud. The ball was virtually impossible to hold on to. Colorado scored first. Then, in the second quarter, Claude Reeds earned a place in the hearts of Sooner fans for generations to come.

Retreating to punt deep in

the Sooner end of the field, Reeds faked the punt and took off. Spectators gasped. The amazing Reeds began to zig-zag, straight-arming and cross-stepping his way through would-be tacklers. Plates of mud flew ten feet high behind his heels as Reeds thundered down the field on a 70-yard touchdown gallop. Few if any had ever seen such a spectacular run. Oklahoma went on to win 14-3. Walter Camp's All-American team of that year carried no mention of Claude Reeds. Ninety-four percent of Camp's selections through the years had come from the East. *Outing* magazine named Reeds All-American, however, the only fullback named from west of the Mississippi. Bennie Owen's words resonate even today. Of Reeds he said, "The harder the game, the harder Claude played."

1914 was a year of national upheaval. World War I began with trench warfare the central tactical standard. The Panama Canal was completed and, reflective of the growing popularity of college football, the Yale Bowl in New Haven, Connecticut, opened, seating 80,000 spectators. In Norman, Owen resolved to embrace the forward pass. "Spot" Geyer's gift was passing the football. "He never had a dime while he was in school but he was good at anything," recalled classmate Hap Johnson. "He was a smart kid and a wonderful mixer." Nearly all of Geyer's pinpoint missiles were thrown on the run, usually following a run fake. Spreading the defense from the long punt formation, Geyer swept to either boundary before heaving the pigskin. Oklahoma passed by Central Normal, Kingfisher College and East Central Teachers of Ada without incident, except for an injury to Geyer's shoulder. At Oklahoma's first homecoming game ever, the Sooners defeated Missouri, 13-0. There weren't

In 1914, the Sooners perfected the end sweep, often concluding the play with a forward pass. Oklahoma successfully threw the football for over a mile during the season.

any old grads in attendance since the first University degree had been bestowed only sixteen years earlier. A big, powerful Texas team defeated the Sooners 32-7 in a game in which Geyer was so injured, he could not raise his arm to throw. The next week against Kansas at Lawrence, Geyer recovered with deadly results. Throwing caution to the wind, Geyer unleashed a spectacular aerial display. The success of the Sooner passing game was offset by

O.U. BAND 1914

the powerful ground game of the opposition. The game ended in a tie, 16-16. Oklahoma did not lose another game in 1914. The Sooners handled the Oklahoma A&M Aggies 23-6, although the Aggies scored on the Sooners for the first time in the ten years that the two schools had been meeting. Homer Montgomery demonstrated his genius as a receiver in Oklahoma's 52-10 victory over Kansas State at Manhattan. Montgomery earned a well-deserved reputation for snaring Geyer's spirals one-handed when necessary. In the first game against Arkansas since 1909, played in Oklahoma City, the Sooners dominated, 35-7. After the game, Lee Field, a substitute team member and track star, raced the interurban train from Oklahoma City back to Norman, an eighteen mile trip. Getting a head start on the electric train, Field was ahead for 17 of the 18 miles, with the train overtaking him just outside of Norman. In his heavy army brogans, Field had averaged six minutes a mile running on the rough track bed. The formidable Haskell Indians were met in Kansas City on November 26. The Haskell players were burly, rough-hewn fellows who gave no quarter. However, Oklahoma instituted its finesse game, winning 33-12. After the game, Owen sent the entire backfield to Claremore to soak out their ailments in steamy mineral baths. Even without Geyer, the Sooners defeated Henry Kendall College in Tulsa, 26-7. The aerial achievements of the 1914 Sooners went largely unnoticed on the coasts. War news dominated the newspapers, with Eastern football obtaining its quota of ink. Far out on the prairie, Bennie Owen had concocted a running/passing formula which was a true discovery. Oklahoma had thrown the football for over a mile in 1914 alone.

Strains of "Boomer Sooner" echoed across the campus from this dedicated group of University bandsmen, 1914.

SOUVENIR PROGRAM

Oklahoma - Missouri Game

OCTOBER 17, 1914

NORMAN, OKLA.

A Golden Year for Oklahoma Football

Owen took Oklahoma into the Southwest Conference prior to the 1915 season, joining Texas, Texas A&M, Arkansas, Baylor, Oklahoma A&M and Georgetown University of Texas. The Lusitania was sunk by a German sub, drawing the United States closer to war. Football in 1915 was the great driving force of college life in Norman. Defeat was considered a campus disaster, while victory was embraced with boundless pride. Bennie Owen's Sooner team of 1915 was placed on a pedestal by the students of the day, not only for its marvelous play, but for its sportsmanship. The Sooners of 1915 employed a new and spectacular offense which grabbed the attention of observers throughout the Midlands and the Southwest. There were few campus diversions in those days – no student union building, no golf course, no movie theater, no drugstore and one tiny restaurant. Students had to walk to town for fun, or pay a nickel to ride an antiquated old Ford jitney, which maintained a route between campus and Main Street. It was a golden year for

Sooner fans gained access to Boyd Field for football games by purchasing a ticket at the booth at left and passing through the gate, 1914.

Oklahoma football. The Sooners swept all the games on the schedule, demonstrating superiority in every facet of the game. The University's first yell-master, Leslie High of Cushing, led an enthusiastic cheering section at Boyd Field contests. The Ruf Neks, a pep body, appeared for the first time in 1915. Owen set about to replace the departed players from the 1914 squad. Two new halfbacks had to be groomed, along with two new linemen. Leon "Red" Phillips of Arapaho won a spot at guard. Twenty-five years later he would be

elected governor of Oklahoma. In the early season tune-ups, the Sooners demolished Kingfisher College 67-0, Southwestern of Weatherford 55-0 and Northwestern of Alva, 102-0. Students on campus directed their fervor to the next game against powerful Missouri. A new yell honoring the ever-popular Hott brothers, Willis "Big Hott" and Oliver, "Little Hott," was introduced. "Big Hott! Little Hott! Red Hott! Too Hott! Wow!" Hundreds of Sooner fans stood in a downpour outside Barbour's drugstore to hear the telegraphed play-by-play. "Spot" Geyer unleashed his aerial attack, inflicting a 24-0 defeat upon old Mizzou. In Norman, chaos reigned. Monday classes were canceled. The Ruf Neks marauded through campus.

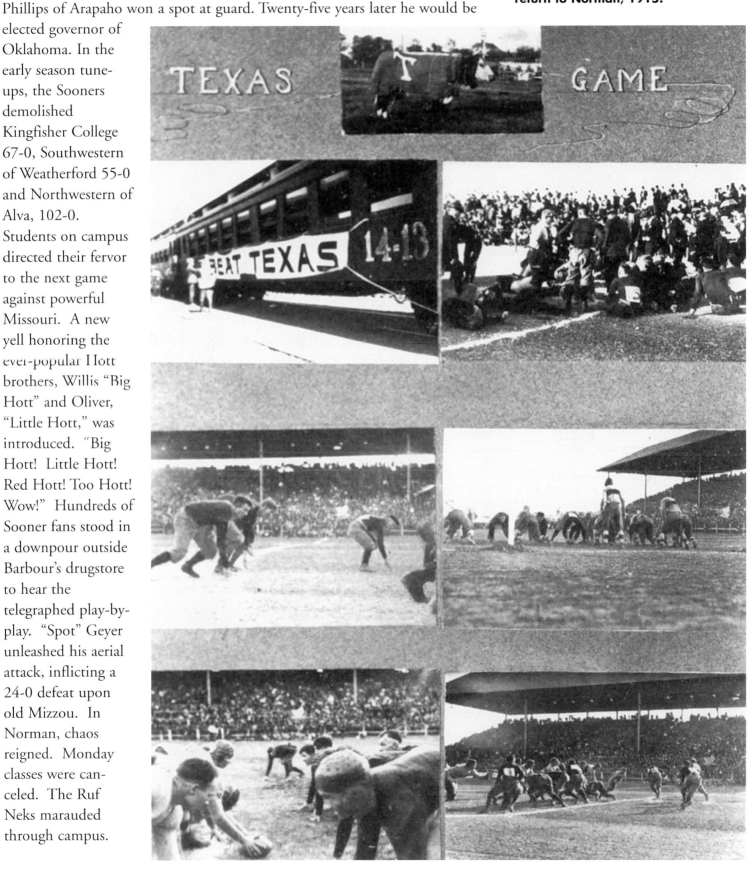

The University band held two dances the same day, raising enough money in donations to send twenty-two bandsmen to Dallas for the next game against Texas.

The largest crowd ever to see a game in Texas, 11,000 partisans crowded the Texas State Fair grandstand to witness the donnybrook. To that point,

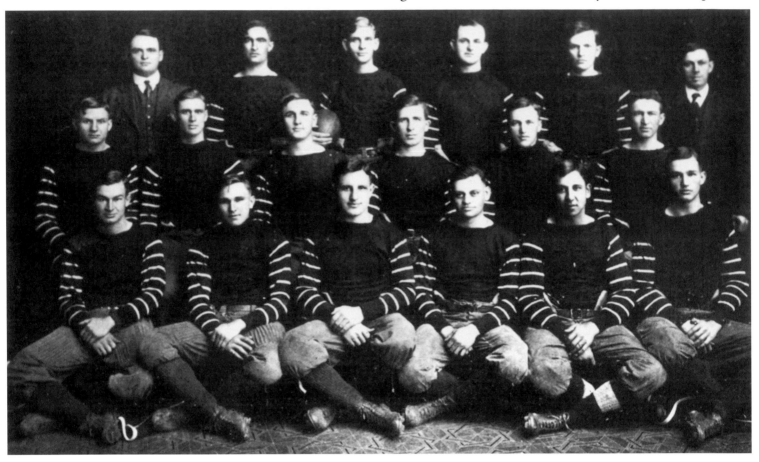

The marvelous Sooners of 1915 – undefeated in all ten contests, superlative in every department, these Sooners constituted OU's first truly great football team.

"Oklahoma absolutely had the cleanest team of all teams we ever played. I would rather have played against them than anybody."

— Kendall College quarterback
Ivan Grove, 1915

the Longhorns had not been scored upon. The game was so thrilling that gasps were as common among the crowd as cheap cigars. With the score tied at 13, "Spot" Geyer booted the game-winning conversion, giving the Sooners the electrifying victory, 14-13. Willis Hott played the game of his life, tackling Longhorn rushers before they could get up a head of steam. Over 4,000 delirious fans greeted the arriving Sooners at the Norman train depot. Homecoming was born as a tradition the following week against the Kansas Jayhawkers. The tough visitors scored first on a pass from quarterback Ad Lindsey, who would later coach at Oklahoma. But Geyer's passes began to whine through the heavy air. His 11 completed passes garnered 288 yards as the Sooners triumphed, 23-14. Against Kendall College at Tulsa, the Sooners met unexpectedly stiff resistance. The Tulsans had meticulously studied Oklahoma's aerial attack. They surprised the Sooners by going out in front 13-7, before late heroics lifted the Sooners to victory, 14-13. The following week against Arkansas in Fayetteville, the Sooners prevailed 24-0, their first ever victory at Arkansas. Kansas State was the next Sooner victim, 21-7. In the season finale against the Oklahoma A&M Aggies, played at Oklahoma City before 5,000 fans at Fair Park, the Sooners completed their all-victorious season, winning 26-7. It was the final game for "Spot" Geyer, the remarkable

captain and fullback who had earned football immortality. He had become the finest forward passer and place kicker of his day. Moreover, Oklahoma was the first football team in America to rely on the forward pass for offensive production. It would be another quarter century, after the football itself was streamlined, for other colleges to utilize the forward pass. For the first time, word of Oklahoma's football exploits reached the media centers of the East. Geyer became Oklahoma's first official All-American. Owen's popularity reached its zenith. Students and fans presented him with a new Hudson Super-Six automobile.

Woodrow Wilson was reelected President in 1916. While World War I raged across the Atlantic, Pancho Villa was terrorizing Texas and New Mexico residents with pillaging raids from across the Mexican border. Bennie Owen was faced with a definite lack of veteran players and an unfortunate rash of injuries. Lack of experience wound up costing the Sooners dearly. The Sooners lost five of 11 games. It was the fightingest, cryingest outfit Owen had ever fielded. "Gee, Cly!" Owen barked repeatedly from the sidelines, as if to vent his frustration. With the season ending with a 41-7 victory over Oklahoma A&M, Owen turned his attention to spring drills and the purchase of 30 acres south of Boyd Field for a future football stadium.

For a while, it looked like the University would have no football games in 1917. The United States had entered the war. Oklahoma's small enrollment meant it was hit especially hard by the departure of youthful and adventurous men. Of the 20 returning lettermen of 1916, 13 went off to war. Colorfully named replacements stepped forward. These included Dewey "Snorter"

Freshman hopefuls report to Coach Owen for fall practice, 1916.

Luster, a wiry little boxer from Chickasha; Earl "Switch" Light, a tackle from Pond Creek; Arlo "Skivey" Davis, a triple-threat back from Norman and Erl Deacon from Tecumseh, a devastating defender. Lawrence "Jap" Haskell joined the squad as well. Later he would become the University's baseball coach, football line coach and athletic director. In the season's second game, the Sooners established a record by defeating Kingfisher College 179-0. Skivey Davis kicked 23 conversions out of 26 attempts, a national record. Hugh McDermott, a great Sooner stalwart, dislocated a shoulder against Phillips and missed the Oklahoma adventure in Urbana, Illinois. The light Sooner 11 was out-manned against a Fighting Illini team which was six-deep at every position. The Illini even stationed marching bands at both ends of the playing field! The Sooners lost to the Illini, 44-0. The next week, the Sooners recovered to beat Texas, 14-0, with Wallace Abbott filling in admirably for the injured McDermott. The war-depleted Sooners struggled through the balance of the season, losing four games and tying one, while winning six. One of the losses was the first ever to Oklahoma A&M by the score of 9-0. Hugh McDermott was elected captain for the 1918 team but shortly left school to become a combat pilot.

The influenza epidemic of 1918 claimed 500,000 American lives. The war came to a merciful end, but not before it dealt its devastation to many of those who had proudly worn the crimson and cream at Oklahoma. Practically all the older players were gone. It was an influx of high school boys who salvaged football at Oklahoma. The new crop of players included Roy "Soupy" Smoot of Lawton and Page Belcher of Medford. There were many others. There was no great concern over the influenza epidemic until October 3, when 1,000 new cases were reported in Oklahoma City within 48 hours. The epidemic paralyzed the University's football program. A campus quarantine was imposed. Games with Missouri and Texas were canceled. In an abbreviated schedule, the Sooners went undefeated, winning all six contests. Oklahoma romped at Kansas, 33-0, and destroyed Arkansas 103-0. The team had become largely a freshman aggregation. At the fairgrounds in Oklahoma City, the Sooners revenged the previous year's loss to the Aggies of Oklahoma A&M. Sooners 27, Aggies 0.

A maturing Bennie Owen led the 1918 squad to an undefeated, but abbreviated, season as World War I and an influenza epidemic burdened the country.

These Ruf-Neks of 1919 appear capable of most anything. The still flourishing spirit group was first organized on campus a few years earlier, in 1915.

Merging Old With New

Boys mercifully came home from the war. Congress enacted the 18th Amendment introducing Prohibition, and Jack Dempsey defeated Jess Willard to become heavyweight boxing champ. In many respects, the Roaring '20s had already begun. At Norman, the campus swelled with 2,608 students. Bennie Owen was faced with a dilemma. Should he play the war vets or play the youthful returnees from the '18 squad? Hundreds of students turned out to watch practice at Boyd Field every afternoon. The Jazz Hounds, a perky little band, was formed on campus. The Hounds attended most games with their instruments in tow, staging some stirring, impromptu shows. Owen merged old with new and the resulting unit showed signs of greatness. Smoot could do things at tackle that no other tackle of his day could do. Erl Deacon and Claude "Big Tub" Tyler were dominant at guard. Phil White, the rebellious quarterback, made the offense go. The Sooners marched through their early opponents before playing Texas at Dallas. Against the Longhorns, the Sooners scored in every way the rules allowed. Myron "Little Tub" Tyler caught a touchdown pass. The Jazz Hounds put on a musical smash at the half. OU won the game 12-7. Oklahoma played Nebraska in Omaha on October 25. The game was played in a snow field. The Nebraska cold was so stinging that the Oklahoma boys took hotel blankets to the game in order to bundle up. The game ended in a 7-7 tie. The next two games were also ties, 6-6 against Missouri and 0-0 against Kansas at Lawrence. The Sooners were upset 7-6 at Arkansas, then finished the season with victories over Kansas State 14-3 and Oklahoma A&M, 33-6. In December, Oklahoma severed its twenty-year ties with the Southwest Conference in order to join the more prestigious Missouri Valley Conference. There was some opposition to Oklahoma's entry because the school was located "so far south." "Snorter" Luster, the diminutive senior end, who tackled so viciously, was elected captain of the team for 1920, a tribute to Luster and the great forward wall of the Sooner defense.

Soupy, Mex and a Championship

Some of Owen's charges in the fall of 1920 needed to hold down jobs in order to make ends meet. The University provided no assistance in this regard. Two boys were employed on the night shift at the fire house. Another worked for a Norman hotel as a porter, meeting trains and carrying luggage. Coach Owen engaged two assistant coaches and a third worked for free. In his sixteenth year of coaching at Oklahoma, Owen's genius at devising offensive stratagems was being compromised by his material. They were heavyweights. That, however, didn't prevent Owen from implementing an effective passing attack. He envisioned long, powerful offensive drives relying principally on the run with passing as a complement. Oklahoma's debut in the Missouri Valley Conference was an impressive one. In fact, the Sooners went undefeated in seven games, tying one. Against Washington University of St. Louis, Soupy Smoot got his front teeth knocked out, an ironic loss for a man who would later become an opera singer. Oklahoma was not only the youngest school in the conference, it was the smallest. Nebraska, for example, had twice as many enrolled students as Oklahoma. Pride in the team, the school and state, however, were in full flower. The Jazz Hounds often managed to accompany the team as did Mex, a new addition. Mex was a tan and white terrier which had stood alongside a company of U.S. soldiers on the Mexican border back in 1917. Mex became the Sooner mascot and one of the early legends of Sooner football. Owen's offense was now clicking with devastating efficiency. Missouri, Kansas, and Oklahoma A&M fell before the Sooner warriors. Motion pictures were first taken of a Sooner squad that everyone wanted to see. The 1920 team enjoyed themselves as much as any squad Owen had ever fielded. Against Kansas State, the Sooners dominated but were tied by the rugged visitors, 7-7. By defeating Drake on

Above: All-American tackle Roy "Soupy" Smoot from Lawton got his front teeth knocked out against Washington University, 1920.

Below: Loyal friend – Mex, the first Sooner mascot, stood proudly on the sidelines for years. One of Norman's largest funerals ever was conducted on campus when Mex died.

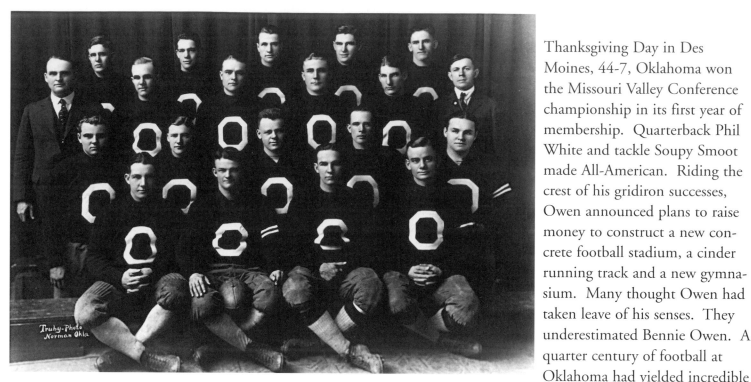

Above: These 1920 Sooners won the Missouri Valley Conference Championship in Oklahoma's first year of membership.

Right: Phil White, All-American quarterback-halfback from Oklahoma City, strikes a powerful pose, 1920.

"We trained. Once a month Snorter and I walked down to the corner and smoked a 15¢ cigar, but that was our only departure off the straight and narrow."

– OU PLAYER ERL DEACON,
REFERRING TO TEAMMATE DEWEY
"SNORTER" LUSTER , 1920

Thanksgiving Day in Des Moines, 44-7, Oklahoma won the Missouri Valley Conference championship in its first year of membership. Quarterback Phil White and tackle Soupy Smoot made All-American. Riding the crest of his gridiron successes, Owen announced plans to raise money to construct a new concrete football stadium, a cinder running track and a new gymnasium. Many thought Owen had taken leave of his senses. They underestimated Bennie Owen. A quarter century of football at Oklahoma had yielded incredible moments of success along with the inevitable moments of disappointment. One thing was clear, however. Football was king at Oklahoma.

Commercial radio had just begun. Women were given the right to vote under the 19th Amendment. Many citizens were troubled by the so-called "Red Scare," with communist threats being perceived in many sectors of American life. Coach Owen was devoting an increasing amount of his energies to his dream of building a new football stadium. Owen benefited by a building boom on campus. President Brooks enjoyed popularity with legislators, students and friends of the university. As a result, by 1922, seven new academic buildings joined the four which had been in place since 1912. Bonds had to be sold to supplement the donations needed to construct the new stadium. The bond package for the stadium was combined with a similar, yet

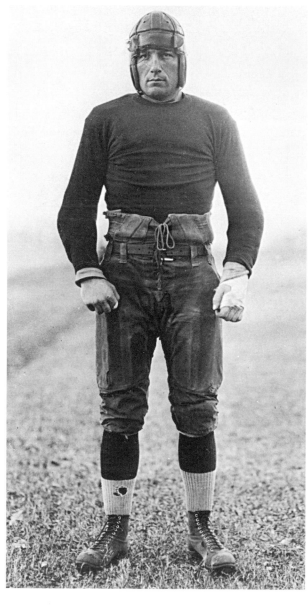

smaller bond proposal for a student union building. In 1923, the first football game was played
at the new field. At that time, the field had no
permanent stands. Steel bleachers taken from
Boyd Field were erected on the east side and temporary wooden bleachers were built on the west.
By 1925, a portion of the concrete west stadium
was completed. It provided 15,000 seats and had
been constructed under the careful supervision of
Bennie Owen. The stadium was named
Memorial Stadium in honor of the World War I
war dead. Later, the field itself would be named

after the pioneer football coach and visionary who conceived, promoted and
built the stadium.

**Above: Bennie Owen envisioned a
new football stadium worthy of a
great university. Construction
commenced on Oklahoma Memorial
Stadium in 1921.**

**Below: The Sooners in action
against conference foe, Washington
University, at old Boyd Field,
October 22, 1921. Oklahoma 28,
Washington 13.**

        The years between the Armistice and the Great Crash were a kaleido-
scope of fragmenting traditions, zaniness and provocation. Prohibition, political chicanery, literary innovation and ethnic myopia were the orders of the
day. American culture bid farewell to days of innocence and youthful naiveté.
Just as F. Scott Fitzgerald's novels reflected contemporary society and his
yearning for afternoons in football pads on the playing fields of Princeton, so
it was in Norman, Oklahoma. Coach Owen not only coached football and
served as athletic director, he was also basketball coach. His first love was, of
course, football. His charges of 1921 could not match the record of the previous year's Missouri Valley Conference champions. However, the Sooner squad
did win five of eight games, including wins over Oklahoma A&M, Kansas and
Rice Institute. The 1923 Sooner yearbook was dedicated to Coach Owen.
The dedication stated, "A sincere belief in the University, an unfaltering confidence in the purest ethics of the game, both on and off the field and a fervent
energy in fostering school spirit has won for him the highest regard both at
home and abroad."
Hugh "Scotty"
McDermott returned
to campus to coach
the freshman squad,
now known as the
"Boomers." Owen
took charge of the var-
sity squad which post-
ed only two victories,
against three losses
and three ties. Against
Nebraska in Norman,
the varsity led at the
end of the first quar-
ter. However, the
defending Missouri
Valley champs from

University of Oklahoma. Norman, Okla.

The University of Oklahoma campus takes shape around the Parrington (North) Oval. Fertile farm land lies south of the administration building, all the way to the South Canadian River, circa 1920.

the North wore down the valiant Sooners, defeating the host 39-7. The next week at Kansas, after a long train ride, the Sooners lost 19-3. On homecoming in Norman, however, the Sooners rallied to defeat Missouri, 18-14. Texas visited Norman next, dispatching the Sooners 32-7. The annual battle with Oklahoma A&M ended with a 3-3 tie, followed by another tie, 0-0, against conference foe Washington University.

The 1923 football season was not entirely fulfilling to Sooner faithful. The opener against Nebraska in Lincoln proved foreboding, as the Sooners lost 24-0. Costly fumbles proved the Sooners' undoing. The varsity recovered to drill Washington of St. Louis 62-7, and defeat Oklahoma A&M 12-0. Only one additional win was posted, coming against Missouri at Columbia. The Sooners of 1924 brought honor to themselves and the University by defeating Nebraska in Norman 14-7. A blocked punt by Sooner Loyal Woodall, who scooped up the ball and ran it in for a touchdown, proved the pivotal play. Otherwise, the season was disappointing, as Owen's men won only one other game, against Washington of St. Louis. The Sooners ended the season of '24 with a record of 2-5-1. Claude Reeds, the great Sooner runner of days gone by, returned to coach the freshman team. Hope for better results in 1925 loomed large.

Rudolph Valentino continued as the cinema's object of feminine affection, while in Tennessee, a school teacher named John Scopes was tried in a rural courtroom in the so-called "Monkey Trial" for teaching the theory of evolution. Bennie Owen's squad was wildly enthusiastic, yet so green that the month of October had expired before the kinks could be worked out. In the fall of 1925, every man had issued to him, a form-fitting leather helmet, coarse duck pants with stiff leather thigh pads, and cleated shoes. In the end, Oklahoma had won four games, losing three and tying one.

He thought it was time. After nearly a quarter of a century as football coach, his Oklahoma teams had won 128, lost 52, tied 13, and came away from every game with the respect of the opposition. Owen's last season as football coach in 1926 began auspiciously enough. His Sooners held off Arkansas 13-6 in Norman, then pasted Drake 11-0. The major disappoint-

"All we got out of football was the fun. It was a sport and that's why we played. If Bennie had offered me board, room and tuition, I wouldn't have played for him."

– OU TACKLE
SABE HOTT, 1910

ment of the season was a heart-breaking loss to Kansas, 10-9. Despite the season's two defeats and one tie against Oklahoma A&M, the team's offense was more effective than it had been for several years. The football program at Oklahoma was on sound footing, drawing spectators from all over the region to the new stadium. Owen relinquished his post as football coach, staying on as athletic director. In a newspaper interview given by former University president Stratton D. Brooks to the *Kansas City Star* in 1926, Brooks said, "There is one man down there who is doing more to teach right living and right thinking to the youth of Oklahoma than anybody. He is Bennie Owen."

Days of Transition

In Norman's garden plots, corn tassels, golden and full of life, withered and died in the face of incessant, fiery south winds. Sewn crops were plucked from the soil and whisked away, leaving barren gray patches of hard pan behind. It was the 1930s. Oklahoma folks didn't want to pack up and move to California. They did so out of desperation. The stock market crash of 1929 had led to the Great Depression. There was no work. "Hoovervilles" sprung up alongside railroad tracks where misery could be shared over open fires. Survival was paramount in the lives of most Americans. Football had to take a back seat. The game, however, would survive on the University of Oklahoma campus.

Adrian Lindsey was a native of Kingfisher, Oklahoma. "Ad" was tall and slender with a serious nature. It had been common in the early days for young men from the northwestern quadrant of the state to identify more closely with the townspeople of Wichita, Kansas, than Oklahoma City. As a result, a number of Oklahoma boys enrolled at Kansas University to pursue their athletic interests. "Ad" Lindsey was among them. Lindsey had played for the Jayhawkers against Oklahoma in 1914, '15, and '16. As a triple-threat quarterback in 1916, Lindsey had led Kansas to a 21-13 victory over Oklahoma, the first such KU triumph in five years. Bennie Owen was impressed with the way Lindsey went about his business on the gridiron. Lindsey had, like Owen, been head man at tiny

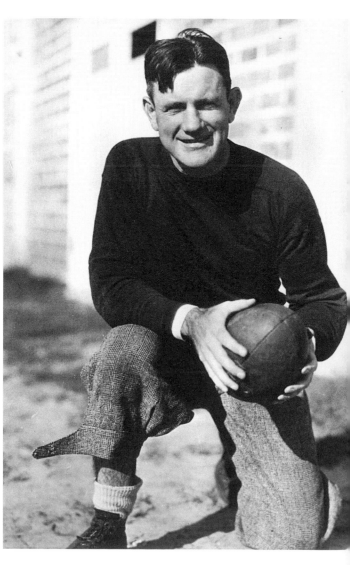

Bethany College in Lindsborg, Kansas. Accordingly, it was Lindsey who replaced Owen as head football coach at Oklahoma in 1927.

Sooners Stun Stagg's Maroons

Lindsey's first game as coach was remarkable inasmuch as he transported his light and inexperienced squad to Chicago to play Amos Alonzo Stagg's University of Chicago Maroons. The game was played before 38,000 noisy Chicago partisans. Lindsey had installed a series of short pass plays in the offense which proved somewhat effective. Passes from Linwood "Bus" Harkins, Sooner halfback, to Mayhew and Crider produced dazzling touchdowns. Oklahoma stunned the Chicago spectators and influential sportswriters by defeating Stagg's squad, 13-7. It was the first ever victory by the Sooners over a Big 10 Conference opponent. The season progressed with

Left: Ad Lindsey's first Sooner squad defeated Kansas, 26-7, in Norman on Homecoming, November 12, 1927.

Below: Sooner pride has been around from the beginning, as evidenced by this on-the-field formation at the 1927 OU-Oklahoma A & M game.

Above: Spring practice roll call, 1928.

Below: The Sooner yearbook called the 1929 football season "semi-brilliant," as these Sooners finished with a record of 3-3-2.

mixed results. A bright spot was the stirring victory over Kansas on Homecoming before 14,000 fans. Ray "Freight Train" LeCrone and Tom Churchill divided the ball-carrying, leading to four lengthy drives. The final was OU 26, Kansas 7. There were two ties in 1927, against Creighton and Central State of Edmond, against three victories and three defeats.

The Missouri Valley Conference was reorganized after the 1927 season. Oklahoma, Missouri, Kansas, Kansas State, and Iowa State invited Nebraska to join with them in constituting the Big 6 Conference. This group of competitors would maintain its affiliation undisturbed for twenty years.

In the fall of 1928, Herbert Hoover was elected President. Walt Disney produced the first animated film featuring a talking mouse named "Steamboat Willie." Ad Lindsey's Sooners met with partial success, utilizing Lindsey's system of short passes on the offense and furious rushes on the opposing passers. Four of Oklahoma's eight opponents were shut out, thus producing Sooner victories. The powerful Nebraska Cornhuskers manhandled the Sooners in Norman, 44-6, while the Sooners rebounded to blank Kansas, Oklahoma A&M and Missouri on successive weekends. The season ended with a Sooner record of 5-3.

Dewey "Snorter" Luster joined Ad Lindsey's coaching staff for the

1929 season, directing line play. The Sooner season was called "semi-brilliant" by the Sooner yearbook writers, due in part to the Sooners' 13-13 tie against Big 6 Champion Nebraska in Lincoln. The series with Texas was resumed, with the Longhorns prevailing over the scrappy Sooners, 21-0. In the end, Oklahoma had won three, lost three and tied two. Team captain and fullback Frank Crider, was named All-Big 6 Conference.

The 1930 season began in stirring fashion as the Sooners trounced the New Mexico Lobos at Memorial Stadium, 47-0. A week later, Nebraska visited Norman, virtually covering the field in warm-ups with its three full teams of players. Nebraska's confidence was shaken when Sooner speedster Buster Mills bolted for fifty yards. The Sooners prevailed 20-7. Losses to Texas, Kansas and Oklahoma A&M marred the season as the Sooners finished at 4-3-1.

Oklahomans comforted themselves, hoping for better weather and better economic times by reading about native son and aviator, Wiley Post. In 1931, Post piloted his plane, the "Winnie Mae" on a successful round-the-world flight. Ad Lindsey was pleased to welcome back Captain "Silly" Guy Warren. A few years before, total blindness threatened Warren. However, after a dangerous operation, Warren's eyesight was saved. Daringly, he returned to the game of football. Warren's daring was not enough to carry the day in several contests, however. The Rice Owls visited Norman in the season opener, only to succumb to Sooner speed. Oklahoma 19, Rice 6. The Sooners returned to earth, losing four contests in a row before edging Kansas 10-0. A charity game was played December 5 against the Oklahoma City University Goldbugs. The Bugs bit the Sooners in a lackluster affair, 6-0. After a victory over Tulsa, 20-7, the Sooners embarked on a long-awaited trip to Hawaii. The first of two Hawaiian encounters was scheduled against an all-star town squad from Honolulu. The Sooners, perhaps dazed by trade winds and hula girls, lost 39-20. In that game, quarterback Bob Dunlap hit fullback Earnest "Iron Mike" Massad with passes sufficient to generate 20 points. Against the University of Hawaii Rainbows, Oklahoma resolved to end their season victorious. The final was Oklahoma 7, Hawaii 0. As a result of the early-season losses, there was considerable grumbling in the state about the football program. Snorter Luster was the first to resign his post as line coach. Ad Lindsey followed suit, and after a season record of 4-7-1, Oklahoma would have a new coaching staff.

William Bennett Bizzell had become President of the University in 1925. He was an extremely able administrator and a first-rate educator. The growth of the state's University accelerated under his leadership until the early 1930s, when growth slowed somewhat. Tuition in 1931-32 was $3.50 per credit hour. The Great Depression was touching every American. Five thousand banks closed. Twelve million citizens were out of work.

Bennie Owen, still at the helm of Oklahoma's athletic department, hired Lewis Woodford Hardage, a Vanderbilt man, to become the school's eighth football coach. Hardage brought along with him John "Bo" Rowland as line coach. Fifty upperclassmen turned out for practice in the fall of 1932, along with an equal number of freshmen. Paul Young from Norman was captain and center of the Sooner eleven. Young was a devastating defender,

Above: Earnest " Iron Mike" Massad, 1931.

Below: A youthful, sinewy Lewie Hardage took over the coaching reins in 1932.

smashing through opposing lines to corral ball-carriers. The speed component in the Sooner arsenal was provided by Bill Pansze, from Fort Smith, Arkansas. It was Pansze's bursts which enabled the Sooners to emerge victorious over Tulsa, 7-0 and over Kansas, 21-6. The Kansas eleven was coached by OU's former coach, Ad Lindsey. Injuries forced Pansze to the sidelines after that, and the

Above: Youngsters sidle up behind the Sooner bench during a game in the fall, 1932.

Below: Art and Bill Pansze reflect the well-scrubbed look of many Sooner hopefuls, 1933.

Sooners were forced to rely on their aerial game. Spirits for a successful season remained high. The University boasted a 110-piece marching band, an aggressive bunch of Ruf-Neks and the infamous Jazz Hounds musical group. Against Texas at Dallas, the Sooners were unable to halt the Longhorns' onslaught, as the Horns won 17-10, their fourth victory in a row over the Sooners. Oklahoma managed subsequent conference victories over Kansas State and Iowa State, while bowing to Oklahoma A&M, Missouri and Nebraska. The season finale was played against George Washington University in Washington, D.C. Sooner stalwart Paul Young suffered an attack of influenza and had to watch from the sidelines as the Sooners settled for a 7-7 tie. Lewie Hardage's first squad finished at 4-4-1.

Little boys stood on dusty street corners along north Porter Street in Norman to watch a single line of Fords and Chevrolets, bumper-to-bumper, make their way to Memorial Stadium for the season opener against the mighty Commodores of Vanderbilt University. A Sooner victory would mean national recognition. Over 18,000 fans attended the game, roaring approval as the Sooners dominated every phase of the game. Only once did the Commodores cross the Sooners' twenty-yard line. Cash Gentry, a tough sophomore tackle for the varsity, savagely attacked opposing runners. The Pansze brothers, Art and Bill, carried the ball with authority. The game was so hotly contested that it ended in a scoreless tie. Against Tulsa a week later, the Sooners wilted, 20-6. Hope sprang anew, however, the following week, when the Sooners traveled to Dallas. Amid the colorful atmosphere on the state fairgrounds, the Sooners stunned the Longhorns, 9-0. It was the University's first victory over Texas since 1919. Against Nebraska in Lincoln, the Sooners sought to dethrone the conference champion Cornhuskers. A Nebraska sportswriter penned, "The Sooners came into the Northland heralded more or less as pushovers, yet these Sooners tore into Coach Dana X. Bible's Cornhuskers like a rip saw. Long and lean, they played a slashing game on the defense that made the highly-touted Husker offense look very poor indeed at times." The Huskers prevailed 16-7 against a Sooner team which impressed everyone with its valor. Returning confident and eager, the Sooners shut out Kansas, 20-0, and routed

Missouri 21-0 at Columbia. The season concluded with losses to Kansas State and Oklahoma A&M, and a record matching that of the season before, 4-4-1. Guards Ellis Bashara and Jim "Red" Stacy, quarterback Bob Dunlap and tackle Cash Gentry made All-Big 6.

Great things had been predicted for the Sooner squad of 1934, principally due to the returning group of 21 veterans plus an impressive array of sophomore additions. "This is Oklahoma's year!" the newspapers heralded in September. After defeating Centenary 7-0 at home, the Sooners awaited the acid test the following week against the Texas Longhorns. The Horns dominated the game, winning 19-0, and effectively compromising Sooner hopes of season honors. Injuries hampered the squad all year. While the Sooners shut out Missouri 31-0, and Iowa State 12-0, there were disappointing losses at Kansas State, 8-7 and at George Washington, 3-0. The Sooners finished tied for third place in the Big 6 Conference.

The University's Board of Regents decided that the entire athletic department needed revitalizing. Lloyd Noble, a wealthy Ardmore oil man, took the lead in achieving the new order. Bennie Owen gracefully stepped down as athletic director. Lewie Hardage exited and Oklahoma took a quantum leap forward with its football program.

Biff Jones Arrives

Lawrence "Biff" Jones had attended West Point, graduating in 1917. Jones was a blunt-spoken, hard-nosed military man. He had coached Army football from 1926-1929. As the head coach of Louisiana State in Baton Rouge, he had refused a request by the "Kingfish," Governor Huey P. Long, to address Jones' Bayou Tigers at halftime of a football game. Thereafter, Jones became available to coach the Sooners. Gene Corrotto, a sophomore-to-be in the spring of 1935, recalls Jones' arrival on campus. "We'd already had one spring practice under Lewie Hardage. When Biff Jones arrived, we had another one." Reflective of Jones' no-nonsense approach, instructions to the players

Above: Coach "Biff" Jones conducted vigorous, para-military style practices in the fall, 1935.

were typewritten and distributed. New wooden lockers replaced coat hooks in the dressing room. Jones looked out for his players. In exchange, he demanded discipline and respect. "Most of the boys were scared of the guy," Corrotto recalls, referring to the 6 foot, 3 inch coach. "When he hollered at you, you didn't jump once, you jumped three times."

While there was renewed interest in the fortunes of Sooner football, inhabitants of Oklahoma were struggling to cope with the effects of the Dust Bowl. "We'd practice in dust storms so thick, you couldn't see the sun. By the end of practice, we were covered in thick dust," Gene Corrotto recalls. Conditioning and toughness were the hallmarks of Jones-coached squads. Popular offensive formations of the day were the single-wing and the double-wing. End sweeps by fleet halfbacks complemented punishing dives by fullbacks. The quarterback received the ball from center some four yards deep, then turned his shoulders towards the line of scrimmage in order to conceal the ball and induce deception. The Sooners featured outstanding tackles in J.W. "Dub" Wheeler and Ralph Brown. Backs Nick Robertson and Bill Breeden would join them in earning all-conference honors. The season opened with blankings of two opponents, Colorado, 3-0, and New Mexico, 25-0. Then came the annual showdown in Dallas. With the smallest crowd ever on hand at Fair Park Stadium for the annual meeting, 16,000, the Sooners fell 12-7. Jones' squad played fiercely all season long, shutting out five of its nine opponents. The Sooners' six wins were the most since 1920. The general feeling among Oklahomans was that Biff Jones would be able to produce victories in very satisfying numbers in the days to come.

"Sarge" Dempsey, the equipment manager, checked out a wire basket full of football equipment, minus a helmet, to each team member. He then lugged a burlap sack out in the middle of the locker room and upended it, sending leather helmets clattering to the concrete floor. "Find you one that fits!" Sarge barked. The home opener against Tulsa on September 26, 1936, was played in a driving rain storm. While the rain was surely welcome, it made football play extremely treacherous. Both teams sloshed about for four

OFFICIAL PROGRAM

TEXAS vs OKLAHOMA

October 10, 1936   Price 25c

quarters before the gun sounded with the score knotted at 0-0. A week later, Oklahoma plastered Colorado 8-0, then headed for Dallas. Thirty-thousand witnessed a thrilling affair which ended in a 6-0 Texas escape. Oklahoma's great end, Pete Smith, caught – then dropped – the football in the end zone as time expired. Webber Merrell and William "Red" Conkright made spectacular cross-country dashes to put away the Kansas Jayhawkers 14-0. The Sooners were not so fortunate against the Nebraska Cornhuskers, who overpowered them in Norman, 14-0. Ties with Iowa State and Kansas State were booked before Missouri surprised the Sooners, 21-14. Against the Oklahoma A&M Aggies in the last game of the season, Sooner back Jack Baer ran wild, leading a five-touchdown assault on the Aggies, who were defeated 35-3. Later, Biff Jones received word that he was being transferred by the Army to Fort Leavenworth, Kansas, requiring him to give up his coaching job at Oklahoma. Before the leaves turned in the fall of 1937, Jones had resigned from the military and had taken over at Nebraska for the legendary Dana X. Bible, who was moving on to the University of Texas. In Norman, more change was in the offing.

There were no athletic dorms in the 1930s. Football players simply took up residence in local boarding houses. A football scholarship consisted of tuition and books. Players were required to work, with their paychecks going to pay for room and board. Gene Corrotto recalls arising at five o'clock in the morning; hustling over to the campus to sweep out classrooms; literally running to make class at 8 a.m.; then practicing football until dark. By that time, dinner was over at the boarding house. The student union was the best place to grab something to eat before heading to the library to study. "Many a night, I was so tired I fell asleep at my study table at the library," Corrotto remembers.

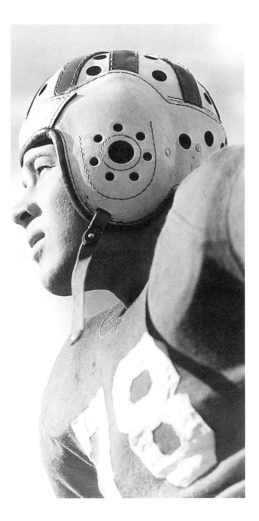

Above: Muskogee native, Pete Smith, played end with distinction, earning All-American status in 1937.

Left: Gene Corrotto leads interference for Jack Baer, in a team drill, 1937.

Stidham, Snorter and Company

Above: Coach Tom Stidham, far left, showcases his coaching staff, 1937.

Right: Roland "Waddy" Young, from Ponca City, played end in 1936-1938, earning All-American honors.

Tom Stidham had grown up in Checotah, Oklahoma. The dark-skinned Stidham, of Indian and Irish descent, had played football at Haskell Indian Institute in 1926 and had been an assistant football coach thereafter at Northwestern University in Chicago. Biff Jones had brought Stidham to Oklahoma to assist him with line play. Now, Stidham added Snorter Luster, the old Sooner, to his own coaching staff. Luster had experienced great success as coach at Norman High School. Other members of the coaching staff were Robert "Doc" Erskine, who had come to Norman with Biff Jones; Harry "Dutch" Hill, a former Sooner back in 1920-21; and Frank "Spec" Moore, who coached the ends. In Stidham's inaugural season, 1937, he posted the best winning percentage by a Sooner head man in 11 seasons – .714. The opener against Tulsa revealed a troubling Sooner weakness, pass defense, as Tulsa triumphed 19-7. Rice University, in those days a Southwest Conference power, visited Norman. The Sooners prevailed 6-0. Quarterback Jack Baer hit end Pete Smith with a touchdown pass in the second quarter for the margin of victory. Against Texas in Dallas, it was a matter of Texas managing a 7-7 tie. The Sooners had reason to wonder when their superior efforts against Texas would finally be rewarded. Another frustration occurred the following week against Nebraska in Lincoln. The Sooners dominated the Huskers, driving into scoring territory 13 times, only to be turned back repeatedly. A muddy field contributed to sloppy play on both sides. With four minutes remaining, Oklahoma place-kicker Raphael Boudreau attempted a 37-yard game winner. Witnesses observed the ball spraying water in pinwheel patterns as it died just short of the cross-bar. Oklahoma 0, Nebraska 0. After dropping a game to Kansas 6-3, the Sooners reeled off four straight victories, defeating Kansas State, Iowa State, Missouri and Oklahoma A&M. Pete Smith was named All-American. Quarterback Jack Baer made All-Conference as did center Mickey Parks and Roland "Waddy" Young.

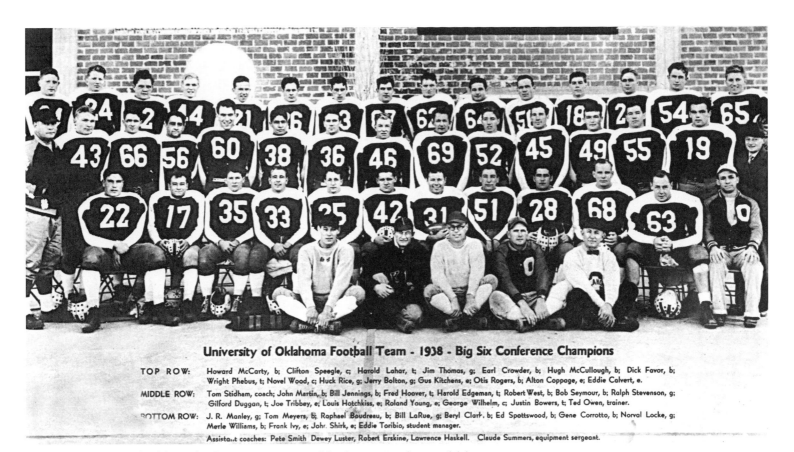

University of Oklahoma Football Team - 1938 - Big Six Conference Champions

TOP ROW: Howard McCarty, b; Clifton Speegle, c; Harold Lahar, t; Jim Thomas, g; Earl Crowder, b; Hugh McCullough, b; Dick Favor, b; Wright Phebus, t; Novel Wood, c; Huck Rice, g; Jerry Bolton, g; Gus Kitchens, e; Otis Rogers, e; Alton Coppage, e; Eddie Calvert, e.

MIDDLE ROW: Tom Stidham, coach; John Martin, b; Bill Jennings, b; Fred Hoover, t; Harold Edgeman, t; Robert West, b; Bob Seymour, b; Ralph Stevenson, g; Gilford Duggan, t; Joe Tribbey, e; Louis Hotchkiss, e; Roland Young, e; George Wilhelm, c; Justin Bowers, t; Ted Owen, trainer.

BOTTOM ROW: J. R. Manley, g; Tom Meyers, b; Raphael Boudreau, b; Bill LaRue, g; Beryl Clark, b; Ed Spottswood, b; Gene Corrotto, b; Norval Locke, g; Merle Williams, b; Frank Ivy, e; John Shirk, e; Eddie Toribio, student manager.

Assistant coaches: Pete Smith, Dewey Luster, Robert Erskine, Lawrence Haskell. Claude Summers, equipment sergeant.

Joe Louis had knocked out Jimmy Braddock to win the world heavyweight championship. In Norman, the Oklahoma Sooners were preparing to win a championship of their own. The Sooners of 1938 won ten straight games before yielding to Tennessee in the University's first ever post-season bowl appearance, that coming in the Orange Bowl. The 1938 Sooners led the nation in rushing defense and won their first Big 6 Conference crown in their first unbeaten season since 1920. Many contributed to the Sooner success. Hugh McCullough, Sooner quarterback, hit 69 of 109 passes and zig-zagged his way on the ground as well. "Waddy" Young and Frank "Pop" Ivy constituted a splendid receiving corps. In Houston, for the season opener against Rice, it was the toe of Raphael Boudreau which saved victory for the Sooners, 7-6. Oklahoma finally overcame the Texas Longhorns, 13-0, due to a steel-knit defensive forward wall, limiting Texas to just two net yards. Over the next eight games, Sooner foes were blanked an incredible seven times. Only Tulsa managed to even get on the scoreboard, earning one single touchdown for six points against third teamers. In a game dubbed the "Orange Brawl," the Sooners were toppled by Major Bob Neyland's Tennessee Volunteers, 17-0. The Vols were penalized sixteen times for 130 yards; the Sooners nine times for 90 yards. The Sooners simply could not penetrate the solid defense erected by the Tennesseans. Oklahoma had, however, elevated itself to national prominence. The names of Roland "Waddy" Young, Cliff Speegle, Gilford "Cactus Face" Duggan, Hugh "Mac" McCullough, Gene Corrotto, Howard "Red Dog" McCarty, Frank "Pop" Ivy and Bill Jennings became known far and wide, synonymous with college football glory.

John Steinbeck published his epic novel, *The Grapes of Wrath*, in 1939. Its poignant tale of anguish and hope among members of Oklahoma's Joad family touched the nation. Meanwhile, the Sooners of Coach Tom Stidham

Below: Frank "Pop" Ivy, a native of Skiatook, was on the receiving end of enough passes to be named an All-American in 1939.

*Gil ("Cactus Face") Duggan
All-America Tackle*

Above: Gilford "Cactus Face" Duggan, All-American tackle, 1939, shown above, sporting the new leather helmet.

Right: Jack Jacobs led the Sooners at quarterback, 1939-1941. Some old-timers say he was the best natural athlete OU has ever had.

sported new leather helmets with a handsome block "O" on the front. At the games, there was a student card section, creating proud symbols. The University band had grown to 165 members. Could the Sooners reprise the successes of '38? That kind of success proved impossible, mostly due to late-season injuries which seemed to drain the spunk out of the squad. A sophomore who had been raised at Holdenville and who had played football at Muskogee began to appear in the press accounts of Oklahoma games. His name was Jack Jacobs. Another back, Beryl Clark, was dubbed the "Sooner Houdini," for his thrilling and totally unpredictable jaunts. "Cactus Face" Duggan, "Pop" Ivy, John Shirk, Justin Bowers and Bob Seymour returned as well. On the opening kickoff of the opening game against Southern Methodist in Norman, Jack Jacobs returned the ball 68 yards. Some observers opined that "Indian" Jack could do anything he wished on the gridiron. He simply had to want to. Fumbles and bumbles by youthful Sooners that day resulted in a 7-7 tie. The day's events, however, seemed to stir the Sooners, as they stormed to six straight victories, shutting out Northwestern 23-0, before defeating Texas 24-12, Kansas 27-7, Oklahoma A&M 41-0, Iowa State 38-6 and Kansas State 13-10. At Columbia the Sooners ran out of steam, losing to Missouri 7-6. A week later at Nebraska, Biff Jones and his Cornhuskers bested the Sooners, 13-7, before 35,000 Husker fans. "You can't expect a grand slam every year," Coach

Stidham retorted. "Pop" Ivy and "Cactus Face" Duggan were named All-Americans.

FDR was once again reelected President, but ominous clouds were gathering over Europe. Hitler's armies had forced an English retreat on the shores of Dunkirk. Americans were agonizingly split over whether to enter the war.

Jack Jacobs was back for his junior year in 1940, displaying a passing ability the likes of which had never been seen in Norman. Bill Jennings, Roger Eason, Harold Lahar, and John Martin paced the Sooners and earned all-conference accolades for their efforts. In the season opener against Oklahoma A&M, the Sooners outlasted the Aggies, 29-27 on the strength of Jacobs' aerial attack. Jacobs played his best game of the year the following week against Texas, but it was not enough as Dana X. Bible's favored Longhorns prevailed, 19-16. Oklahoma returned home to defeat Kansas State 14-0, then traveled to Ames, Iowa, to upend the Cyclones, 20-7. The Sooners wanted to defeat Biff Jones'

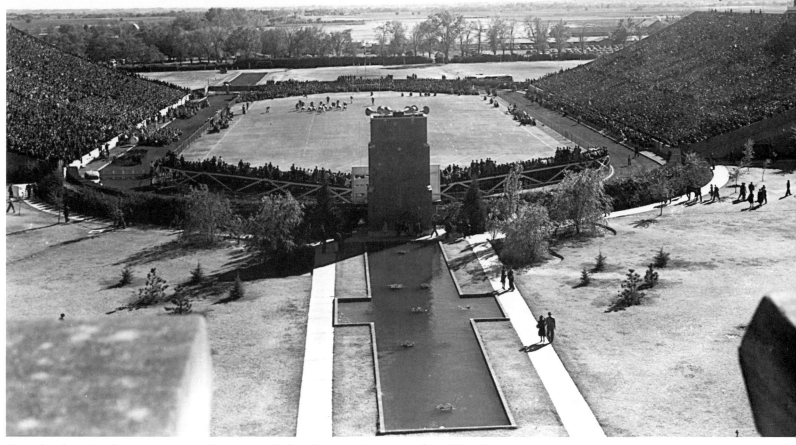

Cornhuskers in the worst way. However, Nebraska was the class of the Big 6. An overflow crowd of 35,000 at Memorial Stadium witnessed the Husker victory, 13-0. The Sooners were never able to free Jacobs to perform his offensive wizardry. Oklahoma dispatched Kansas at Lawrence, 13-0, then set its sights on Missouri and the Tigers' star quarterback, "Passin' Paul" Christman.

The Sooner defense kept Christman in check all afternoon, while Huel Hamm substituted for an ailing Jack Jacobs at Sooner quarterback. Johnny Martin scored the game's lone touchdown from the one-yard line to give the Sooners a 7-0 victory. The Temple Owls were the Sooners' next victims as the Oklahomans coasted to a 9-6 victory. The varsity traveled to the West Coast to play Santa Clara in the season closer. After a fast start, the Sooners were swamped 33-13. The 1940 yearbook stated, "The 35 gridders forgot the defeat as they visited Hollywood before returning." In a surprise move, Tom Stidham announced his resignation in order to accept the head coaching position at Marquette University in Milwaukee. Stidham was also vacating his position as athletic director. Lawrence "Jap" Haskell, the old jock and baseball coach, took over as athletic director, while the wily little gnome, Snorter Luster, was chosen to become Oklahoma's eleventh head football coach.

There had never been a coach at Oklahoma quite like Snorter Luster. Snorter wasn't a polished academic like

Above: A record crowd jammed Oklahoma Memorial Stadium, November 2, 1940, to witness Oklahoma battle the Nebraska Cornhuskers.

Below: Dapper OU cheerleaders pause for refreshments at a stadium concession stand. The photo is from the early 1930s.

Vernon Parrington, nor did he ooze frontier gentility like Bennie Owen. He wasn't a bearish, gruff military-type like Biff Jones, nor was he a somber giant like Tom Stidham. Snorter was different. He was a slightly-built fellow, a bit on the lanky side, with a visage that definitely lingered with the observer. He was trained in law; he was a skilled boxer; he had been a ferocious tackle for Oklahoma back in 1920. All in all, he was as cunning as a coyote and as versatile as a strand of baling wire.

The "Big Red" is Born

William Bennett Bizzell left the university presidency after the summer session of 1941, having contributed 16 years of outstanding leadership. His successor was Joe Brandt, a sandy-haired pipe-puffing scholar. Luster's new coaching staff included Dale Arbuckle, backfield coach; Jap Haskell, line coach; Frank Crider, freshman coach and Jack Baer, assistant freshman coach. Luster preferred to separate the seniors and juniors from the balance of the squad. Out of this organizational arrangement was born a new name for the upperclassmen. They were called the "Big Red." Luster had spent a year in New York, ostensibly to study law at Columbia University. He managed, however, to apprentice on the coaching staff of the New York Giants pro football team.

The Giants were running a marvelous new offensive formation known as the "A" formation. On October 4, 1941, Luster peeled off the covers of his own version of the "A" formation against Oklahoma A&M in Norman. "Indian" Jack Jacobs was without peer that day, running and passing the Sooners to a 19-0 victory. The following week, the largest crowd ever to see an OU-Texas game, 45,000, saw Texas dominate the Sooners 40-7. Jack Crain, a two-time All-American at Texas, scored on gallops of 69 and 72 yards. For the first time, the Texas State Fair awarded the "Golden Hat," a bronze replica of a 10-gallon western hat, to the winners. Against Kansas State, an eager bunch of sophomores, led by Joe "Junior" Golding, employed

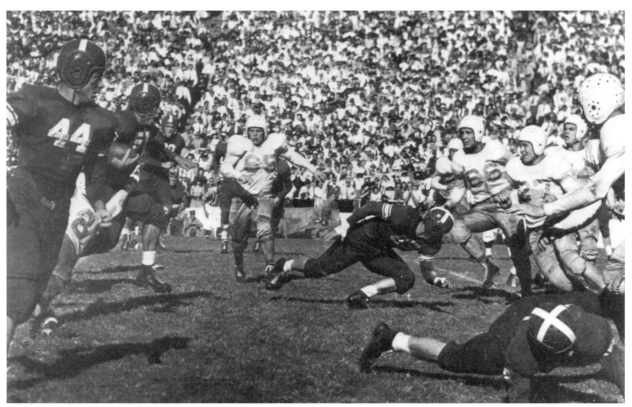

Crisp execution is captured in this photograph from the 1941 OU-Texas game.

the "A" formation to perfection. OU 16, Kansas State 0. Eighteen-thousand fans survived a drenching rain storm at Memorial Stadium to witness a memorable performance by Jack Jacobs against Santa Clara. His punting was nothing short of spectacular. On one occasion, Jacobs punted a sodden pigskin 85 yards to squelch a Santa Clara scoring threat. OU 16, Santa Clara 6. When Kansas came to visit a week later, Jacobs greeted them by completing all eight passes he threw for a total of 111 yards. The Jayhawkers were blanked 38-0 before the Dad's Day crowd. Iowa State was no match for the Sooners either, as substitute quarterback Huell Hamm led a 55-0 rout. At Columbia, Missouri, the Sooners ran into a splendid Tiger squad which stymied the "A" formation and stopped the Sooners cold, 28-0. The following week, Tom Stidham brought his Marquette Hilltoppers to Norman, whereupon Luster's charges walloped them, 61-14. Jacobs scored three touchdowns. In the final game of the season, the Sooners visited Lincoln, Nebraska, with sky-high hopes. The Sooners gained more total yardage and more first downs, yet lost the game 7-6 on a missed conversion. Luster's inaugural season had ended with a record of 6-3.

A week after the season ended, the Japanese attacked Pearl Harbor. Luster later recalled, "Pearl Harbor must have happened on a Saturday night, because I was taking a bath when I heard about it." A common

Iowa State vs. Oklahoma

Official Program
Nov. 8, 1941
Homecoming

Price 25c

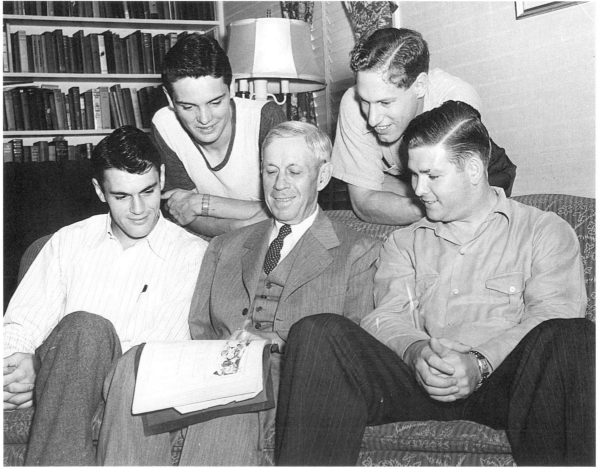

Above: The Sooner squad of 1941 finished its season a week before Pearl Harbor.

Right: The old master, Bennie Owen, is surrounded in 1941 by sons of former greats. Back row, Montfort Johnson, Jr.; Raymond Courtnight, Jr., Front row, Bob Reeds; Owen; Pat Geyer. All Owen's guests were then enrolled at OU.

reaction among young men was a realization that they had played their last football game. The country was at war.

In less than three weeks, 22 OU football lettermen volunteered for military duty. Before the 1942 season opened, all of Luster's assistants had gone off to war as well. The coach was left to build his war-time football teams from among students in the Naval Reserve Officers Training Corps at the University. "They were long on brains but a little short on brawn," Luster remembered. "If we had a boy who weighed 190 pounds, he automatically played left tackle and we called him 'Big John.' Today, even the quarterbacks weigh more than that."

This program from the OU-William & Mary game of 1942 reflected the nation's preoccupation with the war.

The War Years

The opening game at Stillwater against the Aggies accurately reflected the state of college football during the war-torn year of 1942. The final was a scoreless tie, 0-0, with neither team demonstrating much offensive punch. At Tulsa a week later, a passing whiz named Glen Dobbs led Tulsa to a 23-0 victory over the Sooners. Offense was once again absent from OU's performance. In fact, after the first five ballgames, the Sooners had scored in only one game – a 25-0 beating administered to Kansas behind the nifty running and passing of Huel Hamm. The Sooners managed victories over Iowa State, 14-7 and Kansas State, 76-0. The season concluded with a 6-6 tie with Missouri and a loss to William and Mary, 14-7. A persistent woeful lack of offense had been the Sooners' undoing.

The American war machine was whining around the clock. Eisenhower, Patton, and McArthur led the nation's finest young men into battle. In Norman, Snorter Luster's Sooners opened the 1943 season against a group from across town at the Navy Aviation Training Center. Even against this non-collegiate opponent, the Sooners were outweighed 35 pounds per man. However, the Navy men were no match for Luster's cagy tactics as the Sooners won 22-6. Against the Aggies from Oklahoma A&M, the Sooners capitalized on Aggie miscues and won 22-13. A young back for the Aggies, Bob Fenimore, got his first taste of this intense intrastate rivalry.

There was no Texas State Fair in 1943 as the war intensified. There was strict rationing of tires and gasoline. Only 18,500 spectators attended the Cotton Bowl clash. Additionally, only 4 of the 53 players for both teams who had played in the previous year's game were around to play in the 1943 match-up. It was becoming clear that Oklahoma did not have the necessary manpower to successfully execute the complicated "A" formation. The final score was Texas 13, Oklahoma 7. Injuries sustained in the Texas game cost the Sooners the following week as Tulsa passed by the Sooners 20-6. However, the season took a decidedly pleasant turn as Oklahoma opened Big 6 play. The Sooners ran off a string of five straight victories over conference opponents to clench their first Big 6 Conference crown since 1938. In the final game of the

season, the Sooners manhandled Nebraska, 26-7 on the Cornhuskers' home field. OU, behind the running of Bob Brumley and Derald Lebow, outrushed the Huskers 288 yards to 40. The "A" formation was back.

The tide of war had begun to turn in the Allies' favor, as America sighed a collective breath of relief. Ozzie and Harriett were a big hit on evening radio. Meanwhile, Snorter Luster welcomed a scanty crew of gridders to the varsity practice field in September, 1944. The Navy boys from north campus drove over for a game and left with a 28-14 victory. There was substantial work to be done. In the most thrilling game of the season, the Texas A&M Aggies met the Sooners at Taft Stadium in Oklahoma City. After seeing the Sooners take a 14-0 lead, the Aggies battled back to tie the score. An 89-yard drive in the waning moments culminated with Sooner Derald Lebow going over on a short plunge. OU 21, A&M 14. Next, freshman Bobby Layne led the Texas Longhorns to a decisive 20-0 victory over the Sooners in the Cotton Bowl before 23,000 sun-drenched fans. For several years, Big 6 conference play had proven rewarding for the Sooners. It was so in 1944, as the Sooners demolished Kansas State 68-0. Next, the Sooners walloped Southwest Conference champion Texas Christian, 34-19 in Oklahoma City, then played their best game of the season in defeating Iowa State in Ames, 12-7. A hobbled Sooner squad tied Missouri 21-21, then recovering quickly, blasted Kansas in Lawrence 20-0. Derald Lebow passes to Charlie Heard demoralized the Jayhawkers. The Sooners next defeated Nebraska 31-12 in an Oklahoma City match up, then directed their energies toward one of the best Oklahoma A&M Aggie teams of all time. In a fiercely waged contest, All-American Bob Fenimore directed the Aggies to a 28-6 victory. Fenimore played brilliantly on both sides of the ball, providing a spark by stealing a Sooner pass while playing defense. Nevertheless, the Sooners won their second consecutive Big 6 crown, ending the season with a record of 6-3-1.

Seven and one-half million Americans were under arms. FDR died in

Warm Springs, Georgia and Harry S. Truman delivered an ultimatum to the Japanese. Within days, atomic bombs obliterated Hiroshima and Nagasaki. By August, World War II had mercifully concluded. College football rosters remained a hodge-podge of freshmen, military trainees and war veterans. Under special rules of dispensation, service play was not counted against collegiate football eligibility. Old college players from as early as 1941 returned to campus and to their dreams of gridiron glory.

Snorter Luster had been experiencing some health problems. He had every intention of seeing the 1945 season through, however. Against the Hondo, Texas, Army Air Field Comets, sprints by sophomore backs Johnny Steward and Bill Irvin spelled victory for the Sooners, 21-6. Against Nebraska, OU runner Howard Hawkins and husky fullback, Jack Venable dominated the game. Center and placekicker Bob Bodenhamer was making a name for himself in that 20-0 Sooner victory. Texas A&M managed to stave off a late Sooner surge to defeat OU, 19-14. In Dallas, the Sooners once again had trouble getting into the end zone. Despite thoroughly outplaying the Longhorns, Texas prevailed 12-7. The Sooners dominated Kansas, 39-7 in Norman before 13,000 Sooner loyalists, and whipped Kansas State 41-13 in Manhattan. On November 3, Texas Christian solved OU's offensive scheme, defeating the Sooners 13-7. Oklahoma dispatched Iowa State 14-7 before being dethroned from the Big 6 Conference title at Missouri, 14-6. In Norman, on November 24, the Sooners suffered their worst defeat of all time to Bob Fenimore and his Oklahoma A&M Aggies. Thirty-three thousand fans watched as the Sooners proved helpless against the skilled running, passing and special teams play by the visitors from Stillwater. The final score was 47-0.

The Snorter Luster regime at Oklahoma came to a quiet close. Snorter took a position in the OU intramural department, while OU President George L. Cross and the Board of Regents resolved behind close doors to vault the Oklahoma Sooners into the national limelight.

Oklahoma's gridiron hero, Waddy Young, became a war hero as well, piloting his bomber over Europe. Young and his crew were lost in combat, January, 1945.

The Bud Wilkinson Era

Some say he was the greatest college football coach who ever lived. If life is a series of mystical, profound moments connected by long periods of sleepy survival, then we have Bud Wilkinson to thank for allowing us to share with him a few of those mystical, profound, elegant, triumphant moments. To see him on the sidelines of Owen Field didn't merely arouse competitive fires within Sooner fans – it aroused pride which went far beyond football. People simply felt better about themselves – about being Oklahomans – after cheering on Wilkinson and his Sooners. Bud carried something with him throughout his life. It is called grace. Even when he left his Sooners to enter politics, people never had the feeling that he had traded in some essential piece of his dignity. Bud is as much a part of the rich tradition of Sooner football tradition today as he ever was – a legend for the ages. Future generations of Sooner fans will know him through the words of those he touched.

Before Wilkinson, however, there was Tatum. Because of the curious manner in which these men found their way to the county seat community of Norman, Oklahoma, their careers became inextricably entwined.

The decision to engage a new football coach in the cold January days of 1946 hinged more upon a dramatic policy adoption than a mere personnel matter. Oklahoma had weathered the Great Depression, the Dust Bowl, the *Grapes of Wrath* novel, and World War II. There was a perception that despite having endured these adversities, Oklahomans were carrying a great deal of emotional and psychological baggage. If the Broadway musical *Oklahoma!* could have such a positive effect upon the people of the state and indeed, the nation, why couldn't a collegiate football powerhouse do the same? OU regent Lloyd Noble observed that many splendid and experienced football players would be returning to college after military service. Most had played football on outstanding service teams. Hiring a coach capable of luring these players to Norman seemed, to Noble, a master stroke.

Tatum and His Assistants

Athletic director Jap Haskell, who had been on leave of absence to enter the military, felt he knew just the right man. Jim Tatum was a bearish man with a large head and dark features. He had played his football at North Carolina and had been head coach there in 1942. Further, Tatum had been Don Faurot's line coach for the Iowa Pre-flight Sea Hawks and had joined

Faurot at the Jacksonville, Florida naval air station as well. Jim Tatum had made an unusual request prior to interviewing for the position at Oklahoma. He asked if he could bring along a prospective assistant, a young fellow named Bud Wilkinson. The story is often recounted that the OU regents opined that Wilkinson should be hired rather than Tatum. Institutional ethics, it was said, short-stopped that idea. However, Oklahoma's offer to Tatum included a bold condition that Wilkinson be engaged as an assistant. It was a package deal. Tatum resisted the condition, suggesting that the head coach's authority should extend to hiring all members of his staff. In the end, however, Tatum relented and agreed to the arrangement. Wilkinson, who was under pressure to enter the family business in Minneapolis, agreed privately with Tatum to come to Norman for one year. It was, then, a personal favor to Tatum on Wilkinson's part that brought him to Norman and to his football destiny.

Revisionist historians might now agree that Jim Tatum was one of the most interesting, colorful, effective football coaches in Oklahoma's storied history. Tatum was also headstrong and manipulative. These characteristics led to his making a big splash, sending ripples throughout the state. One of the first things he did was to arrange tours of the state, talking up Sooner football, pressing the flesh, eyeing potential recruits. Bud Wilkinson was usually in tow. The two large men, both dapper dressers, made quite an impression. Tatum was always on the move, which led to the stepping on of several toes. He talked rapid fire. He was tireless.

Spring practice in 1946 was like nothing anyone had ever witnessed. Bodies glistening with sweat labored on three separate football fields adjacent to Memorial Stadium. There was a distinct military air to the goings-on. "I never saw so many college football players in my life," Leon Manley, Sooner tackle remembers. "They were swarming in and out carrying suitcases. I never saw so many styles of suitcases, either." Tatum's coaches carried around little note pads. When a prospect

In the spring of 1946, new head coach Jim Tatum and his top assistant, Charles "Bud" Wilkinson, toured the state, promoting Oklahoma football.

creamed his adversary during the one-on-one drills, the coach would halt the drill, ask the kid's name and scribble it down on his pad. But Tatum wasn't through. He hit upon the idea of conducting a summer camp, inviting discharged servicemen, potential transfers and walk-ons to give it a go. There were no limitations regarding off-season practice in those days. The Sooner squad looked promising. Among returnees were Plato Andros, Joe Golding, Tommy Tall Chief and Otis McCrary. The backfield looked particularly promising with quarterback Jack Mitchell having transferred in from the

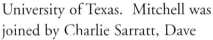

University of Texas. Mitchell was joined by Charlie Sarratt, Dave Wallace, Johnny Allsup and a host of others. John Rapacz, Paul "Buddy" Burris and Norman McNabb added strength in the line as did Wade Walker, a North Carolina transfer. Burris was a transfer from Tulsa University. A skinny war veteran, Myrle Greathouse, was permitted to walk on and try his hand at linebacker. The effects of the frenzied recruiting in the summer of 1946 was, as one sportswriter observed, four years of effective recruiting packed into one steamy summer. Tatum and Wilkinson then set about to install the rudiments of the Faurot-inspired Split-T formation.

Winston Churchill made a speech in Fulton, Missouri, in which he coined the phrase, "The Iron Curtain," referring to conditions in eastern Europe. For the first time, ranch-style homes popped up around the nation. America took a deep breath and plunged into post-war prosperity. The open-ing game of 1946 under Tatum's regime could not have been more challenging. Army was to be played at West Point, New York, September 28, 1946. The Cadets had dominated college football in both 1944 and 1945, going undefeat-ed both seasons. In the Army line-up were shifty halfback Glen Davis and Felix "Doc" Blanchard, a powerful inside runner. Interestingly, Blanchard was Coach Tatum's cousin. The Sooners traveled east, using DC-3 air transporta-tion. It was the first time for Oklahoma to travel by airplane to a football game. Over 25,000 attended the game at Michie Stadium, including President Truman. The first quarter was score-less. OU's scrappy defense was holding firm. Then a blocked punt allowed OU to score. Army's superb execution of the T formation

Above left to right: John Rapacz, All-American center, 1946; Jack Mitchell, All-American quarterback, 1948; Paul "Buddy" Burris, All-American guard, 1946.

Below: Team captain and All-American guard, Plato Andros, joins Coach Jim Tatum in waving farewell to fans at a send-off pep rally, November 30, 1946.

forged a 7-7 half time tie. But in the second half, Army took advantage of the breaks which came their way to win the game, 21-7. The eastern press promptly responded with praise of Oklahoma's effort. OU had outrushed Army, 129 yards to 83. Coach Tatum's sideline intensity is reflected in one story, possibly apocryphal, that after a controversial play, Tatum removed half-back Charlie Sarratt's swollen ankle from a bucket of ice water and took a long swig, then returned the bucket to the ground and stuck Sarratt's foot back in it.

Football intensity in Norman matched that of the new football coach. The following week, OU edged Texas A&M in Norman, 10-7. The offense was lagging behind the splendid defensive line play. That became evident on October 12 in Dallas, as the Texas aerial game spoiled an otherwise sterling Sooner effort. OU once again outgained its opponent on the ground, this time 143 yards to 81, yet fell 20-13. Against Kansas State, halfback Joe Golding exploded for a 43-yard touchdown on his first play of the game and ran 81 yards to score on his last carry of the day. OU 28, K-State 7. Iowa State was destroyed 63-0 in Ames before the Sooners plowed through mud and an inspired team of TCU Horned Frogs to win 14-12. The weather was even worse the next week at Kansas. Playing on a field devoid of grass, the Jayhawks squeezed by the Sooners, 16-13. The pivotal game of the season against powerful Missouri came next. The outcome would determine the direction Tatum was taking the OU program. The game itself was not very close. The Sooners dominated the Tigers, winning 27-6 and followed up that victory with an identical win over Nebraska the following week. Even the Sooners' aerial game was improving. The game against Oklahoma A&M to close the season had taken on special significance due to the Aggies' spectacu-lar wins over OU during the war years of '44 and '45. The great Aggie half-back, Bob Fenimore, watched most of the game from the sideline, nursing an injured knee. Meanwhile, the Oklahoma onslaught commenced. The Sooners rushed for an astonishing 415 yards, while the Aggies gained 7. The final score was OU 73, A&M 12. With that, the Sooners were off to the Gator Bowl in Jacksonville, Florida, the site of Tatum's successes as a military football coach.

Tatum had privately expressed certain concerns about his continued tenure at Oklahoma. There were personnel matters that concerned him. He felt he was underpaid. He felt he deserved a longer contract. President Cross listened patiently to Tatum's musings. However, while the Sooners were in Florida preparing to meet North Carolina State on January 1, Cross got word that Tatum planned to interview for the head coaching job at Maryland. Cross moved quickly to shore up his position with Wilkinson, should Tatum depart. Against North Carolina State, the Sooners' magnificent rushing defense dis-played its awesome power. OU 34, North Carolina State 13. The Sooner rushing defense led the nation, allowing only 58 yards per game. The Sooner season of 1946 concluded with a record of 8-3. Spurred by his success, Tatum pressed his bargain with both Maryland and Oklahoma. It became obvious that while Oklahoma hoped to retain Tatum, the University was equally com-fortable with elevating his youthful assistant, Bud Wilkinson, to the top spot.

Tatum ultimately accepted the position at Maryland, leaving behind an atmosphere of enthusiasm and an inventory of young talent upon which Wilkinson and his new staff could build.

Bud Takes Command

Charles Burnham "Bud" Wilkinson was born Easter Sunday, April 23, 1916, in Minneapolis, Minnesota, the second son to be born to Charles Patton Wilkinson and his wife, Edith. C.P. Wilkinson was a stern, upright and correct mortgage broker with his own Minneapolis business. He had married Edith, a child of Swedish immigrant parents, and had set about to make good for himself and his family. There was an insular quality to life in the upper middle-class neighborhood of south Minneapolis that Bud knew as a child. His paternal grandmother lived in a house on one side of his own, while his Aunt Florence, Edith's sister, lived with her family on the other side. It is said that Bud's early life was stable, safe and secure. But all that changed when Bud's mother died in 1923, having sustained serious injuries in a railroad passenger car derailment. At 7, Bud was without his beloved mother. For months, he could not fall asleep at night. C.P., sensitive to the boy's plight and grieving in silence himself, drew closer to the boy. At the age of 13, however, it was decided that Bud and his brother Bill, would benefit by attending Shattuck Military Academy in Fairbault, Minnesota, some fifty miles south of Minneapolis. C.P. had remarried a lovely woman, Ethel Grace, by this time. Life, it seemed, would be less complicated if the Wilkinson boys received quality instruction a short distance from home. Bud later recalled the first weekend visit by his father and stepmother. The inevitable loneliness of frigid Fairbault overtook Bud and he burst into tears, begging to be allowed to return home. C.P. wouldn't hear of it. Once again, Bud was confronted with the harsh realities of youth and the need to look to the future for strength and reward. Athletics proved a healthy outlet for Bud at Shattuck. He played football, baseball, hockey and, in his senior year, basketball. He became the only four-sport letterman in his senior class. By the fall of 1933, Bud had enrolled at the University of Minnesota and had come under the supervision of the Golden Gopher football coach, the great Bernie Bierman. Through Bierman, Bud's sense of moral authority was sharpened. Bierman was a disciplinarian, though even-handed. He demonstrated to Bud the virtues of hard work. Incredibly, Bud played on three consecutive national championship football teams – 1934, '35 and '36. The first two seasons, Bud played guard but by his senior year, his football savvy prompted Bierman to move him to blocking back in Bierman's single-wing formation. From that position, Bud called signals. Bud became a two-time All-American, winning the Big Ten medal as Minnesota's finest scholar-athlete. As a senior, Bud quarterbacked the college All-Stars to their first-ever victory over a professional team, a 7-0 victory over the Green Bay Packers. Bud's travel with the Minnesota hockey team led to his introduction to his future wife, Mary Shiflett, who was then enrolled at Carlton College. Mary transferred to Minnesota during Bud's

Bud was the only four-sport letterman in his senior class at Shattuck Military Academy, Fairbault, Minnesota, 1933.

CHARLES WILKINSON, '33
Captain 1932

THE TOUCHDOWN CLUB

Lindell Pearson had been a superb football player at Oklahoma City Capitol Hill High School, graduating there in the spring of 1947. Lindell had every intention of enrolling at the University of Oklahoma to pursue his education and his promising football career. He obtained a summer job at the Oklahoma City Coca-Cola bottling plant owned by the Browne family. Henry Browne, Sr. was an ardent OU supporter, having been a four-year letterman in tennis at OU. Mr. Browne enjoyed employing the hard-working athletes over the summers before they departed for Norman, Stillwater and other collegiate destinations. During the summer of 1947, there was a high school all-star football game arranged to be played at Oklahoma City's Taft Stadium. Outstanding athletes from neighboring states were to be matched against Oklahoma's best. In that game, Lindell Pearson had a field day. Afterwards, he was deluged with well-wishers. Some were from Arkansas. These persons offered to make it worth Pearson's while to cancel his plans to attend Oklahoma and to attend Arkansas instead. By early August, Pearson had given notice to his employer, Mr. Browne. Browne assumed Pearson was moving to Norman for fall practice. Browne recalls receiving a telephone call from Dr. C.B. McDonald, an Oklahoma City dentist and fellow OU supporter. McDonald had heard from Wilkinson. Pearson was not on campus – had not reported for practice. There were persistent rumors in town that Pearson had decided to attend Arkansas. Browne and McDonald agreed that something had to be done. If Oklahoma was to continue its climb to the top, rival institutions could not be allowed to surreptitiously lure Oklahoma's finest away unchallenged. With the help of Pearson's girlfriend, it was confirmed that Pearson had in fact been spirited away to Arkansas and was being kept in hiding until time to enroll. Through careful detective work, Browne and McDonald, along with Oklahoma City businessmen Bob Bowers and Gene Jordan, located Pearson in Little Rock and succeeded in convincing him to abandon his new-found friends in Arkansas and return home to Oklahoma. There remained the uncomfortable business matter of reimbursing the Arkansas supporters for their out-of-pocket expenses in dealing with Pearson. A discreet solicitation for funds among Oklahoma City businessmen yielded several thousand dollars – much more than was needed to put the Pearson episode to rest.

What could and should be done to maintain a response mechanism for future crises such as this? A very successful, robust personality named Harrison Smith called a meeting at his home. Oklahoma City's business elite agreed to organize as the Touchdown Club. Smith was elected the club's first president. Paul Brown, an attorney, agreed to draft legal documents to incorporate the organization. On October 8, 1947, the Touchdown Club was formally created. Gordon Brown recalled attending some of the early meetings with his father. "We had a couple of outside barbecues at 'Big Boy' Johnson's home on west Main in Norman." E.G. "Big Boy" Johnson was a prominent Norman businessman, operating Johnson Dairy. Brown continued, "'Big Boy' would open up the door of his back-yard barbecue pit and I'd marvel at how much beef he had in there. It looked like two whole cows to me!" Within three months, Harrison Smith and his merry men had raised $75,000. Over the next few years, the Touchdown Club grew in membership and with that, so did its financial support of Oklahoma football. Men like Dan James, Luther Delaney, Bus Harrington, Dr. D.L. Rippito; Carl Anderson, and even U.S. Senator Robert S. Kerr played roles in the success of the Touchdown Club. In short, the men who shaped the Oklahoma City business community in law, in oil and gas, and in commerce and industry signed on as members of the Touchdown Club. The club's history is not devoid of controversy, however. By the spring of 1954, Oklahoma had experienced sufficient success on the gridiron to generate curiosity. OU president George L. Cross received a comprehensive letter from NCAA executive secretary Walter Byers, implying that wealthy friends of the program were overtly aggressive in the recruiting process. After the Sooners went undefeated in 1954 and had won 19 games in a row, the Sooners were placed on two years probation without sanctions, commencing in April 1955.

Sooner victories continued to follow, however, one after the other. The Touchdown Club flourished both as an integral part of the football program's network of state-wide support but also as a social vehicle. Members simply wanted to be a part of a grand enterprise and Oklahoma football was surely that. Another hiccup occurred after former OU assistant coach Bill Jennings was appointed head coach at Nebraska in 1957. Recruiting wars led to an exchange of terse letters between representatives of both Oklahoma and Nebraska over an extended period of time. Eventually, the dispute, heretofore on simmer, boiled over, with Jennings supplying information to the NCAA regarding a "slush fund" to be used to recruit prospective athletes at Oklahoma during 1952-1954. The fund was ostensibly maintained by Oklahoma City accountant Arthur L. Wood. A letter from Walter Byers to Wood requesting access to records of the account was delivered. However, Wood declined, citing client privilege. The matter deteriorated when, in January 1960, the NCAA placed OU on indefinite probation with sanctions, forbidding post-season play and television appearances. However, a year later, the probation was lifted after Wood had shared certain accounting information and had himself moved to Nevada to pursue other business interests. While there is no suggestion that the Touchdown Club itself, which had maintained a long practice of turning over its funds to the University, had any involvement with Bill Jennings and Arthur Wood, these matters reflect a different time when rules were few and men pursued their football interests in personal ways.

Almost 50 years after its founding, the Touchdown Club continues its support of the Sooner football program. Most recently, the Touchdown Club funded the installation of natural grass on Owen Field, after previously assisting with the acquisition costs of the artificial turf. Other club projects include weight-lifting facilities and the Mosier indoor practice facility. As OU's oldest and most productive support group, it is said that over the last 25 years, 20 percent of OU football scholarships have been funded by the Touchdown Club. Since the inception of The Touchdown Club, over two million dollars have been freely given to assist OU athletic programs. Current club president, Henry Browne, Jr. recalls those early days when his father and others formed the club. "We're all proud to have contributed to our great Sooner football tradition. We plan to continue our work for a long time to come."

Creator of the Tradition

senior year and their romance flowered thereafter.

C.P. Wilkinson was not pleased with Bud's next move, which was to accept an assistant football coaching position under Ossie Solem at Syracuse University. Coaching, C.P. reasoned, was not a suitable profession for someone of Bud's talents. A family strain was emerging. At Syracuse, Bud combined his football coaching with scholarship, earning a master's degree in English. Bud and Mary were married in 1938. Son Pat was born in 1940 and son Jay in 1942. But Bud's five-year exposure to the Syracuse "A" formation had run its course, and the war loomed ahead as well. In 1941, Bud entered the Navy pre-flight program, but not before confronting his father once again

over his career plans. C.P. wanted Bud to join him in the mortgage brokerage business. Bud, on the other hand, had made up his mind. Football coaching combined analytical skills with education, discipline, and physical conditioning. Its lure was something Bud could not escape. At Iowa Pre-flight, Bud tutored centers and quarterbacks for Don Faurot's Sea Hawks. Jim Tatum handled the line coaching chores. The famed Split-T formation, conceived by Faurot, was digested by Wilkinson and Tatum. Later, Bud saw action as a deck officer aboard the aircraft carrier Enterprise. Early in 1946, after his discharge, Bud reluctantly returned to his father's business in Minneapolis. The pace there was just too slow for Bud. Meanwhile, Tatum had migrated to Jacksonville, Florida, as coach of the Naval Air Station Jax Fliers. After posting an 8-2 record there in the fall of 1945, Tatum pursued the football coaching vacancy at Oklahoma with a vengeance. Then came Tatum's call to Bud Wilkinson.

Bud poses with his wife, Mary, and young sons, Jay and Pat, circa 1947.

The short-lived tenure of Jim Tatum had produced splashy successes and an empty OU athletic department bank account. Athletic director Jap Haskell bore responsibility for supervising expenditures and so was discharged. Wilkinson, at age 31, was head football coach and athletic director at Oklahoma.

The casual observer might conclude that a brilliant sun shone continuously on Bud Wilkinson from the day he emerged from a low-slung Hudson automobile onto the OU campus in the winter of 1946. Such was not the

Legendary pair – Bud was always joined by line coach Gomer Jones during a traditional stroll around verdant Owen Field prior to football games.

case. In fact, Bud knew better than anyone of the necessity to win football games at Oklahoma. He set about to do just that. He insisted upon perfection, according to his players. He had an acute eye for detail, which was reflected in everything – even his wardrobe. On game days, he paced the sidelines in a gray flannel suit, white oxford cloth button down shirt, a red necktie and gray fedora. His message was clear. To play at Oklahoma, one must be serious-minded, disciplined and prepared. One of Bud's first tasks was to engage a line coach. He'd been favorably impressed by the coach at Nebraska, a young Ohio State product named Gomer Jones. Gomer was a husky, bespectacled fellow, purposeful yet given to broad smiles. He fit Bud's vision for success perfectly. "Dutch" Fehring was held over from the '46 staff. Four other men, including Bill Jennings, completed the staff. Most fortunately, Bud and his coaches could count on a field general second to none to run the breathtaking, risky Split-T formation. He'd earned the moniker of "General Jack" Mitchell. Thirty-one of Bud's top 33 players were war veterans. Among the youngest was a kid from Hollis, Oklahoma named Darrell Royal. Royal had grown up eagerly awaiting the Saturday afternoon radio broadcasts of OU games. "I'd put a radio on our front porch and have me a solo game in our front yard," Royal recalls. "The play-by-play wasn't so important, but that 'Boomer Sooner' played by the Oklahoma marching band sure was. It lifted me right out of my socks." Among other Sooner recruits was Demosthenes "Dee" Andros, younger brother of Plato, from Oklahoma City. Players like Jim Tyree, Homer Paine, Nute Trotter, Earl Hale, Jim Owens, and Harry Moore were destined to contribute mightily. The genius of the Split-T formation lay in the quarterback's precision handoff to the halfback who received it without looking at the ball. Instead, the halfback was to find the hole quickly and slide off the brush blocks leveled by the forward wall. The scheme required the snap count to be executed flawlessly. Wilkinson's practice sessions became noted for brilliant organization and endless play repetition.

"Siscoed!"

In Wilkinson's debut as a head coach, the Sooners traveled to Detroit to play the Titans of the University of Detroit. Nearly 25,000 fans were in attendance to watch General Jack Mitchell and left halfback Royal share the ball carrying. Wilkinson had every right to be nervous going into the game. Detroit was destined to lead the nation in rushing in 1947, averaging almost

320 yards per contest. The Sooners won the see-saw battle 24-20, launching the season on a successful, if shaky, start. Against the Texas A&M Aggies in Norman on October 4, the Sooners utilized depth in the line, alternating complete lines in order to wear down the opposition. The tactic worked, as 30,000 fans witnessed the Sooner victory, 26-14. One of the most talked about OU-Texas match-ups of all time occurred a week later in Dallas. Wilkinson had primed his defenses to slow down the great Texas passer, Bobby Layne. The Sooners might have managed to survive the Layne aerial display, had not two monumental and highly controversial official's calls greatly altered the course of the game. The official making the calls was Jack Sisco. To this day, Sooner fans refer to Sisco with disdain. To be "Siscoed," it is said, is to

be exploited for the benefit of an adversary. An otherwise cleanly-waged contest was compromised by the calls. In the end, a fine Texas team prevailed, 34-14. A Big 6 Conference showdown took place the following week against Kansas in Norman. Nothing was resolved, as the teams settled for a 13-13 tie. The Texas Christian Horned Frogs visited Norman next, and with five interceptions of Sooner passes, the Froggies managed to cruise to a 20-7 victory over the Sooners. The Sooners outrushed the Frogs 169-93, but breakdowns in their passing game proved lethal. OU rebounded against Iowa State with a

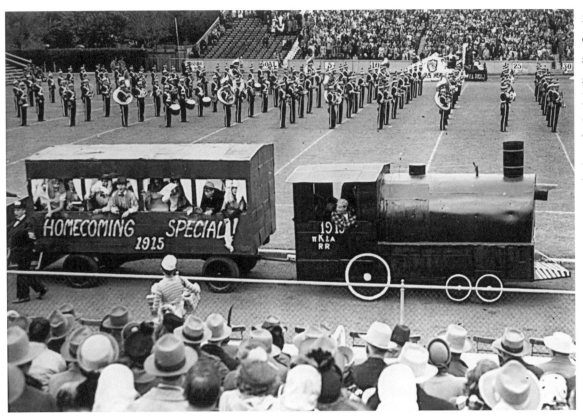

Homecoming was a special event in 1947, as this photo demonstrates.

revamped lineup. Royal opened at quarterback along with Buddy Jones and Johnny Allsup at the halves and Myrle Greathouse at fullback. The Sooners, by fits and starts, managed a 27-9 victory. The Sooners took a 27-13 win over Kansas State at Manhattan before preparing for an out-of-town donnybrook with conference power Missouri. It was the first meeting between Mizzou's Don Faurot and his prize student, Bud Wilkinson. For the first time, Darrell Royal's pinpoint punting affected the outcome of a critical game. As the Sooners fought to come from behind against the Tigers, Royal punted out of bounds at the Tiger one-yard line and again at the four-yard line. Defensively, Oklahoma utilized a seven-man front to stuff the run. Linebackers Rapacz and Greathouse had outstanding success. Great running by George Brewer and a gutty performance by Jack Mitchell sealed the OU victory, 21-12. Wilkinson always believed the miraculous punting by Darrell Royal had saved a pivotal victory for the Sooners – and preserved Wilkinson's fragile mandate with a skeptical public. Oklahoma traveled to icy Lincoln, Nebraska, for a November 22 game with the Huskers. Sub-freezing temperatures hampered the Sooners more than anything. Charlie Sarratt, Junior Thomas, Jack Mitchell and Ed Kreik supplied the rushing prowess as the Sooners held on to win, 14-13. The season closer with Oklahoma A&M required the Sooners to come from behind for the fifth time in their seven victories. Jim Lookabaugh's Aggies performed admirably behind the quarterbacking of Jack Hartman. Guard Buddy Burris forced an Aggie fumble with a jarring tackle, at which point the Sooners erupted from a 13-7 deficit to win going away, 21-13. In Wilkinson's inaugural season as head coach, the Sooners were Big 6 Conference co-champions with Kansas and finished number 16 in the Associated Press poll. Buddy Burris was named All-American. There were mutterings heard over coffee shop table tops that perhaps Bud wasn't mean enough or mature enough to lead a big-time football program. Patience, however, often leads to good things.

Royal, Mitchell and Glory

The 1948 football season was rather peculiar but then the whole year was peculiar. Truman upset Dewey, long-play records appeared for the first

time, and Oklahoma lost only one game, the season opener, to Santa Clara.

It was Wilkinson's idea to get General Jack Mitchell and Darrell Royal into the game at the same time. That meant moving Royal to quarterback and Mitchell to halfback. This offensive move yielded rewards. However, in the opener, Santa Clara exploited a leaky Sooner pass defense. That enabled the Broncos of coach Len Casanova to simply outscore the Sooners, 20-17. On Monday after, Bud placed the fleet Buddy Jones at safety. At home against Texas A&M, the Sooner offensive show hit its stride behind the passing of Royal and Claude Arnold plus the exquisite running of Junior Thomas and Jack Mitchell. A shored-up pass defense limited A&M, and OU triumphed 42-14.

The Sooners, still seething from the 1947 OU-Texas debacle, aimed to take the Longhorns down a notch. With General Jack Mitchell back at the controls, the Oklahoma Split-T hummed with precision. Lindell Pearson and Leon Heath pounded away, while Myrle Greathouse and Buddy Jones stifled Longhorn runners. Oklahoma held a comfortable 20-7 lead before Tom Landry scored for Texas. The final was OU 20, Texas 14, and the Cotton

Bowl was in need of fresh lumber for new goalposts. The Sooners manhandled Kansas State 42-0 at Norman, then escaped Texas Christian at Fort Worth, 21-18. Not only was the Oklahoma Split-T nearly unstoppable, but waves of Sooner players were getting comfortable with. Buddy Burris, Myrle Greathouse and scores of others were making life miserable for the opposition offenses as well. Huge victories over Iowa State,

Above: Quarterback Darrell Royal practices the Oklahoma Split-T hand-off to halfback Lindell Pearson, 1948.

Below: A jubilant group of Sooner gridders join Bud in claiming the Golden Hat in their Cotton Bowl stadium locker room following their victory over Texas, 20-14, in 1948.

Missouri, Nebraska and Kansas assured the Sooners of a Big 6 championship and a lofty national ranking. The peculiar year of 1948 continued November 27 in Stillwater, as a battling Aggie squad fought to tarnish OU's sterling season. Their efforts were to no avail, however, as Royal, Mitchell, Greathouse, Walker, Burris, Owens and friends limped away with a 19-15 win.

North Carolina and Charlie "Choo Choo" Justice awaited in New Orleans at the Sugar Bowl. The central question was whether Oklahoma belonged on the same field with the famed Justice and his mates. After all, the All-American tailback ranked second in the nation in total offense and led the nation in punting. Art Weiner, North Carolina's slender end, constituted another dangerous offensive threat. A strong, well-coached Tar Heel squad somehow managed to stymie the Oklahoma Split-T before the 80,000 fans in the Sugar Bowl stadium. The game was reduced to a defensive struggle, as "Choo Choo" was hampered by a stomach ailment. In the end, Oklahoma prevailed 14-6, with General Jack Mitchell being voted the game's outstanding player in his last college game. Myrle Greathouse had spearheaded the Sooner defense. Justice said of the Sooners, "They've got a good ball club. I don't see how they've been kept down all these years."

After the glorious gridiron successes of 1948, the OU regents

Upper left: "General" Jack Mitchell led the 1948 Sooners to a 10-1 record and a Sugar Bowl victory over North Carolina.

Upper right: Outstanding linebacker, Myrle Greathouse, cradles the 1949 Sugar Bowl trophy.

Below: The successes posted by these Sooners of 1948 merely hastened the beginning of a glorious decade of dominance by subsequent squads.

SUGAR BOWL CHAMPIONS
JAN. 1st. 1949

LEON TRICE
N.O. LA.

approved a $1 million expansion of Owen Field, increasing its seating capacity from 30,000 to 55,000 and providing for a new triple-deck press box with an elevator. The cinder track around the football field was removed and the playing surface lowered six feet, providing thousands of excellent new seats. The following summer, a new type of bathing suit, called a "bikini," began to appear in department stores and Alger Hiss, an alleged spy, went to trial in Washington, D.C., with a California congressman, Richard Nixon, vocally urging on the prosecution.

Those Sooners of '49

Some say the 1949 Sooners were the best ever. There is ample support for the sentiment. The Sooners went undefeated through the regular season and demolished LSU in the Sugar Bowl. They scored 399 points in the season, while allowing only 88. The '49 Sooners finished second behind Notre Dame in the final polls and, of course, were crowned Big 6 Champions. As a reflection of the team's dominance, it led the nation in rushing defense and was second in rushing offense. One key to the success of the team was Wilkinson's introduction of the 5-2 defense. Today, this defensive alignment is commonly referred to around the nation as the "Oklahoma 5-2." Such was its flexibility and devastating effectiveness, that it has survived as a viable defensive alignment for almost half a century. The Sooners were enormously talented, with Leon Manley, Stan West, Norman McNabb, Clair Mayes and Dee Andros opening the holes. Jim Owens and Frankie Anderson anchored the ends. Wade Walker was back for his senior season at right tackle. Pass defense was secure behind Buddy Jones, Darrell Royal and Ed Lisak. George "Junior" Thomas, Lindell Pearson and Leon Heath were fixtures in the backfield. Royal, the cool senior veteran, held steady at the quarterback slot in the Split-T. A splendid group of freshmen toiled away on the practice field. This group included Eddie Crowder, Buck McPhail, Chet Bynum, Jack Santee and Tom Catlin. A mature youngster from Cleveland, Oklahoma, had grabbed the Sooner coaches' attention. He had carried the ball five times in a high school game against Fairfax High and had scored five touchdowns. This muscular youngster was convinced to enroll at OU that fall. His name was Billy Vessels.

Oklahoma began the season with a 46-0 thrashing of Boston College before 36,241 fans at Boston's Braves Field. The following week, Texas A&M visited Norman intent upon heaving the football over the Sooner defenders. By the third quarter, the Sooners had established their awesome ground attack and A&M folded, 33-13. The Texas Longhorns were forced to swallow another dose of Sooner superiority on October 8 before 75,347 Cotton Bowl onlookers. After taking a 7-0 lead, the Horns could not corral Pearson, Thomas, Heath and Royal, as the Sooners defeated the Horns 20-14. Royal's punting continued to awe friends and foes alike. Against Texas, for example, Royal let fly with a 71-yard boot, pinning the Horns on their own 8-yard line. The Sooners dispatched Kansas, 48-26, intercepting six Kansas passes along the way. The juggernaut continued to Lincoln, Nebraska where the Sooners'

"When they blew that whistle, it was like a house a fire."

– OU Quarterback
Jack Mitchell
speaking of the
1949 Sooners

depth, speed and strength spelled disaster for the Huskers. OU 48, Nebraska 0. Iowa State, Kansas State and Missouri were dispatched before Santa Clara came to Norman.

Some folks had whispered that OU would never fill the expanded Memorial Stadium, which now featured 55,000 seats. On November 19, 61,353 fans crowded in while hundreds more were turned away. Many came in search of revenge for OU's lone 1948 loss. They found comfort, if not revenge, in OU's domination of a fine Santa Clara squad which would later play in the Orange Bowl. Three OU fumbles kept the contest relatively close with the Sooners prevailing 28-21, notching a school record 19 consecutive wins. Oklahoma A&M provided little resistance in the regular season finale, falling to OU 41-0. Wilkinson told the press after the game, "They've started something in football at Oklahoma that I am very hopeful we can perpetuate in the future."

Above: This now-famous photograph captures Dr. C.B. McDonald and a police detail apprehending Piggy Barnes at OU's Biloxi, Mississippi, practice field prior to the 1950 Sugar Bowl.

Bottom left to right: All-American tackle Wade Walker anchored the offensive line in 1949. Walker later became OU's athletic director. Jim Owens earned All-American honors at end, 1949. Guard Stan West opened gaping holes for Sooner backs in 1949 and was rewarded by being named an All-American.

The Sugar Bowl game following the 1949 season matched the all-victorious Big 6 Conference champions against the Bayou Bengals of LSU. In preparation, the Sooners had installed a serious of drop-back passes and some defensive wrinkles as well. The game itself was overshadowed by the infamous "spy incident" which occurred in Biloxi, Mississippi, at the Sooners' practice site. Following up on a tip, Sooner supporters discovered a man identified as Piggy Barnes, a former LSU tackle, viewing the Sooners' practices from underneath a blanket stretched between two small buildings. Scratch pads and a pair of binoculars were also recovered. A commercial photographer managed

to snap Barnes' apprehension in a now-famous photograph. Whatever information Barnes might have been able to develop, it didn't help the Bayou Bengals, as OU flattened them 35-0. Leon Heath had rumbled for 170 yards from his fullback position. Pearson and Thomas also found success on the ground. Five members of the team were named All-American – Wade Walker, Jim Owens, Stan West, Darrell Royal and George Thomas. Wilkinson was named Coach of the Year by the National Football Coaches Association.

Far left: All-American Darrell Royal's wizardry as a Split-T quarterback and punter in 1949 remains legendary.

Left: Halfback George "Junior" Thomas was one of five Sooner All-Americans named following the 1949 season.

Below: Bud is pictured accepting Coach of the Year honors in New York, January 12, 1950. He is joined by Joe Williams (center), sports columnist for the *New York World Telegram*, and Dutch Meyer (right), TCU head coach and President of the National Football Coaches Association.

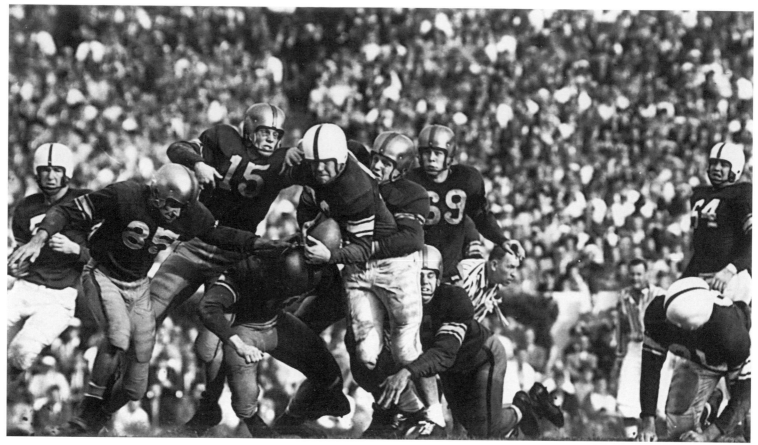

Above: Lindell Pearson bursts through the line against Louisiana State in the January 1, 1950, Sugar Bowl. Oklahoma 35, LSU 0.

Right: Darrell Royal congratulates Bud following the Sugar Bowl victory over LSU which capped an undefeated season, 1949.

Sooner stalwart Ken Tipps mused, "I wonder what that bunch would have been like if put on a weight program?"

By the fall of 1950, people were expecting great things from Wilkinson and his troops. That expectation, it was felt, contributed to the team's success. Meanwhile, America was once again at war, this time in Korea. Americans listened intently to radio broadcasts from the Korean front and to a zany broadcast called "You Bet Your Life."

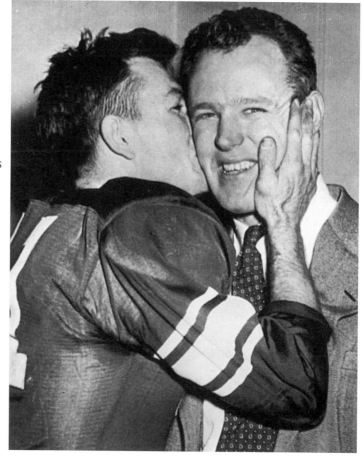

Bud faced a tremendous challenge that fall. Ten of his 11 offensive starters had graduated. Seven valuable reserves were gone as well. The great

PORT G. ROBERTSON

Of all the coaches, of all the administrators, of all the professors who have positively influenced the lives of young men at the University of Oklahoma, none so dramatically influenced young lives as did Port Robertson. The fact that he did so behind the scenes makes his contribution all the more precious to generations of OU football players.

Port, a native of Harrah, Oklahoma, and an OU graduate, had returned to the Norman campus after his military discharge in October 1946. His first position at the University was as wrestling coach, a post from which he would ultimately assist the Sooners in earning three national wrestling championships. Bud Wilkinson was settling into his role not only as football coach but as athletic director. He liked the manner in which Port conducted his affairs. He made Port freshman football coach and gave him additional responsibilities as head of the study program. But to say Port's responsibility stopped there would be to grossly understate the facts. "I was the baby sitter," Port says with a grin. Three times a week, Port inspected dorm rooms in the athletic dorms. Edges of bed spreads were to be hori-

zontal to the floor; clothes were to be picked up, shoes put away. Port wanted study desks straightened up, but open textbooks were okay. (Closed books meant they weren't being used.) If a youngster could not discipline himself, Port would assist him. Seventy-two rows of stadium steps at a brisk pace cured most such ills. There was a side of Port Robertson, however, that even his most reverent supporters have difficulty describing. It is best described by Port's actions. He knew the full name of every young man under his supervision, and he addressed each young man that way. It was a means of making a young man feel special. It made him feel human in a sometimes dehumanizing setting. Port was the father figure. On more than one occasion, he was challenged to take to the wrestling mat by young, strong athletes in his charge. All survived to tell about it. Probably the finest compliment that could be paid to Port Robertson comes not from the serious-minded men who came to Oklahoma to succeed and did so. No, the finest compliment comes from one who came to the campus with a reckless demeanor and

a chip on his shoulder. "You know, I wasn't much of a man when I came to OU, but after spending time with Port Robertson, I learned how to be a man."

freshman class of the previous fall, now sophomores, would have to pitch in. Bud made another tactical decision which was to pay tremendous dividends to the Oklahoma football program over the next thirty years.

Quarterback Claude Arnold led Oklahoma to a national championship in 1950.

Best in the Land

The 1950 season opened with the Sooners dismantling Boston College in Norman, 28-0. It was Claude Arnold's first start at quarterback after an eight-year wait. Arnold had actually come to Oklahoma in 1942. Then came the war interruption and Arnold's patient wait behind Darrell Royal. Now Arnold's time had come. The next game, against Texas A&M in Norman, is still regarded by many as the finest Sooner comeback in history.

Forty thousand spectators at Memorial Stadium collapsed dizzily as the Sooners roared back from a 28-21 deficit in the fourth quarter. Twice the Sooners were forced to conduct 69-yard drives, first in an attempt to tie the

Above: OU trainer, Joe Glander, patches up Coleman "Buck" McPhail during the heat of battle against Texas, 1950. Glander's medical kit, pictured in the foreground, is today, a treasured training room relic.

Below: Sophomore sensation, Billy Vessels, sets sail against Nebraska, November 25, 1950. Oklahoma 49, Nebraska 35.

score and when that failed, to drive to victory with one minute and nine seconds remaining. The final was OU 34, Texas A&M 28. A&M had outrushed the Sooners, 271-205, but Arnold's passing had rectified that imbalance. Leon Heath led the Sooner rushers with 78 yards, while young sophomore Billy Vessels added 56. Against Texas the following week, OU narrowly escaped defeat. Down 13-7 early in the fourth quarter, the Texas punter suddenly froze with the ball while in punt formation. The Sooners, with 4:45 remaining, faked a handoff to Leon Heath and pitched to Vessels, who steam-rolled a tackler and bulled into the end zone from the 11. Jim Weatherall kicked the conversion and OU emerged with a slender one-point win. A homecoming crowd of 38,546 watched OU batter Kansas State 58-0, but the game was significant as two African-Americans, Hoyt Givens and Harold Robinson, became the first of their race to play at Owen Field. Oklahoma dispatched Iowa State, Colorado (the newest member of the conference), Kansas and Missouri, before Nebraska visited Norman on November 25. Nebraska's fabulous Bobby Reynolds shocked the Sooners early, slithering through the lines seemingly at will. At the half, OU trailed Reynolds and company 21-14. One spectator recalls Bud's son, 8-year-old Jay, sobbing in the stands at the half, trying desperately to conceal his tears. But half-time adjustments enabled the Sooners to put a stopper on Reynolds. At the same time, Billy Vessels took over, eventually outrushing Reynolds, 208 yards to 82. Oklahoma 49, Nebraska 35. Oklahoma outran Oklahoma A&M, leading 35-7 at the half. The final in Stillwater was 41-14. That victory led to Oklahoma winning the national championship. Bud declared, "Our squad

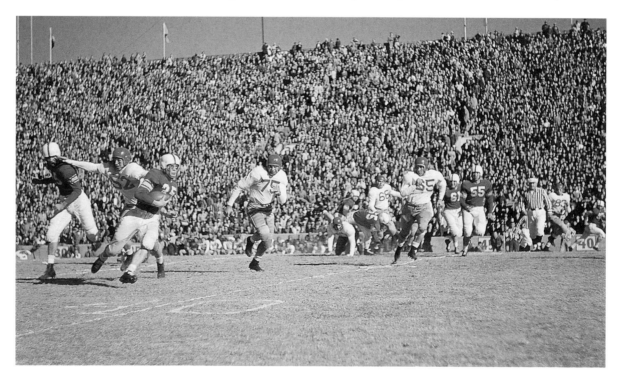

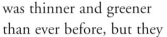

was thinner and greener than ever before, but they improved steadily and despite their physical imperfections proved time and time again that in the qualities of courage, spirit, and poise, they need bow to no other football team anywhere." Four players were named All-American in 1950. They were Jim Weatherall, Frankie Anderson, Leon Heath and Buddy Jones.

Above left to right: All-American tackle, Jim Weatherall, 1950. Frankie Anderson, All-American end, 1950. Fullback Leon Heath, All-American, 1950. Buddy Jones, All-American safety, 1950.

The Sooners had won 31 straight games. The Kentucky Wildcats, coached by Paul "Bear" Bryant, awaited the national champions in the Sugar Bowl. Defense was Bryant's forte. Additionally, Kentucky featured a fine passing quarterback in Vito "Babe" Parilli. Kentucky built a 13-0 lead before Arnold and Vessels could get untracked. The Kentucky defense stiffened, and Kentucky held on to win, 13-7. Oklahoma led in rushing, 189 yards to 84. Kentucky led in passing, but it was error-free execution on Kentucky's part that sealed the victory. Bryant had gotten the best of Wilkinson in the first match up of these gridiron legends.

Oklahoma's football dynasty was clearly in the mak-

Above: Leon Heath rumbles toward the goal against Kentucky in the January 1951 Sugar Bowl.

Right: Bud and Kentucky head coach Paul "Bear" Bryant share the sugar bowl prior to their Sugar Bowl match-up of 1951.

Above: John E. "Buddy" Leake sprints to one of his three touchdowns against Kansas, October 20, 1951. Oklahoma 33, Kansas 21.

Below: The Magician at Work – quarterback Eddie Crowder stuns Oklahoma A & M defenders with his deft ball handling and footwork, December 1, 1951. Oklahoma 41, Oklahoma A & M 6.

ing by the fall of 1951, but off-the-field developments figured just as prominently. While allied forces under General MacArthur repelled the North Koreans as they plunged across the 38th parallel, Bud Wilkinson was coping with a health problem. Surgery was required to remove a cancerous testicle. Moreover, he was seriously considering leaving Oklahoma to work for OU grad Eddie Chiles in the oil and gas industry. OU President Cross had to utilize his best powers of persuasion to convince Bud to remain.

There were other vexing problems to be dealt with. The National Guard had taken several players. Almost everyone else was training in Reserve Officers Training programs along with their football training. However, two new assistant coaches helped address the shortcomings. Pete Elliott, the great Michigan quarterback of 1948 came on board as did Dee Andros to assist Gomer Jones with line tutelage. Eddie Crowder, the Muskogee junior, could be counted upon to lead the offense. Senior tackle Jim Weatherall was back to provide leadership and devastating blocking. A depleted squad suggested that younger players once again would be required to step into the breach. Because of the Korean Conflict, freshmen were eligible to play. Coming on strong were John E. "Buddy" Leake, a Memphis youngster with a pleasing temperament and fierce competitive spirit; Carl Allison from McAlester, who was a quick study; and Gene Calame of Sulphur, a steady quarterback candidate.

The largest crowd ever to witness an Oklahoma home game opener, 38,000, watched as OU throttled William and Mary. Crowder, Vessels, McPhail and Frank Silva opened in the backfield. In the second half, reserves took over. A 152-pound reserve quarterback, Jackie Ging, later a Hollywood actor, scored the final touchdown. OU 49, William and Mary 7. Texas A&M was the next opponent, with the Sooners visiting College Station for the first time since 1907. Forty thousand partisans cheered on the powerful Cadet squad as it shut down the Sooners' Split-T attack. Texas A&M 14, Oklahoma 7. Against Texas, the Sooners doomed themselves by giving up an early safety and fumble. That led to a 9-0 deficit which the Sooners could not overcome. The greatest loss occurred when Billy Vessels was hit hard by tackler Don Cunningham. Vessels had injured a knee which would keep him out the remainder of the season.

Against Kansas in Norman a week later, the famed Oklahoma offense began to engage. Crowder's wizardry as a ball handler was beginning to reap rewards. Buddy Leake stepped forward in place of Vessels and acquitted himself with 121 yards in 15 carries. Fullback Buck McPhail led all rushers with 215 yards rushing on 20 carries. Notably, Eddie Crowder found his touch throwing the ball, completing 5 of 9. Oklahoma 33, Kansas 21. One key to Oklahoma's running success was the blocking of Tom Catlin. It didn't hurt Crowder's marvelous faking either. Against Colorado in Norman, Eddie Crowder took control with his ball handling and crisp passes. OU 55, Colorado 14. Kansas State, Missouri and Iowa State fell aside before the Sooners met the Nebraska eleven on November 24. The Sooners took command with Crowder and Larry Grigg supplying the leadership. The Huskers could get nothing going offensively as the run-pass strategy of the Oklahoma offense resulted in a 27-0 Sooner victory. Oklahoma A&M visited Norman on December 1 as 34,500 spectators witnessed a thorough dismantling of the Aggie defense. OU rushed for 393 yards in winning, 41-6. Some enterprising OU students had stolen the bell clapper from the bell hung in A&M's Old Central Hall. Later, both schools agreed that the victor in the annual game would be awarded possession of the clapper. The season of 1951 ended with Jim Weatherall and center Tom Catlin being named All-American. Although he played in only seven games, Buddy Leake led the Big Seven in scoring with 13 touchdowns and 78 points. Weatherall also won the Outland Trophy and the Sooners were once again conference champs.

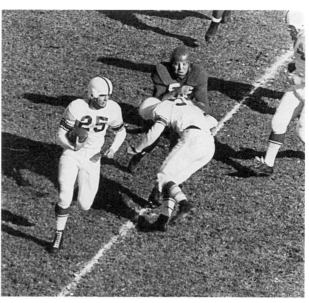

Above: Larry Grigg, #25, returns a punt 72 yards for a touchdown against the Nebraska Cornhuskers in Lincoln, November 24, 1951. Oklahoma 27, Nebraska 0.

Left: Jim Weatherall gives his football shoe a little peck following his last collegiate game in 1951. The All-American had hit on 39 of 47 conversion attempts for the season.

Below: Tom Catlin, center, earned All-American honors in 1951, because of his fierce blocking.

Vessels and the Heisman

A Vessels lateral to Buck McPhail produced big yardage against the Texas Longhorns in 1952. Oklahoma 49, Texas 20.

Daily over the long hot summer of 1952, Billy Vessels kicked off his shoes on the banks of the Arkansas River near his hometown of Cleveland, Oklahoma and ran for miles in the hot, dry river sand. Vessels' knee had to withstand the punishment he would receive on the fast-approaching fall Saturdays. The World War II war hero, General Eisenhower, was elected President that fall. The Korean Conflict ended and panty raids were a popular diversion on college campuses.

The nucleus of an outstanding football squad returned in '52. The backfield of Crowder, Vessels, McPhail and Leake, many believe, might be the Sooners' best ever. In any event, the Sooners were soon to confront adversity in the mountains of Colorado. High altitude, high temperatures and a sky-high Buffalo squad compromised the Sooners all afternoon. The Sooners lost six of seven fumbles. In the end, Oklahoma was satisfied to tie the game with 1:51 remaining. OU 21, Colorado 21. With the Sooner defense faltering a bit, the offense was required to engage as OU outscored Pittsburgh 49-20 in Norman. Reservists, including quarterback Jack Van Pool, Merrill Green, Jack Santee and Jerry Donaghey, applied the finishing touches. Against Texas, Longhorn fans observed in utter disbelief. In the first eleven minutes, Oklahoma produced 29 points as the Sooners stampeded to a 49-20 victory. Wilkinson's brainchild, the counter-option pass, bewildered not only Longhorn defenders, but the game officials and cameramen as well. Substitute quarterback Gene Calame recalls, "The officials would blow the ball dead and Crowder would rise up in another part of the field and throw a forward pass." At one point, the Sooner margin was four touchdowns. Texas tri-captain Jack Barton told the *Dallas Morning News*, "They're the best I've ever seen. They're the hardest playing, yet clean ball club I've ever played against." Kansas had won nine games in a row before Oklahoma came to visit. Receiving the benefit of several turnovers, the Jayhawks made a game of it before losing 42-20. The Sooners trounced Iowa State and Kansas State before preparing for a trip to South Bend, Indiana, in a game against the "Fighting Irish."

This dramatic photo captures the spirit of Oklahoma football during the decade of the '50s. Shown are, left to right, Buddy Leake, Billy Vessels, Eddie Crowder and Buck McPhail.

Notre Dame had been the elite of college football for forty years. Oklahoma aimed at dethroning the king. After all, OU had posted the highest winning percentage in the nation over the previous five years. Even the coaching match-up was titanic – Frank Leahy against Bud Wilkinson. Tickets to the game were impossible to come by. Nine thousand Oklahomans made the trip, many in 13 special trains containing 104 Pullman coaches. Mel Allen's national radio broadcast was heard by more than twenty million people, the largest radio audience ever. Oklahoma took the early lead, 7-0, on a nifty toss to Vessels after a brilliant fake to fullback McPhail. Irish quarterback Ralph Guglielmi knotted the score with a scoring pass to Joe Heap, before Vessels set sail on a brilliant 62-yard touchdown run down the sidelines. The Sooners led 14-7 at the half. Unfortunately, OU guard J.D. Roberts had been tossed from the game after a personal foul. Right tackle Ed Rowland went down with a knee injury. After that, the Sooners had trouble moving the ball. Irish standout Johnny Lattner picked off a Crowder pass and returned it to the OU 7-yard line. After the Irish once again tied the score, the Sooners responded with a spectacular drive, culminating in Billy Vessels speeding 44

yards to a touchdown. OU then led, 21-14. Notre Dame mounted a scoring drive before the fourth quarter began. After a Sooner fumble on the kick-off, the Irish went ahead for the first time, 27-21. Heroic drives late in the game fell a bit short, and the Irish triumphed. Billy Vessels had scored three touchdowns and rushed for 195 yards. On that golden afternoon in South Bend, Vessels had also won the Heisman Trophy.

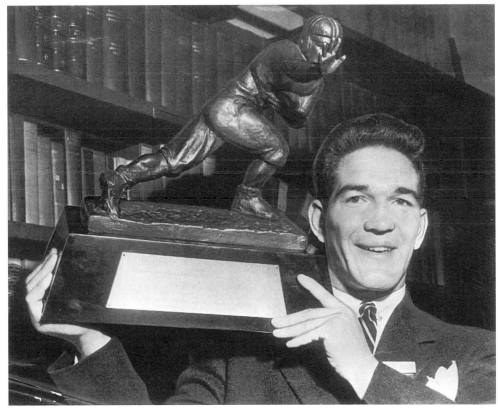

The Sooners of '52 were now a seasoned team, having survived the slings and arrows thrown their way. They demolished Missouri, 47-7 before 44,000 onlookers in Norman, then did the same to Nebraska by a count of 34-13. The Huskers' great runner, Bobby Reynolds, was out of the lineup with an injured leg.

Accordingly, the Sooners breezed to a 20-0 lead, then coasted home. The Oklahoma A&M Aggies were no match for the Sooners, although they scored first on a shocking 96-yard opening kickoff return. After that, it was all Oklahoma as the Sooners cruised, 54-7. Billy Vessels had become Oklahoma's first Heisman Trophy winner. Vessels, Catlin, Crowder and McPhail made All-American. The Sooners of '52 established several rushing records, a tribute to superior talent operating a superior offensive system.

Upper: Billy Vessels speeds to paydirt against the Fighting Irish of Notre Dame, November 8, 1952. Vessels scored three touchdowns in a losing effort but earned national attention.

Above: Oklahoma's first Heisman Trophy winner – Billy Vessels hoists high his Heisman Trophy following his marvelous season of 1952.

While the football season of 1953 would be successful by any standard, the freshman class that fall signaled great things to come. The freshman crop in '53 included Perry quarterback, Billy Pricer; Albuquerque, New Mexico, speedster, Tommy McDonald; Terrell, Texas, tailback, Jimmy Harris; Ada quarterback, Jay O'Neal; Muskogee brothers, Kurt and Bob Burris; and Breckenridge, Texas, center, Jerry Tubbs.

College football had abolished free substitution and two-platoons. Wilkinson recognized that these changes represented opportunity for his Sooners, just as his ancient predecessor, Bennie Owen had done with rules changes over thirty years before. However, it was Oklahoma's misfortune to be opening the season against Notre Dame, everyone's choice to win the 1953 national championship. Losses off the '52 squad left the Sooners woefully

Above: Larry Grigg lunges forward for yardage against Notre Dame, which visited Norman September 26, 1953. Notre Dame 28, OU 21.

Right: Bud ponders his next move against the Fighting Irish in 1953.

outmanned for the likes of the Irish. But the Sooners gave it a valiant try, although both teams suffered opening game inconsistencies. Max Boydston, Buddy Leake and Larry Grigg led OU to a 7-0 start, before the Irish tied the score. A blocked punt allowed the Irish to again tie the game at 14. Additional Sooner miscues permitted the Irish to build a 28-14 lead before OU gathered itself for a final run at victory, which fell short. The final was Notre Dame 28, Oklahoma 21. Traveling to Pittsburgh the following week, the Sooners appeared somewhat lackluster, managing only a 7-7 tie with the Panthers. No one could then have predicted the string of Oklahoma victories which would follow. Personnel changes were ordered. Max Boydston moved from fullback to end. Gene Calame moved in at quarterback. Tom Carroll from Okemah, a Korean War veteran, emerged at left halfback. Bob Burris was switched to fullback. Against Texas, Oklahoma swept to a shocking 19-0 lead. J.D. Roberts led a forward wall which sprung Carroll and Merrill Green time and time again. Calame performed admirably at quarterback. Late efforts by the Longhorns fell short and the Sooners won 19-14. The

Sooners crushed Kansas, 45-0, then struggled past Colorado, 27-20. Kansas State proved no hurdle, 34-0. Larry Grigg personally handled Missouri, 14-0. In that game, Grigg scored both touchdowns and deflected a Missouri pass in the end zone. Big Seven and Orange Bowl honors were clinched by the Sooners as they overhauled Iowa State, Nebraska and Oklahoma A&M in summary fashion. Those victories set up a Orange Bowl match-up between the Maryland Terrapins of Coach Jim Tatum and Wilkinson's Sooners.

The Terrapins had already been crowned national champions and had breezed through their schedule. Jim Tatum visited Norman to scout the Sooners against Oklahoma A&M. "This is the greatest team I have ever coached," Tatum said of his Marylanders. An Oklahoma defense grabbed the spotlight, however, shutting down Tatum's charges. Maryland boasted its own stout defense. Wilkinson, on the other hand, perceived a slight weakness in its defense of sweeps. Taking advantage of that weakness, Sooner halfback Larry Grigg swept left, taking a pitch from Calame, and raced to the corner behind brilliant blocking by J.D. Roberts and Bob Burris. That ended the scoring for the day as the Sooners shut

Below: Crisp blocking springs Larry Grigg against Jim Tatum's Maryland Terrapins in the January 1954 Orange Bowl. Oklahoma 7, Maryland 0.

Lower: A capacity crowd in the Orange Bowl witnesses a splendid halftime show and a Sooner victory over Maryland.

out the national champions, 7-0. Jim Tatum's final lament was, "Bud outcoached me." J.D. Roberts won the Outland Trophy and was named Lineman of the Year by both AP and UPI. The Sooners led the nation in rushing, won the Big Seven Conference and finished fourth in the national polls.

Roger Bannister ran the world's first sub-four minute mile on a cinder track in Oxford, England. The Vietnamese had driven the French out of their country with a military victory at Dien Bien Phu, while Americans cringed at Senator Joseph McCarthy's orchestrated "Red Scare."

Victories All in a Row

The risk inherent in Wilkinson's Split-T attack was that it required seasoning. It was the early season games, then, that afforded opponents an

Upper: The 1953 Sooners closed with nine straight victories, including an Orange Bowl win.

Above: J.D. Roberts earned his All-American sweater as a guard in 1953. He also won the Outland Trophy and Lineman of the Year honors.

Right: Jimmy Harris played brilliantly at quarterback over three seasons, 1954-1956, as the victories piled up in record numbers.

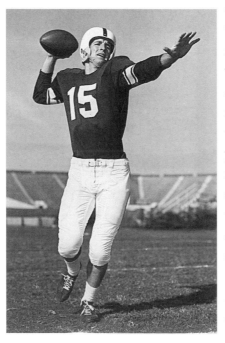

opportunity to succeed against the Sooners. California-Berkeley was host to the Sooners in the 1954 season opener. A national television audience looked in to see the Sooners take advantage of Golden Bear miscues to win, 27-13. End Max Boydston took a Buddy Leake pass and rambled 87 yards to pay dirt. Oklahoma unveiled its next quarterbacking star, Jimmy Harris, against Texas Christian. After Calame left the game with a broken collarbone, Harris directed the Sooners to two fourth-quarter scores to prevail, 21-16.

Never before had so many people witnessed a football game played in the Southwest. Over 76,000 fans filled the

Cotton Bowl on October 9, as the Harris-led Sooners managed a 14-7 victory over a tough Texas squad. The victory hinged largely on a successful fourth-and-one play from the Sooners' own 36-yard line. Bob Herndon rambled 14 yards on that play, which seemed to invigorate the Sooners and spur them to victory. Neither Kansas nor Kansas State were able to score on Oklahoma, falling 65-0 and 21-0 respectively before the Sooners met the Colorado Buffaloes in Boulder. Down 6-0 going into the fourth quarter, the Sooners rallied behind quarterback Gene Calame to squeeze out a 13-6 win. Iowa State was shut out 40-0, before Oklahoma dominated Missouri, 34-13 in Norman. Tremendous offensive line play, led by guard Cecil Morris, crushed the Tiger hopes. Oklahoma was now capable of throwing hordes of quality players against the opposition. This was reflected in the scores. The Sooners humbled the Nebraska Cornhuskers 55-7 before 56,000 celebrants in Norman. Late in the game, the Sooner fourth unit was still jabbing away at the Husker defense. In the season closer against Oklahoma A&M, the Sooners triumphed somewhat indifferently, 14-0. The reason was obvious. Nebraska got to go to the Orange Bowl while the Sooners stayed home. No conference team was permitted to go to Miami in successive years. Center Kurt Burris and end Max Boydston were named All-American. A late public relations campaign by OU Sports Information Director Harold Keith brought Burris from nowhere to finish second in the Heisman Trophy balloting. The Sooners once again reigned as Big Seven Conference champions and finished third in the national polls behind Ohio State and UCLA.

Lawrence Welk and his "champagne music" made its television debut, while rock n' roll was labeled "immoral" in some quarters. In Norman, Bud Wilkinson told the press, "Our 1955 team will be so new that our fans won't recognize it." The team was as strong as Post Toasties inside the tackles, but suspect everywhere else. Young unknowns were, however, starting to emerge. A stringy sophomore from Oklahoma City's Southeast High School, Clendon Thomas, had once found himself on the fifth and last freshman unit. Thomas, however, never even considered quitting. Other young players such as Ross Coyle from Marlow, Joe Mobra, and Don Stiller from Shawnee, were growing up in the program. A two-year probation

Above: Buddy Leake (22) passes to Carl Allison (83) as the Sooners cruise to a 14-0 victory over Oklahoma A & M, in 1954.

Left: Center Kurt Burris, one of the fabulous Burris brothers from Muskogee, was named All-American in 1954 and finished a surprising second in the Heisman balloting.

Below: End Max Boydston, All-American, 1954.

without sanctions had been imposed upon Oklahoma in April 1955. Oklahoma's success was generating curiosity in far-off places.

Back-to-Back National Titles

The 1955 season opener against North Carolina in Chapel Hill was played in such humid conditions that legendary OU trainer Ken Rawlinson observed, "Although the sun was shining brightly, it was raining." With a new quarterback and new ends, OU appeared sluggish offensively. However, they outrushed the Tar Heels, 403-134. A parade of Sooner ball carriers contributed, including quarterback Jimmy Harris, fullback Bob Burris, Tommy McDonald, Billy Pricer, Clendon Thomas, Carl Dodd, Dennit Morris and Jay O'Neal. Applying the traditional Sooner squeeze on defense, the Sooners won, 13-6. Against Pittsburgh in Norman on October 1, the Sooners learned to believe in themselves, holding off a furious Pitt assault to win, 26-14. Linemen Bo Bolinger, Cal Woodworth and Don Stiller provided openings

A fish-eye lens depicts Owen Field on October 1, 1955, a day in which the future national champions defeated Pittsburgh, 26-14.

large enough for Sooner ball carriers to gain yardage. For the fourth year in a row, the Sooners defeated Texas. This time out, it was three Jerry Tubbs pass interceptions and the quick kicking of Billy Pricer and Clendon Thomas that led the way. OU led 13-0 at intermission, and coasted home 20-0. McDonald led the ground attack but as usual, laurels were spread around evenly. Big Seven opponents were, in 1955, no match for the Sooners. By mid-season, Wilkinson was employing his "fast break" offense, which he personally referred to as the "fast recovery." Its intent was to hurry to the line of scrimmage to snap the ball before the defense had time to catch a breath and steel itself for the onslaught.

Sooner mastery was so complete that team members were disappointed if the opponent scored at all. Clendon Thomas recalls, "We wanted to beat

"Remember, never panic and always maintain your dignity."

— COACH BUD WILKINSON

everybody 40-zip." Kansas fell 44-6, followed by Colorado, 56-21, and Kansas State, 40-7. Oklahoma's last four conference opponents, Missouri, Iowa State, Nebraska and Oklahoma A&M did not disappoint Thomas and the other Sooners – they did not score a single point. Waves of Sooners assaulted their foes. The domination was so over-whelming that the records blur the eyes. Oklahoma was awarded the national champi-onship, surely by acclamation. The Sooners led the nation in total offense by a wide mar-gin, netting 410.7 yards a game. Guard Bo Bolinger and little Tommy McDonald were named All-Americans.

Jim Tatum's Maryland Terrapins were spoiling for a fight in the Orange Bowl. UCLA coach Red Sanders tabbed Maryland, "The greatest team of the era." From the outset, it was obvious that Tatum had prepared his team well. The Sooners trailed 6-0 at the half, and Bud was not happy. He ordered Jimmy Harris to start the "go-go" offense. There would be no huddles. Every play would be called at the line of scrimmage. After holding the Terps on downs to start the third quarter, Harris turned on the "go go." "We were running plays while Maryland was still getting up off the ground," McDonald recalls. The Terps began to falter under the intense assault. Big John Sandusky, the fine Maryland defensive lineman rested momentarily on one knee between Sooner snaps, his shirttail dangling out. As teammate Bob Pellegrini attempted to help him up, Sandusky moaned, "Get out of the way! Here they come again!" Indeed. The final was Oklahoma 20, Maryland 6. In addition to being national champions, Oklahoma had won

Above: Coach Wilkinson accepts a 1955 National Championship trophy with the able assistance of All-Americans Bo Bolinger (far left) and Tommy McDonald (far right).

Below: The Oklahoma Sooners of 1955 dominated college football in securing the national championship and posting 11 straight wins.

ALL-VICTORIOUS NATIONAL COLLEGIATE, ORANGE BOWL AND BIG SEVEN CHAMPIONS 1955

their 30th consecutive game.

Remarkable. That's the adjective most often used to describe the 1956 Oklahoma Sooners. Most of the members of the '55 national champions returned, plus a peppering of talented sophomores. Bob Harrison, a Stamford, Texas, sophomore, drove a farm tractor and chopped cotton in the west Texas sun in preparation for the fall wars. Little Jefferson Davis Sandefer III of Breckenridge, Texas, earned a lot of nicknames due to his privileged background. The Sooners simply called him "Jakie." A freshman from Midwest City, Brewster Hobby, had been inclined to play professional baseball before Bud came to his home to visit. Joe Rector, a Muskogee sophomore, readily acknowledged the benefit of organization on the part of the Sooner coaching staff. Rector recalls, "Bud gave us confidence. I always knew exactly what I was supposed to do in every situation. It was automatic."

The opener against North Carolina meant that a Wilkinson-coached team would meet a Tatum-coached team in back-to-back games over two seasons. This was so because Jim Tatum had moved from Maryland to North

Below: A sell-out crowd of over 60,000 attended Oklahoma's home opener against the North Carolina Tarheels, September 29, 1956. Oklahoma 36, North Carolina 0.

Lower: Ruf-neks generate enthusiasm for the Sooners prior to the 1956 battle against Notre Dame. Oklahoma 40, Notre Dame 0.

Carolina, the team he had coached back in 1942. Sixty-thousand spectators turned out in Norman on September 29. With left halfbacks McDonald and Sandefer ailing, the Sooners turned to Bartlesville sophomore David Baker, who sparked the Sooners' second unit to the first score. Thereafter the Sooners exploded to lead 21-0. Brilliant passing by Jimmy Harris baffled the Tar Heels as the Sooners pulled away to win, 36-0. In fact, the Sooners were not scored upon through the first three games of the season. Kansas State folded, 66-0, before the Texas encounter. In that contest, McDonald and Thomas ravaged the Longhorn defense, together accounting for 263 rushing yards. The Sooners had to punt only twice all afternoon while the Sooner defense was intercepting five Horn aerials. The Sooners had won one of the most lopsided victories of the storied OU-Texas series. Oklahoma 45, Texas 0. Oklahoma dispatched Kansas in Lawrence, 34-12, before girding for the Fighting Irish of Notre Dame. The South Bend crowd of 60,128 was an all-time Irish record. Millions more tuned in on television. Notre Dame had not been shut out in 47 straight games dating back to 1951, but on this day, they were humbled 40-0. Paul Hornung, the big Irish quarterback who would later win the Heisman Trophy, was virtually paralyzed by the Sooner defense led by Jerry Tubbs. "Tubbs was the nicest guy in the world until he put on his helmet," Clendon Thomas recalls. Hornung rushed for only 7 yards on 13 carries and was belted into

fumbling three times. Sooner speed and a new flanker offense had won the day. After the game, a jubilant Sooner squad presented the game ball to Bud. "Nothing that has ever happened to me gave me more pleasure," he said. Trailing 19-6 against a fired-up Buffalo squad in Boulder, the Sooners stormed back to win 27-19. Buffalo star Boyd Dowler had created most of the havoc with his punting and precise pitches. "That Colorado crowd was a wild one," recalls Doyle Jennings. "They kept shelling us with snowballs and coke bottle tops. After the game, the field was so snowy from those snowballs, it looked like freshly fallen snow." The Sooners defeated Iowa State 44-0 at Ames, then turned up the offensive heat against Missouri in Norman, winning 67-14. No Wilkinson-coached Sooner team had ever scored as many points. Former OU assistant Pete Elliott was now head man at Nebraska. The Sooners proved less than charitable, however, as they blasted the Huskers 54-6 in Norman on November 24. Clendon

Thomas' rushing was complemented by Harris-to-McDonald tosses. For the second year in a row, Oklahoma defeated the Aggies of Oklahoma A&M by the score of 53-0. This time, in Stillwater, waves of Sooner rushers garnered

520 yards on the ground to A&M's 72. For the second year in a row, OU was crowned national champion. The Oklahoma victory skein was extended to 40 games. Numerous records were set as the Sooners averaged almost 400 yards per game rushing. Tommy McDonald was awarded the Maxwell Trophy, Jerry Tubbs the Walter Camp Trophy. Tubbs was also Lineman of the Year and was joined by McDonald, Bill Krisher and Ed Gray in being named All-American.

Above: Clendon Thomas evades Oklahoma A & M tacklers in a 53-0 Sooner victory at Stillwater, December 1, 1956.

Left: Oklahoma Governor Raymond Gary presents the Walter Camp Trophy to outstanding Sooner defender, Jerry Tubbs, following the 1956 national championship season.

Below: Tommy McDonald, All-American in 1956, pictured here as a cover boy, is best remembered for leaping to his feet at the end of every play, thus leading the "go-go" offense.

Perhaps the finest college football team of all-time had settled all accounts.

The Russians launched the first satellite, Sputnik, and women flooded the stores in search of the new rage, "sack" dresses. Elvis crooned on car radios across the land. In Norman, by Wilkinson's own estimation, he was about to make the most important decision of his legendary coaching career.

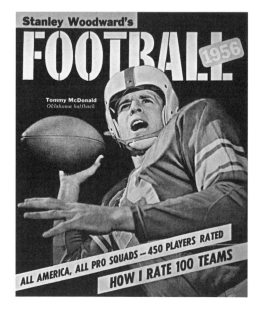

Gautt Becomes a Sooner

Right: Prentice Gautt contributed in many ways to the Sooner successes of 1957-1959 and to the Sooner tradition of excellence.

Below: Jefferson Davis "Jakie" Sandefer III flourished in the one-platoon days of the 1950s, when intelligence and stamina were paramount.

Lower: Bob Harrison blasts Oklahoma State fullback Larry Rundle en route to a 53-6 Sooner victory in Norman, November 30, 1957.

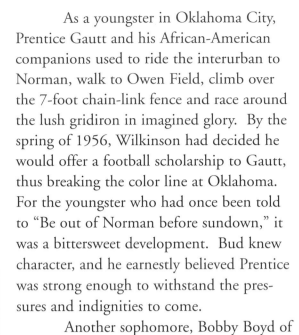

As a youngster in Oklahoma City, Prentice Gautt and his African-American companions used to ride the interurban to Norman, walk to Owen Field, climb over the 7-foot chain-link fence and race around the lush gridiron in imagined glory. By the spring of 1956, Wilkinson had decided he would offer a football scholarship to Gautt, thus breaking the color line at Oklahoma. For the youngster who had once been told to "Be out of Norman before sundown," it was a bittersweet development. Bud knew character, and he earnestly believed Prentice was strong enough to withstand the pressures and indignities to come.

Another sophomore, Bobby Boyd of Garland, Texas, was primed to contribute in 1957, as was wiry Jimmy Carpenter from Abilene, Texas. Hobbs, New Mexico, product Leon Cross arrived on campus, as did Jerry Payne from Breckenridge, Texas. The only returning starters were Stiller, Krisher, Thomas and Buddy Oujesky. A notable loss of speed and experience would be a challenge to overcome. Against Pittsburgh before 58,942 Pennsylvanians on September 21, the Sooners benefited from Panther fumbles to win 26-0. After disposing of Iowa State, 40-14 in Norman, the Sooners turned their attention to Texas. The Longhorns were now coached by Darrell Royal, who had moved to the Austin campus from the University of Washington. Before the traditional full house at the Cotton Bowl, the Sooners utilized smothering defense to hold the Horns in check and win 21-7. Jakie Sandefer led all rushers and collected an interception as well. Next, the Sooners bulldozed Kansas 34-12, before Colorado visited Norman on October 26. Many a spectator at Owen Field experienced heart palpitations before the Sooners escaped by a single point, 14-13. Clendon Thomas had carried the day along with Sandefer and quarterback Carl Dodd. Bud captured his 100th coaching win against Kansas State, 13-0, before the Sooners leveled a tough Missouri squad in

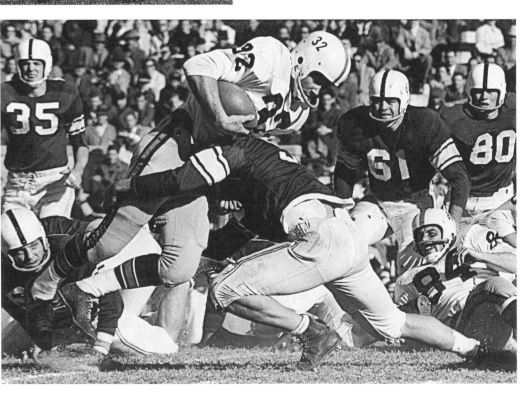

Columbia, 39-14. Prentice Gautt, operating on the third unit, scored his first collegiate touchdown.

The Irish End the Streak

Fifty years to the day after Oklahoma became a state, the Sooners entertained the Fighting Irish of Notre Dame. The Sooners had won 47 straight games, a collegiate record, and had scored in 112 games straight, also a record. Tickets to the game were non-existent. A record crowd of 63,170 jammed Memorial Stadium to greet Terry Brennan's Irish. The Sooners had been flirting with defeat all year and had already secured another Big Seven crown and an Orange Bowl berth. A bit of complacency had set in. Sooner fans sat in disbelief as the Irish halted the Sooner Split-T time and time again. A defensive standoff ensued until late in the fourth quarter when the Irish marched 80 yards in 20 plays behind the bruising rushes of fullback Nick Pietrosante and halfback Dick Lynch. Finally, the Irish faced fourth down and goal from the Sooner 3-yard line. The noise was so deafening that Irish quarterback Bob Williams could not be heard above the din. Television announcers Lindsey Nelson and Red Grange stood with the crowd, explaining the intense scene to millions of viewers. As the Sooner defenders bunched in tight, expecting a bullish thrust from Pietrosante, Williams faked the dive and pitched to Lynch who skirted the end for the score. Remarkably, the Sooner crowd fully expected the Sooners to come back to win. The ear-piercing noise continued as Oklahoma took possession at its own 39-yard line with 1:22 to go. The Sooners advanced to the Irish 36-yard line before an interception ended the threat. Notre Dame 7, Oklahoma 0. For half an hour after the contest, thousands remained in the stadium, somehow expecting the teams to reappear and for the Sooners to ultimately claim victory as they seemingly always had. Wilkinson addressed a tearful squad in the locker room. "You have done something no other major college football has ever done before or will ever do again. You have won 47 straight football games. I am proud of you. You have been just as much a part of this as any other Oklahoma team. The only ones who never lose are the ones who never play."

Many wondered how the Sooners might react to the loss the following week at Nebraska. Those concerns were laid to rest as OU overcame a 7-0 deficit to win 32-7. The Oklahoma A&M Aggies provided little resistance in a 53-6 Sooner victory in Norman. Clendon Thomas once again led all rushers.

The Duke Blue Devils were matched against the Sooners in the Orange Bowl. The big strong Duke squad withered however, in the humid afternoon air of the Orange Bowl and the relentless attack of the Sooner offense. By the fourth quarter,

Above: A disconsolate Bud Wilkinson shares defeat with his Sooners. Oklahoma had won a record 47 straight games before falling to Notre Dame, 7-0, on November 16, 1957.

Below: The Orange Bowl queen and her court greet Coach Wilkinson along with team co-captains Don Stiller and Clendon Thomas prior to the January 1, 1958, Orange Bowl Classic.

Upper: In 1957, these Sooners posted a 10-1 record, including a 48-21 Orange Bowl victory over the Duke Blue Devils.

Above: Halfback Clendon Thomas (35) and guard Bill Krisher (65) were All-American standouts in 1957.

Oklahoma was dominating the game, pulling away to win 48-21. Red Smith, New York newspaper sports columnist, marveled at the Sooner onslaught. "For the football fan, watching Oklahoma is a treat. Going at top speed and employing their talents with confidence and polished precision, Wilkinson's operatives create excitement." The Sooners were once again Big Seven champs and finished fourth in the national polls. Clendon Thomas and Bill Krisher were named All-American.

A huge box, twice the size of a washing machine, was developed by the Xerox company to make document reproductions. Ike was re-elected President. There seemed no limit for those steeped in the virtues of the American dream. Those kinds of dreams filtered down to Norman, where several national magazines predicted Oklahoma would win its fourth national title. Prentice Gautt had been moved to fullback and was hitting his stride there. Unfortunate injuries over the summer, however, eliminated promising linemen Leon Cross and Jerry Thompson. Meanwhile, a recruiting controversy had erupted over Stamford, Texas, product Mike McClellan. McClellan had originally enrolled at Baylor. When he grew disenchanted there, he attempted to enroll at OU. Baylor officials cried foul. By the fall of 1958, however, McClellan was residing in Norman and pursuing his football career. There was the additional controversy stemming from the recruitment of a Nebraska youth, Monte Kiffin. Nebraska coach, Bill Jennings, took exception to OU's interest in Kiffin after the youngster had expressed an interest in attending Oklahoma. Jennings, the OU grad and former Oklahoma assistant, was sufficiently exercised that Oklahoma eventually became the target of an NCAA investigation and probation.

Oklahoma utilized its new "smorgasbord" offense to dispose of the West Virginia Mountaineers in Norman, 47-14. The odd assortment of flankers and spread formations allowed quarterbacks Bobby Boyd and David Baker to succeed with the forward pass. Oregon, however, solved the "smorgasbord," using its own speed on defense. It was not enough, however, as Oklahoma roasted the Ducks, 6-0 in Norman. For six seasons, Texas had suffered at the hands of the Sooners. On October 11, the Horns finally retaliated. As the stadium announcer intoned, "Lackey under," Horn quarterback Bobby Lackey worked some late magic, flipping a quick pass to end Bob Bryant for a touchdown and a 14-14 deadlock. Lackey's conversion gave the Longhorns a 15-14 lead which stood up as time expired. Over the next seven

contests, four Oklahoma opponents would fail to score, while none of the other three would score more than seven points each. Jack Mitchell's over-matched Jayhawks fell 43-0, followed by lopsided Sooner victories over Kansas State, Colorado, Iowa State, Missouri and Nebraska. Against Oklahoma State, the Sooners were forced to defend against outstanding Aggie quarterback Dick Soergel, in a quagmire. As a result, little offense was generated by either team with the Sooners winning, 7-0.

The 1958 Sooners finished fifth in the national polls and were matched against the Syracuse Orangemen in the 25th anniversary Orange Bowl game. David Baker had been declared ineligible to play due to academic problems. That meant Wilkinson had to elevate another quarterback to the starting eleven. He selected Bob Cornell, an Oklahoma City sophomore. Prentice Gautt helped the Sooners to get off on the right foot with a 42-yard touchdown run, followed by a spectacular 79-yard touchdown toss from halfback Brewster Hobby to end Ross Coyle. Late in the third period, OU led 21-0 but Syracuse didn't fold. The Sooners ultimately prevailed, 21-6. The Sooners were Big Eight champions, and they led the nation in scoring defense. Center Bob Harrison was named All-American.

While Alaska and Hawaii were celebrating statehood, Americans celebrated the return to Earth of its space-flying monkey duo, Abel and Baker. One hundred-forty men reported to Norman for fall football practice,

Upper: Sooner Jim Davis (53) is swarmed by jubilant teammates after his theft of the football and touchdown return run against Texas, 1958.

Above: This 1958 Sooner starting eleven was Big Eight Conference champion, led the nation in scoring defense and defeated the Syracuse Orangemen in the Orange Bowl.

Left: 1958 All-American center, Bob Harrison, excelled at both blocking and tackling.

Right: Senior quarterback Bobby Boyd discusses strategy with Coach Wilkinson, 1959.

Below: Ronnie Hartline, fullback, sped 31 yards to score against OSU, November 28, 1959. Oklahoma 17, OSU 7.

Lower: The starters of 1959 – (front row left to right) RE Jerry Tillery; RT Marshall York; RG Billy Jack Moore; C Jim Davis; LG Jerry Thompson; LT Gilmer Lewis; LE Wahoo McDaniel; (back row left to right) RH Brewster Hobby; FB Prentice Gautt; QB Bobby Boyd; LH Jimmy Carpenter.

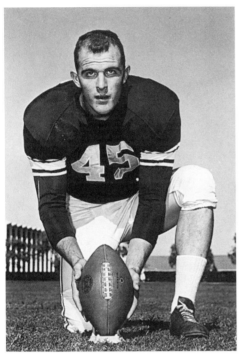

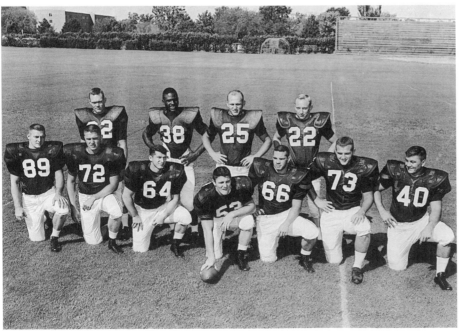

103 of the these walk-ons. Freshman coach Port Robertson set about to thin out the group. Ten quit the first day, such was the intensity of the workout. The Sooners were without the seasoned line veterans which Gomer Jones had so skillfully developed in prior years. Plus, the season opener was against Ara Parseghian's Wildcats of Northwestern University. What happened next mystified sports observers across the nation. The night before the game, the Sooners were victimized by food poisoning, ostensibly caused by adulterated fruit cocktail. Only Prentice Gautt and Wahoo McDaniel avoided illness. Further, during the game, the heavens opened and deluged the crowd for most of the first half. Oklahoma, operating on shaky legs, quickly fell behind. In the end, Northwestern had dealt the Sooners a stunning defeat, 45-13. The Sooners recovered by clubbing Colorado, 42-12 in Norman, as sophomore Mike McClellan earned his spurs in a fine rushing performance. The Sooners met Texas the following week and fell 19-12 behind the splendid Longhorn attack featuring quarterback Mike Cotton and senior halfback Rene Ramirez. The Horns had come back from a 12-0 deficit to doom the Sooners. The Sooners hammered Missouri, 23-0 in Columbia, before dealing with an inspired Kansas squad in Norman. Jayhawk John Hadl added a record punt of 94 yards as the Sooners nudged Kansas 7-6. The Sooners were shocked in Lincoln, 25-21, by a Husker squad using a variety of scoring methods to achieve success. It signaled the first time a conference opponent had defeated an OU team coached by Wilkinson. After thumping Kansas State 36-0, the Sooners looked to a visit by the Black Knights of Army. The temperature plunged to 28 degrees as anxious Sooner fans strained to see Army's famed "Lonesome End," Bill Carpenter, demonstrate his considerable talents. While Army had success throwing the football, it could not contend with Oklahoma's ground game, which ground out 201 yards to Army's 91. Outstanding play on both sides made the Sooner victory, 28-20, even more rewarding. Oklahoma handled Iowa State's "Dirty Thirty" by a count of 35-12, before

closing out the season with a 17-7 triumph over Oklahoma State at Norman. Fullback Ronnie Hartline was the hero, rambling 31 yards to score in the fourth quarter. Cowboy heroics by quarterback Dick Soergel and halfback Tony Banfield were not enough as the Sooners closed out the season victorious. The Big Eight title was once again Oklahoma's and lineman Jerry Thompson made All-American.

An End to "Oklahoma and the Seven Dwarfs"

The end of the decade of the '50s gave way to enormous change in the country. John F. Kennedy had been elected President in a razor-thin election win. There was a space race with the Russians under way. The Oklahoma Sooners had won an incredible 14 consecutive conference crowns. However, part of the new order was an end to "Oklahoma and the Seven Dwarfs." Oklahoma's indefinite probation posed a burdensome problem and the Sooners were denied permission by the Big Eight to schedule a game in Hawaii. In the 1960 season opener against Northwestern in Norman, a crowd of 61,289 hoped to see Oklahoma avenge the previous year's loss to the Wildcats. It was not to be as OU had trouble generating offense, losing 19-3. Against Pittsburgh in Norman, a dramatic contest unfolded with both teams moving the ball well, but meeting resistance close in. In the end, OU managed a one-point victory, 15-14. The Sooners fell to Texas 24-0 in Dallas behind the running of Ray Poage and a thrilling 78-yard interception return for a touchdown by Pat Culpepper. Texas had won its third straight over OU, and many Sooner fans were forced to admit that the Sooners of 1960 were indeed, human after all.

Legendary athletic trainer Ken Rawlinson shows off his immaculate training room located beneath Memorial Stadium, circa 1960.

The Sooners were underdogs to ninth-ranked Kansas, led by halfback Bert Coan. By sustaining long drives at the beginning of both halves, OU fashioned a 13-13 tie. Next, the Sooners defeated Kansas State with a 49-point barrage. The final was 49-7 and Wilkinson became Oklahoma's all-time winningest coach. The Colorado Buffaloes of Coach Sonny Grandelius featured a superb middle linebacker in Joe Romig. With Romig stuffing the Sooner drives, Colorado needed but a single touchdown to defeat Oklahoma, 7-0. The Sooners fell to Iowa State at Ames, 10-6, upon the strength of fullback Tom Watkins and the old Iowa State single-wing attack. Missouri, ranked number 2 in the nation and sporting a 8-0 record, visited Norman and returned home victorious, having vanquished the Sooners 41-19. Nebraska came to Norman, riding the talents of quarterback Pat Fischer and fullback Bill "Thunder" Thornton. The Sooners couldn't bring down Thornton, and

"The truly vital factors of success in football remain the same. There is no substitute for desire to win, physical condition and good athletes. Any team that has the three elements listed above and that is well coached in a sound system of attack will be successful."

– BUD WILKINSON

Above: Fellow linemen pile up on All-Big Eight tackle, Billy White, on bottom, in September, 1961.

Below: Halfback Jimmy Carpenter hangs up his pads for the last time following a Sooner victory over OSU, 21-13, in 1961.

Below right: Halfback Mike McClellan rambles 75 yards to paydirt against the Black Knights of Army in a spectacle played at New York's Yankee Stadium, November 8, 1961. Oklahoma 14, Army 8.

the Huskers won 17-14. By defeating Oklahoma State 17-6 at Stillwater, the Sooners closed their only losing season under Wilkinson at 3-6-1. Oklahoma's best player in 1960 was Billy White, a devastating 197-pound blocker who made All-Big Eight.

Some observers speculated that Bud's enthusiasm for coaching was beginning to wane. Certainly recruiting was getting tougher, the competition stronger. That spring, Bud was asked by President Kennedy to become Special Consultant on Youth Fitness. He graciously accepted and thereafter suffered from a case of low-grade Potomac fever. The injury bug struck the Sooners with a vengeance. Promising Tulsa sophomore quarterback, Bill Van Burkleo suffered a severely sprained ankle. In short, the Sooners were woefully thin, especially given the caliber of the competition. Notre Dame, Texas and Army joined the imposing Big Eight opponents on the schedule. The Sooners were destined to lose their first five ball games. The Sooners lacked their usual depth and speed. They were not short of pride, however. After the fifth loss of the season, to Colorado, Wilkinson told his squad on Sunday morning that they would win their last five ball games. Bud had sensed improvement sufficient to accomplish this goal. He later made the same declaration to the public on his weekly television show. Amazingly, that's precisely what the Sooners did. The Sooners posted road victories against Kansas State and Missouri before facing Army at Yankee Stadium in New York.

With statues of Babe Ruth, Lou Gehrig and Miller Huggins as a back drop, the Sooners set about to upset the Black Knights before their New York fans. Wilkinson had installed a bit of trickery – a no huddle quick snap, intended to catch the Army defense asleep at the wheel. After a Sooner running play, the Sooners pretended to return to the huddle, then quickly set up at the line. Jimmy Carpenter received the snap and shoveled the ball along the line to a waiting Mike McClellan. Seventy-five yards down the field, McClellan crossed the goal line. Oklahoma went on to win 14-8. The Sooners were the talk of Gotham the rest of the fall. Against Nebraska in

Lincoln, the Huskers led 14-0 behind the passing of Dennis Claridge before the Sooners engaged and scored thrice in the second half to win, 21-14. The Sooners concluded the season of '61 with a crisp 21-13 victory over Oklahoma State in Norman. Mike McClellan led the way with brilliant sideline dashes. In an Associated Press poll, sportswriters voted Oklahoma's November rally as the greatest sports comeback of 1961.

Rentzel, Looney and Flynn, Oh My!

While Americans held their breath during the Cuban naval blockade, a comedian named Johnny Carson was readying a new late-night talk show called "The Tonight Show." Only two starters, Leon Cross and Wayne Lee, returned to anchor the Sooners of '62. New blood was desperately needed. Fortunately, the sophomores of 1962 represented a wonderful array of talent. They included Glen "Moose" Condren, Purcell's Rick McCurdy, John Flynn from Washington, D.C., Ralph Neely from Farmington, New Mexico, Lance Rentzel from Oklahoma City, Jim Grisham from Olney, Texas, Tommy Pannell from Norman and Ronnie Fletcher, a local walk-on.

Most intriguing, however, was a junior college transfer by way of Lawton's Cameron Junior College and Fort Worth, Texas. His name was Joe Don Looney. Looney, a gifted athlete, was also adverse to authority figures. That would prove to be a problem all the way around. Eight days before the season opener, Pannell went down with a broken ankle. Wilkinson scrambled to prepare lightly regarded senior, Monte Deere. In the season opener against powerful Syracuse in Norman, the game ratcheted down into a defensive struggle, with OU trailing 3-0 late in the fourth quarter. The mercurial Looney, who had never played a down for Oklahoma, asked Bud to put him in the game. Two minutes and twenty seconds remained on the stadium clock and Oklahoma was 60 yards away from victory. Into the game trotted Joe Don. "Gimme the ball and I'll score a touchdown!" Joe Don growled to Deere. At the snap, Looney took the hand-off and plunged to the left. Emerging from a swarm of tacklers, he rumbled down the sideline to a touchdown. All he could do was hold the ball up in the air. With that one play, Looney became an Oklahoma football legend. The Sooners had won, 7-3, and Looney was written up in the *New York Times*. Thereafter, the Sooners struggled, losing to Notre Dame, 13-7, and Texas, 9-6, on succeeding Saturdays. Texas scored all its points in the first half. No one shall ever forget the spectacular touchdown combination of Ronnie Fletcher tossing to Lance Rentzel in the waning seconds of the first half. Rentzel, in fact, had not made the traveling squad and had

Above: A youthful Lance Rentzel hitchhiked a portion of the way to Dallas before snaring back-to-back aerials from little Ronnie Fletcher. The second one, pictured here, was for a touchdown which electrified the OU-Texas Cotton Bowl crowd just prior to halftime, October 13, 1962.

Left: Sprint to victory – Joe Don Looney escaped Syracuse tacklers and flashed to a touchdown in the waning moments of a 1962 defensive struggle. Looney thus earned himself an eternal, and oft controversial, national reputation. Oklahoma 7, Syracuse 3.

Below: Sooner players carry Bud off the field in triumph following their 34-6 victory over the Nebraska Cornhuskers in 1962.

hitchhiked a por-
tion of the way to
the Cotton Bowl.
Soon after, the
Sooners found
their defensive sea
legs, winning the
next seven games,
and allowing only
three of those
opponents to score
at all. Joe Don
Looney proved to
be the nation's best
punter, leading the
nation in that cate-

Right: President Kennedy visits
Bud and the Oklahoma squad in
their Orange Bowl locker room
prior to the bowl contest against the
Alabama Crimson Tide, New Year's
Day, 1963.

Below: Joe Don Looney was an All-
American in 1962 and was the
nation's top punter as well.

**Right: Center Wayne Lee (51) and
guard Leon Cross (61) were named
All-Americans after leading the
1962 Sooners to another Big Eight
Championship and a berth in the
Orange Bowl.**

gory with a 43.4 yard average. On defense, Sooner lines had halted four great backs. Gale Sayers of Kansas had been limited to 23 yards; Dave Hoppmann of Iowa State, 23 yards; Johnny Roland of Missouri, 9 yards; and "Thunder" Thornton of Nebraska, 32 yards. While holding lofty rankings in several national statistical categories, the Sooners were also ranked seventh in both national polls.

Oklahoma, as Big Eight champion, carried that banner to the Orange Bowl to meet Bear Bryant's Crimson Tide of Alabama. Bryant and Wilkinson prepared to meet once again. President Kennedy visited the Sooner locker room before the game. Across the way, Alabama quarterback Joe Namath and linebacker Lee Roy Jordan waited patiently. Namath roll-outs proved difficult to defend. Alabama quickness ultimately prevailed, as the Tide defeated the Sooners 17-0. It was a bitter loss for Wilkinson, who had lost to Bryant's Kentucky team in the 1950 Sugar Bowl. Leon Cross, Wayne Lee and Joe Don Looney were named All-Americans.

History tends to be forged in fits and starts. The American public had settled quietly in front of their television sets to watch "Bonanza," "Perry Mason" and "Leave It To Beaver." All seemed bright for the nation's future. Oklahoma had lost its senior U.S. Senator, Robert S. Kerr, on January 1, 1963. Governor Edmondson had appointed himself

to fill the temporary vacancy, pending a special election in the fall of 1964. Bud Wilkinson was growing restless in his position at Oklahoma. National politics continued to interest him. When fall practice commenced, the Sooners appeared to be a seasoned squad composed mostly of juniors. However, sophomore Mike Ringer from Pauls Valley had impressed in fall drills, as had White Deer, Texas, linebacker, Carl McAdams. In the season opener in Norman, Oklahoma toppled Clemson, 31-14. The number one-ranked Southern California Trojans were to be met next on the field of the Los Angeles Coliseum. Los Angeles was smoldering under a record heat wave with temperatures of 110 degrees all too prevalent. Trojan coach John McKay sug-

Above: Crimson-clad Sooner fans swarm the playing field after Oklahoma's startling reversal of fortune against Syracuse, September 22, 1962.

Left: A double reverse sprang Joe Don Looney, #33, to a 19-yard touchdown against the Southern Cal Trojans, September 28, 1963. Oklahoma 17, USC 12.

gested to Wilkinson that the game be postponed to the evening hours. Bud refused. The Sooners went out for pre-game warm-ups, helmet-less, in white T-shirts and light pads, while the Trojans toiled in full battle gear. Looney opened the scoring with a 19-yard jaunt off a double-reverse. The Trojans stormed back. Trojan quarterback Pete Beathard and halfback Mike Garrett led the assault. It was a see-saw battle witnessed by millions on national television. The Sooners eventually prevailed, 17-12. With that, they became the top-ranked team in the country.

For the first time in history, the OU-Texas match-up featured the first and second-ranked teams in the nation. The Sooners were in for a rough time of it, however, as the Longhorns stormed to a 21-0 lead behind quarterback Duke Carlisle and halfback Tommy Ford. Mike Ringer had been sidelined before the game after slicing his elbow in an oscillating fan. John Hammond took over at his position. An inexplicable flatness befell the Sooners who were soundly defeated, 28-7. The following Monday, Wilkinson dismissed Looney from the squad. Seven conference games remained. Kansas, Kansas State, Colorado, Iowa State and Missouri fell to the Sooners in order before the Sooners were scheduled to travel to Lincoln, Nebraska, in late November. Then came word of President Kennedy's assassination. Many thought the game should be postponed. The game went on as scheduled, however, and the Sooners were less than enthusiastic.

In the game, field position doomed the Sooners. Oklahoma yielded seven turnovers, Nebraska five. With Nebraska able to capitalize on errors more effectively, they prevailed, 29-20. Against Oklahoma State in Stillwater, Phil Cutchin's squad led 10-7 into the third quarter. However, OU fullback Jim Grisham, recovering from an injured ankle, repeatedly lanced the Cowboy defensive front. OU linebacker Carl McAdams likewise repelled Cowboy runners. OU 34, OSU 10. The Sooners received an invitation play in the Bluebonnet Bowl, but Bud's heart was not in it. The following February, he resigned as football coach and athletic director in order to run for the United States Senate. During Wilkinson's seventeen years as head coach, his Oklahoma teams won 139, lost 27 and tied 4 regular season games for a winning percentage of .837 percent. Wilkinson's loss to Fred Harris in the Senate election was, he said, the second greatest sorrow of his life, after the premature death of his mother. Bud went on to a successful career as a businessman and sportscaster. He coached the NFL St. Louis Cardinals in 1976-77. When Bud died in February 1994, the *Daily Oklahoman* headline read in part, "They were the best of times."

"They were the best of times." After 17 seasons, Bud Wilkinson resigned his posts as head football coach and athletic director in 1964. That fall, he ran unsuccessfully for the United States Senate.

Gomer Fills the Void

The Beatles were a stage sensation in the fall of 1964, and the Oklahoma Sooners were led by Wilkinson's affable former assistant, Gomer Jones. Everyone wanted Gomer to succeed, but following a legend is a chore for anyone. After a season opening victory over Maryland in College Park, 13-3, the Sooners faltered three weeks in a row. Southern Cal clobbered the Sooners, 40-14 in Norman, followed by a 28-7 setback to Texas. At Lawrence, the Jayhawks prevailed, 15-14. The Sooners were committing too many errors. Penalties were becoming a real problem. Jones recognized this and the Sooners improved with victories over Kansas State, Colorado and Iowa State. A tough Missouri squad tied the Sooners 14-14, before the Sooners overcame Nebraska, 17-7 in Norman. The regular season concluded with a Sooner victory over OSU in Stillwater, 21-16.

The Gator Bowl extended an invitation to the Sooners. They were to play Florida State, featuring quarterback Steve Tensi and wide receiver Fred Biletnikoff. The Sooners could not defend the pass in Jacksonville, as the Seminoles outscored the Sooners, 36-19. The Sooners finished their first season under Gomer Jones with a record of 6-4-1. Carl McAdams was named

Above: Two-time All-American tackle, Ralph Neely paced the Sooners under head coach Gomer Jones in 1964.

Below: Oklahoma linebacker Carl McAdams steals a pass intended for Florida State's Fred Biletnikoff in the 1964 Gator Bowl.

All-American.

Pop artists Sonny and Cher wailed their version of "I Got You, Babe." The United States continued its build-up in South Vietnam. In Norman, football observers were anxious to see whether Gomer Jones could fill the rather large shoes of Bud Wilkinson. The season of '65 would be the acid test. Three straight losses scuttled any chance Jones had of settling into his position. The Sooners simply were not able to generate a consistent offensive attack. Victories were posted mid-season over Kansas and Kansas State. After losing to Colorado at home, 13-0, the Sooners defeated Iowa State 24-20 on the same field. Missouri and Nebraska handled the Sooners prior to the season finale against OSU in Norman. Some measure of comfort could be salvaged with a victory over the Cowboys. It was not to be, as OSU edged the Sooners on their home field, 17-16. It was Gomer Jones' last game as head coach. Never having been totally comfortable with the public aspects of being head coach, Gomer gracefully stepped down, retaining his job as athletic director. Six years later, in 1971, Gomer was standing on a New York subway platform when he died of a heart attack. His final act was to offer encouragement to a team of Sooner basketball players playing a game far, far from home.

Above: Carl McAdams was named All-American twice, 1964 and 1965, for his outstanding defensive skills.

Right: Gomer Jones stepped down as head football coach following the 1965 season but continued as athletic director until his death in 1971.

Mackenzie
and
Friends

Darrell Royal, almost halfway through what would be a 20-year coaching career at the University of Texas, was not interested in returning to his alma mater when OU sought a replacement for Gomer Jones. When offered a six-year contract at $32,000 a year, he politely declined.

It was December 1965, and Oklahoma was conducting a genuine search for the first time since Jim Tatum was hired in 1946. OU turned its attention to the Southeastern Conference, where a couple of young head coaches had made names for themselves.

In 1965, Doug Dickey had coached Tennessee to a 7-1-2 record and a Bluebonnet Bowl berth against Tulsa. It was the Vols' first winning season in four years. Likewise, Georgia's Vince Dooley appeared to have turned around the Bulldogs, going 7-3-1 and 6-4 his first two years at a program that, until his arrival, had suffered three straight losing seasons. Dickey and Dooley would go on to splendid careers. Dickey would coach 15 years at Tennessee and Florida, going 104-58-6 with 10 bowl trips. Dooley would coach Georgia for 25 seasons, compiling a 201-77-10 record and winning the 1980 national championship. However, both turned down the Sooners. Dooley rejected OU on Dec. 19, and Dickey preferred to wait until after the Dec. 18 bowl game to talk with Oklahoma officials.

Feeling pressed to make a decision and avoid compromising recruiting, OU president George L. Cross and the board of regents turned to an obscure assistant at

Superlative staff – Jim Mackenzie assembled a notable coaching staff in the spring of 1966. (front row, left to right) Chuck Fairbanks, Pat James, Mackenzie, Homer Rice, Barry Switzer. (back row, left to right) trainer Ken Rawlinson, Galen Hall, Billy Gray, Swede Lee, Larry Lacewell, Port G. Robertson.

Arkansas. It was the best thing to happen to Oklahoma football since Tatum brought a young Bud Wilkinson to the state twenty years earlier.

Jim Mackenzie would lead the Sooners for only sixteen months. On April 28, 1967, he was felled by a heart attack and died at the age of 37. His one season, 1966, was both memorable (victories over Texas and Nebraska) and forgettable (a second straight loss to Oklahoma State). But his coaching legacy lives on. That is to say, Mackenzie assembled a coaching staff that, with the benefit of almost 30 years of retrospection, can be labeled nothing short of superlative. As coordinators, he engaged Pat James (defense) and Homer Rice (offense), who would have distinguished careers as assistant coaches. He added a former NFL quarterback to be receivers coach. Galen Hall would go on to be OU's offensive coordinator during the fabulously successful 1970s, then head coach at Florida. To coach freshmen, Mackenzie hired Larry Lacewell, who would devise the incredible Sooner defenses of the 1970s, be an 11-year head coach at Arkansas State, and eventually become director of scouting for the Dallas Cowboys. Chuck Fairbanks was hired to work with the defensive secondary. Fairbanks would replace Mackenzie in May 1967 and coach OU to an Orange Bowl victory and the No. 2 national ranking a mere eight months later. In six years with Fairbanks as head coach, the Sooners would go 52-15-1. Later, Fairbanks would turn the New England Patriots from a hapless franchise into a powerful NFL contender.

Finally, Mackenzie hired a brash young man from Crossett, Arkansas, whom he had lured into coaching at Arkansas. Barry Switzer would eventually take the Sooner reins and fashion the fourth-best winning record in the history of college football.

"In one year's time we brought Oklahoma back to the top of college football with what was already here," Switzer said, referring to the 1967 season. "Jim was responsible for that. Jim was dead, but Jim Mackenzie was why that happened."

Mackenzie was a 1953 graduate of the University of Kentucky where he played for Bear Bryant, was a three-time all-Southeastern Conference tackle and a member of the Kentucky team that beat Oklahoma 13-7 in the 1951 Sugar Bowl. That game ended the Sooners' 31-game winning streak.

Mackenzie seasoned himself at the high school and junior college levels before joining Frank Broyles' staff at Missouri in 1957. The following year, Mackenzie followed Broyles to Arkansas and became part of some remarkable Razorback coaching staffs. Accordingly, Arkansas became a national power, highlighted by an 11-0 season in 1964. Mackenzie eventually became Broyles' assistant head coach, and in his last six years at Arkansas, the Razorbacks

Head coach Jim Mackenzie cranes his neck to see the action against Nebraska, as defensive secondary coach Chuck Fairbanks obscures his view, November 24, 1966. Oklahoma 10, Nebraska 9.

played five times in either the Sugar Bowl or the Cotton Bowl.

Arkansas assistant coaches in the early 1960s included Mackenzie, Switzer, Doug Dickey, Hayden Fry and Johnny Majors. Ironically, when Dickey was hired at Tennessee in 1964, he attempted to take Switzer with him but Switzer already had decided to be patient until Mackenzie became a head coach and follow him.

When Switzer finished his playing days at Arkansas, he was called into active duty in the armed services. "He would come by here on weekends," recalled Mackenzie's widow, Mrs. Sue Disney. "He was talking about what he wanted to do and Jim asked him if he had ever considered coaching. Barry said no. 'Well,' Jim said, 'You know more about football than a heckuva lot of coaches do.' So he worked and got Frank to hire Barry." Broyles offered Switzer a job in the summer of 1960 and after a letter-writing campaign to military officials, Switzer was released from the army in time to join the Razorbacks in the fall of 1961. He immediately impressed Mackenzie, who, when he brought Switzer to Oklahoma would say, "He's a real fine recruiter, makes a fine appearance and he's intelligent. I think Barry has a fine future."

Mackenzie's lone season at OU was a roller-coaster ride. In fact, 1966 is the only year in their history that the Sooners beat both Texas (18-9) and Nebraska (10-9) but lost to Oklahoma State (15-14). The Sooners also were defeated 38-0 by Notre Dame. However, their 6-4 finish was a positive indicator after the difficulties of 1965. In his only recruiting class, Mackenzie assembled a freshman class that included three eventual first-round NFL draft choices - Steve Owens, Jim Files and Steve Zabel. Expectations for the future rose to new heights.

Right: ABC sportscasters Bud Wilkinson (left) and Chris Schenkel (right) broadcast the nationally televised action from Owen Field in the Sooner victory over the Nebraska Cornhuskers, 1966.

Below: Sooner defensive back Bob Stephenson returns an intercepted pass against the Texas Longhorns, October 8, 1966. OU 18, Texas 9.

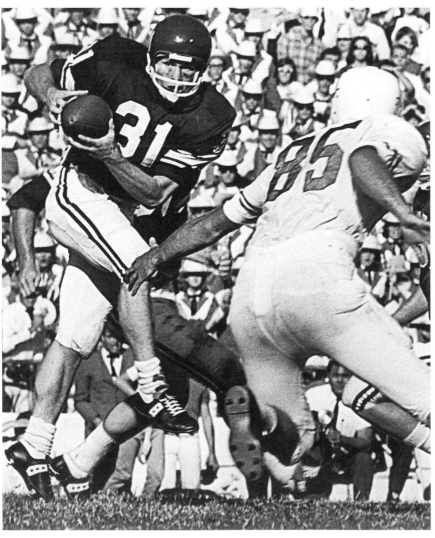

Fans flocked to Owen Field on September 17, 1966, to see the unveiling of Jim Mackenzie's first and, regrettably only, Sooner squad. Oklahoma 17, Oregon 0.

Shockingly, that 15-14 loss at Stillwater would be the last football game of Jim Mackenzie's coaching career. Mackenzie was a heavy smoker back in the days when smoking wasn't considered the health risk it is today. On the day of the Texas game in Dallas in 1966 - a game that would end with the Sooner players carrying their new coach off the field on their shoulders in triumph - Mackenzie smoked five packs of Camels. He had been gaining weight, and there were other warning signs. Numbness in his left arm. Occasional chest pains. On April 27, Mackenzie prepared to fly to Amarillo, Texas, to recruit blue-chip quarterback Monte Johnson, who eventually would sign with Texas but later transfer to OU and become a starting safety. On his way out of the office, Mackenzie stopped to chat with Switzer. "Barry," he said. "I'm going to get us a quarterback. Promise me one thing. Don't run anybody off today." Switzer still remembers that last conversation with his mentor. "I just said, 'Coach, we're not going to do that. Good luck.' He walked out and I never saw him again. I'll never forget, that was the last statement Jim Mackenzie made to me." Mackenzie's return flight landed back in Norman around 9:10 p.m. that night and he seemed fine. But at home around midnight, the chest pains returned. Mackenzie called his doctor, took an extra dose of medication and was suddenly stricken by a massive heart attack. Switzer was awakened about 1 a.m. by a phone call from OU trainer Ken Rawlinson. Pat James and Fairbanks picked up Switzer and they rushed to the hospital but they arrived too late. Jim Mackenzie was dead at the age of 37. "I never forget the anniversary of his death," Switzer said. "Not one time. He was a great friend, too. I think he was a man's man. Anybody that knew Jim Mackenzie loved Jim Mackenzie."

More than 600 people attended the memorial service at St. John's Episcopal Church in Norman. Switzer, Fairbanks, James, Hall, Gray and Carl Nystrom were pallbearers. On May 2, four days after Mackenzie's death, President Cross promoted Fairbanks to head coach. Mackenzie's widow still has a tape of the 1951 Sugar Bowl and occasionally watches. "Lots and lots of memories. When Jim died, I felt for those who loved him. But I never felt sorry for Jim. It upset me, but he died living the life he wanted to live and doing the things he liked to do best."

Without Mackenzie's death, "I probably never would've been the head football coach at Oklahoma," Switzer said. "I probably would've made a move to take an opportunity elsewhere. But you never know what happens. Life unfolds, unknowing to us what's ahead. But I can look back and think that probably would've happened."

On the 25th anniversary of Mackenzie's death, Switzer said, "The tragedy of his death is the fact that had he lived, he would've still been the head football coach and enjoyed all the success that I have enjoyed and all that since. And I wish it would've happened, cause I wish Jim Mackenzie were alive today and enjoyed the success he brought to Oklahoma."

A Cat Nap

Oklahoma's hiring of Jim Mackenzie almost didn't happen, and not because the Sooners first courted Darrell Royal, Vince Dooley and Doug Dickey. The OU-Mackenzie match appeared star-crossed before it began. When Dr. Cross first tried to contact Mackenzie, he was unsuccessful. Cross telephoned Mackenzie's Fayetteville, Arkansas, home for a week with no answer. Finally, Cross discovered he was calling another Jim Mackenzie, an Arkansas student who had left campus for semester break. Arkansas head coach Frank Broyles put Cross in touch with Mackenzie and an interview was scheduled. There were additional problems. Mackenzie overslept on his connecting flight from Dallas to Oklahoma City and flew on to Colorado Springs, Colorado, missing his appointment in Norman. Mackenzie hurriedly called OU officials to apologize. Later he joked, "Well, I heard Royal didn't interview and he was offered the job."

The Winning Edge

Jim Mackenzie was a compulsive note-taker his entire coaching career. "Every day of practice he put down what he planned," said Mrs. Sue Disney. He wrote about the practice and the effect it had on the next day's practice. "He kept adding to it. It was something he gained through experience and coaching, as well as a player."

That note-taking evolved into a series of principles Mackenzie called "The Winning Edge." It was, said his protégé Barry Switzer, "Jim's philosophy, the things he learned from coaching. His Bible. What he believed in. It applies in life and every other way, not just football. It applies in everything you do in life to be a success."

Here is Mackenzie's "The Winning Edge:"

1. Play the percentages!
2. Avoid losing first!
3. Play field position football.
4. Every coach knows more than he can teach.
5. Don't coach caution into good players.
6. Nothing is accomplished without enthusiasm.
7. Look for and recognize your mistakes in coaching.
8. Little things are done by winners.
9. Having a good team just gives you a chance to win.
10. Physical conditioning precedes mental toughness. Discipline precedes morale.
11. Players, not coaching, win. Poor coaching loses.
12. Be yourself, not an actor. Players recognize phonies.
13. Play like you practice. Make second effort part of your personality.
14. Know the rules, players and coaches.
15. Football is a game of critical situations.
16. Kicking game is one-third of football. This is the phase of the game where big breaks occur.
17. Prepare for the psychological lifts and letdowns.
18. Know what to expect of your offense, defense, kicking game and personnel.
19. Always have a plan and believe in it.
20. Form a team of winners. Surround yourself with players and people to whom football means a lot.

"I'll never forget Jim Mackenzie's influence on me," Switzer said. "Obviously, my tutoring in the game of football, philosophy, coaching, our success, my success, came because of my association with him. He was definitely a great influence in my professional career."

Switzer still has the original composition of Mackenzie's "The Winning Edge."

Wishbone Wonderland and Other Mysteries

The ringing phone jarred Biggie Munn from a deep sleep in his East Lansing, Michigan, home. He shook himself into semi-consciousness, looked at his alarm clock, and discovered it was 3 a.m. Who would call a retired football coach at three o'clock in the morning?

It was September 27, 1970, and Munn was 17 years out of coaching. He had been a head coach only seven seasons, but his name still carried weight in the upper Midwest. In those seven seasons at Michigan State, Munn's teams went 54-9-2. Among the men he tutored were Bob Devaney and Dan Devine who would go on to win national championships at Nebraska and Notre Dame, respectively. Munn also was the mentor of Chuck Fairbanks, a letterman at Michigan State in the early 1950s who had gone into coaching and found himself the head man at Oklahoma in 1967.

It was Fairbanks on the phone that early morning. Back in Oklahoma, Fairbanks was desperate. His Sooners were struggling, Sooner fans were getting restless, and his offensive coordinator, Barry Switzer, had this crazy idea. A few hours earlier, OU had lost 23-14 to Oregon State. The newly installed veer offense was not working. All the coaches now agreed it had been a mistake to adopt the veer. Switzer, a young, volatile guy, now wanted to make a bold move. The Sooners had two weeks before their next game, the annual showdown against Texas in Dallas, and Switzer wanted to scrap the veer in those two weeks. Change offenses in the middle of a season? You just don't do that. First of all, it makes people think you don't know what you're doing. More importantly, it makes your players doubt your commitment to the next offense. And Switzer didn't want to go back to the I formation, which the Sooners had run in Fairbanks' first three years as head coach. No, Switzer wanted to try a revolutionary offense that Texas was running with amazing results but still was considered somewhat experimental.

He wanted to install the wishbone.

Switzer says his idea wasn't so crazy. "We weren't worth a ——," he said of OU's 2-1 start in 1970, which included ho-hum victories over SMU (28-11) and Wisconsin (21-7).

"Tell Barry that's easier'n hell for him to say," Fairbanks says. "He didn't have to make the choice. I didn't sleep too good making that one. It was a big gamble, a tremendous gamble. I wouldn't advise anyone to do it."

Abandoning the veer would be "an admission we made a mistake back in the spring. What we were doing, we'd probably done all right against some of the teams we were playing, but to play against the really good teams..." That's why he called Munn. Fairbanks was torn, and maybe his mentor could shed some light on the decision. "I told him I was thinking about making a change, told him why and asked him for his advice," Fairbanks said. "He said, 'I'm not going to answer you. It's too important. I need to stay up and think about it. I'll call you at nine o'clock in the morning.'"

Fairbanks waited. He reflected back on his OU coaching career. He had joined Jim Mackenzie's staff in 1966, and when Mackenzie was killed by a heart attack in April 1967, Fairbanks was elevated four days later to OU's head coach. It was a tenuous situation at best. For one thing, defensive coordinator Pat James thought he (James) was the natural replacement for Mackenzie and left the staff. For another, Fairbanks had been appointed by out-going

Chuck Fairbanks led the Sooners for six seasons, 1967-1972, and took the leap of faith which brought the wishbone formation to Oklahoma.

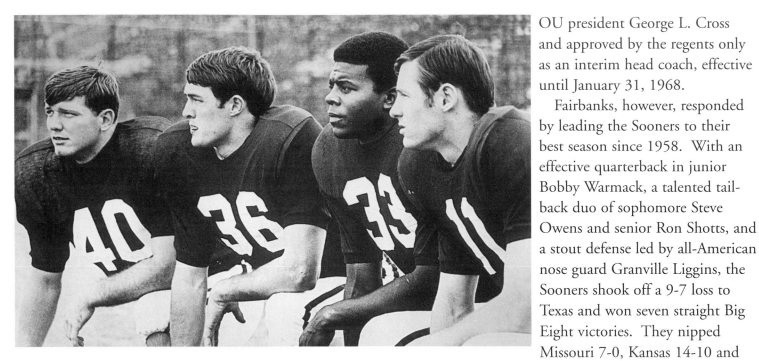

OU president George L. Cross and approved by the regents only as an interim head coach, effective until January 31, 1968.

Fairbanks, however, responded by leading the Sooners to their best season since 1958. With an effective quarterback in junior Bobby Warmack, a talented tailback duo of sophomore Steve Owens and senior Ron Shotts, and a stout defense led by all-American nose guard Granville Liggins, the Sooners shook off a 9-7 loss to Texas and won seven straight Big Eight victories. They nipped Missouri 7-0, Kansas 14-10 and Nebraska 21-14.

Above: The Sooner backfield of 1968, left to right, fullback Mike Harper, tailback Steve Owens, flanker Eddie Hinton, and quarterback Bobby Warmack, constitutes the most notable Oklahoma offensive weaponry of the 1960s.

Below left to right: Senior Ron Shotts (left) and understudy Steve Owens (right) became a formable tailback tandem in 1967. Bob Kalsu was an All-American tackle in 1967. Later, Kalsu was killed in action in Vietnam. Granville Liggins literally defined the noseguard position in 1966-1967. "Granny" was rewarded by being named a two-time All-American and was Lineman of the Year.

Ranked third nationally entering the Orange Bowl, OU upset No. 2 Tennessee 26-24 to cap a 10-1 season. Warmack scored on a 7-yard run and threw a 21-yard touchdown pass to Eddie Hinton. Owens scored from a yard out to give the Sooners a 19-0 halftime lead. Bob Stephenson's 24-yard pass interception in the fourth quarter helped stave off a Tennessee rally, and OU had its first bowl victory since defeating Syracuse in the 1959 Orange Bowl Classic.

Fairbanks had earned his job on a permanent basis and hopes remained high after the Sooners recovered from a 2-3 start in 1968 to tie Kansas for the Big Eight championship. After a 41-27 loss to Colorado, the Sooners won five straight. They beat Kansas 27-23 and routed Nebraska 47-0. However, a 28-27 Bluebonnet Bowl loss to Southern Methodist left OU at 7-4.

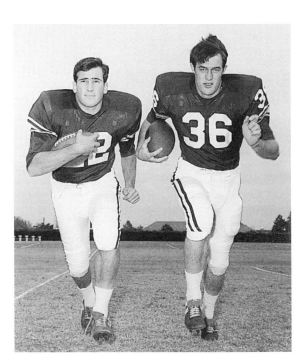

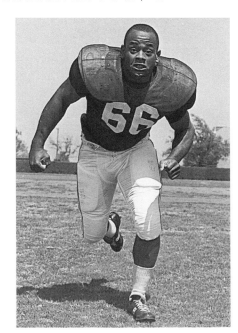

STEVE OWENS

Steve Owens sat in the stands at Super Bowl XXVIII in Atlanta, Georgia, when he was recognized by a stranger, who urged his young son to ask for an autograph of the 1969 Heisman Trophy winner. "The kid didn't know Steve Owens," Owens recalled. "But he knew the Heisman."

Winning the Heisman means membership in one of sport's grandest fraternities. The day Owens went to New York City to receive his award, he was told, "Your life's never going to be the same." The observation proved accurate, from the autographs to being dubbed "Harry Heisman" as a Detroit Lion rookie to the personal relationships with fellow winners like Roger Staubach and O.J. Simpson. But those aren't the faces Owens sees when he looks at one of the planet's most famous pieces of hardware. "I see the faces of my teammates," said Owens. "That's why it means so much to me. I think of Mike Harper and Steve Zabel and Jack Mildren. I think of Chuck Fairbanks and Barry Switzer and all the guys." It's safe to assume they often think of him.

Owens did not lead Oklahoma to a national championship, and his Heisman-winning year was one of the more disappointing seasons in Sooner history, a 6-4 record and no bowl game. But Owens won more than the Heisman with his sterling performance in 1969. He won a reprieve for a coaching staff that included Chuck Fairbanks, Barry Switzer, Larry Lacewell, and Galen Hall. Owens already had been announced as the Heisman winner when the Sooners played Oklahoma State at Stillwater on November. 29. However, OU was 5-4 and a loss to the Cowboys would not bode well for Fairbanks and his staff. The previous three times the Sooners had ended a season with a loss to their Bedlam Series rival -1945, 1965 and 1966 - it was the final game for OU's head coach. "To save our coaching staff, we really needed to win that game," Owens said.

The Sooners won it, 28-27, thanks to a failed 2-point conversion by OSU in the final 1:15 and a yeoman effort by their Heisman-winning tailback. Owens carried the ball an incredible 55 times that day, an NCAA record, and gained 261 yards. In the third quarter alone, Owens carried 20 times, still an NCAA record for one period, and gained 97 yards. During that excruciating third quarter, when the Sooners turned a 21-14 deficit into a 28-21 lead with 13:56 left in the game, Owens was exhausted. In the quarter, he had carried seven straight plays during one stretch and six straight during another. He asked Mildren, OU's sophomore quarterback, to call timeout. From the pressbox, Switzer, then the offensive coordinator, barked over the headset, wanting to know who called timeout. Mildren told Switzer that Owens was tired. "Well, I'll tell you what," Switzer says he told Mildren. "You go inform that big stud he ain't supposed to get tired. Tell him to saddle up ... because we're not going to a bowl, so he can rest all spring."

Owens didn't hold a grudge. After a successful six-year career with the Lions, Owens returned to Norman. "The day I retired, I told my wife, call the moving van," he said. "We're going back to Oklahoma. I've enjoyed this university and this city so much. Playing here meant so much to me."

In 1969, when Steve Owens rewrote the Sooner record book, the honeymoon with Fairbanks began to wane. The '69 Sooners had three players who would become first-round NFL draft choices – Owens, tight end Steve Zabel and linebacker Jim Files – but after a 27-17 loss to Texas, OU failed to summon up its traditional rally. On October 25, the Sooners were blindsided by a gifted quarterback, Lynn Dickey, and routed 59-21 by Kansas State. Oklahoma had beaten K-State for 32 straight seasons, a still-standing NCAA record for victories between annual opponents. The Sooners were in for two

Right: Heisman Trophy winner Steve Owens (36) bulls forward behind the familiar blocking of fullback Mike Harper (40) against Nebraska, 1969.

Below left: Center All-American Ken Mendenhall anchored an offensive line which opened the holes for Steve Owens in 1969.

Below right: Steve Zabel was a dominating player on both sides of the ball. Accordingly, he was named an All-American following the 1969 season.

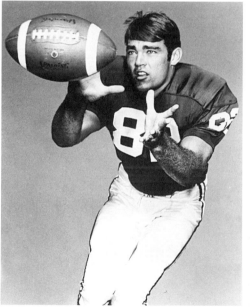

more clobberings – 44-10 by Missouri and 44-14 by Nebraska – and Fairbanks might have lost his job had OU not survived Oklahoma State 28-27 in the season finale. "You never know what would have happened," Switzer said. "I didn't know what Chuck's position really was."

To turn things around in 1970, he installed the veer offense, which the Sooners hoped would showcase quarterback Jack Mildren, who had started as a sophomore. The Abilene, Texas, native was a tough runner and a capable passer. The veer was an offense that set up in a pro-style formation but relied heavily on option plays. But the veer proved ineffective. In those first three games of 1970, the Sooner offense could not sustain drives. "We wanted to control the ball," Switzer said. The veer "was hit and miss. We knew we had to do something. Our staff was totally sold. It was no gamble." After the loss to lowly Oregon State, Fairbanks was tempted.

At 9 a.m. that Sunday morning, Biggie Munn called back. Munn asked Fairbanks, "Are you convinced making this change is the right thing to do?" Fairbanks said yes. Then Munn said, "I want to ask you one more question. Can you convince your team and your coaching staff it's the right thing to do?" Yes, Fairbanks told him. Munn responded, "Don't look back."

No Sooner ever did.

The Oklahoma wishbone was born that Sunday morning, and when it finally was laid to rest twenty years later, the Sooners had sustained an offensive reign of terror over all of college football.

With the wishbone, Oklahoma:

• Won three national championships;

• Fashioned winning streaks of 28 and 20 games;

• Eight times led the nation in rushing, including an NCAA record 472.4 yards a game in 1971;

• Scored at least 50 points 38 times;

• Begot a series of legends, from slick-operating quarterbacks to hello-goodbye halfbacks. Jack Mildren, Steve Davis, Thomas Lott, J.C. Watts and Jamelle Holieway. Greg Pruitt, Joe Washington, Elvis Peacock and Billy Sims.

"We used to score as fast running the ball as most teams did throwing the ball," said Pruitt, an OU all-American in 1971 and 1972. "We had a lot of confidence in our offense. We felt we could score at any time, from anywhere on the field."

Pruitt was the prototype wishbone halfback. A short (5-foot-9) bundle of speed and power, Pruitt was playing split end in the Sooner veer. He was moved to halfback in the wishbone, and a star was born. "You add 4.3 speed to your backfield, and there is no way the defense is going to be able to stop you," Pruitt said. "That was our approach." Before the re-creation of the Oklahoma Land Run, however, and establishing the NCAA records, and before all of college football came to fear the offensive lightning of Oklahoma's Big Red, Fairbanks & Company had to sell those frustrated 1970 Sooners on the idea.

Fairbanks and Switzer had a chat with Mildren that Sunday afternoon. "He was a key guy, the one who had to make it work," Fairbanks said. "It was kind of an affront to Jack ... I knew he had to be ready to accept the challenge." Going to the 'bone would end Mildren's days as a passing quarterback, and that could have been a problem. "Jack had a lot of self-confidence in his ability to throw the football," Fairbanks said. "But the part of the throwing game that Jack lacked most was his ability to throw intermediate, possession-type passes that required a lot of velocity on the ball." Mildren was stunned by the news. "I was 20 years old," he said. "I was not a willing convert, particularly. We frankly ... weren't pleased. You really don't want to change. You don't want to think that what you've been doing is wrong. Coach Fairbanks just told everybody that's what we were going to do."

Then things really got interesting. OU had 13 days to install an alien offense for the October 10 game against Texas, a team which not only used the wishbone itself but practically invented the offense. The Longhorns were using the formation en route to a winning streak that would reach 30 games before a Cotton Bowl loss on January 1, 1971.

Mildren still winces at the sacrifices the coaching staff had to make that October. "As many hours as they put in anyway, I bet those guys didn't go home very often during the first month," he said. "I'm sure many, many

Below: Two-time All-American halfback Greg Pruitt, it was suggested, should have had "hello" on the front of his jersey and "goodbye" on the back.

Lower: All-American quarterback Jack Mildren was the key to the most prolific ground offense in college football history, 1971.

long nights were part of it."

The players weren't spared, either. These were the days before the NCAA limited practice time. The Sooner offensive units went to work on the mechanics of the wishbone: the quarterback-fullback option, where Mildren would read the defensive tackle and decide whether to hand the ball to Leon Crosswhite or pull it back and head outside; and the quarterback-halfback option, where Mildren would read the defensive end and either cut upfield or pitch the ball to Pruitt, Joe Wylie or Roy Bell, the trio of halfbacks which emerged in the wishbone.

"We probably couldn't have done it without a quarterback like Jack," said Galen Hall, an OU offensive assistant that season and later Switzer's long-time offensive coordinator. Mildren remembers "a 15-yard strip where we practiced the quarterback-fullback exchange. It was a second home to most of us, we spent so much time there. We had to start from day one, learning that first step. Gosh, we were having to worry about mechanics. We were having to learn to crawl."

On October 10, the Sooners unveiled their version of the wishbone – with predictable results. The No. 1-ranked Longhorns hammered Oklahoma 41-9. The drubbing was "every bit as bad as it sounds," Mildren said. But there was a glimmer in the eyes of the OU coaches as they saw the potential of the 'bone. Hall said, "I feel we came away from that game knowing we had a chance to control the football. The players got confidence in it." Switzer said there was no doubt: "I knew it was the right decision. I knew it when we played Texas and moved the ball up and down the field (212 yards rushing). We had better players than Texas. We proved that the next year." The incredible Oklahoma wishbone ride didn't really begin until the following fall. "It was a very courageous decision," Mildren said. "It could have come tumbling down on the coaching staff. And everything wasn't all positive. We had plenty of bumps and bruises. The Kansas State game is the one that sticks in my craw 20 years later—things you just let happen because you're not playing well." The week after Texas, OU beat Colorado 23-15 but then was stunned by Kansas State 19-14 at Owen Field, the Sooners' second straight loss to KSU and OU's first at home to the Wildcats since 1934. There was no turning back. Gradually the Sooners became accustomed to the wishbone. "You learned things every day," said Hall.

Right: Roy Bell, halfback from Clinton, was one of those players critical to the mid-season conversion to the wishbone in 1970.

Below: Long-striding Joe Wylie made All-Big Eight in 1970 as a fine runner and punter.

OU rallied to beat Iowa State 29-28, defeated Missouri 28-13 and edged Kansas 28-24. Then came a showdown with Nebraska, which was on its way to the national championship. The Huskers seemed baffled by the 'bone and narrowly escaped with a 28-21 victory. The following week, the explosion came. In a foretelling of the 1971 season, the Sooners beat Oklahoma State 66-6. "Toward the end of the year, we were pretty damn good," Fairbanks said.

Late in the 1970 season, Fairbanks got a note from Munn, who would suffer a stroke in 1971 and die in 1975 at the age of 65. "I'm proud of you," Biggie wrote.

In the Bluebonnet Bowl, the Sooners changed the face of college football for a decade. OU and Alabama played to a 24-24 tie in Houston and Crimson Tide coach Bear Bryant was so impressed with the wishbone, he installed it himself. In 1971, Alabama began running the 'bone and such was its success that the Crimson Tide matched OU's two national titles in the '70s. "It not only turned Oklahoma around, it turned a lot of teams around," Switzer said. Bryant, like Fairbanks, was struggling. Alabama in 1969 and 1970 had gone 6-5 and 6-5-1. Fairbanks in those two seasons was 6-4 and 7-4-1. But in the decade of the 1970s, only two schools won 100 football games—Oklahoma and Alabama.

Above: Oklahoma defensive back Steve O'Shaughnessy zeroes in on a fumble by Missouri's Mel Gray in 1970. Oklahoma 28, Missouri 13.

Below: Steve Owens signs an autograph for a fan while under the watchful eye of legendary Owen Field gatekeeper and resident philosopher, Morris Tennenbaum.

That Magnificent Wishbone

"Who would have dreamed OU would have the offensive success it did?" Mildren asked. "That's why I give credit to Barry Switzer, Galen, people like that who worked very hard to teach it." The Sooners proved to be good students. By September 1971, the Oklahoma wishbone was far more than a well-oiled machine. Machines, devoid of personality, sometimes need repair. The '71 Sooners, brimming with personality, never broke down. "The thing I remember about our offense is that everybody seemed to understand what we were trying to do," Pruitt said.

Playing against teams in 1971 that didn't yet fully understand how to defend the triple option, the Oklahoma wishbone was simply terrorizing. The Sooners scored 55 points against Pitt, 33 against Southern Cal, 48 against Texas, 45 against Colorado, 56 against Kansas and 58 against OSU. They were held under 30 only in a 20-3 victory at Missouri. In what was known then, and probably forever, as the Game of the Century, the Sooners lost, but don't blame the 'bone — Nebraska, 35-31.

GAME OF THE CENTURY

The Game of the Century, they call it still today. But to anyone who played in it or coached in it or even merely watched it with baited breath and pounding heart, the Thanksgiving Day epic that matched the two best teams of 1971 simply was the Game of a Lifetime.

"That game has taken on a life of its own," said quarterback Jack Mildren, the Sooner star that day. "It is absolutely amazing that a game played by 21-year-olds more than 20 years ago would still be raved about."

No. 1-ranked Nebraska. No. 2 Oklahoma.

The Cornhuskers won 35-31 and went on to win the national championship. The Sooners settled for the No. 2 final ranking. More than a generation after the spectacle at Owen Field, the memories of the Game of a Lifetime are not bitter ones. It indeed mattered who won or lost, but it also mattered how they played the game.

"As I campaigned throughout the state, people would come up and reminisce about this game," said Mildren, who was elected Oklahoma's lieutenant governor in 1990 and who lost the gubernatorial election in 1994. "People have a nice feeling about that game. A positive feeling. "It wasn't 0-0, 3-3, 7-7. There were points scored. The referees didn't take control of the game (each team was penalized just five yards). People perceive that OU played well. It's just too bad we lost."

The game was the crowning achievement in the career of Nebraska coach Bob Devaney, who would retire following the 1972 season. In 1971, Devaney had produced what some consider the greatest college team of all time.

The Thanksgiving shootout against OU "was the only game all year we had to play hard in," Devaney said. "That was the thing that stood out. The team rose to the occasion very well. I talk to a lot of people who say that's the most interesting football game they've ever seen."

November. 25 1971, dawned cool, cloudy and crisp. A capacity crowd of 61,000 filled Owen Field to watch America's most dominant college football teams. Oklahoma was 9-0 and averaging 479 yards rushing per game without breaking a sweat - a 33-20 win over Southern Cal was the Sooners' closest call. Defending national champion Nebraska was 10-0 and also unchallenged.

Colorado would finish the season 10-2

and rank third nationally. The Buffs won road games at Louisiana State and Ohio State and routed hometown favorite, Houston, in the Bluebonnet Bowl. But CU was blasted 45-17 at OU and 31-7 at Nebraska.

ABC televised the game, President Nixon attended and prior to the game two coaches renewed old acquaintance at midfield. Devaney had been an assistant coach at Michigan State when Chuck Fairbanks played there in the early 1950s. Devaney remembered Fairbanks as a "good offensive player." But in 1952, single-platoon football returned, and Fairbanks found his playing time reduced. "He was a good receiver, but when it came to defense, he was a foreigner," Devaney said. "So he didn't play as much. He probably didn't think I was a very good fellow."

In 1968, when OU routed the Huskers 47-0, Devaney reminded Fairbanks of the 1952 season. "That's probably why you had (Steve) Owens score that last touchdown." Fairbanks remembers Devaney trying "to tell me that would be his last year to coach. I think he tried to make me feel sorry for him." Fairbanks laughs at the memories. "Bob is a great friend and is to this day. He's a wonderful friend. I always enjoyed going against friends, because I knew it would be a straight-up competition."

Nebraska got the jump when Johnny Rodgers made what amounted to his campaign bid for the 1972 Heisman Trophy, returning a punt 72 yards for a

touchdown less than five minuets into the game.

"The thing I look back on is how many times we practiced on our specialty teams," said OU all-American halfback Greg Pruitt, who was part of the Sooners' punt coverage. "I was the first guy to miss Johnny on that punt return. There was great competition between us, and I got excited. I had him and let him go." To this day, Oklahoma fans claim Pruitt was clipped on the play, and Devaney mischievously smiles at the suggestion. "Borderline," he calls the block. "A few years ago, I saw the kid, and he said he had his head in front."

Johnny Rodgers was a fabulous player, a wingback who returned kicks, ran reverses and caught passes. Husker defensive back Joe Blahak – who threw the final block on Rodgers' TD – said, "We had a certified game-breaker in Johnny. I don't think there's been another player collegiately that has been as good. He could do so many things."

OU needed a hero to counter. All eyes turned to Pruitt. The remarkably quick

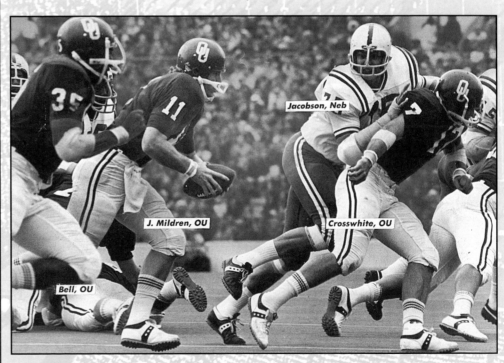

but strong scatback from Houston had exploded onto the national stage in 1971. He would finish the season with 1,665 yards rushing and an NCAA record 9.4 yards per run. Pruitt was third in the Heisman voting. The Huskers, however, were determined not to let Pruitt beat them. They assigned a defender to shadow Pruitt on every play. "He was the guy who could break it on one play," Devaney said. "We took the pitch away, but we gave up a little more inside and Mildren hurt us. He was a real star that day." Mildren would finish with 130 yards on 31 carries and 137 passing yards, completing five of 10. He scored two touchdowns and threw for two more. But a Sooner squad averaging 472.4 rushing yards per game would be held to 279. Pruitt managed just 53 yards on 10 carries, and frustration set in.

"I remember getting upset and going to (Barry) Switzer during the game, asking why I wasn't getting the ball," Pruitt said. "He told me Nebraska was keying on me. I remember saying, 'Hasn't every team we've played this season keyed on me?' My feeling was that until you stop me for no gain, I haven't been stopped. Nebraska did take me out of the wishbone offense, but we had other formations and other plays where I could have gotten the ball."

Pruitt's frustration is understandable. A big game and an OU victory likely would have made him the 1972 Heisman favorite, and as it was, he finished second to Rodgers in '72 and OU finished second to Nebraska in '71.

"I think about what happened and what a difference it would have made if we had won," Pruitt said. "I could have won the Heisman ... in that one game, we not only lost the Big Eight championship, but the national championship."

The Nebraska defensive star was middle guard Rich Glover, who played sensationally against OU all-American center Tom Brahaney. Glover dominated the interior, and with the Huskers tailing Pruitt everywhere, OU's only effective plays were passes and keepers by Mildren. "Rich Glover played a tremendous game that day," Devaney said. "We slowed the wishbone down. We didn't stop it. That triple option wishbone was relatively new. People were experimenting. We had some good defensive coaches. You've gotta have somebody play the fullback, the quarterback, the pitch man. It's a difficult offense. We made 'em look like quite a passing team. They threw quite effectively."

Mildren's old Abilene, Texas, high-school buddy, split end Jon Harrison, became a surprise hero that day. He caught four passes for 115 yards and two touchdowns and threw a 51-yard completion to tight end Albert Chandler. "There was no different plan for that game," Mildren said. "A play or two,

maybe. The pass defense Nebraska played was no different than other teams had played against us. We just threw the ball more in that game than we had previously." Harrison had only 17 catches all season. "A lot of times, I felt like I was a split guard out there," he said. "We threw just to make a big play." Harrison provided those against Nebraska. He twice recovered the lead for the Sooners. Nebraska took a 14-3 lead, but the Sooners went on top 17-14 just before halftime on a Mildren-to-Harrison touchdown pass. The Huskers regained command 28-17, but back came OU, and another Mildren-to-Harrison connection made it 31-28 with 7:10 left in the game.

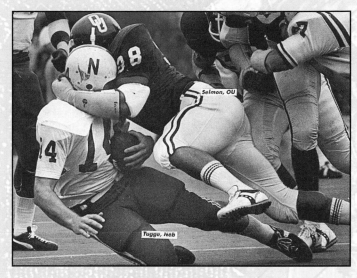

A victory would have been sweet for Mildren and Harrison. There are Texans alive today who will argue that the Game of the Century was not the biggest game in the lives of Mildren and Harrison. Playing for Abilene Cooper, they lost the 1967 Texas state championship game 20-19 to Austin Reagan. "I don't know if I've gotten over either of the losses," Harrison said.

The Huskers won it with the most famous drive in their storied football history. Taking over at its 26-yard line with 7:10 left, Nebraska went 74 yards in 12 plays. Tailback Jeff Kinney - a plow horse who would finish the game with 174 yards on 31 carries - ran seven times for 50 yards on the drive.

"I always thought Kinney was a great player, but he did have a great day," Fairbanks said. "I was most impressed with him on that last drive." The part of the drive that haunts Fairbanks was a 3rd-and-8 play from the OU 46. Sooner defensive end Raymond Hamilton pressured Husker quarterback Jerry Tagge, but Tagge scrambled free and hit Rodgers for an 11-yard gain. "Raymond got ahold of Tagge and missed the tackle," Fairbanks recalled. "If he had made that tackle, they'd have had to punt." Instead, the Huskers drove in, and Kinney's two-yard touchdown run with 1:38 left in the game put Nebraska in front. "Both teams scored almost every time they got

the ball," Fairbanks said. "It was a case of who had it last. If we'd have had enough time, I'm certain we would have scored."

OU's wishbone was, however, not a hurry-up offense. OU took over deep in its own territory. On first down, Mildren overthrew an open Harrison - a pass he still laments. Mildren gained four yards on a second-down option run, was sacked by massive tackle Larry Jacobsen on third down and threw a pass that was batted down by Glover on the Sooners' final play.

With 1:10 left, Oklahoma was out of chances.

"I'm still sick about it," OU defensive coordinator Larry Lacewell said more than 20 years later. "It's just something that's never really left my mind."

Has Fairbanks replayed a few of those pivotal snaps? "Not over a few thousand times," he said. "I'd love to play it over again with the same teams. I like our chances just as much as I did then."

OU went on to rout Oklahoma State 58-14 in the regular-season finale and Auburn 40-22 in the Sugar Bowl. Nebraska went on to trample Hawaii 45-3, then rip unbeaten Alabama 38-6 in the Orange Bowl.

"There was a lot of talent in that game," Devaney said of the Oklahoma-Nebraska shootout. "We beat Alabama, and Oklahoma beat the hell out of Auburn."

A quarter of a century later in the memories of Sooners, pride still has just as much a claim as disappointment on the Game of a Lifetime.

"I felt that way at the time," Fairbanks said. "I always had a lot of pride in the way our players played. I told 'em not one of them ought to hang his head."

Of 1971, Fairbanks said, 'We had to quit practicing our offense against our defense. We couldn't stop 'em, and we had a pretty good defense in 1971." Indeed. OU's '71 defense included future NFL players Raymond "Sugar Bear" Hamilton and Derland Moore. "I know this," Fairbanks said. "It was the best offense I've ever coached from the standpoint of having the entire football team understand what we were trying to accomplish. They knew when the defense was out of position. The linemen knew it, the backs knew it, the quarterback knew it, the coaches knew it. We had probably one of the best offenses that ever played college football."

Many members of that '71 squad credit Mildren. Maybe he wasn't the greatest OU optioneer of them all. Steve Davis won more games. Thomas Lott was smoother. J.C. Watts was better in the clutch. Jamelle Holieway was flashier. Overall, none was better than Mildren. "To me, Jack Mildren was the best wishbone quarterback ever," said Pruitt, not limiting his views to Oklahoma. "I've never seen another option quarterback turn the corner like Jack did. He used to square it off and head up the field, and he would cuss you out if you didn't follow him. If you were tailing him, he wouldn't hesitate to pitch the ball to you 20 yards down the field.

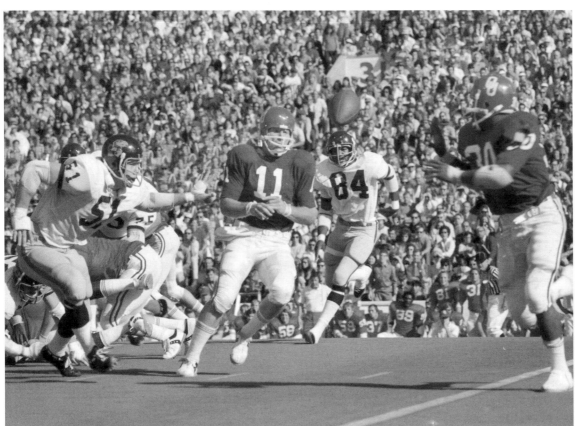

Below: The legendary pitch on the corner – Quarterback Jack Mildren (11) pressures the Kansas defense, then pitches to trailing jet Greg Pruitt (30), who bolts to the sideline corridor, 1971. Oklahoma 56, Kansas 10.

Lower: Tom Brahaney was named All-American twice, 1971 and 1972, as a devastating, blocking center in the Sooner wishbone.

"Jack was like a coach and a quarterback on the field. He understood what he was doing. He was tough." Pruitt drew most of the attention that landmark season. He rushed for 1,665 yards and averaged 9.4 yards per carry. Crosswhite, Bell and Wylie also ran wild. "We had a host of running backs," Fairbanks said. "They were small and quick, ideally suited for the wishbone, but the No. 1 guy ideally suited for it was Jack Mildren." Mildren rushed for 1,140 yards on 193 carries, including quarterback sacks. No Sooner quarterback has ever rushed for more yards in a single season.

In the mature days of the wishbone, defenses fortified the corner, and the home-run play became the exception. In those early days, however, it was the rule. "The Texas wishbone was more of a power offense," Pruitt said. "What we did was take the wishbone and add speed. Our whole concept was that we were going to get the defense in a 3-on-1 mismatch, at best, or no worse than 2-on-1." Said Mildren, "I think OU was on the leading edge of

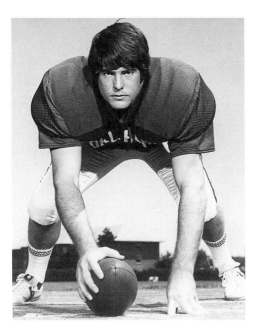

how to run that offense. OU's wishbone was always a little different, a little special. It had its own flavor, because of the players. Texas really didn't have quite the speed at halfback that we did." The wishbone was the perfect offense for a man like Switzer, who in 1973 would replace Fairbanks as head coach. Switzer "was an offensive genius," said Pruitt, who concluded his OU career in 1972. The wishbone was high-risk, yet conservative. It required disciplined, yet highly skilled, players to execute. It was a ground-oriented offense that frequently shocked opposing defenses with a spectacular pass play.

It was, truly, an enigma. And so was Barry Switzer.

Hundreds of high school bandsmen join the Pride of Oklahoma marching band in creating this memorable halftime formation on Band Day, 1971.

Switzer & Sooner Magic

He was a "Bootlegger's Boy," the title of his autobiography. He made enemies but made many more friends. He flouted NCAA rules he thought were not only absurd but inhumane – like getting a winter coat for a wind-chilled kid who didn't have one – but earned the respect of straight-arrows like Joe Paterno. He also was the ultimate competitor. Switzer and his Sooners were at their best when their backs were against the wall.

"Sooner Magic," it came to be called after sensational victories over two decades in some of college football's most famous games. Indeed, there seemed to be something magical about the man. "The magic was in the players," Switzer simply said. Perhaps. Switzer certainly had great players. Thirty-one all-Americans in 17 years as Oklahoma's head coach. A Heisman Trophy winner (Sims). A two-time Butkus Award winner as the nation's best

"When you beat the University of Texas, I don't care what your won-lost record is, it's the biggest day of your life."

– BARRY SWITZER AFTER HIS FIRST WIN OVER TEXAS, 52-13, IN 1973

linebacker (Brian Bosworth). Two Lombardi Award winners (Lee Roy Selmon and Tony Casillas). Two Outland Trophy winners (Selmon and Greg Roberts). One Jim Thorpe Award winner as the nation's best defensive back (Rickey Dixon).

Oklahoma had the outstanding players, and it also had a coach – a remarkable, blessed, charming, roguish, magical coach. In 17 years as head coach – the same tenure as Wilkinson – Switzer achieved what many thought impossible: he surpassed Wilkinson's record. Wilkinson was 145-29-4 at OU. Switzer was 157-29-4.

Barry Switzer achieved what many thought impossible – he surpassed Bud Wilkinson's winning record.

Switzer's record, however is not unblemished. In 1973, he took over a program on NCAA probation, and when he left in June 1989, the Sooners were once again on probation. He had publicized run-ins with opposing coaches and even talented players, like Marcus Dupree and Brian Bosworth. He gave players a long leash. Occasionally the leash turned into a noose. But the people who know him best – the people who played for him and worked with him – swear by the man. There never was anything phoney about Barry Switzer, they say. The loyalty of Switzer's admirers is legendary. "Barry Switzer's the same today as he was when I met him at a junior high track meet in Crossett, Arkansas, in 1949," said Lacewell, who eventually buried the hatchet with Switzer and in 1994 recommended him to Dallas Cowboy owner Jerry Jones. Jones hired Switzer as head coach in one of the most noteworthy sports stories of the '90s.

Joe Paterno, the long-time coach at Penn State who carries the nickname St. Joe, became an admirer of Switzer because "Barry has many qualities I admire," he wrote in a foreword to Switzer's book. "Loyalty, a lack of hypocrisy, a warmth for young people and friends, a deep and honest concern for poor black athletes, a zest for life, and, most of all, a devotion to his children and unswerving appreciation and respect for their mother."

Steve Owens said of Switzer, "Other than my dad, he influenced my life more than anyone. Barry always challenged me, didn't allow me to become complacent. He made me feel good about myself as a player. I'm a big Barry Switzer fan because of what he did for me." Jim Mackenzie planted the seeds and Chuck Fairbanks reaped the initial harvest, but it was Switzer who returned the Sooners to the glory days of the 1950s. He didn't lose in his first 30 games as head coach, and when he finally lost, 23-3 to Kansas on November 8, 1975, Switzer rallied his troops to a national championship. After a temporary swoon in the early '80s (three straight four-loss seasons) Switzer did what Wilkinson failed to do—put the Sooners back on top, winning the 1985 national title and four straight Big Eight championships. Long-time *Dallas Times Herald* and *Dallas Morning News* writer Blackie Sherrod, often a sharp critic of Switzer and the Oklahoma football program, nevertheless tagged Switzer "the best combination recruiter/coach since Bear Bryant."

Switzer proved ideal for Oklahoma in the early '70s. While Southwest Conference schools were just beginning to racially integrate their sports teams, OU had a comparatively long history of acceptance of black athletes. Switzer exploited that advantage, relentlessly recruiting the state of Texas and getting more great athletes from south of the Red River than any school.

In the '70s, when black players still were rare at Texas and Arkansas, Switzer had black co-captains, black quarterbacks and black assistant coaches. Switzer admits that back in the '60s and early '70s he used to tell Texas high school kids, "If you signed with a Southwest Conference team, just think how lonesome it would be to look around in the huddle and see nothing but honky faces." The foundation for Switzer's success was in place by January 1973, when Fairbanks suddenly resigned to become head coach and general manager of the NFL's New England Patriots. Though those '71 Sooners lost the Game of the Century, they routed Auburn 40-22 in the Sugar Bowl and finished No. 2 in the nation.

In the fall of 1972, OU was almost as good. Only a 20-14 loss at Colorado, on a slippery field, kept the Sooners from an unbeaten season. Defensively, OU was extraordinary. Only Colorado, Nebraska and Oklahoma

Coach Switzer displays on Owen Field the treasure trove of hardware which accompanied his teams' successes.

State scored more than seven points on the Sooners. Hamilton and Moore, the future NFL defensive linemen, were joined by future stars Rod Shoate and Randy Hughes, both sophomores, and OU shut out both Texas (27-0) and Penn State (14-0 in the Sugar Bowl). Offensively, the Sooners weren't quite as prolific as in '71, but Pruitt remained a threat on every option, and senior quarterback Dave Robertson became an accomplished passer. Future stars emerged. When Pruitt was slightly injured, freshman Joe Washington stepped in and showed the flash that was to grace the Sooner wishbone the next three years. And an unheralded freshman split end, Tinker Owens, became a late-season star. Oklahoma trailed Nebraska 14-0 in the second half at Lincoln, but Owens had five catches for 108 yards, Washington ran for a spectacular touchdown and John Carroll kicked a field goal to win the game 17-14. In the Sugar Bowl, Penn State proved no threat at all, falling to the Sooners, 14 - 0.

Above: Greg Pruitt goes airborne against the Missouri Tigers in Norman, November 11, 1972. Oklahoma 17, Missouri 6.

Below left: While the wishbone offense received the publicity, All-American defensive tackle Derland Moore spearheaded a smothering defense in the fall of 1972.

Below right: By the fall of 1972, linebacker Rod Shoate was focused on a legendary career which would include All-American status each year from 1972-1974.

But twenty-six days later, Fairbanks resigned. Bowing to tradition, OU's regents turned to a current staff member and selected the 35-year-old Switzer to replace him. The program at that time appeared in fine shape. The nucleus of the '71-72 teams was gone – only two of OU's eight all-Big Eight players from '72 would return—so another 11-1 season seemed a stretch, but expectations were high. Then came the blow of NCAA probation. In April 1973, the NCAA announced that OU was guilty of using two players with altered high-school transcripts.

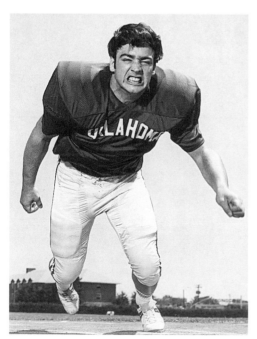

The probation sanctions were harsh. OU was made to forfeit three Big Eight victories in which freshman quarterback Kerry Jackson had played in 1972, plus the Sooners were handed two years of sanctions: no televised games in the 1974 and 1975 seasons, and no bowl game following the 1973 and 1974 seasons. The ramifications of the probation, plus the loss of Jackson, who was declared ineligible for one year, compromised the outlook for the 1973 season. Jackson was considered the next great OU quarterback. He had been Robertson's backup in 1972 and had shown flashes of brilliance. Without him in '73, the quarterback prospects were completely unknown.

The Sooners were picked as low as fourth in the conference, and

Switzer, armed with only a one-year contract, seemed to be piloting a boat that had sprung a leak. But Switzer's competitiveness arose. While Sooner fans questioned how good Oklahoma might be in '73, Switzer remained confident. He told a group of Tulsa alumni shortly after the probation, "I'm a fighter. I'm a competitor. I'm a winner. And nothing is going to stop our team. I'd better go now. I'm double-parked, and I may get another year for that." A team picked fourth in the Big Eight instead finished No. 3 in the nation, and there are

respected observers who consider the 1973 Sooners to be Oklahoma's best team of all time.

Steve Davis, a sophomore from Sallisaw who was also a Baptist minister, became the quarterback. He would lose only one game in his three-year career. Joe Washington became a superstar. Eddie Foster and John Roush anchored an all-star offensive line. But it was on defense that OU had a team for the ages. The Selmon brothers from Eufaula, Oklahoma, senior Lucious and sophomores Lee Roy and Dewey, anchored the line. Rod Shoate was an all-American linebacker. Gary Baccus was an all-Big Eight end and Randy Hughes was an all-Big Eight safety. The '73 Sooners didn't completely shut down opponents like their '72 predecessors – just when they had to. In their biggest games of the season, against Southern Cal and Nebraska, OU allowed a total of only 20 points.

Against USC in the Los Angeles Coliseum, the Sooners faced an all-star lineup. The Trojans had Pat Haden at quarterback, Anthony Davis at tailback and Lynn Swann at flanker. It was Switzer's second game as head coach, and the Oklahoma defense was superb, even though Lee Roy Selmon missed the game with a heart ailment, pericarditis. USC got only a first-half touchdown pass from Haden, finished with 161 total yards and escaped with a 7-7 tie only because OU missed three field goals.

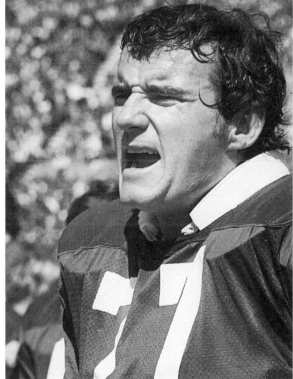

THE SELMON BROTHERS

The bus carrying the 1973 Sooners from their Fort Worth hotel to the Cotton Bowl was rocking with jocularity. A few guys were yelling to one another. Some were singing. One of the Sooner co-captains was not amused. This was the Texas game. Didn't anyone realize it? He had never lost to those despised Longhorns and wouldn't start now. So Lucious Selmon stood up. That soft voice of his turned commanding. "I WANT IT QUIET IN HERE AND I WANT IT QUIET NOW!" The merriment vanished in the autumn air. Game faces replaced hijinks as the OU bus rolled into Fair Park. Then Lucious Selmon and the suddenly serious Sooners thrashed the Longhorns 27-0.

Leadership.

With Lucious leading the way for his younger brothers, Lee Roy and Dewey, the trio teamed to forge the most amazing brother act in college football history. Lucious' initial demonstration of leadership came when he preceded his brothers to the OU campus from their hometown of Eufaula. Barry Switzer still recalls the first time he ever laid eyes on the little brothers, who went on to be all-American defensive linemen for the Sooners. In his autobiography, Switzer recalled the winter of 1969-70, when Lucious was being recruited by OU assistant coach Larry Lacewell and visited the OU campus, accompanied by his brothers. In the cafeteria, Lee Roy and

Dewey were "piling food a foot high on their trays," Switzer said. "Who's that?" Switzer asked Lacewell.

"Those are Lucious's two little brothers, they're high school sophomores,"

Lacewell responded. Switzer gulped. But Lucious was much more than just the carrot who got Lee Roy and Dewey to become Sooners. He too was an all-American, as a senior nose guard in 1973, and the leader of what many observer consider the finest football team in OU history. He put that game-day leadership to good use, becoming an OU assistant coach for 19 years before moving on to the NFL coaching ranks in

1995. He began the Selmon legend. Today, Selmon remains a sacred Sooner name.

The Selmons came from tiny Eufaula and won over a state with all-American

play and all-American quiet dignity. "If you get to be too boisterous, I don't know how much attention is paid to you," Lucious says. The Selmons are truly unique. They played side by side by side on the 1973 defensive line, anchoring perhaps OU's most suffocating defense ever. Those Sooners held USC, Texas, Nebraska, Colorado and Missouri to a combined 30 points.

Dewey would go on to earn a Ph.D. in philosophy and play professional football as well. Lee Roy, arguably the greatest Sooner player regardless of position, was the first pick in the 1976 NFL draft. In 1995, he became the first former Sooner to be voted into the Pro Football Hall of Fame.

Lee Roy and Dewey were not twins – Dewey was 11 months older – but they were in the same grade because when Dewey went off to first grade, Lee Roy cried so much Mrs. Lucious Selmon, Sr., the boys' mother, sent him off with Dewey on the second day.

Fifteen years later, at the conclusion of the pre-game prayer at Sooner home football games, the OU student section would chant "God Bless Mrs. Selmon!" It was a fitting declaration, for Mrs. Selmon truly had blessed Oklahoma.

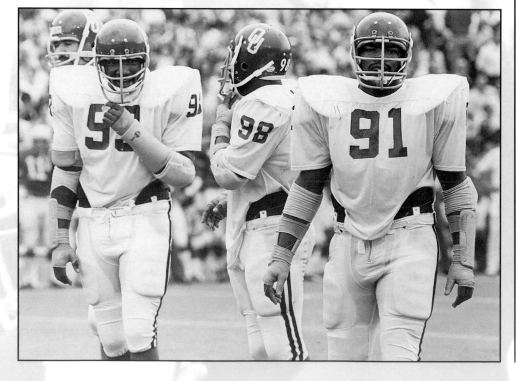

Against Texas in the Cotton Bowl, OU applied to the Longhorns the most lopsided decision in the rivalry since the '50s and the third-largest ever. The Sooners won 52-13, as Washington threw a halfback pass to Tinker Owens for a touchdown and Davis threw long TD passes to Owens and Billy Brooks. OU gained 225 yards passing in the scoring avalanche.

Against Nebraska and left-handed quarterback David Humm in OU's last televised game until January 1, 1976, the Sooner domination was complete. The Huskers crossed midfield only once, and fumbled away the ball on the play, meaning they never snapped the ball from Sooner territory. The final was OU 27, Nebraska 0.

Unbeatens Notre Dame and Alabama played in the Orange Bowl with the Irish winning. The best college football team of 1973 almost certainly was the Oklahoma Sooners, but by the end of the season they found themselves in NCAA purgatory.

Oklahoma went from December 31, 1972, until January 1, 1976, without playing in a bowl game. It went from November 23, 1973, until January 1, 1976, without appearing on live television. The Sooners were, as *Sports Illustrated* dubbed them in 1974, "The Best Team You'll Never See."

Above: Center Kyle Davis (50) bear hugs quarterback Steve Davis (5) after a touchdown in Oklahoma's 1973 victory over Texas, 52-13.

Below left: The national championship of 1974 featured All-American guard John Roush.

Below right: Randy Hughes became one of Oklahoma's most outstanding defensive backs ever in 1974 and was named All-American.

The Marvels of '74 & '75

"My 1974 team was probably the best all-around group I ever coached," Switzer said. "If we had been on television in 1974 and 1975, Joe Washington would have won the Heisman Trophy at least once." Instead in those years, Ohio State's Archie Griffin became the only man to win two Heismans. Members of the American Football Coaches Association, who voted in what was then the United Press International poll and what is now the CNN/USA Today poll, voted in January 1974 to exclude all teams on probation from their rankings. Thus, the Sooners weren't even eligible for one of the mythical national championships. Switzer claims the rule is a good one but maintains to this day that the decision amounted to a frontal assault on OU's dominating football program. The result was a team on a mission.

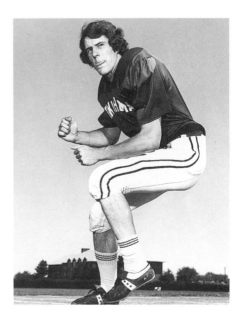

Playing in anonymity, the '74 Sooners went 11-0 and won The

Associated Press national title. They led the nation with 507.7 yards per game, the second-best in OU history, including 438.8 rushing yards per game. Incredibly, half of Oklahoma's starting lineup made all-Big Eight. Tight end Wayne Hoffman, split end Tinker Owens, Joe Washington and linemen Jerry Arnold, John Roush and Terry Webb on offense. End Jimbo Elrod, linemen Lee Roy and Dewey Selmon, Shoate and Hughes were named on defense. Eight Sooners made at least one all-America team: Washington, Owens, Roush, both Selmons, Shoate, Hughes and center Kyle Davis.

After rallying with three fourth-quarter touchdowns to beat Baylor 28-11 in the season opener, Oklahoma had only two close games – predictably, Texas and Nebraska – and answered the bell in both. The Sooners had beaten Texas three straight years and the Longhorns were primed to end the domination. Texas led 13-7 in the fourth quarter, but OU used an Austin native against the Horns. Wide receiver Billy Brooks took a reverse pitch from Steve Davis and raced 40 yards for a tying touchdown. Though OU missed the extra point, the Big Red defense stepped up. Texas freshman fullback Earl Campbell, who would terrorize college football the next three seasons with his battering runs, took a vicious hit from Elrod and fumbled the ball at midfield. With five minutes left, Tony DiRienzo kicked a 37-yard field goal, and the Sooners exited the Cotton Bowl 16-13 winners. "In the dressing room, of course everyone was very happy," said OU offensive tackle Mike Vaughan. "I just wanted to find my locker and sit down. I felt like I was going to pass out. But then I saw Jerry Arnold passed out and spread across the floor, and another player down from exhaustion. I didn't dare pass out because there weren't any trainers left to look after me."

Above left: Little Joe Washington electrified Sooner fans with his soaring dives and silver shoes, 1972-1975.

Above right: Tinker Owens became a two-time All-American end in 1974 and 1975, cradling passes like this one.

Right: Joe Washington takes flight against the Texas Longhorns, 1974. Oklahoma 16, Texas 13.

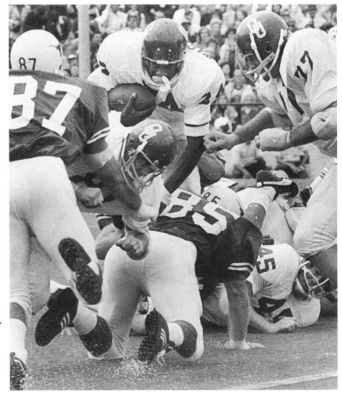

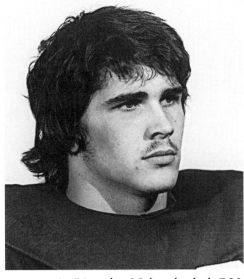

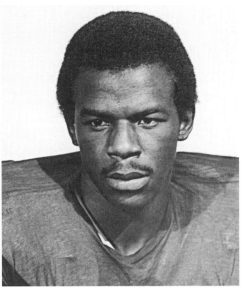

At Lincoln, Nebraska led OU 14-7 in the third quarter as quarterback David Humm played well against the mighty Sooner defense. But Davis executed three long touchdown drives, Randy Hughes intercepted two fourth-quarter passes and OU had a 28-14 victory. The following week, the Sooners ended their season with a 44-13 rout of Oklahoma State. Washington's spectacular 57-yard punt return sparked OU from a 13-10 deficit in the third quarter.

While the '74 Sooners were dominant, the '75 Sooners proved amazingly resilient. It is doubtful any national championship team ever played so many dramatic games. OU beat Miami 20-17 in the Orange Bowl Stadium. The Sooners also won two Big Eight games, 21-20 over Colorado and 28-27 over Missouri, thanks to missed extra points by opposing placekickers. They beat Texas 24-17 with a late touchdown. They routed Nebraska 35-10 only with a fourth-quarter explosion. They edged Bo Schembechler's Michigan

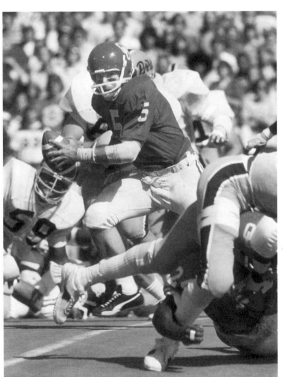

Wolverines 14-6 in the Orange Bowl. "Like I always say, you've got to be lucky – and we had our share in 1975," Switzer said. While lady luck played a hand, the Sooners still had the Selmons, Joe Washington, Steve Davis, Jimbo Elrod, Tinker Owens and Billy Brooks, plus a huge offensive line led by Mike Vaughan and Terry Webb.

Oklahoma routed a fine Pittsburgh team 46-10 in Norman, the game made famous when strong safety Scott Hill made a flying tackle that crumbled Pitt tailback Tony Dorsett. It is remembered as the most dev-

Above left to right: Jimbo Elrod endeared himself to Sooner fans with his jarring tackles, 1973-1975. He was named All-American in 1975. Guard Terry Webb was a senior in 1975 when the Sooners were national champions and he earned All-American honors. Austin, Texas, native Billy Brooks was as dangerous on the end-around play as he was as a pass receiver. He was an All-American in 1975.

Left: Memorable day – Sooner signal caller Steve Davis leads the Sooner rout of Pittsburgh and Tony Dorsett, September 20, 1975. OU 46, Pitt 10.

Above: Deck the house – Oklahoma Memorial Stadium expands with an added upper deck and new press-box along with other improvements, 1974.

Below: Sooner stand-out defenders Daryl Hunt (85) and Basil Banks (17) prepare to sandwich a Texas runner on the floor of the Cotton Bowl.

astating hit in Sooner history. "It was the greatest one-man effort to stop a play that I've ever seen in a crucial situation," said Larry Lacewell. But after the victory over the Pitt Panthers, Oklahoma had its series of close calls. Playing at Miami – OU's first game in the Orange Bowl Stadium since beating Tennessee at the conclusion of the 1967 season – the Sooners held on for a 20-17 victory over a team that did not reflect the Miami powerhouses of the 1980s. In fact, the week of the game, there was a published report that Miami was considering dropping the sport. Instead, OU almost dropped the game, taking a 20-7 halftime lead and then holding on. After scoring a touchdown with 7:09 left in the game, Miami trailed 20-17 and got one more chance which was snuffed out mainly by nose guard Dewey Selmon.

The Sooners survived Colorado 21-20 thanks to a crucial error. The Buffaloes had driven 68 yards to score on David Williams' 8-yard touchdown pass to tailback Billy Waddy with 1:19 left in the game. Down one point and on the verge of ending OU's 23-game winning streak, Coach Bill Mallory ordered a conversion kick to tie. Tom Mackenzie promptly missed it. Then came Texas, which had lost four straight to the Sooners but was not the pushover of 1971-73, when OU won by an average of 29 points. Sophomore Earl Campbell had developed into a superior running back and Marty Akins was a seasoned quarterback. The game developed into a defensive struggle, with Sooner defensive end Mike Phillips recovering a fumble in the end zone for a touchdown. Two OU turnovers led to ten Texas points in the second half and a 17-17 tie with eight minutes to play. But the Sooners drove 79 yards, the final 33 on a brilliant run by Horace Ivory, a young man playing fullback in a halfback's body. With 5:31 left, OU led 24-17. With 2:25 on the clock, the Sooners had the ball but faced 3rd-and-8 from their own 10-yard line. Offensive coordinator Galen Hall ordered a quick kick, with Washington taking a pitch from Steve Davis and unleashing a surprise punt. The play had been practiced in recent years but never used. This appeared to be the perfect time for it. Washington's kick flew, bounced, rolled and died at the Texas 14-yard line, a 76-yard quick-kick that effectively doomed the Longhorns. "It (the game) was an old-fashioned slobber knocker," said Lacewell. As Mike Vaughan told a Longhorn opponent after the game, "They don't make 'em like that every day."

Then came three routine victories before the improbable happened – OU lost. Eight Sooner turnovers, on consecutive possessions, led to a 23-3 Kansas victory at Owen Field. "We've been avoiding bullets all year long," Lacewell said. "But we got one right between the eyes out there today." It was Switzer's first loss as head coach and the only one he would suffer in his first 40 games. "You all helped us a lot and we'll take it any way we can get it," said Kansas coach Bud Moore.

OU's funk continued the next week at Missouri, when a 20-0 Sooner lead evaporated into a 27-point Missouri explosion. Oklahoma was ultimately saved by Joe Washington's memorable 71-yard run off a fourth-and-one option and his subsequent two-point run conversion, but the Sooners also got a few breaks from an opposing kicker. After Missouri took a 27-20 lead, kicker Tim Gibbons missed a conversion for the first time all season. After Washington's touchdown, Gibbons missed two field-goal attempts, one from 35 yards away and one from 50.

"Smoke through a keyhole."

– TEXAS COACH DARRELL ROYAL
DESCRIBING SOONER HALFBACK
JOE WASHINGTON, 1974.

Little Joe

His real name ended with Junior. His nickname started with Little. He's most famous for a punt return (against USC) when he lost yardage, and his longest play from scrimmage (against Texas) was a quick-kick.

Little Joe Washington never won a Heisman Trophy like Steve Owens or Billy Sims. He didn't have the raw speed or prolific rushing numbers of Greg Pruitt. He didn't have the inside toughness of Stanley Wilson. But Little Joe held the franchise on Sooner excitement. Whether he touched the ball – on a handoff, a pitch or a kick – every fan in Memorial Stadium immediately rose. They didn't want to miss an instant of a Washington performance.

Texas coach Darrell Royal said Washington was like smoke through a keyhole. "Every time Joe tucked the football under his arm, there was a sense of anticipation," said Barry Switzer, "like you were about to witness something that you had never seen before. We called it Showtime."

Washington came to OU from Port Arthur, Texas, where he played high-school football for his father, Joe Washington, Sr. Little Joe made his mark as a freshman with a spectacular touchdown run against Nebraska, then made himself legendary with a punt return in OU's 7-7 tie against Southern Cal in 1973. Washington took a punt return and faded back, back, back, back – he seemed to dance backward forever, looking for an opening. He finally circled, found a

crease and darted up the sideline before the Trojan masses finally swarmed him under. Washington took what seemed an eternity and the breath of 86,000 fans in the Los Angeles Coliseum, all for a punt return that netted a minus nine yards.

Washington was always great against Texas; he threw a touchdown pass to Tinker Owens against the Horns in 1973 and uncorked a 76-yard quick-kick in 1975. Washington remains the career rushing leader at Oklahoma, his 3,995 yards surpassing Owens' 3,867 and Sims' 3,718.

Most importantly, Oklahoma has a national championship largely because of Washington. In 1975, the week after Kansas handed OU its first loss in three years, the Sooners were struggling. They were 8-1 and ranked sixth, but Missouri outplayed them at Faurot Field. The Tigers led 27-20 late in the game, and OU faced 4th-and-1 from the Missouri 29-yard line. "Eleven Hammer" was the play called by OU offensive coordinator Galen Hall. It was an outside option, with a fake to the full-back. Switzer barked at quarterback Steve Davis to make sure Washington got

the ball. Washington got the ball all right. He cut between blocks by halfback Elvis Peacock and tight end Victor Hicks, broke two tackles and cut back to the middle of the field. An unbelievable 71-yard touchdown run it was, and with little over three minutes left in the game, OU had a chance at victory. The Sooners went for a two-point conversion and Hall called "Eleven Lead," virtually the same play as before. Washington took the pitch, was hit at the 2-yard line, squirmed, leaped and fell to earth on the chalk line. Oklahoma won 28-27 and went on to the 1975 national title.

Switzer shrugged off the high-stakes risk. "What's high-risk about giving the ball to the best back in the country?"

A pall settled over Norman, Oklahoma, the evening of November 8, 1975. It was a Saturday night in a bustling college town, but the streets seemed strangely quiet, the people dazed. It was as if the city had been transported into some kind of parallel universe – a universe where the university football team actually could lose a game. The feeling had not been felt since the Oklahoma-Notre Dame game of 1957.

Earlier in the day, the Oklahoma Sooners had been defeated. After 37 games and 37 months, Oklahoma's invincibility had expired. Kansas beat the Sooners 23-3, OU's first defeat since a 20-14 loss at Colorado on October 21, 1972. The Sooners had won 28 straight games and had gone 37 games without a defeat. Kansas quarterback Nolan Cromwell slew the Sooners with their own deadly poison – he ran the wishbone to perfection and didn't throw a single pass. Halfback Laverne Smith also performed well. Meanwhile, Oklahoma self-destructed, committing turnovers on eight consecutive possessions.

Sooner Steve Davis, a senior in his next-to-last home game, had quarterbacked Oklahoma for three years and had never experienced defeat. Against the Jayhawks, he threw four interceptions. Running onto the field late in the game, he was booed. On the sidelines, Switzer comforted the stunned Davis, who admitted it took him several days to get over the treatment. In the locker room, Switzer told his players, "Hold your heads up. You are a great ballclub. We rode this train a long time and it had to stop sooner or later. We have nothing to be ashamed of."

On Thursday the next week, the electricity to the coaches' offices temporarily was cut off while technicians made repairs. OU defensive coordinator Larry Lacewell greeted visitors to the darkened complex by saying, "See men, this is what happens to you down here when you lose a ballgame." Earlier in the season, when the Sooners still were undefeated, Lacewell received a letter from a fan critical of his television show: "I've never seen such a farce ... HoHo the Clown has a show for clowns ... maybe you had better join his show. This football business is a serious thing and if you have time to work a little more on defense ... the coaches at Podunk don't have a TV show, and if you don't shape up the team you'll wind up at Podunk." At the time, OU had gone 32 straight games without a defeat.

Despite the booing at the Kansas game, Lacewell discovered the true feelings of Sooner fans. That week, he and the defensive unit had received hundreds of letters, almost all of them in support. One letter was from an inmate in an Oklahoma prison. "It really points out the class of the Oklahoma fans," Lacewell said. "You know, you get all wrapped up in what's going on around here and you forget the guy in one of those small, faraway towns, who maybe works in a gas station and lives from Saturday to Saturday just to listen to OU football. It really means something to him. I'll tell you, that's the kind of person that makes this program what it is."

Unbeaten Nebraska followed. Three times in Switzer's 17 years as head coach, Oklahoma would ruin an unbeaten Nebraska season. The first time was in 1975. The Huskers were ranked second, while the Sooners had dropped to seventh in the national-title race. OU led 7-3 at halftime, thanks to a half-ending play on the goal line, when Anthony Bryant and the Selmon brothers stacked up tailback Monte Anthony for no gain. The teams traded touchdowns in the third quarter, but in the final period, the floodgates opened. The Sooners scored three fourth-quarter touchdowns. The beleaguered Nebraska offense and quarterback Vince Ferragamo, meanwhile, would finish with six turnovers and just nine second-half yards. Suddenly, Oklahoma was back in the national-title hunt. OU rose to third in the polls after routing Nebraska, and a week later No. 2 Texas A&M lost to Arkansas. That gave the Sooners a fighting chance going into the bowl games, which would include Oklahoma for the first time since Switzer became head coach.

OU was to play Big Ten runner-up Michigan in the evening January 1 Orange Bowl after the conclusion of the Rose Bowl, where No. 1 Ohio State played a rematch against UCLA (the Buckeyes had blasted UCLA 41-20 in September). As the Sooners warmed up in the Orange Bowl that night, fans throughout the stadium erupted. There was good news from Pasadena. The Bruins trailed just 3-0 at halftime, and when the Sooners returned to their locker room just prior to the Orange Bowl kickoff, they got the final word: UCLA had beaten top-ranked Ohio State 23-10. "Boy, this game got big all of a sudden," said Galen Hall. The Sooners were up to the challenge. Both defenses were dominant – Michigan quarterback Rick Leach constantly was harassed – but OU used big plays from its split ends to take the lead. Tinker Owens made a sensational catch for a 40-yard gain to the Wolverine 39-yard line, and on the next play Billy Brooks

Above: All-American noseguard Reggie Kinlaw (62) upends a Cornhusker in the 1977 OU-Nebraska game won by the Sooners, 38-7.

Left: Quarterback Steve Davis tucks the ball under his arm against the Michigan Wolverines in the Orange Bowl Classic, January 1, 1976. Oklahoma 14, Michigan 6.

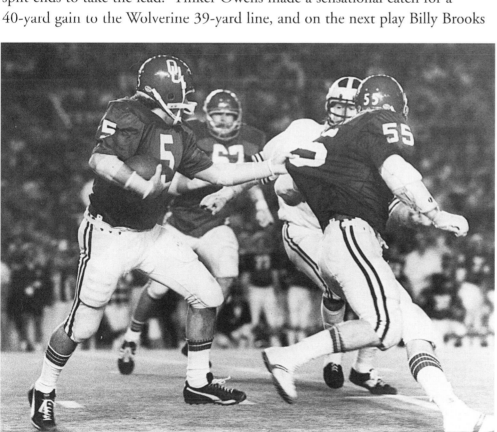

took a reverse pitch and glided 40 yards for a touchdown. In the third quarter, backup Sooner fullback Jim Culbreath motored 21 yards to the Michigan nine, and two plays later Steve Davis darted to a 10-yard touchdown that put the Sooners in command. Michigan's late TD came on a two-yard drive after an OU fumble. The Sooners won 14-6.

They were national champions.

Switzer would say, "I'd like for our program to say that the young men who were a part of it would someday look back and feel a great pride and a feeling that they had something better than most thousands that played the game." The 1975 season was an example of that. The Sooners had ridden a roller coaster of narrow victories, a history-making defeat and dominating victories to their second consecutive national title.

The Colorful Decade

It would be ten more years before another national championship found its way to Norman, but what a marvelous ten years it was. Billy Sims. Thomas Lott. George Cumby. Reggie Kinlaw. Greg Roberts. Uwe von Schamann. Darrol Ray. Daryl Hunt. J.C. Watts. Terry Crouch. Stanley Wilson. Buster Rhymes. Marcus Dupree. Rick Bryan. Tony Casillas. Brian Bosworth. It was a splendid cast of high-caliber players, not to mention colorful characters, and though there was no No. 1 ranking in the final polls, the Sooners still won big.

In the nine seasons between 1975 and 1985, OU won six Big Eight titles, played in five Orange Bowls and went 83-22-3. Switzer endured his first slump – 12 losses in three seasons, 1981-83 – and emerged to rebuild the Sooners into a national champion less than two years later.

In those nine seasons, the Sooners suffered frustration against Texas, going just 2-5-2, losing mostly tight games, but continued their fourth-quarter mastery of Nebraska. The Huskers finally won three straight during the slump years, but Switzer would win 12 of his first 16 games against Nebraska.

And those nine seasons included some of the most memorable non-Texas, non-Nebraska games in OU history. For example, there was the epic 29-28 victory at Ohio State in 1977, won on von Schamann's last-minute 41-yard field goal. There were the back-to-back Orange Bowl victories over Florida State that stamped J.C. Watts as a winner. There was the 28-24 loss to top-ranked Southern Cal in 1981, when the Sooners were ranked No. 2. There was the 32-21 loss to Arizona State in the 1983 Fiesta

Below left: Zac Henderson played air-tight pass defense for four years, 1974-1977, and earned All-American honors as a senior.

Below right: The "U.S.S. Vaughan," offensive tackle Mike Vaughan, was a mammoth presence along the offensive line, earning All-American status in 1976.

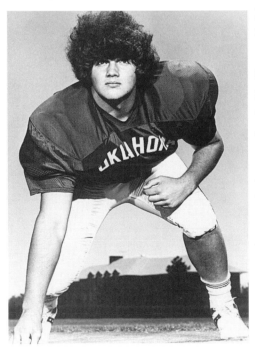

Bowl, when Dupree ran for 239 yards on 17 carries. There was the miraculous 21-20 victory over Oklahoma State in 1983, when Jimmy Johnson's Cowboys led 20-3 in the fourth quarter.

Below: Horace Ivory uses his explosive speed to gain yardage against the Florida State Seminoles in 1976. Oklahoma 24, Florida State 19.

In October 1976, Switzer had been head coach three and a half years, and OU's record was an astounding 36-1-1. But October was a cruel month. Against Texas, in a game even more bitter than the usual Red River riot, the teams tied 6-6. Prior to this, in his final OU-UT game, Longhorn coach Darrell Royal had accused the Sooners of spying on a Longhorn practice. Switzer later would admit an OU booster, unbeknownst to the coaches, indeed did spy on the Horns.

Royal desperately wanted to upset the top-ranked Sooners, and his underdog squad played valiantly, leading 6-0 late in the game. But the bandannaed Thomas Lott, who was making his starting debut, finally got the OU wishbone in gear, and fullback Horace Ivory scored the tying touchdown on a one-yard run. However, center Kevin Craig's snap was high, holder Bud Hebert failed to handle the ball, and OU was left with a 6-6 tie.

Injuries began to decimate the Sooner secondary, and OU's defense paid the price. Oklahoma State stunned the Sooners 31-24 at Norman, as tailback Terry Miller ran 73 yards for a touchdown and quarterback Charlie Weatherbie aptly directed the Cowboys. Colorado gave OU a two-game losing streak with a 42-31 victory, as defensive backs Terry Peters, Sidney Brown and Scott Hill sat out with injuries.

The Big Eight, however, was experiencing a peculiar year. Not before nor since has the conference football champion had more than one defeat. In 1976, Colorado and Oklahoma State were tied for the Big Eight lead with 5-2 records when OU and Nebraska, each with 4-2 records, played on November 26. In retrospect, the Sooners were certainly the equals of the Huskers. But that day at Lincoln, OU seemed outmanned, and Hill – then a senior co-captain – in his pre-game prayer in the locker room whispered, "Please, dear Lord, don't let the best team win."

The Sooners won, despite trailing 17-13 with three minutes left and being 84 yards from pay dirt. Sophomore Woodie Shepard threw a halfback pass that freshman end Steve Rhodes caught with a sensational dive for a 50-yard gain. A minute later, OU faced 3rd-and-19. Backup quarterback Dean Blevins was inserted to throw a hook-and-lateral. It worked stupendously. Rhodes caught

Below: Quarterback Thomas Lott was as well-known for the colorful bandanna under his helmet as he was for his many victories at the helm for the Sooners of 1976-1978.

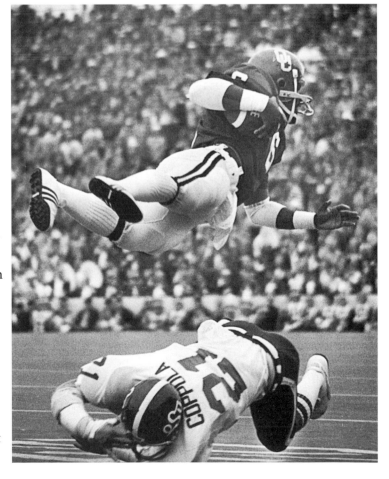

a short pass, then pitched the ball to trailing halfback Elvis Peacock, who sprinted down the sideline to the 3-yard line. Peacock scored a touchdown in the last minute, and the Sooners won 20-17.

"Sooner Magic," Switzer called it.

In the Fiesta Bowl, OU finished 9-2-1 by trouncing a Wyoming team coached by Fred Akers, 41-7.

In 1977, the Sooners no longer were a young, rebuilding team. They were simply loaded. Lott was a seasoned quarterback. Peacock and Billy Sims were the halfbacks, Kenny King, the fullback. Greg Roberts had emerged as a dominant blocker. On the defense, four Sooner defenders made all-American: linebackers George Cumby and Daryl Hunt, nose guard Reggie Kinlaw and safety Zac Henderson.

Above: During the 1970s, an Oklahoma Decade of Dominance, there was perhaps no finer blocker than guard Greg Roberts. He was a two-time All-American, 1977 & 1978.

Below: The Kick – On September 24, 1977, placekicker Uwe von Schamann earned immortality with a single swing of the leg. Oklahoma 29, Ohio State 28.

What a Kick!

On September 24, Oklahoma played in one of the most amazing games in college football history. If you polled Sooner fans, they very well might pick the 1977 Ohio State game as their favorite. "One of the greatest things I ever saw or participated in," Switzer said. The spectacle pitted Ohio State's Woody Hayes, in his 27th and next-to-last season coaching the Buckeyes, against the upstart Switzer.

OU took a 17-0 lead at halftime that grew to 20-0 early in the third quarter. But Thomas Lott had been knocked out of the game. So had Billy Sims. Back came the Buckeyes, scoring 28 straight points to lead 28-20.

When Ohio State stopped OU's 2-point conversion with 1:29 left in the game, the Sooners appeared mortally wounded. But miraculously, OU recovered von Schamann's onside kick—and Blevins completed a pass to Rhodes at the Buckeye 24 with three seconds left. OU called timeout while von Schamann took the field. Then Ohio State called timeout, trying to psyche out von Schamann. As the Ohio State crowd chanted "Block that kick! Block that kick!" von Schamann did a curious thing. He raised his arms, in the manner of an

orchestra conductor, leading the fans' chants. An electrified crowd stood on its tip-toes. Then the ball was snapped, the hold was down and von Schamann's 41-yard field goal was strong and true. "You never heard 90,000 people so silent," Switzer said.

Texas, however, soon cured OU's delirium. Fred Akers, a former Arkansas teammate of Switzer, had been hired away from Wyoming to replace Royal. Akers made his Red River Riot debut a success, thanks to two remarkable athletes. The first, tailback Earl Campbell, was en route to the 1977 Heisman Trophy, and he dented the OU defense with a 24-yard touchdown run. The Longhorns didn't again threaten the Sooner goal line, but with a placekicker like Russell Erxleben, it didn't matter. The amazing Erxleben booted field goals of 64 yards in the second quarter and 58 yards in the fourth quarter, as Texas defeated OU 13-6. Akers would go on to have a record of 5-2-1 against the Sooners but Switzer recalls that first one hurt the worst.

The Sooners quickly recovered, and by the end of the season, they were playing very well indeed. OU thrashed Colorado 52-14 and Nebraska 38-7 in the final two games. An Orange Bowl date against

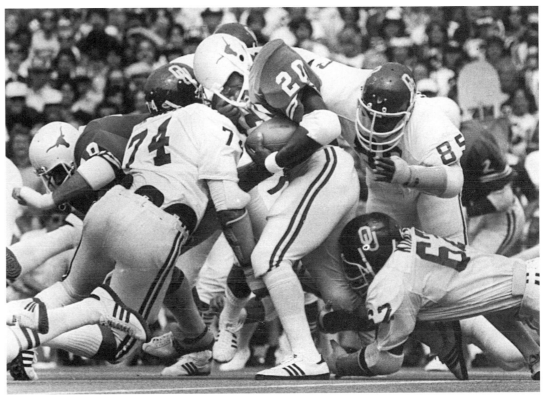

Arkansas presented national-championship ramifications. Notre Dame had dumped unbeaten Texas 38-10 in the Cotton Bowl and OU had a legitimate claim to be No. 1 if it could dispose of Arkansas, a 17-point underdog. Razorback coach Lou Holtz had suspended four of his players for disciplinary reasons, and despite a 10-1 record, Arkansas was considered vulnerable. It was, however, Oklahoma that proved vulnerable. "We were the poorest prepared emotionally of any team I ever coached," Switzer said. "Lou Holtz had done a hell of a job." Backup tailback Roland Sales rushed for 205 yards on 23 carries, Arkansas led 24-6 at halftime and won in a 34-6 rout. "I have never been so humiliated," Switzer said.

Upper: Linebackers George Cumby (28) and Daryl Hunt (85) do their part as the Sooners continue their mastery over Nebraska, this time in the 1977 contest. OU 38, Nebraska 7.

Above: Texas Heisman Trophy winner Earl Campbell (20) is stopped by Sooner defenders Phil Tabor (74), Daryl Hunt (85) and Reggie Kinlaw (62) in the 1977 game won by the Longhorns, 13-6.

BILLY SIMS

When Billy Sims was winning one Heisman Trophy and nearly winning another, he was embraced by Oklahoma fans. But down in Hooks, Texas, folks merely rocked on their porches and smiled all the while. Dale Hanes, a Hooks native and businessman, says, "I remember what Dizzy Dean said about Satchel Paige. I say the same about Billy Sims. 'We done seen him, and we saw him first.'"

From first to last, anyone who ever saw Billy Sims run with a football never will forget it. From Hooks to OU to the Detroit Lions, Sims was something far more than special. He wasn't as big as Marcus Dupree or as shifty as Joe Washington or as fast as Greg Pruitt or as tough as Steve Owens.

But he was the best. His final two seasons, 1978 and 1979, Sims was all the running back a football team could ever want. He gained 1,762 yards as a junior and won the Heisman, then rushed for 1,506 yards as a senior, including an incredible finishing kick - 282 yards in a 24-22 victory at Missouri and 247 yards in a 17-14 squeaker over Nebraska.

"The Oklahoma days were the most rewarding," Sims said. However, it all started in Hooks, the tiny village in the northeast corner of Texas, just outside Texarkana. Sims moved in the eighth grade from the St. Louis ghetto to live with his grandmother in Hooks, which soon became more than just a dot on Lone Star maps. "You had to admire him for more than just the way he played football," Hanes said. "We saw what he did for his school and his community."

Sims was the nation's most ballyhooed school boy recruit in 1975, and OU coach Barry Switzer won the sweepstakes when Sims decided to become a Sooner. "I was as close to him as anyone," Switzer said. "He got out of the projects in St. Louis and escaped what he knew would have been a tough situation. Hooks was such a small town, he was god-like."

But things weren't always smooth at OU. There were flashes of brilliance - Sims scored a touchdown as a freshman in the Sooners' 35-10 rout of Nebraska, and he bolted 20 yards for a memorable TD in the 1977 game at Ohio State - yet Sims was plagued by ankle injuries. He received a medical redshirt in 1976, and Sims often thought about quitting. He even did, once. Switzer persuaded him to come back, and Sims hasn't forgotten. "Coach Switzer is a player's coach. He is a guy who would give you the shirt off his back. He was always in my corner."

Much of the nation was in Sims' corner in November 1979, when he lost the Heisman vote to USC's Charles White despite his amazing stretch run. Many voters already had cast their ballots. Had they had waited to see Sims rumble against Missouri and Nebraska, Sims likely would have joined Ohio State's Archie Griffin a a two-time Heisman winner. "One's enough for me," Sims said.

The 1978 Sooners might have been Switzer's best team. The great recruiting class of 1975—Lott, King, Sims, Kinlaw, Roberts, Hunt, Ray, von Schamann, the Tabor twins, Phil and Paul— had borne fruit. Oklahoma was a veteran, talented team. In short, it was a powerhouse.

The Sooners survived eight fumbles and beat Stanford 35-29 in their opener, then hit their stride, including a 31-10 pasting of Texas. Then, with Lott injured, OU escaped Kansas 17-16 when the Jayhawks missed a two-point conversion with 15 seconds left. Young quarterback, J.C. Watts, replaced Lott in that game and spent most of the game handing the ball to Sims, who rushed for 192 yards on 30 carries. Sims was only getting warmed up. He rushed for more than 200 yards in three straight games and became the leading candidate for the Heisman Trophy going into the November 11 game against Nebraska. But at Lincoln, the Sooners lost six fumbles and were beaten 17-14. It was Switzer's first loss to Nebraska. It had seemed impossible that he could actually lose to the Huskers. OU was in position for its patented "Sooner Magic" comeback, but with 3:27 left in the game, on the end of a twisting 19-yard gain, Sims fumbled and Nebraska recovered at the 3-yard line. Sims gained 153 yards on 25 carries, and won the coveted Heisman Trophy a few weeks later. The fumble at Nebraska, did, however, cost OU the national title. Alabama and Southern Cal went on to split the final No. 1 rankings, though both finished with 11-1 records, the same as Oklahoma. On November 18, a truly remarkable day, OU routed OSU 62-7 and Missouri shocked Nebraska, making the Sooners and Huskers co-champions of the Big Eight. In a momentous decision, the Orange Bowl Committee voted to invite OU to play Nebraska, in a rematch. The Sooners were ecstatic about their opportunity and made the most of it, beating the Huskers 31-24 in a game that was 31-10 until the closing minutes.

In 1979, the Sooners faced a crossroads. Sims and Darrol Ray returned as fifth-year seniors, and George Cumby was an all-American line-backer. Otherwise, there were troubling holes left by the departed class of '75. Switzer had had only two true starting quarterbacks in his six-year career,

Above: Quarterback J.C. Watts demonstrates his talent running the triple option against Kansas at Lawrence, 1978.

Left: Billy Sims poses enormous problems for Texas tacklers in this 1978 game action. Oklahoma 31, Texas 10.

Below: The scoreboard tells the tale as the Sooners cruise to a 62-7 victory over Oklahoma State in the final regular season game of 1978.

Davis and Lott, and now he faced the prospect of developing a new leader. J.C. Watts was worthy of the task. Like Steve Davis, he was a Baptist preacher. Like Thomas Lott, he was a skilled optioneer in the OU wishbone.

In the Sooners' first nine games of 1979, they had only one tough game and lost it, 16-7 to Texas. An ill-advised call, a bomb late in the first half that Switzer regretted, led to an interception and Texas' only touchdown. However, in the final two games, Sims ran wild. He gained 282 yards in a 24-22 victory over Missouri and 247 yards in a 17-14 victory over unbeaten Nebraska. A late interception by cornerback Mike Babb preserved the win over the Huskers and put OU in the Orange Bowl against unbeaten Florida State. Watts scampered 61 yards for a touchdown on an option play and Sims rushed for 164 yards as the Sooners rolled 24-7 and finished No. 3 in the nation.

Watts Provides the Power

In 1980, the Sooners' enormous reservoir of talent was evaporating a bit. All of Switzer's prior teams had been heavily decorated with post-season honors, but in 1980 OU had only one all-American, guard Terry Crouch, and three other all-Big Eight selections, defensive tackle Richard Turner, offensive tackle Louis Oubre and tight end Forrest Valora. But Watts was a winning quarterback. Behind his leadership, the Sooners made it back to the Orange Bowl after a strange season. OU was routed by Stanford and John Elway, then only a sophomore but already one of the nation's premier quarterbacks. In the rain at Owen Field, Elway guided Stanford to a 31-14 victory. The next week at Boulder, the Sooners responded with their most explosive game of the wishbone era. Halfback David Overstreet rushed for 258 yards on 18 carries. Freshman halfback Buster Rhymes scored four touchdowns. Backup quarterback Darrell Shepard gained 151 yards — on three carries. Freshman Jerome Ledbetter returned a kickoff 99 yards. The final score was 82-42 over Colorado. NCAA records were set for total yards (OU's 875), rushing yards (OU's 758), touchdowns by two both teams (18) and points by both teams (124). Ironically, one victim was CU coach Chuck Fairbanks, in his second year back in college football.

The next week, Texas pinned a 20-13 loss on the Sooners in what was another Longhorn defensive

Stanford quarterback John Elway (7) is shown a split second before being sacked by OU defensive tackle Richard Turner (96) in a game won by Stanford, 31-14, on a rainy day in Norman, September 27, 1980.

masterpiece. OU committed eight turnovers but had a 13-10 lead in the fourth quarter. Oklahoma native Rod Tate scored on a 1-yard run to give the 'Horns the lead with 8:13 left in the game.

On November 1, unbeaten North Carolina invaded Owen Field with the No. 5 national ranking and all-star linebacker, Lawrence Taylor. The Tar Heels limped out of Norman with a tarnished record and a 41-7 defeat. J.C. Watts rushed for a career high 139 yards as Carolina was clueless against the wishbone, giving up 495 rushing yards.

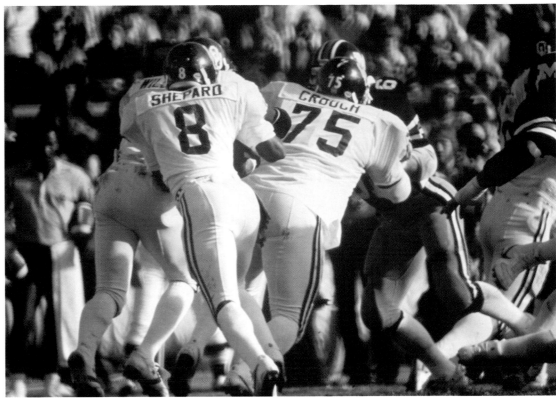

The OU-Nebraska showdown once again became the Big Eight title game, and once again in Lincoln, the Sooners appeared overmatched. The loser would be headed for the Sun Bowl in El Paso, Texas – Switzer had appeared on NU coaching legend Bob Devaney's television show and offered Devaney a sack of tacos – and that appeared to be OU when the Huskers took a 17-14 lead with 3:16 left in the game. But Buster Rhymes, a freshman from Miami, Florida, who had become a force late in the season, reeled off a 43-yard gain via a wishbone pitch, and after Watts hit Bobby Grayson with a 13-yard gain to the one, Rhymes scored with 56 seconds left. "Sooner Magic" had once again prevailed.

In the Orange Bowl rematch against Florida State, "Sooner Magic" mysteriously appeared even though Nebraska was not in sight. OU trailed 17-10 with 2:37 left, but Watts took the Sooners on a 76-yard drive. He hit fifth-year senior Steve Rhodes, who four long years before had made a huge catch against Nebraska, with a 42-yard gain and then with an 11-yard touchdown pass 1:27 before the end. Watts' two-point pass to Forrest Valora gave the Sooners an 18-17 victory, and Watts became the first player to win Orange Bowl MVPs in successive years.

In eight years, Switzer's record was 83-9-2. Led by three wishbone wizards, a stable of incredible running backs and a defensive wealth of talent that went on to fill NFL rosters, Oklahoma had achieved the impossible – it had matched the success of the Sooner squads of the 1950s. But most of the

Upper: Sooner quarterback Darrell Shepard follows behind the block of All-American guard Terry Crouch (75) against the Missouri Tigers, 1981.

Above: George "Buster" Rhymes flashed brilliance at times. He is shown gaining yardage against the Texas Longhorns in 1981.

great talent was gone. "I knew we were going to miss them, but I didn't realize how much," Switzer said.

Then came the four-loss seasons of 1981, 1982 and 1983. OU's nine-year reign atop the Big Eight ended, as Nebraska won three straight conference titles. In 1981, Switzer found himself with a losing record for the first time in his career – 1-2-1 after four games. After 10 games, OU was 5-4-1. On September 26, the Sooners, ranked second, played No. 1 Southern Cal at the Los Angeles Coliseum. OU twice led by 10 points but lost five fumbles, and the game, 28-24. "We turned a rout into a defeat," Switzer said. Quarterbacks Kelly Phelps and Darrell Shepard alternated and each scored touchdowns. But Marcus Allen, kicking off his successful Heisman Trophy campaign with 208 yards rushing, scored a touchdown with 7:37 left in the game to cut OU's lead to 24-21. Then with two seconds to go, quarterback John Mazur rolled left and dumped a 7-yard TD pass to tight end Fred Cornwell.

The Sooners went into free fall. Iowa State, which had lost to OU every year since 1961, managed a 7-7 tie at Owen Field, and the Sooners were fortunate to get it. Alex Giffords, ISU's talented kicker, missed field goals of 23 and 50 yards late in the game. Texas routed the Sooners 34-14 even though OU led 14-3 at halftime. Oklahoma got down 21-0 at Kansas State but won 28-21 on Shepard's 49-yard touchdown run with 2 1-2 minutes left. Missouri took advantage of eight turnovers and whipped the Sooners 19-14.

Quarterback Kelly Phelps (7) receives sideline instruction during a 1981 contest from (left to right), assistant coach Mike Jones, Coach Switzer and assistant coach Merv Johnson.

Steve Sewell attempts to get outside against Southern Cal at Owen Field, September 25, 1982. USC 12, Oklahoma 0.

Nebraska buried OU 37-14, and this time there was no Orange Bowl rematch. In the Sun Bowl, OU scored 30 fourth-quarter points to blast Houston 40-14. Shepard, a senior who had transferred from Houston, was named the game's outstanding player. Freshman fullback Fred Sims gained 181 yards, all in the second half, despite having gained just 179 yards during the entire regular season.

1982 was the year of Marcus Dupree, a fabulous freshman halfback whose blend of speed and power is unsurpassed in OU history. Dupree played sparingly early in the year, and for the third straight season the Sooners lost twice to non-conference foes. West Virginia quarterback Jeff Hostetler threw for 321 yards and four touchdowns as the Mountaineers pulled a 41-27 stunner at Owen Field. Two weeks later, USC beat OU 12-0 at Owen Field, ending the Sooners' NCAA record of 181 straight games without being shut out. Switzer responded by junking his beloved wishbone. With Dupree and the tough Stanley Wilson alternating at tailback in the I formation, OU beat Iowa State 13-3. The tailback duo combined for 159 yards on 37 carries. The next week, Dupree took center stage. He dashed 63 yards for a first-quarter touchdown against Texas, and the Sooners went on to a 28-22 victory. Fullback Weldon Ledbetter had 144 yards, including a 59-yard TD run, but the game's star was Dupree.

Dupree followed with a 75-yard TD run against Kansas, a 30-yard score against Oklahoma State, a 77-yard punt return at Colorado, an 80-yard touchdown against Kansas State and a 70-yard score against Missouri. Sooner victories all. "He plays in a different league than everybody else," Switzer said.

In the showdown with Nebraska for the Orange Bowl berth, Dupree responded with an 86-yard touchdown run that brought the Sooners to within 21-17 in the third quarter. But Husker quarterback Turner Gill directed the Huskers to another score – backup tailback Roger Craig, replacing the injured Mike Rozier, scored from the three – and Nebraska held on 28-24.

In the Fiesta Bowl, Dupree rushed for 239 yards on only 17 carries, including gains of 56, 56 and 48 yards, though he didn't score. Arizona State, playing on its home field, outscored OU 14-0 in the fourth quarter and won 32-21. The 1982 season thus ended at 8-4 for the Sooners, but the corner apparently had been turned. With Dupree returning, and three all-conference defenders – tackle Rick Bryan, end Kevin Murphy and linebacker Jackie Shipp – back, the Sooners were expected to be powerful indeed in 1983.

MARCUS DUPREE

Danny Gregory was a prophet of sorts. Gregory was Marcus Dupree's high-school principal in Philadelphia, Mississippi, and before Dupree left home in August 1982, for his freshman year at OU, Gregory said this about Dupree's future. "There won't be an in-between with him. He can't go out there and be an ordinary freshman ballplayer." As his collegiate football career unfolded, Dupree achieved almost instant stardom, and never was he anything resembling ordinary.

Barry Switzer rattles off the names of the best runners from the '70s and '80s. "Earl Campbell, Herschel Walker, Bo Jackson, Eric Dickerson, Billy Sims, Joe Washington . . . I am here to tell you that Marcus Dupree could have been the best of them all." Instead, Dupree became a fleeting star. He burst upon the national spotlight with a series of amazing performances as a freshman but was gone less than halfway through his sophomore year. "Marcus just didn't like to play football as much as all the rest of the world wanted him to," Switzer said.

Dupree signed with OU in February 1982, after one of the most ballyhooed recruiting tussles in history. OU, Texas, UCLA and Southern Mississippi went round and round for the marvelously talented tailback. When Sooner assistant coach Lucious Selmon heard the news that Dupree had picked OU, he said, "I tell you how glad I was. I was so glad I

got a headache!" Dupree was an incredible blend of speed and power. He was a 4.3 sprinter who weighed 230 pounds. He had every physical tool imaginable.

Dupree played sparingly his first three games as a Sooner, but Switzer then junked the wishbone in favor of the I formation, to which Dupree responded. He had sprints of at least 50 yards in seven of OU's final nine games, finishing with 905 total yards rushing, not counting an amazing 239 in 17 carries against Arizona State in the Fiesta Bowl. But he played the Fiesta Bowl at 240 pounds, and though he had runs of 56, 56 and 48 yards against the Sun Devils, he was caught and tackled on all three plays.

In the spring of 1983, Dupree did not practice due to a variety of minor ailments. While he played the first five games of the '83 season, he did not produce the explosive results of his freshman season, and after a 28-16 loss to Texas in which he rushed for only 50 yards, Dupree went home to Mississippi and never returned. Within a year, Dupree signed a contract with the United States Football League, suffered a severe knee injury and his career effectively was over, although he did make a brief appearance with the Los Angeles Rams many years later. Switzer labeled Dupree's abbreviated career a tragedy and said he considered his inability to communicate with Dupree "a real failure in my coaching career."

Adversity, however, lay ahead. OU struggled to win 27-14 at Stanford, then Ohio State held Dupree to 30 yards rushing as Buckeye quarterback Mike Tomczak engineered a 24-14 victory. By the Texas game, Dupree had shown his brilliance on two Saturdays – 138 yards versus Stanford and 151 at Kansas State – and the Longhorns were waiting for him. This time, the game's star was from Texas. Edwin Simmons galloped 67 yards for the clinching touchdown in the third quarter of UT's 28-16 win. Dupree gained only 50 yards. He went home to Mississippi following the game and never returned.

The next week, armed with a 3-2 record, Oklahoma traveled to Stillwater and seemed on the verge of defeat. OSU led 20-3 with 10 minutes left in the game. Victory was saved by a couple of freshman walk-on players. Derrick Shepard, from Odessa, Texas, was the little brother of two highly touted OU recruits, Woody and Darrell. Derrick started it all against the Cowboys. Quarterback Danny Bradley's little dump toss to Shepard was turned into a 73-yard touchdown by Shepard, who broke away from two defenders. Bradley then hit Buster Rhymes, now a split end after one and a half years away from the squad, for consecutive 14-yard gains. Spencer Tillman's 5-yard touchdown and Earl Johnson's conversion catch from Bradley brought OU within 20-18 with 2:40 left. Switzer debated about

Above: The Sooners were behind late in the game, but the Pride never gave up, continuously cheering and pounding out "Boomer Sooner." After OU's comeback win, Coach Switzer awarded a game ball to the band – the first such instance in history. October 15, 1983. OU 21, OSU 20.

Below: Two-time All-American defensive tackle, Rick Bryan, elevates his game in this 1983 action.

Spencer Tillman sets sail against Texas on the rain-soaked Cotton Bowl turf in 1984. The controversial game ended in a 15-15 tie.

an onside kick, and at first, one was ordered. Then he changed his mind, and the kickoff team planned for a deep kick. In the commotion, no one told Lashar, the team's kicker all of four weeks and a non-recruited walk-on player from Plano, Texas. Lashar dutifully squibbed an onside kick that no other Sooner was expecting. The ball caromed off the helmet of OSU's Chris Rockins, and into the hands of OU's Scott Case, who recovered at the Cowboy 49-yard line. More "Sooner Magic." With 1:14 left in the game, Lashar nailed a 46-yard field goal, and OU had secured a miraculous 21-20 victory. Lashar would go on to have a record-setting Sooner career, but he never kicked a longer field goal.

Still, the Sooners struggled. They lost to Missouri 10-0, never penetrating the Tigers' 10-yard line. The Nebraska game loomed as a mismatch for the Sooners. The unbeaten Huskers were ranked No. 1. Many were touting Nebraska as the greatest football team of all time. The Sooners, however, rose to the challenge. Spencer Tillman had a 39-yard touchdown run and Danny Bradley threw a 73-yard TD pass to Buster Rhymes. Nebraska trailed the Sooners 21-14 in the third quarter, but Turner Gill took the Huskers to two third-quarter scores. Then Nebraska held off OU after the Sooners had reached the Husker 2-yard line in the final minutes.

To close out the season, OU played at Hawaii and escaped, 21-17, capping another 8-4 season that left the Sooners 23-12-1 in three years. Some OU supporters were calling for a coaching change. Switzer was wily enough to have obtained the copyright on the phrase, "Bury Barry." "I didn't need a bumper sticker to make me understand that I couldn't have another four-loss season," Switzer said.

The Old OU Returns

In 1984, the Sooners were back. They were back in an option offense, though it often remained an I formation, and they were back with young defensive stars like nose guard Tony Casillas, linebacker Brian Bosworth and safety Keith Stanberry. "Our guns were loaded," Switzer said. "I knew we were going to be studs on defense." For the first time since 1979, OU reached the Texas game undefeated. The Sooners easily had bulldozed through a tough schedule that included Stanford, Pitt and Baylor. "The old OU is back," said Danny Bradley, the senior quarterback.

On the rain-slick Cotton Bowl turf, Texas led 10-0 at halftime. The Sooners stormed back with 15 third-quarter points, then relied on their defense. The defense proved reliable. Texas freshman Kevin Nelson broke free for an apparent touchdown, but OU cornerback Andre Johnson ran him down at the Sooner 2-yard line, whereupon Oklahoma mounted a spectacular goal-line stand, with Tony Casillas leading the charge. Texas failed to get in the end zone, and with 2:10 left OU took an intentional safety. The Longhorns had one last chance, and Jerome Johnson's fumble appeared to end Texas' hopes. But officials ruled he

Above: Freshman quarterback Troy Aikman rambles for yardage against Missouri in Norman, November 3, 1984. Oklahoma 49, Missouri 7.

was down prior to the fumble. Quarterback Todd Dodge moved UT to the Sooner 10-yard line with 10 seconds left, then lofted a pass in the end zone that Keith Stanberry intercepted as he fell onto the end zone turf. But shockingly, officials ruled him out of bounds on the interception. Jeff Ward kicked a 32-yard field goal on the game's final play to give Texas a 15-15 tie. "A game that still eats at my stomach," Switzer says.

Two weeks later, OU was playing at Kansas without the services of the injured Danny Bradley. Switzer pulled out of redshirt status a strapping young freshman quarterback from Henryetta with worlds of potential. Troy Aikman was his name. That Saturday at Lawrence, however, the youthful Aikman showed little of the promise that would later make him an all-pro quarterback

Left: (Left to right) Sonny Brown, Jim Rockford and Brian Hall celebrate a 1984 victory over Oklahoma State, 24-14, and an invitation to the Orange Bowl.

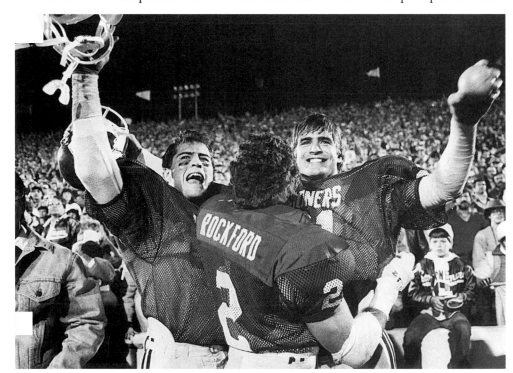

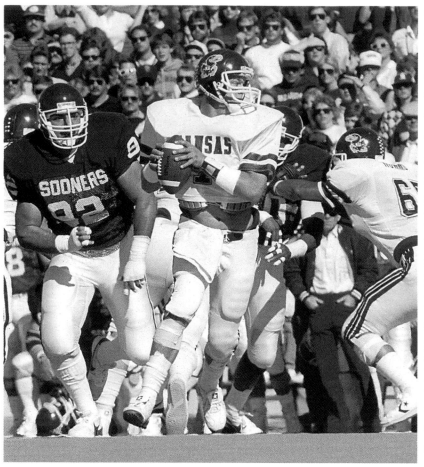

Above: Tony Casillas was twice named an All-American noseguard. Here he prepares to wrap up a Kansas quarterback in the 1985 game won by Oklahoma, 48-6.

Below: An appearance by the Sooner Schooner, pulled by the twin ponies, Boomer and Sooner, signal a touchdown and the spectacle of another Big Red tradition.

with the Dallas Cowboys. Aikman completed just two of 14 passes. With Oklahoma's offense sputtering, Kansas won 28-11. The weekend turned even grimmer later that night back in Norman, when star defensive backs Stanberry and Johnson were severely injured in an auto crash that effectively ended their careers. Somehow, the Sooners regrouped. Bradley was back at quarterback the next week, and OU began building steam. The Sooners reached the November 17 showdown at Nebraska with a chance to reach the Orange Bowl, though the unbeaten Huskers were ranked No. 1 in the nation. Lashar's 32-yard field goal two plays into the fourth quarter gave the Sooners a 10-7 lead, then another magnificent Sooner goal-line stand stonewalled Nebraska. On 3rd-and-goal from the one, linebacker Dante Jones stopped fullback Scott Porter. On fourth down, cornerback Brian Hall snuffed out tailback Jeff Smith's sweep. A fumbled punt set up Bradley's 29-yard touchdown run with 56 seconds left, and OU had achieved a magnificent 17-7 victory.

Oklahoma State remained, and the Cowboys entered the game with a glittering 9-1 record. OU and OSU were ranked second and third in the polls, with the order in each reversed. The winner of the bedlam series matchup won the trip to the Orange Bowl. OSU took a 14-7 lead in the third quarter on a 77-yard touchdown pass from Rusty Hilger to Malcolm Lewis. Back came the Sooners, driving 72 yards to Spencer Tillman's 3-yard touchdown run. Fumble recoveries by Dante Jones and Kert Kaspar set up 10 more Sooner points. The 24-14 victory put Oklahoma in the Orange Bowl against Washington.

Unbeaten Brigham Young was ranked No. 1 but wasn't playing on New Year's Day – they would defeat a 6-5 Michigan team in the Holiday Bowl. Switzer touted the Orange Bowl, No. 2 OU against No. 4 Washington, as the national title game. He was rewarded with a sewage treatment facility in Midvale, Utah, named in his honor. The issue became moot. Washington beat Oklahoma 28-17 in a game made notable for the 15-yard penalty assessed against the Sooner Schooner, OU's mascot. But there was no reason for discouragement. The '84 Sooners, 9-2-1, were an extremely young team, and Switzer thought they still were two years away from full bloom. He was wrong. They only were one year away.

Sooners Crowned Again

1985 was one of the most wild, wonderful seasons in Sooner history. The season started late, September 28, and ended late, December 7. OU had played only two games prior to Texas, and when Aikman, the starting quarter-back, suffered a broken leg on October 19, there still were seven regular-season games remaining. A national championship seemed a ridiculous goal for most of the season, but it was accomplished on New Year's night. "Often the best things in life happen when you are not really expecting them," Switzer said. Despite the presence of Aikman, a 6-foot-4 pure passer, the Sooners were back in the traditional wishbone, and it was a somewhat awkward arrangement. OU struggled against Minnesota, winning 13-7, and Texas, winning 14-7, but the Sooners held the Longhorns to just four first downs and 70 total yards. "The greatest defensive performance by an Oklahoma team since I have been here," Switzer said. Patrick Collins' 45-yard run off an option broke a 7-7 tie early in the fourth quarter.

However, against Miami the next week at Owen Field, trouble brewed. Both Aikman and Hurricane quarterback Vinny Testaverde were on fire. Testaverde would complete 17 of 28 passes for 270 yards touchdowns; early in the second quarter Aikman had completed six of seven. But with a second-quarter sack, Miami tackle Jerome Brown broke Aikman's leg just above the ankle. Aikman never again would play for OU. Faced with a choice between two freshman quarterbacks, Jamelle Holieway and Eric Mitchel, Switzer inserted Holieway. Of course, he struggled. But only that day. Miami went on to a 27-14 victory. Holieway set a course for stardom.

The mighty Oklahoma wishbone – plays, personnel and philosophy – was back. Holieway was a diminutive, deft magician who was ideal to run the option. In his first four games as a starter, no opponent came within 31 points of the Sooners. "From that day on," Switzer said, "with Jamelle at quarterback, we became a truly great option football offense. If Troy hadn't broken his ankle, I don't know how long it would have taken Jamelle to hit the field. But once he took charge,

Kevin Murphy was named a 1985 All-American as a defensive end for plays like this one against Stanford in a 1984 contest won by the Sooners, 19-7.

Right: "Ice Bowl" played in Stillwater, November 30, 1985. Blinding sleet and frigid temperatures did not prevent Oklahoma from posting a 13-0 shutout over the Oklahoma State Cowboys.

Below left: Jamelle Holieway directed a Sooner wishbone attack which led to a national championship in 1985.

Below right: Enid native Lydell Carr combined speed and power as a splendid fullback for the Sooners over four seasons, 1984-1987.

our offense was suddenly racing up and down the field, like our wishbone of old."

In the annual showdown against Nebraska, the Sooners thoroughly dominated. Tight end Keith Jackson raced 88 yards on a spectacular reverse three and a half minutes into the game. Holieway added touchdown runs of 43 and 17 yards as OU triumphed 27-7. The Huskers had scored only on a 76-yard fumble return with 26 seconds left in the contest. Remarkably, the Sooners still had two games left. In the Ice Bowl at Stillwater, OU beat OSU 13-0. With temperatures in the '20s and a blinding sleet falling on a frozen turf, neither offense had a chance. OSU didn't get closer than the OU 21-yard line. "The worst conditions I ever saw," Switzer said. The Sooners took care of business the next week, dispatching Southern Methodist 35-13 on Pearl Harbor Day.

On New Year's night, No. 3 Oklahoma played No. 1 Penn State in the Orange Bowl, while No. 2 Miami played No. 8 Tennessee in the Sugar Bowl. At that stage of his career, through 152 games, Switzer's record was 124-24-4 with two national titles. Through the first 153 games of Bud Wilkinson's career, Wilkinson's record was 125-24-4 with three national championships.

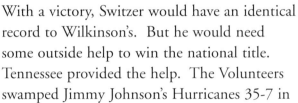

With a victory, Switzer would have an identical record to Wilkinson's. But he would need some outside help to win the national title. Tennessee provided the help. The Volunteers swamped Jimmy Johnson's Hurricanes 35-7 in the Sugar Bowl. Meanwhile, OU was battling Penn State.

Penn State took a 7-0 lead, but Lashar responded with the first of his four field goals. Keith Jackson hauled in a 71-yard touchdown pass from Holieway. As the fourth quarter began, the Sooners led 19-10. The Nittany Lions missed a short field goal, and with 1:42 left, Sooner fullback Lydell Carr burst 61 yards for a touchdown. OU won 25-10, and with the victory, its first national title in 10 years. Switzer was carried off the field by his proud defense, which allowed only three touchdowns in the final seven games of the season. Casillas, Bosworth and Murphy were all-Americans. Casillas won the Lombardi Award as the nation's best lineman and Bosworth won the Butkus Award as the nation's best linebacker. The Sooners had begun a three-year run in which they would have nine all-Americans, four national award winners, raise their Big Eight winning streak to 25 games and go 33-3 overall.

If not for one nemesis, Oklahoma might well have won three consecutive national titles and been considered among the greatest college football teams of all time. That nemesis was Miami. Jimmy Johnson's Hurricanes pinned three defeats on the Sooners in 1985-87. OU was 30-0 against the rest of the world; 0-3 against Miami. "If it just hadn't been for Miami..." Switzer said. The Sooners had spectacular teams in 1986 and 1987. In 1986, OU led the nation in all four major defensive categories: total, rushing, passing and scoring. In 1987, the Sooners were first in all but rushing defense. They had big, strong, fast players at every position, the likes of which included safeties David Vickers and Rickey Dixon, end

THE BOZ

He wore a rainbow of colors in his hair. He claimed to have purposely dropped loose bolts in auto doors while working at a GM plant. He wrote an outrageous book. He said outrageous things. He insulted old people, women and even his teammates. Bob Hope, he called "No Hope." UCLA, he said, played football like girls. The NCAA, he called the National Communists Against Athletes. Texas, he said, was the Shorthorns. He went from being an unknown high school player to a folk hero to a comic-book character to an icon of the counterculture, who played a little pro football, did a little acting and earned himself millions of dollars. He alienated more Sooners than he won over, including his fellow OU

all-Americans, who demanded that his portrait be removed from the wall in Memorial Stadium.

He was the Boz.

But what occasionally is forgotten about Brian Bosworth is what kind of player he was. "One of the greatest players ever to play for the University of Oklahoma," said Barry Switzer, one of Bosworth's greatest admirers and, likewise, one of his severest critics. "There have been very few linebackers in the history of the game who could play in his class."

Bosworth, who played at OU from 1984-86, was a two-time all-American, the winner of the first two annual Butkus Awards as the nation's best linebacker. He finished fourth in the 1986 Heisman Trophy voting. He was the cover boy of *Sports Illustrated's* 1986 college football preview. He was a model student, graduating in four years with a 3.6 grade-point average in business.

Bosworth was superb on OU's 1985 national championship team and even better in 1986. His performance in a 28-16 loss to Miami in September 1986 - when Bosworth made 19 tackles, was all over the field until the final gun and then collapsed, dehydrated, in the locker room - was as fine a game as a Sooner ever played.

Brian Bosworth, the man, invented The Boz, the action hero who drew attention from all over America with his scandalous statements, his haircut and his steroid use. Juicing up, it was claimed, made him ineligible for his final college game, the 1987 Orange Bowl.

Switzer has said he is honored to know Brian Bosworth, "but I have some problems with this guy you call the Boz." Bosworth wrote in his book "The Boz: Confessions of a Modern Anti-Hero," that the Switzer-Bosworth relationship was star-crossed from the beginning because two were so much alike. "Switz

and I are a lot alike," Bosworth wrote. "He's brash and outspoken. So am I. He likes to step on toes for fun. So do I. He's colorful and a partier. So am I. He was an honor student at Arkansas

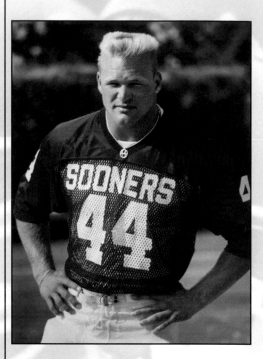

and a damn good college football player who loved the game. So was I. We both know our way around people. We've been to a hundred of the same cocktail parties and we can both adapt and fit in - whether it's rednecks in NUKE PHIL DONAHUE hats or history professors in bow ties. We're both overachievers, guys who want to win at all costs and will walk over anybody to do it." He could have mentioned that when both are smiling just so, they even look alike. "But that was the problem," Bosworth said of their similarities. "It's like those old westerns. Norman, Oklahoma, just warn't big enough for the two of us, pilgrim."

Darrell Reed, and linebackers Bosworth and Jones.

In 1986, OU played only two games decided by fewer than 19 points. The Sooners blasted UCLA 38-3. They routed Texas 47-12. They shut out five opponents and held two others to a lone field goal. But in September, OU played Miami in the Orange Bowl Stadium and lost 28-16. Hurricane quarterback Vinny Testaverde was even better than the year before; he set up his Heisman Trophy season by completing 21 of 28 passes for 261 yards and four touchdowns, two to Michael Irvin. Oklahoma was not, however, derailed by the loss. The Sooners were 9-1 going into the Nebraska game on November 22 in Lincoln, and what transpired was what Switzer called the finest example of "Sooner Magic."

Oklahoma trailed Nebraska 17-7 in the fourth quarter and 17-10 with 4:10 left in the game, when a Husker punt pinned the Sooners 94 yards from the Nebraska end zone. Holieway fumbled on a fourth-down play at the OU 15, but a facemask penalty gave the Sooners new life. Holieway responded with a 35-yard pass to Derrick Shepard, and with 1:22 left, all-American Keith Jackson snagged an 18-yard TD pass. Switzer then ordered a kick, not wanting to risk a 2-point conversion. A 17-17 dead-lock seemed likely. On the contrary, Nebraska quarterback Steve Taylor threw three straight incompletions, and OU got the ball back. On 3rd-and-12 from the Sooner 45, Holieway threw to Jackson, who made a sensational one-handed catch and sprinted down the sideline for a 41-yard gain. With nine seconds left, Tim Lashar came on and kicked a 31-yard field goal that handed OU a glorious 20-17 victory.

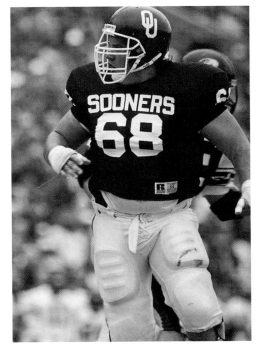

Above left: Anthony Phillips was an All-American guard on a 1986 Sooner squad which went 11-1 and defeated Arkansas in the Orange Bowl.

Above right: Keith Jackson was a fine musician as well as a two-time All-American tight end for the Big Red in 1986 and 1987.

Left: Sooner conquerors raise the Orange Bowl trophy in triumph after their defeat of the Arkansas Razorbacks, 42-8, January 1, 1988.

The Sooners went on to rout Arkansas 42-8 in the Orange Bowl, giving Switzer a measure of revenge for the fiasco in the 1978 Orange Bowl. Unbeatens Penn State and Miami played in the Fiesta Bowl for the national title. Penn State emerged as national champion while OU was relegated to No. 3 in the final polls.

194

Cottony clouds and a full house greet the Oklahoma Sooners in their 1987 season opener against North Texas. Oklahoma 69, North Texas 14.

"You Will Shock the Nation"

In 1987, the Sooners were equally dominant. They had five Associated Press all-Americans: tight end Jackson, defensive end Darrell Reed, linebacker Dante Jones, safety Rickey Dixon and offensive lineman Mark Hutson. None of their first nine opponents came within 19 points. OU walloped Texas by 35 points for the second straight year, 44-9. The Sooners scored at least 59 points on four opponents. However, on November 7 against Oklahoma State, the magnificent Holieway suffered a career-shattering knee injury. Ripping an anterior cruciate ligament in the open field, he hobbled into the arms of OSU head coach Pat Jones. The Sooners' chances now rode on the slender shoulders of redshirt freshman Charles Thompson from Lawton, whose speed and quickness surpassed Holieway's. The Sooners struggled against OSU, winning 29-10 only after fourth-quarter interceptions by Troy Johnson and Dixon were returned for touchdowns, and against Missouri, winning 17-13 with Scott Garl's fourth-quarter interception holding off the Tigers.

All-American linebacker Dante Jones corrals an opposing quarterback in 1987, a year in which he recorded 118 tackles.

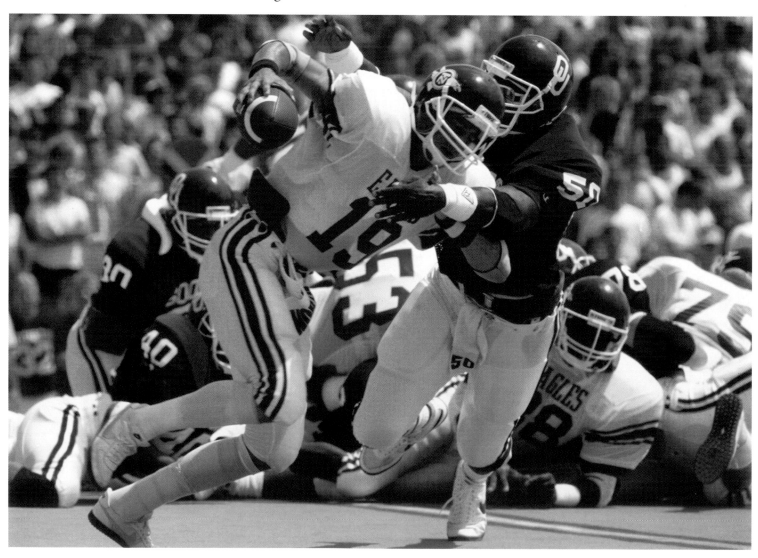

On November 21 at Lincoln, OU and Nebraska staged Game of the Century II. The Huskers were No. 1, the Sooners No. 2 and both were 10-0. Oklahoma appeared vulnerable without Holieway, and for once it was Nebraska that was brash, with linebacker Broderick Thomas promising victory. Switzer pointed out that the Huskers had scored only three offensive touchdowns in three years against OU. Privately, he told Thompson, "You will shock the nation." Thompson and the Sooners did. OU outgained Nebraska 444-235 in total yards and dominated the game. Fumbles handicapped the Sooners in the first half, but Dixon's interception set up Anthony Stafford's 11-yard touchdown run that forged a 7-7 tie in the third quarter. Patrick Collins raced 65 yards for a touchdown with 1:39 left in the third and R.D. Lashar nailed a clinching field goal with 7:40 remaining. Collins, backup fullback Rotnei Anderson and Thompson all rushed for more than 100 yards, and OU had accomplished its first perfect regular season since 1974.

Below: The Sooner defense was stifling in 1987, led by All-American defensive end, Darrell Reed, shown here sacking an opposing quarterback.

Lower: All-American defensive back Rickey Dixon was, in 1987, as tough against the run as he was against the pass. Here, he brings down North Carolina fullback Kennard Martin. Oklahoma 28, North Carolina 0.

All that remained was Miami in the Orange Bowl for the national championship.

The Sooners battled valiantly. Holieway would have come in handy against Miami, an aggressive, physical team that wore out the spindly Thompson. Miami quarterback Steve Walsh played solidly, throwing two touchdowns, and the Hurricanes' Greg Cox nailed a 56-yard field goal. OU persevered, and with 2:05 left, Mark Hutson scored on a 29-yard fumblerooski play that brought the Sooners within 20-14. But there was no more magic. So ended an incredible three-year run: 33-0 against the world, 0-3 against Miami.

1988 would be Switzer's last season as coach. It became a laborious season after Southern Cal bumped OU 23-7 on September 24. Holieway was attempting to return to form but was a shadow of his former self. The Sooners beat Texas 28-10 as Anthony Stafford sprinted 86 yards for a touchdown and Kert Kaspar returned an interception for a touchdown with a sensational run. Oklahoma survived Colorado 17-14, then nipped Oklahoma State

31-28 in a wild affair in which redshirt freshman Mike Gaddis from Midwest City ran wild.

"Sooner Magic" fell short against Nebraska, which beat OU 7-3 at Owen Field. In the game's final offensive series, Charles Thompson suffered a broken leg – the third time in four years OU's quarter-back suffered a season-ending injury – and the 9-2 Sooners were headed to the Citrus Bowl in dubious form.

Then, on December 18, the NCAA handed OU a two-year probation. It included a two-year bowl ban, a one-year television appearance ban and scholarship cutbacks. But probation was only symptomatic of OU's troubles. Clemson beat the Sooners 13-6 in the Citrus Bowl, with a crippled Holieway unable to ignite much offense. Over the next five weeks, the program developed internal problems. There was a series of disciplinary problems which led to suspensions and even some criminal charges. The program was in turmoil, the national publicity decidedly negative. On June 19, in a press conference, Barry Switzer resigned. He claimed he was tired of dealing with all the off-field requirements of coaching, of being responsible for the actions of 100 young men. "It's no fun anymore," he said. "I'm drained. I don't have the energy level to go compete in this arena today. We need new leadership. We need someone to fight the tough times ahead. And it is going to be tough ahead. I don't think I am the person for that job at this present time."

Running back Leon Perry expressed the sentiment of many Sooner players when he said, "It's more than losing a coach. It's losing a friend and someone you have a lot of respect for. A lot of the players came here because of him." Steve Owens, who arrived on campus in 1966, the same year Switzer came as a young assistant under Jim Mackenzie, said, "Barry was a player himself. He has great feelings for the players and what they're going through. The thing I remember about him more than anything else is he wouldn't let me get complacent. He kept dangling the carrot in front of me to make me a better player. It takes a special coach to be able to do that. I love him. With the possible exception of my father, Barry Switzer's been the biggest influence in my life. He's a great influence to a lot of men's lives. I care a lot about Barry Switzer – that's what's important to me."

And so ended the Oklahoma coaching career of the man who helped Jim Mackenzie rebuild the foundation for greatness in the program, the man who 19 years before had urged a beleaguered Chuck Fairbanks to throw caution to the wind and install a wild new offense called the wishbone, a man who in 17 seasons compiled the fourth-best winning percentage in college football history, .837, going 157-29-4.

Keith Jackson, who, like Switzer, came out of Arkansas to make a name for himself at Oklahoma, put it best: "It's gonna be impossible to replace him."

FORGING A NEW RESPECT

The Oklahoma-Texas game, Gary Gibbs once observed, takes on a life of its own. That is to say, the annual gridiron battle has implications far beyond the fortunes of victory or defeat. It certainly took on a life of its own during Gibbs' head coaching career with the Sooners. In six seasons as the OU head coach, 1989-94, Gibbs went 1-5 against the Longhorns. The Sooners were seemingly over-matched in only one of those five defeats. In a couple of cases, it was Texas that was overmatched, though OU suffered defeat.

Perhaps a reversal of fortune in the 1990 OU-Texas game would have changed everything. Perhaps if the Sooners could have gotten five yards closer to the Longhorn goal line, five yards closer so R.D. Lashar's field-goal attempt would have died *after* it fell over the cross bar, Gibbs' coaching career would have accelerated skyward.

Perhaps a reversal of fortune in the 1991 OU-Texas game would have changed everything. Perhaps if the toughest Sooner on the squad hadn't fumbled and allowed Texas to score a touchdown the only way – defensively – it ever was going to on that Saturday in the Cotton Bowl, Gibbs would have shared the limelight with a deserving group of warrior-heros.

Perhaps if Gibbs had experienced just a little more luck he wouldn't have sat down on the afternoon of November 21, 1994, and resigned from the job to which he always had aspired. As it was, Gibbs left with the singular legacy of forging a new respect for the tradition-rich Sooner football program.

The past is, indeed, prologue. Succeeding a coaching legend almost always is a rigorous journey, and not just at OU, where Gomer Jones experienced the feeling in 1964 and 1965. Fred Akers felt it at Texas, succeeding Darrell Royal. Ray Perkins at Alabama, succeeding Bear Bryant. Earle Bruce at Ohio State, succeeding Woody Hayes. All were winners. All coached championship teams. All, however, left because of the devastating pressure of matching the feats of their legendary predecessors.

"I haven't thought about it and I'm not concerned about it," Gibbs, the day he was hired, said of following a legend like Barry Switzer. It was the kind of resolute statement that became Gibbs' trademark. "I know what I can do. I know the people that I'm associated with, I know the great program we have – the tradition and the people involved. We're going to be successful at Oklahoma."

And he was successful. In his six seasons as head coach, OU never won a Big Eight title or played in a New Year's Day bowl. The Sooners beat Nebraska only once, Texas only once and Colorado not at all. Gibbs' 2-15-1 record against that trio led to the firestorm that prompted his resignation. But Gibbs' overall record was 44-23-2. He was 2-1 in bowl games, beating Virginia in the 1991 Gator Bowl, Texas Tech in the 1993 John Hancock Bowl and losing to Brigham Young in the 1994 Copper Bowl. He took over a program saddled with a two-year probation, a sagging national image and a critically low number of scholarship athletes. In his first season as head coach, 1989, the Sooners would play at Nebraska with less than 50 scholarship athletes available to suit up.

Promises Kept

Five years later, in 1994, Gibbs left the program fully stocked in numbers and reflecting a talent level that had new head coach Howard Schnellenberger raving about the potential of the squad. "The mandate I was given in '89 directed me to bring integrity to the university football program, emphasize academic achievement, field a competitive team and save the program from a complete collapse," Gibbs said on the day he resigned. "While

A convincing win over Virginia, 48-14, in the 1991 Gator Bowl gave Coach Gary Gibbs and quarterback Cale Gundy reason to smile.

we did not reach a championship level, we have achieved the 19th-best record in the country over the past five years while having the highest graduation rate of any of the Big 12 schools this past year. Our players have represented the university with class at all times, and I'm proud of what we have accomplished."

Gary Gibbs was born on August 13, 1952. He was an unassuming high school football player whose coach had no clue he was mentor to a boy who one day would take over one of the nation's most notable college football programs. Gibbs toiled in relative obscurity for four years before becoming a start-

Gary Gibbs had chosen Oklahoma
as the place he wished to play
football and receive his education
before OU chose him to lead its
football program in 1989.

ing linebacker as a senior on the Sooners' only perfect-record season in the last 40 years. He was a quiet, effective assistant coach at his alma mater, where he considered leaving football and putting his business degrees to good use. Finally, he was a contrite, laconic head coach, preferring to remain intensely private in arguably the state's most public job.

"You didn't worry about a guy like Gary," said Paul Register, Gibbs' head coach at Houston's Spring Branch High School in 1968 and 1969 and later a long-time assistant coach at Texas A&M. "I could tell big things were down the road for him. You knew he was going to be a success at whatever he did. He was an over-achiever as far as athletics. Just an outstanding young man." Register remembers Gibbs as "a guy that got along with all the players. Just a team guy all the way around." He was a Sooner reserve in 1972 and 1973, then started alongside all-American Rod Shoate at linebacker in 1974. Those '74 Sooners went 11-0 and won the Associated Press national championship. His most rewarding game was also his best – Gibbs had 19 tackles in a 28-14 victory at Nebraska.

Gibbs earned his bachelor's degree in marketing in the spring of 1975 and, after a brief tryout with Chuck Fairbanks' New England Patriots, entered graduate school and became a student assistant coach at OU. Two years later, Gibbs was about to receive his master's degree in business administration. A prestigious Dallas accounting firm offered Gibbs a job. Barry Switzer advised him to take it. Switzer wasn't making a judgment of Gibbs' coaching ability. He simply knew what a tough business coaching was, how it could chew up the toughest of men, and he knew, like Paul Register back in Spring Branch, what a bright future Gibbs would have no matter his line of work. "I remember that conversation with Barry, and obviously I'm glad I did not take his advice and pursue the business endeavors," Gibbs said. "I've always aspired to be a coach. As soon as I got through playing and got the opportunity to be a graduate assistant at OU, I knew my calling. This was exciting and I liked it, so even though Barry gave me that advice, I knew deep down that I wanted to coach."

Almost immediately, Gibbs became successful. He became a full-time assistant in 1978 and was defensive coordinator by 1981, at the youthful age of 29. Gibbs' reputation as a defensive mastermind preceded his elevation to coordinator. In the summer of '81, Southern Cal head coach John Robinson attempted to hire Gibbs as the Trojan defensive coordinator. OU and USC were scheduled to play in September 1981, a game that eventually turned into a marquee matchup of No. 1 vs. No. 2, and Switzer figured he couldn't afford to lose a staff member to a rival he needed to beat in a few months. Gibbs was promoted to defensive coordinator, and OU's defense took off. During Gibbs' eight years as defensive coordinator, the Sooners allowed just 12.6 points a game and earned nine shutouts. In the final four years, 1985-88, OU opponents averaged only 8.9 points a game.

Thus, in 1989, when circumstances prompted the resignation of Switzer, Gibbs was an obvious choice for the job. He was young (36 years, 10 months), he was polished and articulate. He was a loyal Sooner; after high school, Gibbs never played or coached anywhere besides Oklahoma. "The University of Oklahoma has had a history of having young football coaches rise to the top," athletic director Donnie Duncan said on June 20, the day he recommended Gibbs be hired. "Bud Wilkinson, Chuck Fairbanks, Jim Mackenzie, Barry Switzer." Indeed, all four men were Sooner assistants with no head-coaching experience when they were hired.

Gibbs, in essence, agreed. "I feel comfortable that I have all of the qualifications, that I can get the job done," he said the day he was hired. "I've always aspired to be the head coach here someday. This is my school. This is where I played. These are the people I believe in. I came to Oklahoma because of the people and now I have an opportunity to pay something back to those people."

Gibbs set about to make the most of his opportunity. The task was formidable, indeed. Even Switzer was sympathetic with Gibbs' plight. "It was disgusting, the things that Gary and his staff had to put up with from compet-

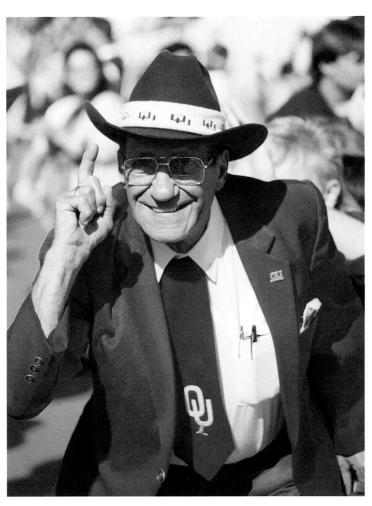

OU's No. 1 fan – Cecil Samara built his life around his love for the Oklahoma Sooners.

ing recruiters," Switzer said. Gibbs said he had a simple solution to changing OU's image when he took over in 1989: Do The Right Thing. "You do what's right; you don't do what's wrong," he said. "It's simple. We've got great people. This is a great institution with a great program. We've got great tradition here. I will be in complete control of the football program so that the university and its supporters will feel proud to be Oklahoma Sooners."

In 1989, the competitive landscape of college football was changing. The balance of power had shifted south to Florida. Miami had become the nation's most dominant program. Florida State had emerged as a national power. Florida was en route to achieving the same status. Recruiting had truly become national in scope. And in the Big Eight, Bill McCartney had transformed Colorado into a powerful force.

What Gary Gibbs faced in 1989 was national gridiron competition toughened considerably and Big Eight competition increased geometrically. The conference championship was no longer decided automatically by the Oklahoma-Nebraska game. There were additional burdens associated with NCAA probation: scholarship reductions by seven in 1989 and five in 1990; no television appearance in 1989; no bowl games following the 1989 and 1990 seasons, and one

Above: Mike Gaddis flies against Oklahoma State in 1989. It is hard for fans not to think about what might have been, had he remained healthy.

Right: Dewell Brewer scoots away from Colorado defenders in the 1991 game won by Colorado, 34-17.

less field recruiter in 1989.

Gibbs' woes surfaced two games into his head-coaching career. Starting quarterback Steve Collins, a redshirt freshman, suffered a broken finger in a 33-7 rout of Baylor and was lost for several weeks. The next Saturday, OU was ranked sixth nationally but had to use another novice quarterback, Chris Melson, and lost 6-3 at Arizona on a 40-yard field goal with two seconds left in the game. And thus began an uneven inaugural season under Gary Gibbs. Tink Collins, yet another redshirt freshman, settled in at quarterback and played well – he even had OU in position to beat Texas. However, in the third quarter, promising sophomore tailback Mike Gaddis suffered a torn anterior cruciate ligament in his knee. He would be sidelined for the next season and a half. In the fourth quarter, OU rallied to take a 24-21 lead. But capping a 65-yard, 7-play drive, Longhorn quarterback Peter Gardere threw a 25-yard touchdown pass to Johnny Walker with 1:33 left in the game, and the Sooners were defeated 28-24 despite outgaining the 'Horns 346-273 in total yards.

OU survived a 43-40 shootout at Iowa State, lost 20-3 to Colorado and ended the season 7-4 after a 42-25 loss at Nebraska. The Sooners had three all-conference selections – linebacker Frank Blevins and defensive linemen Dante Williams and Scott Evans – their fewest since 1970. The 1989 season was widely considered a prelude to better days.

In the fall of 1990, the Sooners featured considerable talent. Fourteen juniors and seniors on the squad would eventually be selected in the NFL draft. Quarterback Steve Collins was seasoned and OU's option offense was shelved, replaced by a traditional I formation that featured tailback

Left: Defensive tackle Stacey Dillard (77) wraps up an opposing quarterback with the help of his Sooner mates.

Below: Dewell Brewer, takes the sideline route to the end zone in this 1991 action shot.

blasts.

The first six weeks of the 1990 season were the highlight of the Gibbs era. The Sooners intercepted five passes and beat UCLA 34-14 in a game played in Pasadena's Rose Bowl Stadium. The Sooners returned to Owen Field and routed highly-touted Pittsburgh 52-10, with three running backs – Kenyon Rasheed, Ike Lewis and Dewell Brewer – all rushing for at least 100 yards. Tulsa fell to the Sooners 52-10. Kansas went down 31-17.

Cale Gundy (12) signals touchdown against the Nebraska Cornhuskers at Owen Field, November 23, 1990. Oklahoma 45, Nebraska 10.

Gundy Takes the Controls

The next week at Oklahoma State, freshman sensation Cale Gundy made his quarterbacking debut. He had been Collins' backup, but with the clock running down in the first half at Lewis Field and OU trailing 14-7, Gundy was inserted to make use of his passing ability. The clock appeared to run out with OU on its own 48-yard line, and the Pride of Oklahoma band began taking the field. However, the officials ruled that OSU coach Pat Jones had called for a timeout. Jones apparently wanted the Sooners to punt. Instead, Gibbs ordered a Hail Mary pass into the Cowboy end zone. Gundy launched a deep spiral. Tight end Adrian Cooper sprinted to the goal line and caught the pass amid several Cowboy defenders as the gun sounded. That

Kenyon Rasheed resembles a
locomotive leaving the station
against Pittsburgh, September 15,
1990. Oklahoma 52, Pittsburgh 10.

gave OU a remarkable 14-14 halftime tie, and Gundy went on to lead the
Sooners to a 31-17 victory.

Texas was next, and Gibbs' Sooners found themselves ranked fifth in the
national polls. Collins remained the starter, but when the OU offense stalled,
Gundy came on and took over the job he would hold for the next three and a
half years. The Sooners led 13-7 late in the game, but Peter Gardere, then a
sophomore, took Texas on a desperation drive, 91 yards, and with a minute
left in the game he flipped a 16-yard touchdown pass to 6-foot-5 receiver
Keith Cash. Gundy brought the Sooners back, completing a succession of
passes, desperately trying to set up for a game-winning field goal. But a draw
play didn't develop, and on the game's final play, OU had to settle for a
48-yard field-goal attempt by Lashar. Such a kick was well within his range –
he would finish his career with four field goals longer than 48 yards – but this
one fell short. It started true but fell away, dying a few yards shy of the cross
bar. A victory in the Cotton Bowl would have made the Sooners 6-0 and
ranked in the top five nationally. Instead, OU was 5-1 and soon to be 5-3
with its first three-game losing streak since 1965.

Iowa State stunned the hung-over Sooners 33-31 the next week at
Norman, with gimpy-legged Chris Pederson running crazily on quarterback
draws. He finished with 148 yards on 29 carries and took the Cyclones on a
game-winning, 80-yard drive in the final two minutes, scoring on a sneak with
35 seconds left in the game, giving Iowa State its first victory in the series
since 1961.

At Colorado, which would go on to win the national title, the Sooners
played valiantly. However, leading 18-17 in the fourth quarter, OU was

stopped on 4th-and-1 from the Buff 11-yard line, and on the next play Colorado quarterback Darian Hagan threw an 85-yard touchdown pass, igniting a 32-23 CU victory.

OU played superbly the rest of the way, routing Missouri 55-10, Kansas State 34-7 and Nebraska 45-10. The Huskers committed seven turnovers, gave up the most points in the 19-year Tom Osborne era and OU completed an 8-3 season on an emotional high. Defensive standouts such as linebacker Joe Bowden, end Reggie Barnes and backs Jason Belser, Terry Ray and Darnell Walker were returning. Gundy and a talented stable of running backs were returning as well. 1991 figured to be the Sooners' year.

In 1991, the Sooners went 9-3, matching their best record under Gibbs. They had Nebraska on the ropes with the Orange Bowl on the line, and played poorly only against Colorado. But the Texas bug bit OU once again.

Upper: A solid Sooner defense plants Nebraska's Lance Lewis in the 1990 match-up won by Oklahoma.

Above: The traditional glories of OU-Texas games are captured in this 1991 game photo. A resolute Sooner defense awaits the snap.

The Sooners were 4-0 going into the Cotton Bowl, with Gundy throwing for big yardage and setting school records of 18 completions and 31 attempts in a 27-17 victory over Virginia Tech. Against Texas, Gundy hit Ted Long with a 24-yard touchdown pass in the first quarter, and the Sooners appeared to be bound for glory. But they didn't score again. UT mustered a field goal, then OU fullback Mike McKinley, considered the toughest player on the squad, fumbled, and Texas defender Bubba Jacques returned the fumble 30 yards for a touchdown with 13:30 left. Ironically, 1991 was the first season for the rule that allowed fumbles that hit the ground to be returned by the defense. Texas had a 10-7 victory despite being outgained 269-223 in total yards.

The next week, Colorado wizard Darian Hagan threw three first-quarter touchdown passes and the Buffs unleashed two 99-yard TD drives en route to a 34-17 victory. No other opponent threatened the Sooners until the

November showdown at Lincoln, where OU took a 14-0 lead but lost to Nebraska 19-14 on Calvin Jones' 15-yard run with 2:57 left in the game, capping an 80-yard drive.

Mike Gaddis Flashes Brilliance

The 1991 Sooner season was bolstered by the recovery of Mike Gaddis. He began the season on the third team; he ended it all-Big Eight and having rushed for 1,240 yards, seventh-best in OU history. Gaddis got 120 yards against Colorado and two weeks later kicked into high gear, gaining 611 yards in three games: 191 vs. Kansas State; 217 vs. Missouri, and 203 vs. Oklahoma State. The latter total gave Gaddis a remarkable 690 yards in three career games against OSU, an NCAA record for yards against a single opponent.

In the Gator Bowl, it was Gundy's turn to set records: in 31 passes, his school record 25 completions went for a school record 324 yards and two touchdowns. He completed 11 passes in a row during one stretch, as the Sooners dominated

Above: All- American linebacker Joe Bowden was a shining star in 1991 and throughout his lengthy career.

Left: Corey Warren (2) seals off an Iowa State tackler, enabling Mike Gaddis (32) to accelerate, October 5, 1991. Oklahoma 29, Iowa State 8.

the Virginia Cavaliers. Many Sooner faithful believed great things were in store for the Sooners of 1992.

Gundy had another hot hand in the 1992 season opener at Texas Tech, completing 12 straight and 22 of 28 overall for 341 yards in a 34-9 victory. That was the highlight of a disappointing season. The Sooners led USC 10-0 in the fourth quarter, but Trojan quarterback Rob Johnson threw a 51-yard touchdown pass. Kenyon Rasheed's fumble was returned nine yards for a USC score and OU was beaten 20-10. Texas quarterback Peter Gardere joined Bobby Layne as the only starting quarterbacks to go 4-0 in the OU-UT series, completing 18 of 32 passes for 274 yards in a 34-24 victory. The Longhorns stormed to a 34-10 lead and survived Gundy's 276 passing yards, a series record.

The next week, for the first time under Coach Gibbs, OU rallied to avoid a post-Texas swoon. The Sooners had Colorado on the ropes. With Buff quarterback Kordell Stewart sidelined by injury, OU forced seven Buffalo turnovers and led 24-14 late in the fourth quarter. But a Rasheed fumble set up a Buff touchdown. Then reserve kicker Mitch Berger toed a 53-yard field goal on the game's final play to give Colorado a 24-24 tie.

Cale Gundy suffered a shoulder injury as Kansas defeated OU 27-10. With Steve Collins back at quarterback, the Sooners nipped Kansas State 16-14 and blasted Missouri 55-17. Gundy returned the following week at OSU, yet the Cowboys tied OU 15-15. The teams traded field goals in

Above: The Sooners entertained the Southern Cal Trojans in 1992. Here, Sooner defenders Rickey Wren (98) and Joe Correia (92) apply pressure to the placekicker. Sooner William Shankle blocked the attempt.

Lower left: Darnell Walker (28) upends a Trojan runner in the 1992 contest in Norman. USC 20, OU 10.

Lower right: Reggie Barnes storms in from his defensive end position to pressure Missouri quarterback Jeff Handy in 1992. Oklahoma 55, Missouri 17.

the final 80 seconds, with OU settling for Scott Blanton's tying 27-yarder with one second to go. The tie dropped OU to 5-3-2. Against Nebraska, the Huskers turned a tight 10-9 halftime lead into a 33-9 rout, and the Sooners suffered a 5-4-2 record for 1992. OU had one all-conference pick, cornerback Darnell Walker.

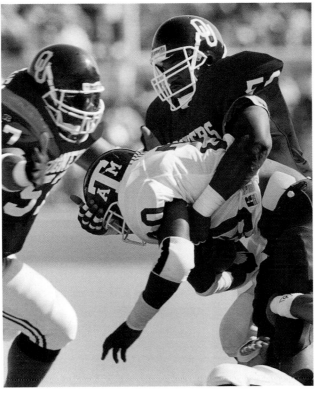

In 1993, Gibbs rallied the Sooner program. In OU's best game of the Gibbs era, the Sooners routed fifth-ranked Texas A&M 44-14, ending the Aggies' 22-game regular-season winning streak. OU led 13-0 at halftime, scored 24 points and took advantage of six A&M turnovers. Gundy completed 13 of 24 passes for 167 and two TDs.

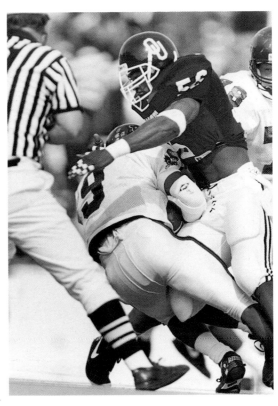

Above left: Sooner stalwarts, Cedric Jones and Paul Oatts, halt a Texas A & M ball carrier in OU's 1993 victory over the Aggies, 44-14.

Above right: Aubrey Beavers uses his strength to take down an opposing runner during the 1993 season.

And in the Cotton Bowl, the monkey was cheerfully removed. "That was a gorilla!" cracked Gibbs after a 38-17 Sooner thrashing of Texas. Senior defensive end Aubrey Beavers led an assault with two sacks. Gundy overcame a sore hip to rush for three touchdowns and OU scored on four consecutive second-half possessions to turn a 10-3 halftime lead into a cross-country romp. As the final gun sounded, Gibbs jumped into the arms of assistant coach Lucious Selmon and pumped his fist into the air.

The euphoria, however, didn't last. Colorado was next, and the Buffs were talent-laden. Flanker Charles Johnson caught five passes for 136 yards, tailback Lamont Warren rushed for 182 yards and threw a touchdown pass, and Colorado stormed to a 20-3 halftime lead. OU fought back, trailing 20-10 in the fourth quarter, but at the conclusion of a 28-yard scramble, Gundy suffered a concussion and missed the final 11 minutes. The Sooners didn't threaten again and lost 27-10.

Two weeks later, OU ran into a buzzsaw at Kansas State, which was enjoying its finest season since World War II. The Wildcats would finish 9-2-1 and win the Copper Bowl. On a bitterly cold day at Manhattan, KSU beat OU 21-7, its first victory over the Sooners since 1970. OU fumbled eight times, matching the total of their first seven games, and lost three. Gundy threw for 335 yards, but the Sooners didn't score until 4:28 remained in the game. KSU quarterback Chad May didn't match Gundy's numbers – he was 13 of 31 for 203 yards – but he threw for two TDs and ran for another.

The Sooners still could have forged their finest season under Gibbs with an upset of unbeaten Nebraska. OU, at times, dominated the Huskers, but still lost 21-7. OU outgained NU 294-179 in total yards and held Husker tailback Calvin Jones to 82 yards on 25 carries. The Sooners, however, committed four turnovers, leading to two Nebraska touchdowns. The Huskers weren't required to drive farther than 38 yards for their scores.

In the season-capping John Hancock Bowl in El Paso, Texas, OU swamped Texas Tech 41-10 as Gundy finished his Oklahoma career in a blaze of glory. He completed 15 of 26 passes for 215 yard and three touchdowns, and finished owning virtually every passing record in Sooner history. His 6,142 career passing yards were 2,615 more than the No. 2 man on the list, Bobby Warmack, and no other Sooner was within 175 completions or 300 passes of his totals. The Sooners proclaimed themselves Southwest Conference champions, having beaten Texas, Texas Tech, Texas A&M and Texas Christian.

Days of Transition

For 1994, Gundy was gone, and OU broke in a new quarterback, junior-college transfer Garrick McGee. It was, in many ways, a wrenching season. The Sooners finished 6-6, their first non-winning season since 1965, and Gary Gibbs resigned four days before the regular-season finale against Nebraska. Season highlights included an amazing comeback to beat Syracuse and a gutty comeback to beat Kansas. The Sooners beat the eventual Southwest Conference Cotton Bowl representative, Texas Tech, 17-11, and had eventual national champion Nebraska down for the count at one point. Yet, the Sooners also were stormed by Texas A&M, lost another hand-wringer to Texas and were beaten by Kansas State for the second straight year.

In the Rocky Mountains, Colorado handed Oklahoma perhaps its most embarrassing defeat of all time. The Buffs blasted OU 45-7, and it was 45-0 until 23 seconds remained in the game. Eventual Heisman

Coach Gibbs meets with the media in a post-game press conference held in the Big Red room beneath Memorial Stadium, 1993.

Trophy winner Rashaan Salaam ran for 161 yards, and Kordell Stewart completed 10 of 13 passes as the Buffs dominated. The season had started with great promise, as McGee demonstrated clever skills. OU led Syracuse 24-0 at halftime, and McGee was on his way to a 12-of-23, 276-yard passing night in the Carrier Dome. But as Sooner flanker P.J. Mills was about to complete a 70-yard touchdown play that would have made it 30-0, Syracuse defender Bryce Bevill ran down Mills, stripped the ball at the 1-yard line and it rolled through the end zone for a touchback. Remarkably, the Orangemen rallied. Quarterback Kevin Mason had a horrific night – 6 of 17 – but got hot and twice hit Marvin Harrison for long touchdown passes. The latter, of 48 yards, gave Syracuse a 29-27 lead with 1:01 left in the game. But facing 4th-and-13 from his 33-yard line with no timeouts left, McGee hit Albert Hall for an 18-yard gain. He then nailed Hall for another 18-yard gain. Scott Blanton came on and kicked a game-winning, 48-yard field goal with 11 seconds left.

Above: Quarterback Garrick McGee (8) retreats to pass behind solid blocking during the 1994 season.

Below: OU tailback James Allen challenges a Texas defender in the 1994 clash. Allen's last carry of the game ended, agonizingly, at the Texas goal line.

But the Sooners' resilience didn't hold. Texas A&M avenged its 1993 defeat with a 36-14 victory at College Station, Texas. OU committed five turnovers and A&M just one, as Aggie quarterback Corey Pullig was nearly flawless. The Sooners were within 19-14 in the fourth quarter, but costly turnovers yielded the rout.

Against Texas, OU's Cotton Bowl frustrations rose again. OU outgained UT 440-346 and led 7-0 at halftime. However, freshman quarterback James Brown rallied the 'Horns to 10 third-quarter points. Then, OU tail-

Sooner wide receiver P.J. Mills goes high to catch a pass against an OSU defender in the 1994 game won by the Sooners, 33-14.

back James Allen threw an ill-fated pass that was intercepted, setting up another Texas touchdown. Blanton's field goal with 6:40 left drew OU closer at 17-10. McGee led the Sooners to one last daring hurrah. They reached the Texas 3-yard line. Two passes fell incomplete. As the capacity crowd roared in anticipation, on a fourth-down tailback reverse, Allen was nailed at the goal line by nose guard Stoney Clark. It was a bitter defeat for the Sooners, which was followed by the Colorado debacle.

Amazingly, OU didn't fold. The Sooners were down 17-7 at Kansas but scored 13 fourth-quarter points to win 20-17. Blanton's 39-yard field goal with 1:38 left won the game. The next week, OU challenged a Kansas State squad that had suddenly become a power. In the first half, KSU had only three first downs and 45 total yards. But the Wildcats led 7-3, thanks to a blocked punt returned for a touchdown. In the second half, Wildcat quarterback Chad May warmed up, and K-State went on to a 37-20 victory.

After a 33-14 win over Oklahoma State, the Sooners were 6-4 and apparently bound for the Copper Bowl. On November 21, Gibbs sat down at his weekly news conference and instead of discussing the upcoming Nebraska game, he resigned. "The question I had to face was, 'Am I being fair to my family and the team to continue as head football coach?'" he said. "The answer is, I will resign my position as head football coach, effective at the end of the season. This decision was made without any conversation with the board of regents." Garrick McGee was present at the news conference. "I was expecting to hear coach Gibbs talk about Nebraska, and I hear my coach resign," he said. "We didn't expect this at all. We've gone through a lot this season, but this is the biggest shock of all. We had to deal with being

214

SOONER CENTURY

not as good as we thought we were. But this is much harder to deal with."

"This is my decision," Gibbs said. "There have been times I've been disappointed with the final score, but I have never been disappointed by the effort of the players or their willingness to lay it on the line. I've had the great privilege to work with some of the finest coaches in the game and I certainly appreciate everything they've done in bringing this program back. Many have been responsible for laying a solid foundation that will serve this program well in the future. I feel proud of my contribution and I feel good about the Sooner football program."

Albert Hall was a reliable pass receiver for the Sooners during his career, 1991-1994.

The Sooners went out the day after Thanksgiving and played mighty Nebraska to a near standstill. It was 3-3 at halftime and 6-3 Nebraska after three quarters. The Huskers finally resorted to the pass, and quarterback Brook Berringer completed 4-of-4 passes for 81 yards as NU went 82 yards for a fourth-quarter touchdown and won 13-3.

Only the Copper Bowl against Brigham Young was left, and by the time the Tucson, Arizona, game was played, OU had hired Howard Schnellenberger to replace Gibbs. Schnellenberger watched from the pressbox as Gibbs coached his last game. McGee had contracted an illness in December and was unable to play. The Sooners were forced to use Terence Brown, an option-type quarterback, in their pass-oriented offense. BYU quarterback John Walsh threw for 454 yards, and the Sooners were steamrolled 31-6.

The final gun brought to an end a 25-year Oklahoma playing and coaching tenure for Gary Gibbs. At times, his tenure had brought such glory. At other times, painful disappointment had visited him and his Sooner charges. There was little doubt, however, that new respect for Sooner football had been forged. The Sooners were now primed to restore their former dominance on the playing fields of the nation.

SCHNELLENBERGER AND THE SECOND CENTURY

History does repeat itself. Twenty-nine years after the University of Oklahoma turned to a tough Kentucky disciple of Bear Bryant to revive its football program, it did it again. Until December 16, 1994, Howard Schnellenberger had no connection with OU, unless you count his 40 years of respect for the crimson and cream. However, on that December day, Schnellenberger became a Sooner.

"The rest of my life," Schnellenberger responds, when asked how long it will take to get the Oklahoma program to the top level. He wants to get the Sooners back to the level of the 1950s when OU was winning national championships under Bud Wilkinson and Schnellenberger was learning his craft under Bryant at Kentucky.

"My thinking of Oklahoma is much that of any fan. One of the premier, dominant football powers of the '40s, '50s, '60s, '70s, '80s," Schnellenberger said. "We equated Oklahoma football with hard-hitting, sell-out defense. A running attack that was stoppable by few. A high-scoring, relentless team that won more games than anybody in my lifetime. Won more conference championships and on top of that more national championships than anybody in my lifetime."

Schnellenberger was born March 16, 1934, in St. Meinrad, Indiana, and grew up in Louisville, Kentucky. He played for Bryant at Kentucky and began a coaching career that led him to labor beside some of the most colorful, successful men in the history of the game. Bear Bryant, Blanton Collier, Don Shula and George Allen. Like Jim Mackenzie, Schnellenberger is inextricably linked to Bryant but he discounts too many analogies to Mackenzie. Schnellenberger arrived at the University of Kentucky after Mackenzie had departed, but he knew the reputation of the man. "I know the folklore of Jim Mackenzie," Schnellenberger said. "Tough, hard-nosed, disciple of Bryant. Football was the epitome of his existence. Would've carried a very proud and hard-nosed program forward had he lived." Is such a description equally fitting for Schnellenberger?

"I wouldn't say that," Schnellenberger said. "I've been fortunate to live a lot longer than he did. Fortunate to coach for Don Shula and Blanton Collier. I've had my own teams for fifteen years. He had one for sixteen months. It may have described me at his age pretty well."

Schnellenberger was the head coach at the University of Miami for five years, going 42-15 and winning the 1983 national championship. He then spent ten years at Louisville, 1985-94, going 54-56-2 but taking the downtrodden Cardinals to the 1991 Fiesta Bowl, where they beat Alabama 34-7 to cap a 10-1-1 season.

Schnellenberger knows little about Mackenzie's sixteen months at OU, but his observations are pretty accurate. When told that Mackenzie's 1966 Sooner squad went 6-4 but created a lot of waves, Schnellenberger said, "That sounds about right. I'll bet you there were a lot of guys that started with him that didn't finish his tenure with him. I'll bet you there were some faint-hearted that decided being a student was more comfortable." Correct. Mackenzie's off-season training camp down on the south base remains notable for its physical demands and the players who didn't last. That, Schnellenberger speculates, parallels with Mackenzie's background with Bear Bryant. By the time Schnellenberger joined his old college coach as an assistant at Alabama in 1961, Bryant had mellowed somewhat and Mackenzie was coaching for Frank Broyles at Arkansas.

"I saw a kinder, gentler Bryant," Schnellenberger said. "And he was probably at his finest the years that I coached with him." Schnellenberger was at Alabama from 1961-65. Over that span, the Crimson Tide won three national titles and lost four games in five years. "Still tough as nails," Schnellenberger stressed. But "already a legend, he didn't have to die to become one. And the players responded to him so well. Without even raising his voice, he could command respect. Jim saw him only in that young, Bryant vintage. I had the good fortune to see him some years later. You still have to

Coach Howard Schnellenberger aims to take Oklahoma back to the top.

have the same toughness all great coaches have had. But you've also got to have a pinch of love for your team, genuine respect. Am I like Bryant, am I like Shula, am I like George Allen, am I like Blanton Collier? I'd say no. But I'd like to think that somehow I may have assimilated some of their winning ways. Some of the things that helped them. They were all great coaches. I have to believe no matter how I would try to orchestrate it, I've learned some good things and hopefully avoided some shortcomings. That doesn't mean I'm anything close to perfect. I'm obviously not. But if living to age 60 and coaching for 35 years has any value, maybe I'm prepared for this job."

Schnellenberger coached under Allen with the Los Angeles Rams from 1966-69, then joined Shula's Miami Dolphins in time to win two Super Bowls, including Super Bowl VII, which gave Miami the only perfect record (17-0) in modern NFL history. He had an abbreviated stint as head coach of the Baltimore Colts (1973-74), then returned to Shula's Dolphin staff before getting the job at the University of Miami. Ironically, Miami had been considering dropping football. Instead, under Schnellenberger's leadership, the Hurricanes were transformed into one of college football's perennial powers.

A Firm Foundation

The day he took the OU job, Schnellenberger started talking national championship. "It is exciting for a 60-year-old coach who has been coaching for a lot of years to be given the assignment and the trust and the confidence to lead this program. You'll have to bear with me a little bit because I'm not used to leading a great program and dropping into the shadow of Bud Wilkinson and all the other great coaches you have had here. I am not used to coming into a program that has already achieved national championship status, not just once but six times. I'm not used to having the raw materials, the young men, the facilities and all those things necessary to bring this great program back, and I assure you that is my avowed goal."

Schnellenberger spent the previous fifteen years building programs from the bottom, but before that he saw what coaches like Bryant and Shula could do with firm foundations, and that prospect excites him. "For the first time in my life as a head coach, I've started halfway up the mountain," he said. "At Baltimore, we started under the ground. At Miami, we started under the ground. At Louisville, we started under the ground. We had to build foundations, put in sewers, electric conduits, ducts for the air conditioning and heating. As you know, most skyscrapers are as deep as they are tall. It takes longer to come out of the ground than it does to reach the Christmas tree. We don't have to do that at Oklahoma. There is a foundation."

Manifest changes accompany the new coaching regime. The venerable wishbone, for example, is gone. The Oklahoma 5-2 defense, invented by Bud Wilkinson and Gomer Jones, will be replaced with the 4-3 alignment.

"I'm still waiting for the earthquake to happen," Schnellenberger said. 'For the first time since 1946, '47, the University of Oklahoma will not run the Oklahoma defense. Be now assured the manifesto has been put out.

We're recruiting in that direction. I think our squad we have in place will best suit that style." Actually, the Sooners ran the 4-3 for a year or so in 1969-70 under Chuck Fairbanks, but they quickly returned to the 5-2. That likely won't happen under Schnellenberger. "For us to win the national championship, we've got to be able to beat Florida or Florida State or Miami," he said. "Somewhere along the line, we've gotta beat Kansas State. Obviously, we've still gotta beat Nebraska, Oklahoma State, Texas, and Texas A&M. You can do that with a four-man line. I think it's very difficult to do with an odd scheme. The 4-3 adjusts to more things, including the option and power attack. It adjusts to all those things. What it also does, it simplifies assignments. You don't have to go through 44 calls. You're sitting there with four down guys, they're going to do the same thing every time, just like in the National Football League."

Schnellenberger also is married to an NFL-type offense. At Oklahoma, he will implement what he calls the Miami Dolphin offense, 1970s vintage, which utilized a variety of passing options along with a solid running attack. "We're starting the modern era now," he said. "Futuristic. It has to be, going from the wishbone and the variations thereof to the pro style offense." He admits he was concerned how Sooner fans might take to such wholesale changes. "I thought maybe I'd be ridden out of town on a rail or presented with an olive branch and eulogized," he said. "Hasn't been either one. I guess I'm puttin' more emphasis, more importance on it than anybody else is. They want to win, whatever it takes."

But the man who played and coached for Bear Bryant and has been to Orange Bowls and Super Bowls promises his coaching regime will respect the Oklahoma football legacy. "We're not going to flaunt tradition," he said.

Coach Schnellenberger introduces his coaching staff to the media in the spring of 1995, and acknowledges his respect for the tradition of Oklahoma Sooner football.

Tradition, Respect, Pride

Schnellenberger can become a bit sentimental just sitting in his office at Memorial Stadium. He holds a quiet reverence for Owen Field. At Miami, Schnellenberger's teams played in the historic Orange Bowl, but it was city-owned and off campus. At Louisville, the Cardinals played in a converted baseball park on the state fairgrounds. By contrast, the Sooners play in a grand stadium in the middle of campus. Schnellenberger is inspired by that prospect. He had a sign placed on the outside stairwell at Memorial Stadium directing visitors to walk up there instead of using an inside stairwell - that route provides a dramatic view of the expansive new grass field. "It's big and it's on campus," Schnellenberger said. "And on Saturdays, it's full of loud,

boisterous people. What else is there to like about a stadium?

"I know the fathers and forefathers of this great university put this stadium in the middle of this campus, just like they did at Harvard back in 1875. That's a big stadium, still is a big stadium." Schnellenberger quotes from a *Sports Illustrated* story of 20 years ago, when the Harvard president was asked, "You're in the Ivy League. Why do you have this big stadium?" Schnellenberger relishes the answer. A big stadium in the middle of campus "reminds us of our heritage," Schnellenberger recited. "Without football, Harvard wouldn't be what it is today. Football has more to do with the development of Harvard and Yale and Princeton and Cornell than the educators did. It's symbolism, the center of campus. Everything revolves around it."

Schnellenberger added, "I see the same thing here. It's still the symbol for Oklahoma football in this state. You want to go through campus, you've gotta go around the stadium. I'm proud to be a renter, hopefully a lessee of this position."

To that end, Schnellenberger has taken steps to embrace fans into the OU football family. When

he arrived in Norman, his office was adorned with awards, memorabilia and replicas of the three Heisman Trophies won by Sooner players. Schnellenberger promptly had a trophy case installed in the lobby of the football offices to display such battle relics. "I've got these three Heisman Trophies back here," he said. "They shouldn't be in the coach's office. They ought to be out there where the fans can see them, people who have earned the right to see them. They need to be out where fans and the players and the staff, everybody that has had a lifetime commitment to this program can see them. We coaches just enjoy the luxury of the position. The position belongs to the University of Oklahoma."

A hundred years after a few upstarts laid a pigskin down on a sun-drenched prairie field in Norman, Oklahoma, one sentiment somehow remains. The pride that wells up inside us all when young men in crimson and cream take to the gridiron will be there not only for Oklahoma's second century, but for always.

Lettermen from A to Z
(1895-1994)

According to intercollegiate athletic records, the following men lettered at Oklahoma in the years indicated:

Abbott, George C.	1916
Abbott, Wallace	1917
Acker, Mark	(T)*
Acker, Neal W.	1972
Acree, Jim	1949,52,53
Acton, Owen E.	1905,06,07
Adkins, David	1975(M)
Adkins, Kevin	1983,84,85
Alfred, Joey	1993
Ahrens, Conrad	1934,35,36
Aikman, Troy	1984,85
Alexander, Stephen	1994
Alfieri, Jerry	1963,64,65,66
Aljoe, Mike	1983,84,85
Allen, Fred	1907
Allen, James	1993,94
Allen, Keith	1994 (M)
Allen, Robert L., II	1992, 93,94
Allen, Russell	1990,91,92,93
Allen, Sam	1951,52
Allford, V. Larry	1963,64,65
Allison, Carl	1951,52,53,54
Allsup, John V.	1946,47
Allton, Joe	1940,41
Ambrister, Hubert	1910,11,12,13
Andarakes, Drake	1973,74
Anderegg, Dan	1947
Anderson, Bruce	1972(T)
Anderson, Frank G.	1947
Anderson, George	1914,15
Anderson, Jerry O.	1975,76
Anderson, John	1991,92,93,94
Anderson, Rotnei	1985,86,87,88
Anderson, Vickey Ray	1977,78
Andros, Dee G.	1949
Angel, Keith F.	1980
Antone, Tony	1977,78
Arbuckle, Dale	1923,24,25,26
Armstrong, Tyrone	1973
Arnold, Gerald K.	1972,73,74
Arnold, Lee	1900
Aston, Roscoe	1901
Atkins, Arthur	1994
Atyia, Darren	1983
Austman, George	1967
Austin, John	1944
Avent, Bob	1945
Aycock, Steve	1969,70,71
Babb, Mike	1976,77,78,79
Baccus, Duane	1974,75,76
Baccus, Gary	1970,72,73
Backes, Tom	1987,88,89,90
Baer, Jack	1935,36,37
Bagby, Boots	1966
Bagwell, Paul W.	1966
Bailey, Calvin	1988
Bailey, Manley	1916
Bailey, Warren	1921
Baily, Gary	1974
Baker, Boone	1942,43
Baker, Charles	1967
Baker, David	1957,58
Baker, Frank	1916
Balcer, Frank	1916
Baldischwiler, Karl	1975,76,77
Baldridge, Richard D.	1967,68,69
Baldwin, James	1989
Ball, Fred S., Jr.	1935,36,37
Ballard, Hugh C.	1951,55,56
Banks, Basil M.	1977,78,79

Barkett, Woody	1945
Barnes, Reggie	1989,90,91,92
Barnoskie, Gary	1974
Barr, Johnny	1968,69
Barresi, John	1973,74
Barrett, J. Rodney	1986(T)
Barrett, Steve J.	1966,67,68
Barrow, Edwin	1896,97
Base, Micheal	1963,64,65,66
Basham, Jim	1945
Bashara, Ellis	1931,32,33
Bass, Maurice	1918
Baublit, Randy	1993 (M)
Bayles, Marion	1963
Beattie, Richard L.	1961
Beavers, Aubrey	1992, 93
Bechtold, Earl	1917,19
Bechtold, William B.	1979,80,81
Beck, Wesley W.	1933,35
Becker, Max	1902
Beckman, William	1950
Belcher, Page	1918
Bell, Curry	1913,14,15
Bell, Glenn	1988
Bell, John H.	1954,55,56
Bell, Roy Lemount	1969,70,71
Belser, Jason	1988,89,90,91
Bene, Fred	1895
Benien Jr., Paul F.	1959,60,61
Benien, John David	1961
Bennett, W. Gary, Jr.	1985,86,87
Benson, Thomas	1980,81,82,83
Bentley, David P.	1975
Berg, Robert P.	1973,74
Bergman, Deroy	1945
Berry, Curtis	1928,29,30,31
Berry, Harry L.	1926,27,28
Berry, John	1901
Berry, Mike	1978
Berry, Roger E.	1910,11,12
Berryhill, Darin	1981,83,84,85
Bibb, Boyd	1946,47
Bigby, Byron	1966,67,68
Birge, Laddie V.	1940,41
Birks, Mike	1974,75,76
Bishop, Bobby	1979,81
Bishop, Gary	1975
Blake, John	1979,80,81,82
Blanton, Scott	1991,92,93,94
Blevins, Dean	1974,75,76,77
Blevins, Frank	1987,88,89,90
Blodgett, Mark	1988,89,90
Blubaugh, Tom	1984(M)
Boatright, Lloyd	1922
Bobo, Robert,	1987(M)
Bodenhamer, Bob	1945,47,48,49
Bodin, Jeffrey R.	1974,75
Bodine, Hugh	1904
Bogle, Clyde	1899,1900,01,02,03
Bolinger, Bo	1953,54,55
Boll, Virgil Lloyd	1961,62,63
Bolton, Jerry	1937,38,39
Bookout, Billy	1951
Borah, Oren	1930,31
Bosworth, Brian K.	1984,85
Boudreau, George	1941
Boudreau, Raphael	1936,37,38
Bourland, Joe	1991(T)
Bowden, Joe	1989,90,91
Bowen, Jim	1957(M)
Bowers, Justin	1938,39
Bowles, R.C.	1921,22,23
Bowman, Charles "Chuck"	1957
Bowman, Dick	1951,52,53
Boyd, Bobby	1957,58,59

Boyd, James	1989
Boydston, Max	1951,52,53,54
Boyle, Dorsey	1917,19
Braden, Kent	1951,52(M)
Bradford, Kent	1977,78
Bradley, Danny L.	1981,82,83,84
Bradley, John	1988,91
Bradley, Lester E.	1959
Brady, Rickey,	1990,91,92,93
Brahaney, Tom	1970,71,72
Brauninger, Brian	1990,91
Breathett, Sherdeill H.	1980,81
Brecht, Martin B.	1974
Breeden, Charles	1943
Breeden Joe, Jr.	1943
Breeden, J.W.	1935,36
Brewer, Dewell	1989,90,91,92
Brewer, George W., Jr.	1946,47,48,49
Brewer, Otto	1916
Brewington, Carl	1941
Bridges, John	1935
Bridges, Richard	1984
Briggs, Larry	1975
Brindley, Bob	1945
Brinkman, Wade	1988(M)
Briscoe, Albert	1916,19
Bristow, J. Gordon "Obie"	1922,23,24
Britt, Jodie Dean	1985
Brockman, Ed	1923,24,25
Brooks, Bill	1973,74,75
Bross, Eric B.	1986,87,88,89
Bross, Larry A.	1968
Brown, Sidney, Jr.	1974,75,76
Brown, C.D. "Sonny"	1983,84,85,86
Brown, Don K.	1952,53,54
Brown, Gordon	1963,64,65
Brown, Jim	1905
Brown, Joe A.	1917
Brown, Joe	1994
Brown, Larry	1963,64,65
Brown, Mart	1925,26,27
Brown, Melvin	1950,52,53
Brown, Ralph	1934,35,36
Brown, Terence	1993,94
Brown, Victor Larue	1975,76
Brown, William H.	1955,56
Browne, Howard	1907
Broyles, J. Henry, Jr.	1955,56
Brumley, Bob	1943
Bryan, Mitch W.	1982,83
Bryan, Rick D.	1980,81,82,83
Bryan, Steven R.	1983,84,85
Bryant, Anthony	1973,74,75,76
Bryce, C.F.	1942
Buchanan, Dennis	1972,73,75
Buchanan, James N.	1909
Bullard, David	1994
Bumgardner, Allen W.	1962,63,64
Bunge, Paul,	1972
Burch, Wyatt	1901,02,03,06
Burgar, Jim	1966,67
Burgert, Eran Omer, Jr.	1943,44,45
Burgess, Rickey T.	1966
Burget, Barry	1976,77,78,79
Burget, Grant	1972,73,74
Burkett, Vernon D.	1964,65,66
Burks, Brent	1982,83,84
Burns, Artis	1993
Burns, Greg	1964
Burns, Mike	1965
Burris, Kurt	1951,52,53,54
Burris, Lynn	1956
Burris, Paul "Buddy"	1946,47,48
Burris, Robert R.	1953,54,55
Burson, H.T.	1896

Burton, Newton	1962,63,64	Collier, Perry	1993,94	Davis, Sam A.	1961
Burton, Sam	1910,12	Collier, Terry	1992,93,94	Davis, Skivey A.R.	1917,19,20
Bush, Larry	1992,93,94	Collins, Egean	1983	Davis, Steve	1973,74,75
Butts, Wes	1965,66,67	Collins, Herve T.	1914	Davis, Thomas "Eddy"	1941,42,46,47
Buxton, C.C.	1930	Collins, Patrick	1984,85,86,87	Davis, Wendell	1994
Byerly, Jim	1959	Collins, Steve	1989,90,91,92	Dawson, Chris	1993,94
Byford, Lyndle	1979,80,81	Collins, Tink	1989,90,91,92	Dawson, Russell Scott	1977,79,80,81
Bynum, Chester L.	1951,52	Comeaux, Glenn	1973,74,75	Day, Ernest B.	1955,56
Cabbiness, Carl	1985,86,87,88	Comer, Jason	1992,93,94	Day, Lionell	1968,69,70,71
Cabbiness, Chris	1988,89,90	Condren, Glen P.	1962,63,64	Dayton, Max	1971
Cagle, Gene	1965,66,67	Conkright, William	1934,35,36	Deacon, Erl E.	1917,18,19,20
Calame, Gene	1965,66,67	Conrad, J. R.	1992,93,94	Deere, Monte M.	1960,61,62
Calonkey, Steve	1973	Coody, Reed	1972	DeLoney, Bruce Edward	1969,70,71
Campbell, Bill	1940,41,42	Cook, Edward	1904	Delozier, Brown	1980,82
Campbell, Chris	1993,94	Cook, James Duane	1960,61,62	Dempsey, Jackie L. "Bud"	1962
Campbell, David	1992,93,94	Cook, Paul	1987	Denton, Sammy L. "Bo"	1967,68
Campbell, Ralph	1907,08	Cookman, Jeff	1986(T)	Denton, Tim	1994
Campbell, Roy	1908	Cooper, Adrian	1987,88,89,90	Depue, L. Dale	1956,57
Cantrell, Marshall	1973	Coots, Earl	1910	DeQuasie, Brent	1992, 93, 94
Capshaw, Elmer	1912,13,14,15	Copher, Brian	1985(M)	DeQuasie, Greg	1988,89,90,91
Capshaw, Fred	1908,09	Coppage, Alton	1937,38,39	Derr, Bruce J.	1968,69,70
Carey, Orville J.	1931,32,33	Corbitt, Dick	1957,58	Derrick, Robert	1954,55,56
Cargill, Brett	1976,77	Corbitt, Tom R.	1964(M)	Desmond, Jim	1943
Carlyle, Bill	1964,65	Corey, Orville J.	1931,32,33	Dewberry, Glenn	1969,71
Carman, Jack P.	1927	Cornelius, George R.	1950,51,52	Dickey, Donald F.	1960
Carnahan, Sam D.	1950	Cornell, Bob	1958,59,60	Dickson, Wayne	1987,88,89
Carner, James	1978,79,80	Correia, Joe	1992,93	Dillard, Stacy	1988,89,90,91
Carollo, Joe	1993	Corrotto, Albert	1935,36,37	Dillingham, David	1983,84
Carpenter, Dick	1957,58,59	Corrotto, Eugene F.	1936,37,38	Dillingham, W. David	1969
Carpenter, E.J.	1958,60,61	Coshow, Larry	1980	Dillon, Richard	1984,86,87,88
Carr, Lydell	1984,85,86,87	Couch, Jeffrey A.	1979	Dinkins, Merle L.	1943,44,46,47
Carroll, Hugh	1904	Counter, Ron	1987	DiRienzo, Tony	1973,74,75
Carroll, John	1971,72,74	Courtright, Raymond	1911,12,13,14	Dittman, Barry Robert	1975,77,78,79
Carroll, Tom M.	1953,54	Covin, Bill	1951	Dixon, Greg	1987,89
Carter, Bobby	1984	Cowan, Jackie R.	1961,63	Dixon, Rickey	1984,85,86,87
Carter, David,	1981,82	Cowling, L.A.	1941	Dobbs, James Mark	1982(M)
Carter, Gary	1972	Cox, R.A.	1934	Dodd, Carl	1955,56,57
Carter, Melvin	1989,90	Cox, Thomas S.	1959,60,61	Dodd, Gary Steve	1971,72,73
Cartwright, Roy	1954	Coyle, Ross	1956,57,58	Dodd, Sidney	1982,83
Case, Scott	1982,83	Crafts, Jerry	1988	Dodds, James Lawrence	1974,75,76
Casey, Clay	1936	Craig, Kevin	1976	Dodson, Ted E.	1963
Casillas, Tony	1982,83,84,85	Craig, Robert Edward	1965,66,67	Dollarhide, Louis	1944
Cason, Owen T.	1933	Crider, Frank	1927,28,29	Donaghey, Jerry	1953
Casteel, Steve	1968,69,70	Crook, Justin	1988(M)	Douglas, Alfred G.	1917,18
Catlin, Tom A.	1950,51,52	Cross, D. Leon	1960,61,62	Douglas, Willard	1906,09
Cavil, Ben	1991,92,93,94	Cross, Jerry L.	1953	Dowell, Charles	1947,48,49
Cawthon, Pete W., Jr.	1941,42	Cross, Rick D.	1980	Downing, Dewayne	1979,82
Chambers, Evans E.	1931	Cross, W.J.	1904,05,06,07	Downs, Albert	1942
Chandler, Albert M.	1970,71,72	Crosswhite, Kenneth	1975	Drake, Bruce	1927,28
Chandler, Dwayne	1992,93,94	Crosswhite, Leon M.	1970,71,72	Drane, Dwight	1980,81,82,83
Chase, Martin	1994	Crosswhite, Rodney	1964,65,66	Driscoll, Mark W.	1970,71
Cherry, Fred	1930,31	Crouch, Terry	1979,80,81	Dubler, Rick	1984
Chiles, Clay	1933	Crowder, Earl F.	1936,37,38	Duggan, Gilford	1937,38,39
Chilless, Bill	1947,48,49	Crowder, Eddie	1950,51,52	Duke, Richard Lawrence	1975
Choate, Phillip	1988(T)	Crowder, Stan	1965,66	Duncan, Terry	1990
Chrisman, Gary	1968,69,70	Crudup, Derrick	1985,86,87	Dunkleberger, Scott	1993 (T)
Christian, Brian	1994(M)	Crutchmer, Larry	1965,66,67	Dunlap, Robert L.	1931,32,33
Christmon, Drew	1990,91,92	Culbreath, James C., Jr.	1975,76	Dunn, Bert	1895
Churchill, Tom, Sr.	1927,28,29	Cullen, Ronald J.	1920,21,22	Dunn, Lewis	1943
Clammer, Sam	1927	Culver, David	1982	Duong, Holly	1993 (T)
Clapam, Jasper	1895,96,97,98,99	Culver, Ed	1978,79,80,81	Dupree, Marcus	1982
Claphan, Sam	1976,77,78	Culver, Max	1944	Durant, W.E.	1916,17
Clark, Bert	1949,50,51	Cumby, George	1976,77,78,79	Durham, Jere	1957,58
Clark, Beryl	1938,39	Cummings, Jim	1979(M)	Dutton, Richard L.	1974
Clark, Carl	1919	Cummings, Millard	1944	Dutton, Todd	1975
Clark, Glenn C.	1909,10,11,12	Cunningham, Glenn	1959	Dye, Alan	1973
Clark, Waymon	1973	Cunningham, Joe	1950	Dykes, Billy	1988,91
Clark, William	1912,13,14	Curnett, E. Lee	1931	Earnest, Rick	1988(M)
Clark, William, N.	1905	Curtis, Joe	1976,77	Earthman, Bill	1982,83,84
Clay, Nigel	1988	Cutchall, Dean B.	1935	Eason, Roger	1939,40,41
Clearman, David	1970(M)	Dalke, Bill	1975,76	Eck, Robert	1988
Clements, Alex	1902,03	Dambro, Guntar	1972(M)	Ederer, John	1955,56,57
Clewis, Paul	1981,82,83	Darnell, Bobby J.	1952,53,54,55	Edgeman, Harold C.	1938
Clopton, Mike	1983	Daughtry, Tim	1994	Edmonson, A.V.	1920,21,22
Coast, Mike	1978,79,80	Davis, Arlo	1917,19,20	Edmonson, Charles Van	1920,21,22
Coats, Michael	1990,91,92,93	Davis, Danny	1979(M)	Elam, Willis	1954
Cobbs, John	1978	Davis, Don W.	1966	Elfstrom, W.W. "Bill"	1967,68,69
Cockrell, Gene	1954	Davis, Ernest	1945	Ellington, Sidney	1983(M)
Coffman, Randy	1972	Davis, George	1975	Ellis, Harry H.	1933,34,35
Cohane, Tim	1967	Davis, Heath	1994(T)	Ellis, Richard F.	1951,52
Coker, Jeff	1933,34	Davis, James W.	1957,58,59	Ellstrom, Marvin	1931
Cole, J.W.	1949,50	Davis, Jim	1951,52	Ellsworth, Ferd	1933,35,36
Coleman, Royce	1979	Davis, Kyle	1972,73,74	Elrod, James W.	1973,74,75

Emel, Thomas Jeffrey	1974	Fischer, Max	1941,46,47	Fultz, Eric	1988,89,90
Emerson, Thomas E.	1954,55,56	Fisher, Rod	1988,89,90	Funk, John H.	1941
Emerson, John	1978	Fitch, Ken	1943	Fuqua, Karey A.	1933,34,35G
Emmert, Darryl L.	1969,70,71	Flanagan, Orlando	1980,81	Gaddis, Mike	1988,89,91
English, Porter	1908,09	Flanagan, Robert	1965	Gaines, Ryan	1993 (T)
Ervin, Greg	1990,91	Fleetwood, Harold E.	1932,33	Gambill, Jess	1898
Erwin, Bill	1945	Fleming, L.B.	1923	Gambrell, Bob	1944
Estep, Robert	1943,44	Flemons, Tommy	1980,82,83	Gambrell, Rick E.	1971,72,73,74
Estes, H.O.	1960	Fletcher, Ron	1964	Gammil, Floyd	1916
Evans, Chez	1973,74,75,76	Flint, Earl	1928,29	Garl, Michael Scott	1985,86,87,88
Evans, J.C.	1895	Flood, Alger W.	1969	Garrett, John C.	1962,63,64
Evans, Richard	1958Evans,	Flynn, John	1962,63	Gary, Keith	1979,80
Richard W.	1974	Fogle, Anthony	1993,94	Gassoway, Jim	1943
Evans, Scott	1987,88,89,90	Foley, Mark J.	1980	Gatewood, Evan	1983,84,85
Evans, Tommy	1993(M)	Fontenette, Johnny	1980,82,83	Gaut, Robert N.	1951,52
Ewbank, James B.	1948,52	Ford, Harry	1896,97,98	Gautt, Prentice	1957,58,59
Ewing, Darrell L.	1929,30	Forrest, Dugan	1987	Gaynor, Joe	1951
Farley, Gerald	1992	Foster, Ed	1970,71,72	Geerts, Greg	1985(M)
Farthing, Jody	1976,77,78	Foster, Jerry	1975	Gentry, Cash	1933,34
Fauble, Don	1942	Foster, Raybourne	1915	Gentry, Malcomb	1914
Favor, Richard E.	1938,39	Fox, Dave	1908	Gentry, Weldon C.	1928,29
Feagan, Jimmy	1958	Francis, William Raleigh	1933,34,35	Geren, David R.	1971
Ferguson, Glenn	1981	Franklin, Willie	1970,71	Geyer, Forest	1913,14,15
Ferguson, Milton	1899	Franks, Charles	1988,89,90,91	Gibbons, George	1941,42
Ferrer, Paul G.	1981,82,84,85	Frazer, David P.	1968	Gibbs, Gary L.	1972,73,74
Fields, Jess	1914,16	Frazier, Jeff	1994	Giese, Warren	1946
Fields, Mike	1991,92	Freeman, Mario	1992,93,94	Giles, Barry	1994
Fields, Robert D.	1928,29,30	Friday, Elmer	1945	Giller, Tre	1987,88
Fields, Troy	1984	Friedrichs, L.G.	1939	Gilstrap, Jimmy R.	1961,62,63
Files, Jim	1967,68,69	Fulcher, Rick	1972,73	Ging, Jack	1951,52,53
Finch, Lonnie	1985,86,87	Fulghum, Gale	1943	Glenn, Ledell	1985

Goad, Robert W.	1946,47,48,49	Harris, Jerome	1976	Hewes, Elmo "Bo"	1934,35,36
Goff, Duane	1953,54,55	Harris, Jim	1954,55,56	Hicks, Victor	1975,76,77
Golding, Joe	1941,46	Harris, Ralph	1939,40,41	Higginbotham, John	1977
Goldsby, Jerry	1963,64	Harrison, Bob	1956,57,58	Hill, Harry F.	1918,19,20,21
Goodall, Buddy	1942	Harrison, Jon	1970,71	Hill, Houston "Bus"	1925
Goode, James	1988,89,90	Hart, Ben	1964,65,66	Hill, Howard W. "Bill"	1962,63,64
Goodlow, Daryl	1980,82,83	Hartford, Glen	1922,23,24	Hill, James	1945
Goodman, John	1976,77,78,79	Hartline, Ronnie	1958,59,60	Hill, Kyle	1991,93
Goodwin, Rick	1965,66,67	Harts, John A.	1895	Hill, Scott	1973,74,75,76
Gordon, Murray	1927	Harvel, Everett	1945	Hillis, James H.	1982(T)
Gordon, Tracy	1988,89,90	Haskell, Lawrence	1918,19,20,21	Hines, Percy	1983,84
Gorka, Bryan	1991,92,94	Haskins, A. Lynwood	1926,28	Hinton, Eddie	1966,67,68
Graalman, Gordon	1931	Hatcher, Mickey	1976	Hobby, Brewster,	1959,60
Grace, George	1936,37	Haught, Richard	1960	Hoffman, Wayne	1972,73,74
Graham, Bobbye	1993 (M)	Hawkins, Howard	1945	Hogan, Patrick	1963
Graham, Elbert	1979,80,81	Haworth, Steve	1979,80,81,82	Hoge, John	1979
Graham, Hershel A.	1918,19,22	Hawpe, Mike	1969,72	Holieway, Jamelle	1985,86,87,88
Graham, Thomas	1916,17	Haycraft, Hugh	1896	Holland, J.D.	1912
Gravitt, Bert W.	1962	Hayden, Jerry	1963	Holland, Lonnie	1956
Gray, Edmund	1954,55,56	Hayes, Jim	1983(M)	Holland, Weaver	1910
Gray, Tom	1948,49,50	Haynes, Ray	1964,65,66	Holloway, Don	1983(M)
Grayson, Bobby	1979,80,81	Heape, Gene G.	1946,49	Holman, Jay	1975
Grayson, Joseph P.	1967	Heard, Charles	1943,44	Holt, Jack D.	1958,59
Greathouse, Myrle	1942,46,47,48	Hearon, Darlon N. "Doc"	1951,52,53	Hood, Fred,	1955
Green, Fred	1901,03	Heath, Leon	1948,49,50	Horkey, Joe R.	1948,49,50
Green, John	1987	Heatly, Dick	1949,50,51	Hotchkiss, Lewis	1938
Green, Karl	1973	Hebert, Bud	1976,77,79	Hott, Oliver	1913,14,15,16
Green, Merrill	1950,52,53	Hefley, John	1896,97,98,99	Hott, Sabert	1910,11,12,13
Green, Stanley	1942	Helms, Randy	1985(T)	Hott, Willis	1913,14,15,16
Green, Tremayne	1992,94	Henderson, Joseph S.	1965	Houston, Brandon	1989,90,91
Greenberg, Alan	1945	Henderson, R. Alan	1964,65,66	Hover, Lee	1975,76,77
Greene, Emmitt "Mickey"	1986	Henderson, Rod	1993,94	Howard, James	1979
Greenlee, C. Wayne	1954,55	Henderson, Zac R.	1974,75,76,77	Hubbard, Edward	1934
Griffin, Bennett	1916	Hendricks, Earl	1920,21,23,24	Hubble, Rocky	1981,82
Griffis, Russell D.	1977,78	Hendricks, Viene	1921,23,24	Huddleston, Woody	1935,36,37
Grigg, Larry	1951,52,53	Herndon, Bob D.	1953,54	Hudgens, David	1976,77
Grimmett, Tom	1931	Hetherington, Jerry	1969	Huffman, Bill	1945
Grisham, Jim C.	1962,63,64	Hetherington, Rickey	1966,68,69	Huffman, Eric	1990(M)
Guess, Arthur	1987,88,89,90	Hettmannsperger, Harry	1966	Hughes, Harry	1904,05,06
Guffey, Roy	1923,24,25				
Gundy, Cale	1990,91,92,93				
Gwinn, Richard L.	1956,57,58				
Gwinn, Robert,	1989(M)				
Haag, Heinie W.	1931				
Haberlein, Jack	1940,41				
Haddad, David	1979				
Hake, Jeff	1983,84,85				
Hale, David	1984				
Hale, Earl P.	1946,47,48				
Hale, Joe Cliff	1974				
Halfman, Peter F.	1970,72				
Hall, Albert	1991,92,93,94				
Hall, Bernard	1987				
Hall, Brian	1980,82,83,84				
Hall, Charles E. "Ed"	1964,65,66				
Hall, Larry	1963(T)				
Haller, W.C.	1925,26,27				
Hallett, Bill D.	1944,45				
Hallum, Ken	1955				
Hamilton, Raymond L.	1970,71,72				
Hamilton, William	1926,27,28				
Hamm, Huel	1940,41,42				
Hamm, W. Dow	1918,19,21				
Hammert, Pete, Jr.	1922,23				
Hammond, John	1963,64,65				
Hamon, Claude L.	1960,61				
Han, Tony	1990				
Hancock, Roy	1916				
Hardin, Lawrence,	1981				
Hardin, Robert W.	1979				
Hardy, Russell	1918,19				
Harley, John, Jr.	1943,44				
Harley, John, Sr.	1910				
Harman, Jason	1994				
Harmon, Ronald E.	1962,63				
Harold, James	1921				
Harp, Laddie J.	1947				
Harper, Gary	1966,67,68				
Harper, Mike	1967,68,69				
Harrell, Joe	1945				
Harris, Bill	1956				
Harris, Calvin Roy	1974				
Harris, Jack	1933,34,35				

Hughes, Randy	1972,73,74	Kidd, Summie	1926,27	Lisak, Edward J.	1948,49,50
Hull, Ronn	1993	Killingsworth, Joe	1967,68,69	Little, Kenneth	1933,34,35
Hunt, Daryl	1975,76,77,78	Killingsworth, T.K.	1974(M)	Littlejohn, Wray	1951,52,53,54
Husack, John E.	1946,47,48	Killion, Kirk	1973,74	Littrell, Jim	1973,74,75
Hussey, Pat	1972,73,74	Kilpatrick, Darren	1984,85,86,87	Lively, William Prentice	1915
Hutson, Mark	1984,85,86,87	Kimball, Robert L.	1977,78	Locke, Norval	1936,38,39
Ingram, Austin	1952	Kindley, Don L., Jr.	1965,66	Lockett, David M.	1949,50,51
Ingram, Jerry	1950,51,52	King, Aubrey	1985,86	Lohmann, Phil Jay	1959,60,61
Inman, Richard Walton	1961	King, David W.	1967	Loman, Brad	1980(M)
Irmscher, Chris	1987(M)	King, Glenn	1969,70,71	Long, Beede	1934,35
Irvin, Darrell	1978,79	King, Kenny	1976,77,78	Long, Bert	1895
Irvin, Kyle	1984	Kinlaw, Reggie	1975,76,77,78	Long, Charles	1899
Irvin, Oliver	1906	Kirby, Darrell	1990	Long, Delbert	1954,55,56
Ivory, Horace	1975,76	Kircher, Omer*	(M)	Long, Frank	1904,05,06,07,08
Ivy, Frank	1937,38,39	Kirk, Clyde	1928,29,30	Long, Ted	1988,89,90,91
Jackson, Alvin	1921,22	Kitchell, Charles Abe	1928	Looney, Joe Don	1962
Jackson, Elvin E.	1943,44	Kitchens, Gus	1938,39	Lott, Thomas	1976,77,78
Jackson, Grady	1931	Klitzman, Robert	1969	Loughridge, Robert E.	1953,54,55
Jackson, James Ray	1966	Knapp, Jim	1961	Lovall, Gerald	1945
Jackson, Keith	1984,85,86,87	Knight, Alford Eugene	1965	Lowe, Marcus	1987
Jackson, Kerry	1972,74	Koller, John	1965,66,67	Lowell, Gary	1978,80,81,82
Jackson, Mickey	1957,59	Koontz, Brent	1990,91,92	Luckey, Stirling	1994
Jacobs, Jack	1939,40,41	Kosmos, Mark	1965,66	Lucky, Mark	1977,78,79,80
Jacobs, Jay	1982	Kramer, Forrest	1916	Ludwig, Stephen Lee	1974
Jamar, Gary	1968	Kramer, Kyle	1994	Lund, Craig M.	1975
James, Harold L.	1921	Kreik, Edward	1946,47	Luster, Dewey	1917,18,19,20
Janes, Charles Art	1949,50	Krisher, Bill	1955,56,57	Mabry, Jeffrey C.	1974
Jarman, George W.	1961,63	Krivanek, Louis	1994(M)	MacDuff, Larry	1968,69
Jenkins, Delbert	1899	Kulbeth, Ralph L.	1975	Mackey, Paul	1896,97,98
Jenkins, William	1899	Kunkle, Steve	1975	Malone, Fred R.	1966,68
Jenkinson, Steve	1974	Kusiak, Joe	1968,69	Maloney, Don J.	1985
Jennings, Bill	1938,39,40	LaCrosse, Clane	1993	Maloney, Pete	1931
Jennings, Doyle D.	1955,56,57	La Rosa, Vince	1969,70	Manley, Leon	1947,48,49
Jennings, Steve	1956,57,58	Ladd, Benton	1955,56,57	Manly, J.R.	1937,38,39
Jensen, Chris	1991	Lahar, Harold W.	1938,39,40	Manning, Terran	1987,88,89,90
Jensen, Lester	1945	Lamb, Roy	1923,24	Mantle, Mike	1983,84,85
Jensen, Robert M.	1971,72	Lamb, W.G.	1940,41,42	Manuel, Rod	1993,94
Jimerson, Jay	1977,78,79,80	Lambert, Chris P., Sr.	1942	Marcum, Delton	1949
Johnson, Andre	1984	Lancaster, Eddie	1967,68	Marks, Richard W.	1985,86,87
Johnson, Corey	1990,91	Land, Proctor	1989,90,91	Marsee, Jack	1939,41,42
Johnson, Darrius	1992,93,94	Lane, Lester	1952	Marsh, James H.	1918,19,20,21,22
Johnson, E.B.	1921,22,23,24	Lang, Noland W., Jr.	1949	Marsh, Victor	1927,28,29
Johnson, Earl	1983,84,86	Lang, Vernon	1958,59,60	Marshall, Everett	1969,70,71
Johnson, Graham B.	1916,17	Langston, Chuck	1992,93,94	Martin, Bob	1956
Johnson, Greg	1984,85,86,87	Larghe, Steve	1976	Martin, Howard C.	1925,26
Johnson, Keith	1978(M)	Larue, William	1938,39	Martin, Fred	1918
Johnson, Mark D.	1980(M)	Lashar, R.D.	1987,88,89,90	Martin, Jason	1994(M)
Johnson, Mickey R.	1955,56,57,58	Lashar, Tim	1983,84,85,86	Martin, John	1938,40
Johnson, Montford	1914,15,16	Latham, Bob, Jr.	1985,86,87,88	Martin, Leo	1974,75,76
Johnson, Montford T. III	1969,70	Laurita, Al	1984,85,86,87	Martin, Randy	1984
Johnson, Neil R.	1913,14	Lawrence, J. Adair	1918	Martin, Robert	1911
Johnson, Oscar	1900,01	Lawrence, Jim	1956,57,58	Martin, William A.	1938,39,40,41
Johnson, Troy	1984,85,86,87	Lea, Paul	1961,62	Mason, Rick	1969,70
Johnson, Wallace	1961	Leake, John E. "Buddy," Jr.	1951,52,53,54	Massad, Ernest L.	1929,30,31
Johnson, Wally	1982	Lear, Alvin	1962	Mathes, Donald E.	1922
Johnston, Paul X.	1918,19,20	Leavell, Ron	1959,60(T)	Mathews, Orville	1939,40,41
Johnston, Ross	1916,17,18	Lebow, Derald	1943,44	Mathis, Reggie	1976,77,78
Johnston, W.R.	1916,17,19	Lecrone, Leroy	1925,26,27	Mattox, William	1940,41,42
Jones, Cedric	1992,93,94	Lecrone, Ray	1925,26,27	Maxfield, Ralph*	
Jones, Danté	1984,85,86,87	Ledbetter, Jerome	1980,83,84	Mayes, Clair S.	1948,49,50
Jones, Harold	1989	Ledbetter, Weldon	1979,80,82	Mayfield, Corey	1989,90,91
Jones, Jim	1979,80,81	Lee, Frank	1930	Mayfield, R.C. "Bob"	1943,44
Jones, Ken	1970,71,72	Lee, Hillory	1929,30	Mayhew, J.A. "Al"	1927,28,29
Jones, Russell	1991,92	Lee, John	1928,29	Mayhue, Charles D.	1962,63,64
Jones, W.D. "Buddy"	1947,48,49,50	Lee, Steve	1988	Mays, Ed B.	1946,47,48,49
Jordan, Phil	1969,70,71	Lee, William Wayne	1960,61,62	McAdams, Carl	1963,64,65
Joyce, Micheal R.	1980	Legg, Jerry A.	1980	McBride, Brad	1984,85,86,.87
Joyner, Barry	1978,79,80	Leggett, Scott	1983	McCain, Frank	1915,16,17
Judkins, John F.	1986	Lemon, William	1907	McCall, Aubrey	1945
Kalsu, Bob	1965	Lester, Chuck	1977(M)	McCampbell, Richard	1976
Kaltanbaher, Jim	1984	Levonitis, Bill	1959	McCartney, John	1900
Kaspar, Kert	1984,87,88	Levy, Tony	1990,91	McCarty, Howard W.	1937,38
Keadle, Robert D.	1960	Lewis, Fred	1994	McCasland, T. Howard	1914,15
Kearney, Vic	1970,71,72	Lewis, Gilmer A., Jr.	1957,58,59	McClellan, Mike	1959,60,61
Keeling, Mike	1979,80,81,82	Lewis, Hardie	1930,31	McCloud, Marc Dwight	1974
Keeton, Durwood	1972,73	Lewis, Ike	1989,90	McClure, Bruce	1994
Keith, Jason	1990,91,92	Lewis, Johnnie	1978,79,80,81	McClure, Daniel Edwin II	1974
Keith, Olen	1939,40	Liggins, Granville	1965,66,67	McCoy, James P.	1961
Keller, Troy Kay	1950,52,53	Light, Earl	1917	McCreary, Byrom	1902,03,04,05
Kennedy, Jon R.	1964,65,66	Link, Donald	1943	McCullough, Hugh	1937,38
Kennon, Doug,	1986(T)	Link, Emery A.	1953	McCurdy, Rick	1962,63,64
Kennon, Lee V.	1943	Linn, Jim	1968	McCutcheon, Bill	1896,97
Key, Don	1979,80,81,82	Linzy, Marceline Chavez	1974	McDade, Billy	1991

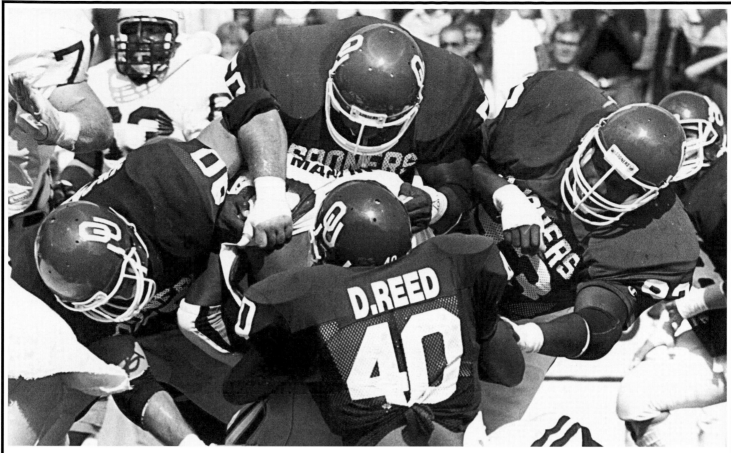

McDade, Laddie Burl	1949	Milburn, Glyn	1988	Muldrow, Alvin	1928
McDaniel, Edward "Wahoo"	1957,58,59	Mildren, Jack	1969,70,71	Muldrow, Hal	1925,26,27
McDaniel, Mike	1994	Mildren, Richard	1973	Mullen, John Daniel	1970,71,72
McDannald, Morris Robert	1933,34,35	Miles, Mitch	1990(M)	Mullen, Michael L.	1969
McDermott, Hugh V.	1916,17,19	Miller, Jeff	1989,90	Mullen, Ray R.	1941,42
McDonald, Chris	1991(T)	Miller, T.B.	1933,34	Munn, Jeff	1986(T)
McDonald, Jeff	1981	Mills, Bus	1928,29,30	Munsey, J.S.	1939,40,41
McDonald, Tommy	1954,55,56	Mills, P.J.	1992,93,94	Murphy, Kevin	1981,82,83,85
McDonough, Kevin	1979	Mills, Ron	1981	Murray, Richard	1974,75,76,77
McFadden, Alfred	1922,23	Milstead, Jon	1970,71,72	Nairn, James	1908,09,10,11
McFerron, George	1916	Milstead, Karl	1959,60,61	Needs, Al	1945,48,50
McGee, Garrick	1994	Ming, Leslie L.	1948	Neely, Ralph E.	1962,63,64
McGee, Reece	1948	Miskovsky, John	1933,34,35	Neher, Lee Roy	1941,42,46,47
McGehee, Perry E.	1969	Mitchel, Eric	1985,86,87,88	Nelson, Don	1957
McGlothlin, Claude	1916,17	Mitchell, Jack	1946,47,48	Nelson, F. Wayne	1967
McGraw, Joseph	1898	Mobra, Joe	1953,54,55	Nelson, George N.	1954
McKim, Jay D.	1978,79,80	Monnett, Jim	1902,03,04,05,06	Nelson, Roger D.	1951,52,53
McKinley, Mike	1987,89,90,91	Montgomery, Homer	1914,15,16	Nelson, Roy	1929
McKinley, William	1920,21	Montgomery, Sam	1916	Nemecek, Vivian	1934,35
McLaughlin, John	1971,72	Mooney, Prentiss	1926,27	Newland, Scott	1982,83,84
McLaughlin, Mike	1971,72	Moore, Billy Jack	1957,58,59	Newton, Charles E.	1968
McMichel, Ken	1986,87,88,89	Moore, Derland	1971,72	Nicholson, John	1970
McNabb, Norman	1946,48,49,50	Moore, Dewayne	1987(M)	Nixon, Fred	1976,77,78,79
McPhail, Coleman "Buck"	1950,51,52	Moore, Frank	1979	Noles, Dan M.	1969
McPhail, Gerald	1954,55	Moore, Grant	1993 (T)	Nolte, David	1982(M)
McQuarters, Ed L.	1962,63,64	Moore, Harry	1948,49,50	Nordgren, Geoffrey E.	1969,70,71
McReynolds, Edwin C.	1910	Moore, Jerald	1993,94	Norris, Granville T.	1925,26,27
McReynolds, Joe	1973,75	Moore, John	1925,26	Northcutt, Ken	1954,55,57
Meacham, Bill	1960	Moore, Kirk	1988	O'Gara, Bill	1977,78
Meacham, Edgar	1911,12,13	Moore, Obie	1973,75,76,77	O'Grady, Kevin	1969,70
Meacham, Randy	1966,67,68	Moreno, Dennis	1986(M)	O'Neal, Preston, Jr.	1953,54
Mears, Gene	1952,53,54	Morford, Clare E.	1941,42	O'Neal, Benton	1958
Medice, Larry	1988,89,90	Morford, Robert B.	1957,58,59	O'Neal, Jay	1954,55,56
Medlock, Newt	1895	Morford, R. Brent	1960	O'Neal, Pat	1951,52,53,54
Meinhert, Lloyd	1943	Moriarty, Paul	1991,92	O'Neal, Roberto	1992
Melendez, Jaime H.	1973,75,76,77	Morris, Lee A., Jr.	1985	O'Shaughnessy, Stephen M.	1969,70,71
Melson, Chris	1988,89,90,91	Morris, Bill	1941,42,46,47	Oatts, Paul	1993
Mendenhall, Ken	1967,68,69	Morris, Cecil	1953,54,55	Ogilive, Frank A.	1920
Merkle, Fred	1896,97,98,99	Morris, Dennit E.	1955,56,57	Orendorff, Bill	1972
Merkle, Joe	1896,97,98,99	Morris, Max	1958,60	Orr, Charles	1912
Merrell, Webber	1936,37	Morrison, C.E., "Ram"	1920,21,22,24	Orr, Ellis	1928,29
Metcalf, L.A. "Butch"	1962,63,64	Morter, Ray A.	1909,10	Oubre, Louis	1978,79,80
Meyer, Clifford	1915	Morton, Don	1975	Oujesky, Joseph B.	1954,55,56,57
Mickey, Joey	1989,90,91,92	Moseley, Donald G.	1976,77,78(T)	Overstreet, David	1977,78,79
Migliazzo, Paul	1983,84,85,86	Moss, William B.	1911	Overton, Milton	1992,93,94

Owens, Jim	1946,47,48,49	Potters, Gary	1975	Reed, Chester	1904,05
Owens, Roger Ray	1976	Potts, Frank	1925,26	Reed, Darrell	1984,85,86,87
Owens, Roy	1983	Powell, Raymond R.	1949,51,52,53	Reed, Richard	1984,85
Owens, Steve	1967,68,69	Powell, Roland	1956	Reeds, Artie	1909
Owens, Tinker	1972,73,74,75	Powers, Clyde J.	1971,72,73	Reeds, Clarence	1904
Paaso, Dick	1966,67,68	Poynor, Ben	1933,34,35	Reeds, Claude E.	1910,11,12,13
Pace, Bobby W.	1962,63,64	Preston, Gene	1945	Reese, Jerry	1974,75,76
Pace, Harrison W.	1950	Price, Harry	1906,07,10	Reilly, Mike	1977,79,80
Page, Bobby	1962,63,64	Price, King	1923	Remy, William E.	1949
Page, G. Robert	1957,58,59,61	Price, Lance	1985,86,87	Rentie, Caesar	1984,85,86,87
Page, Harland	1934	Price, William	1945,46,47,48	Rentzel, Lance	1962,63,64
Paine, Charles W.	1949	Pricer, Billy C.	1954,55,56	Resler, Jeff	1991,92,93,94
Paine, Homer	1946,47,48	Prickett, John	1895	Rhodes, Roy	1945
Pair, Gayle	1945	Prince, Blair	1985(M)	Rhodes, Steve	1976,77,78,80
Pangburn, Sam L.	1926	Prince, Tony	1987	Rhymes, George	1980,81,83,84
Pannell, Larry	1962	Pruitt, Greg	1970,71,72	Rhynes, Gary	1972
Pannell, Tommy	1963,64,65	Qualls, Albert	1969,70,71	Richardson, Joe A.	1945
Pannell, William	1962	Quinn, Daniel	1965,66,67,68(T)	Richey, Joey	1993 (T)
Pansze, Art	1932,33,34	Radcliffe, Earle	1907,08,10	Riley, James	1964,65,66
Pansze, William N.	1931,32,33	Raley, John	1979	Ringer, Mike	1963,64,65
Parham, Duncan	1986,87	Randolph, John	1976	Ripley, J.M. "Mickey"	1967,68,69,70
Parker, James	1960,62	Randolph, Tim	1981,83,84	Risinger, R.L.	1895
Parker, Kenneth W.	1947,48,49	Rapacz, John J.	1946,47	Roach, Larry	1970,71,72
Parker, Paul	1981,82,83	Rasheed, Kenyon	1989,90,91,92	Roberson, Broderick	1991,92,93,94
Parks, Edward Mickey	1934,37	Ray, Darrol	1976,77,78,79	Roberts, Donald H.	1968
Parks, Jerry	1988	Ray, John	1898	Roberts, C.C.	1896,97,98,1900
Parrish, George	1933,34	Ray, Terry	1988,89,90,91	Roberts, Fred	1901
Parsons, Hillard, Jr.	1943	Rayburn, Tony	1983,84,85,86	Roberts, Greg	1975,76,77
Pasque, Dan	1985(M)	Rector, Joe D.	1956,57,58	Roberts, Harold	1929,30
Patterson, Mark	1990(M)	Reddell, Brad	1989,90,91,92	Roberts, Hugh	1908
Patterson, William A.	1922,24	Reddell, John C.	1950,51,52	Roberts, J.D.	1951,52,53
Paul, Byron	1978,79,80				
Paul, Harold	1971				
Payne, James H.	1959,62,63				
Payne, Jerry	1957,58,59				
Payne, Ron	1959,61				
Peacock, Elvis	1974,75,76,77				
Pearce, Joe	1967,68,69				
Pearson, Douglas B.	1974				
Pearson, Lindell	1948,49				
Pearson, Tom	1954				
Peddycoat, Dick	1944				
Pegues, Rod	1978,80,81,82				
Pellow, Johnny	1956,57,58				
Pemberton, Jerry	1982(T)				
Pena, Tony III	1992				
Pennick, James	1922,23,24				
Penny, JaJuan	1992,93,94				
Perini, Dale	1960,61				
Perry, Ed*					
Perry, Fred	1895				
Perry, Leon	1985,86,88,89				
Perryman, A.G.	1970				
Peters, Tony L.	1973,74				
Peters, Karl	1979				
Peters, Terry	1975,76,77				
Peters, Tyrell	1993,94				
Peters, Zarek	1989				
Pettibone, Jerry	1961				
Pfrimmer, Don	1967,68				
Phebus, Wright	1938				
Phelps, Kelly	1978,79,81,82				
Philips, Leon C.	1915				
Philips, Marland	1928				
Philips, Martin	1927				
Phillips, Anthony	1985,86,87,88				
Phillips, Forb L.	1968,69,70				
Phillips, Jon	1984,85,86,87				
Phillips, Michael F.	1974,75,76				
Phillips, T. Ray	1932				
Phipps, Mike	1994				
Pickard, Claude	1904,05,08				
Pickett, Jeff	1983,84,85				
Pierce, Clovis	1941				
Pitchlynn, Thurman J.	1966				
Porkorny, Charles D.	1922				
Pomeroy, Gary	1982,83				
Pope, Eric	1982,83,84,85				
Pope, Kenith	1971,72,73				
Porter, Jack D.	1966,67,68,69				
Porterfield, John L.	1962,63				
Poslick, Joe	1965,66,67				
Potter, Byron	1939				

Robertson, Dave	1971,72	Schreiner, Henry F.	1945,49	Simpson, Travis	1983,84,85
Robertson, Melbourne	1933,34,35	Scott, Bob	1956,57	Sims, Billy	1975,77,78,79
Robinson, Bobbie	1965,66	Searcy, Byron	1955,56,57	Sims, Fred	1981,82
Robinson, Eric	1984	Sellmyer, Greg	1976,78,79	Sims, Jerry L.	1968,69,70
Robison, Leroy	1933,34	Selmon, Dewey	1972,73,74,75	Sims, Richard	1930,31
Rockford, Jim	1980,81,83,84	Selmon, Lee Roy	1972,73,74,75	Singletary, Hinston L.	1928
Rogers, Tyrone	1988	Selmon, Lucious	1971,72,73	Sitton, Ken	1979,80
Rogers, Charles E.	1911,12,13	Severin, Robert	1904,05,06	Skidgel, Wesley A.	1962,63
Rogers, J.W. "Jim"	1907,10	Sewell, Steve	1981,82,83,84	Slater, Bob	1981,82,83
Rogers, Jimmy	1974,76,77,78	Seymour, Bob	1937,38,39	Slough, Elmer	1923,24
Rogers, Otis R.	1936,37,38	Shadid, Mitch	1940,41,42	Smalley, Harley	1944
Roland, Phil	1977	Shane, Dan S.	1967	Smith, C. Lyle	1939,40,41
Rolle, David	1956,57,58	Shankle, William	1991,92,93	Smith, C. Michael	1970
Rollins, Zerrick	1993	Shanks, Patrick	1941,42	Smith, David	1972,73
Rose, Michael	1994	Sharp, Basil	1944,45	Smith, Dean C.	1948,49,50
Rosenberg, Collin	1993,94	Sharp, Mike	1973(M)	Smith, Fred	1949,50,51
Ross, Alvin	1981,83	Sharpe, Louis	1939,40,41	Smith, Fred C.	1927
Ross, Dwight M.	1920	Shaw, Clinton	1917	Smith, John L.	1899
Ross, Eugene	1964,65,66	Shearer, Clifton	1928	Smith, Leon L.	1927
Ross, H. Grady	1909	Shelley, John A.	1969,70,71	Smith, Michael G. "Mike"	1973
Ross, Ronald K.	1978	Shepard, Darrell	1980,81	Smith, Norman W.	1962,63,64
Rousey, Tom	1940	Shepard, Derrick	1983,84,85,86	Smith, Pete	1935,36,37
Roush, John	1972,73,74	Shepard, Woodie	1976	Smith, Ray	1897
Rowe, William J.	1959	Sherrod, Dale	1955,56,57	Smith, Robert E.	1968(M)
Rowland, Ed	1950,51,52	Shields, Bennie	1961,63	Smith, Todd	1983,84,85
Royal, Darrell	1946,47,48,49	Shields, Larry	1963,64	Smith, Travian	1994
Royter, (Unknown)	1895	Shilling, Jack C.	1957,58	Smitherman, Don	1986,88,89
Runbeck, Leonard	1905	Shipp, Jackie	1980,81,82,83	Smoot, Roy	1918,19,20,21
Russell, Clyde	1973,74	Shirk, John	1937,38,39	Snell, Ernest B.	1930,31
Russell, Kleyn	1972	Shoate, Myron	1974,76	Snodgress, M.H.	1925
Russell, Dan	1970,71,72	Shoate, Rod	1972,73,74	Songy, Darrell	1979,80,82
Salmon, Don E.	1960	Shoemaker, David	1987,88	Soult, Timothy A.	1984(T)
Sandefer, J.D. "Jakie" III	1956,57,58	Shores, Phillip	1982	Sparkman, Homer	1943,44
Sanders, Jerry	1978,80,81,82	Short, Dan	1900,01,02,03	Sparks, Keith	1992,93,94
Sandersfield, Melvin	1959,60,61,62	Short, Gacicuis,	1927	Spears, Roy A.	1911,12,13
Santee, Jack H.	1951,52	Short, Harvey	1898,99	Speegle, Cliff	1938,39,40
Santee, Robert P.	1954	Short, Tom M.	1936,37	Spencer, Micheal L.	1975
Sarratt, Charles	1946,47	Shotts, Ron	1965,66,67	Spottswood, Ed	1938
Saunders, Thomas W.	1970,71,72	Shotts, Steve	1970	Stacy, James	1932,33,34
Sawatzky, Mike	1988,89,90	Silva, Frank R.	1948,49,50,51,52	Stacy, Ronnie Lee	1970,71
Sawyer, Steve	1944	Simcik, Douglas W.	1976,77	Stafford, Anthony	1985,86,87,88
Schaefer, Herbert	1922,23,24	Simmons, Homer	1940,41,42	Stahl, William	1921
Schmitt, Pete	1989,90,91,92	Simmons, Milton E.	1953,54	Stamps, Harry, Jr.	1992,93,94
Scholl, Robert	1958,59	Simms, Dick E.	1930,31	Stanberry, Keith	1981,82,83,84
Schreiner, Carl S. III	1963,64	Simon, E.N.	1973,74	Stanley, Raymond	1929,30
Schreiner, Carl S., Jr.	1945	Simpson, Broderick	1993,94	Steele, David A.	1969

Name	Years	Name	Years	Name	Years
Steele, Jack	1940,41,42	Titsworth, John	1966,67,68	West, Mark	1993 (T)
Steinberger, Clinton C.	1922,23	Todd, Nelson Page	1969,71	West, Stanley B.	1946,47,48,49
Steinbock, Delmar	1934,35	Tolbert, James R.	1916	Wetherbee, Phillip L.	1965
Stell, Damon	1984,85,87,88	Tribby, Floyd	1912	Whaley, Steve	1979,80,81
Stensrud, Bruce	1967,68,69	Trotter, Jess	1946,47,48	Wheeler, Gordon	1967
Stephens, Sam,	1941,42	Trousdale, J.R.	1987(T)	Wheeler, J.W.	1933,34,35
Stephenson, Robert L. "Bob"	1965,66,67	Truesdell, George	1905,06	Wheeler, Jeff	1994(T)
Stevenson, Ralph	1937,38,39	Truitt, John	1981,83	Whisenant, John B.	1916
Steward, J.N.	1945	Tubbs, Jerry	1954,55,56	White, Billy	1959,60,61
Stidham, J. Thomas	1966	Tupper, Jeff	1982,83,84,85	White, Brad	1973
Stiller, Don	1955,56,57	Turner, Richard	1977,78,79,80	White, C. Lazelle,	1922,23,24
Stogner, C.H.	1930,31	Tyler, Claude	1919	White, Derrick	1984,85,86,87
Stoia, Sam	1984	Tyler, George	1918,19,20,21	White, Phil E.	1918,19,20
Stokes, George	1961,62,63	Tyree, James E.	1941,42,46,47	Whited, Marvin	1939,40,41
Stokes, Ricky	1971,73	Uhles, Ric	1981,82,85	Whittington, Claude L.	1931,32,33
Stone, Clifford O., Jr.	1945	Unruh, Dean	1970,71,72	Wickersham, Taylor	1994
Stout, Mark	1987(T)	Vachon, Mike	1966,67	Wilcox, John	1923
Stover, Albert	1944,45	Vallance, Chad Y.	1941	Wilhelm, George	1937,38,39
Stover, Robert L.	1944	Valora, Forrest	1977,78,79,80	Wilhite, Otto	1909
Strouvelle, C.E.	1922	Van Burkleo, Bill	1961	Wilkins, Greg	1991
Struck, Mike	1971,72,73	Van Camp, Eric	1973,74,75	Williams, Chad	1987(M)
Sturm, Bill	1955	Van Horn, Bruce	1957,58,59,60(M)	Williams, Charles A.	1966
Sullivan, David	1974	VanKeirsbilck, Mark	1986,87,88,89	Williams, Curtice	1985,86,87,88
Sullivan, Glenn	1986,87	Van Osdol, Scott	1979	Williams, Dante	1986,87,88,89
Sumpter, R.O. "Bob"	1926	Van Pool, Jack	1951,53	Williams, Dewey	1979
Suntrup, Tom	1977	Vardeman, Robert	1963,65	Williams, Earnest	1990,91,92
Sutton, Anthony P.	1974	Vaughan, Mike	1974,75	Williams, Edward	1976
Swank, Floyd	1905	Venable, Jack	1945	Williams, Gregory	1987,89
Swanson, Garry F.	1969	Venable, Jim	1944,45	Williams, Jeff	1977,81
Swanson, Lance	1988,89,90	Vermillion, Larry	1962,63	Williams, Robert	1983,84
Swanson, T.M.	1922	Vessels, Billy	1950,51,52	Williams, Steve	1979,80,81,82
Swartz, P.W.	1909	Vickers, David	1984,85,86,87	Williams, Troy	1981
Swatek, Charles	1915	Vickers, Mike	1989,90(T)	Wilmoth, Evert G.	1916,17
Swatek, Roy E.	1918,19,20,21	Vitito, Tim	1991	Wilson, Bryon	1989(M)
Swofford, Joe	1931	Vogel, Al	1944,45	Wilson, Charles Hugh	1930,31
Tabor, Dion	1983(T)	Vogle, Daniel O.	1922	Wilson, Chris	1988,89,90,91
Tabor, Paul	1977,78,79	Voiles, John David	1962,63,64	Wilson, Corey	1991,92
Tabor, Phil	1975,76,77,78	von Schamann, Uwe	1976,77,78	Wilson, Danny	1980,81,82,83
Talbott, George V.	1957	Von Tungelin, Rudolph	1916	Wilson, Keith	1977
Tallchief, Tom	1945	Wade, Greg	1989(M)	Wilson, Matt	1991,94
Tanner, Barron	1994	Waggoner, Roy	1904,05,06	Wilson, Remardo	1989
Tarlton, Stephen F.	1968,69,70	Waggoner, F.E. "Gene"	1929	Wilson, Stanley	1979,80,81,82
Tate, Larry Wayne	1974	Walker, Ab D.	1930,31	Winblood, Bill	1960
Taton, Bruce	1977,78,79	Walker, Barrion	1980,81	Winchester, Mike	1984,85,86
Tatum, John E.	1960,61,62	Walker, Barth P.	1935,36,37	Winfrey, Ronald M.	1965,66
Taylor, Ben	1925,26,27	Walker, Darnell	1990,91,92	Wingate, Robert	1899,1900
Taylor, Fenton	1928,29	Walker, Wade	1946,47,48,49	Winters, Chet	1979,80,81,82
Taylor, Jim	1972,73,74	Wallace, Dave	1946,47	Wise, Mike	1987,88,89
Taylor, L. Geary	1961	Wallace, Polly	1924,25,26	Wolf, Key	1905,06,07,08
Taylor, Otis	1989,90,91,92	Wallace, Randy	1988,89,90,91	Wolfe, Zetta	1925
Taylor, Ron	1971(M)	Walling, Vernon	1906,07,08	Wolverton, M.E. "Woody"	1953,54
Taylor, Sherwood A.	1977,78,79	Walrond Jr., George A.	1976,77	Wood, Eddie*	
Teel, Charles	1930,31	Wantland, C.W.	1907,08	Wood, Steven Norvel	1938,39,40
Teeter, George Howard	1938,40,41	Ward, Allan	1982	Woods, Billy Joe	1958,59,61,62, 63(M)
Tennyson, Dewey	1932,34,35	Ward, Bob	1957,58		
Terrell, David	1967	Ward, Dennis	1961,62	Woods, C.A. "Tony"	1985,86,87,88
Thomas, James A., Jr.	1973,74,75	Ward, Jeffery C.	1977,78	Woods, Mort	1909,10
Thomas, Chuck	1981,82,83,84	Ward, Paul	1926,27,28	Woodson, Paul	1939
Thomas, Clendon	1955,56,57	Ward, Stanley	1958	Woodsworth, Calvin	1953,54,55
Thomas, George C.	1946,47,48,49	Warmack, Bob	1965,66,67,68	Wooten, W.G.	1942,43,44
Thomas, Jamie	1973,74,75	Warren, Corey	1990,91,92,93	Wren, Ricky	1991,92,93
Thomas, Jim	1936,37,38	Warren, Guy	1929,30	Wright, Curtis Truman	1947,48
Thomas, Keith	1973,74,75,76	Washington, Joe	1972,73,74,75	Wright, John W. "Bill"	1944
Thomas, W.S.	1964	Waters, Ron L.	1972,73,74	Wright, Lonnie Gene	1975
Thompson, Bobby	1968	Watkins, Chris	1991	Wright, Sonny Thelton	1942,43
Thompson, Charles	1987,88	Watkins, Smith	1931	Wright, Willie	1978
Thompson, James	1921,22,23,24	Watkins, Steve	1981(M)	Wyatt, Bobby J.	1961
Thompson, Jerry	1957,58,59	Watson, Johnny A.	1968,69,70	Wylie, Gary	1960,61,62
Thompson, Kevin	1986,87,88,89	Watts, Bennett	1957,59,60	Wylie, Joe	1970,71,72
Thompson, Michael	1992	Watts, Bill	1959	York, Marshall R.	1958,59,60
Thompson, Scott	1989	Watts, Elbert	1981	Young, Dalton	1990
Thompson, Scott	1985	Watts, J.C.	1978,79,80	Young, Gary L.	1973,74
Thompson, Travis	1990	Weatherford, Jennifer	1994(T)	Young, Herbert	1979,80
Thomsen, Todd	1985,86,87,88	Weatherall, James	1948,49,50,51	Young, Paul	1930,31
Tigart, Thurman	1943,44,45	Webb, Terry D.	1973,74,75	Young, Waddy	1936,37,38
Tillery, Jerry	1958,59,60	Weddington, Darrell	1984	Zabel, Steve	1967,68,69
Tillman, A.M. "Pete"	1946,47,48	Weddington, Mike	1979,80,81,82		
Tillman, Donald	1943,45	Weedn, Henry	1911,12		
Tillman, Spencer	1983,84,85,86	Welch, Tim	1971,72,73	* Date unavailable;	
Timberlake, R.W.	1954,55,56	Wells, Ben D.	1958	(M) indicates manager; (T) trainer	
Tippens, Trey	1989,90,91	Wenzl, Troy	1989,90(T)		
Tipps, Ken	1947,48,49	Wesley, Maylon	1992,93,94		
Tipton, Greg	1993(M)	West, John	1944,45		

Sooner All-Americans
(1895-1994)

1991 **JOE BOWDEN***
Linebacker • Mesquite, Texas

1988 **ANTHONY PHILLIPS***
Guard • Tulsa, Oklahoma

1987 **MARK HUTSON***
Guard • Fort Smith, Arkansas
KEITH JACKSON*
Tight End • Little Rock, Arkansas
RICKEY DIXON*
Defensive Back • Dallas, Texas
DANTÉ JONES*
Linebacker • Dallas, Texas
DARRELL REED
Defensive End • Cypress, Texas

1986 **BRIAN BOSWORTH***
Linebacker • Irving, Texas
KEITH JACKSON*
Tight End • Little Rock, Arkansas
ANTHONY PHILLIPS
Guard • Tulsa, Oklahoma

1985 **BRIAN BOSWORTH***
Linebacker • Irving, Texas
TONY CASILLAS*
Noseguard • Tulsa, Oklahoma
KEVIN MURPHY
Defensive End • Richardson, Texas

1984 **TONY CASILLAS***
Noseguard • Tulsa, Oklahoma

1983 **RICK BRYAN***
Defensive Tackle •
Coweta, Oklahoma

1982 **RICK BRYAN***
Defensive Tackle •
Coweta, Oklahoma

1981 **TERRY CROUCH***
Guard • Dallas, Texas

1980 **TERRY CROUCH**
Guard • Dallas, Texas

1979 **GEORGE CUMBY***
Linebacker • Tyler, Texas
BILLY SIMS*
Halfback • Hooks, Texas

1978 **BILLY SIMS***
Halfback • Hooks, Texas
REGGIE KINLAW
Noseguard • Miami, Florida
DARYL HUNT
Linebacker • Odessa, Texas
GREG ROBERTS*
Guard • Nacogdoches, Texas

1977 **ZAC HENDERSON***
Defensive Back •
Burkburnett, Texas

DARYL HUNT
Linebacker • Odessa, Texas
GEORGE CUMBY
Linebacker • Tyler, Texas
GREG ROBERTS
Guard • Nacogdoches, Texas
REGGIE KINLAW
Noseguard • Miami, Florida

1976 **MIKE VAUGHAN***
Tackle • Ada, Oklahoma
ZAC HENDERSON
Defensive Back •
Burkburnett, Texas

1975 **LEE ROY SELMON***
Defensive Tackle •
Eufaula, Oklahoma
DEWEY SELMON*
Noseguard • Eufaula, Oklahoma
TERRY WEBB
Guard • Muskogee, Oklahoma
MIKE VAUGHAN
Tackle • Ada, Oklahoma
BILLY BROOKS
Split End • Austin, Oklahoma
JIMBO ELROD*
Defensive End • Tulsa, Oklahoma
TINKER OWENS
Split End • Miami, Oklahoma
JOE WASHINGTON
Halfback • Port Arthur, Texas

1974 **JOE WASHINGTON***
Halfback • Port Arthur, Texas
ROD SHOATE*
Linebacker • Spiro, Oklahoma
LEE ROY SELMON
Defensive Tackle •
Eufaula, Oklahoma
DEWEY SELMON
Noseguard • Eufaula, Oklahoma
TINKER OWENS
Split End • Miami, Oklahoma
JOHN ROUSH*
Guard • Arvada, Colorado
RANDY HUGHES
Defensive Back • Tulsa, Oklahoma
KYLE DAVIS
Center • Altus, Oklahoma

1973 **ROD SHOATE**
Linebacker • Spiro, Oklahoma
EDDIE FOSTER
Tackle • Monahans, Texas
LUCIOUS SELMON
Noseguard • Eufaula, Oklahoma

1972 **TOM BRAHANEY***
Center • Midlands, Texas
ROD SHOATE
Linebacker • Spiro, Oklahoma
GREG PRUITT*

Halfback • Houston, Texas
DERLAND MOORE
Tackle • Poplar Bluff, Missouri

1971 **JACK MILDREN**
Quarterback • Abilene, Texas
TOM BRAHANEY*
Center • Midland, Texas
GREG PRUITT*
Halfback • Houston, Texas

1969 **STEVE ZABEL**
Tight End • Thornton, Colorado
STEVE OWENS*
Halfback • Miami, Oklahoma
KEN MENDENHALL
Center • Enid, Oklahoma

1968 **STEVE OWENS***
Halfback • Miami, Oklahoma

1967 **GRANVILLE LIGGINS***
Noseguard • Tulsa, Oklahoma
BOB KALSU
Tackle • Del City, Oklahoma

1966 **GRANVILLE LIGGINS**
Noseguard • Tulsa, Oklahoma

1965 **CARL McADAMS***
Linebacker • White Deer, Texas

1964 **CARL McADAMS**
Linebacker • White Deer, Texas
RALPH NEELY*
Tackle • Farmington, New Mexico

1963 **JIM GRISHAM***
Fullback • Olney, Texas
RALPH NEELY
Tackle • Farmington, New Mexico

1962 **LEON CROSS**
Guard • Hobbs, New Mexico
WAYNE LEE
Center • Ada, Oklahoma
JOE DON LOONEY
Halfback • Fort Worth, Texas

1959 **JERRY THOMPSON**
Tackle • Ada, Oklahoma

1958 **BOB HARRISON***
Center • Stamford, Texas

1957 **CLENDON THOMAS***
Halfback • Oklahoma City,
Oklahoma
BILL KRISHER*
Guard • Midwest City, Oklahoma

1956 **JERRY TUBBS***
Center • Breckenridge, Texas
BILL KRISHER
Guard • Midwest City, Oklahoma

TOMMY McDONALD
Halfback •
Albuquerque, New Mexico
ED GRAY
Tackle • Odessa, Texas

1955 **BO BOLINGER***
Guard • Muskogee, Oklahoma
TOMMY McDONALD
Halfback • Albuquerque,
New Mexico

1954 **KURT BURRIS***
Center • Muskogee, Oklahoma
MAX BOYDSTON*
End • Muskogee, Oklahoma

1953 **J.D. ROBERTS***
Guard • Dallas, Texas

1952 **TOM CATLIN**
Center • Ponca City, Oklahoma
EDDIE CROWDER
Quarterback • Muskogee,
Oklahoma
BILLY VESSELS*
Halfback • Cleveland, Oklahoma
BUCK McPHAIL
Fullback • Oklahoma City,
Oklahoma

1951 **JIM WEATHERALL***
Tackle • White Deer, Texas
TOM CATLIN
Center • Ponca City, Oklahoma

1950 **LEON HEATH***
Fullback • Hollis, Oklahoma
JIM WEATHERALL*
Tackle • White Deer, Texas
BUDDY JONES
Safety • Holdenville, Oklahoma
FRANKIE ANDERSON
End • Oklahoma City, Oklahoma

1949 **WADE WALKER**
Tackle • Gastonia, North Carolina
STANLEY WEST
Guard • Enid, Oklahoma
DARRELL ROYAL
Quarterback • Hollis, Oklahoma
JIMMY OWENS
End • Oklahoma City, Oklahoma
GEORGE THOMAS
Halfback • Fairland, Oklahoma

1948 **BUDDY BURRIS***
Guard • Muskogee, Oklahoma
JACK MITCHELL
Quarterback • Arkansas City,
Oklahoma

1947 **BUDDY BURRIS**
Guard • Muskogee, Oklahoma

1946 **BUDDY BURRIS**
Guard • Muskogee, Oklahoma
PLATO ANDROS
Guard • Oklahoma City, Oklahoma
JOHN RAPACZ
Center • Kalamazoo, Michigan

1939 **FRANK "POP" IVY**
End • Skiatook, Oklahoma
GILFORD DUGGAN
Tackle • Davis, Oklahoma

1938 **WALTER YOUNG***
End • Ponca City, Oklahoma

1937 **PETE SMITH**
End • Muskogee, Oklahoma

1935 **J.W. "DUB" WHEELER**
Tackle • Davis, Oklahoma

1934 **CASH GENTRY**
Tackle • Lawton, Oklahoma

1927 **GRANVILLE NORRIS**
Tackle • Laverne, Oklahoma

1920 **PHIL WHITE**
Halfback • Oklahoma City,
Oklahoma
ROY "SOUPY" SMOOT
Tackle • Lawton, Oklahoma

1915 **FOREST "SPOT" GEYER**
Fullback • Norman, Oklahoma

1913 **CLAUDE REEDS**
Fullback • Norman, Oklahoma

(*) **Consensus All-American**

THREE-TIME ALL-AMERICANS
1946-48   Buddy Burris
1972-74   Rod Shoate

TWO-TIME ALL-AMERICANS
1950-51   Jim Weatherall
1951-52   Tom Catlin
1955-56   Tommy McDonald
1956-57   Bill Krisher
1963-64   Ralph Neely
1964-65   Carl McAdams
1966-67   Granville Liggins
1968-69   Steve Owens
1971-72   Greg Pruitt
1971-72   Tom Brahaney
1974-75   Tinker Owens
1974-75   Dewey Selmon
1974-75   Lee Roy Selmon
1974-75   Joe Washington
1975-76   Mike Vaughan
1976-77   Zac Henderson
1977-78   Reggie Kinlaw
1977-78   Greg Roberts
1977 & 79   George Cumby
1977-78   Daryl Hunt
1978 79   Billy Sims
1980-81   Terry Crouch
1982-83   Rick Bryan
1984-85   Tony Casillas
1985-86   Brian Bosworth
1986-87   Keith Jackson
1986 & 88   Anthony Phillips

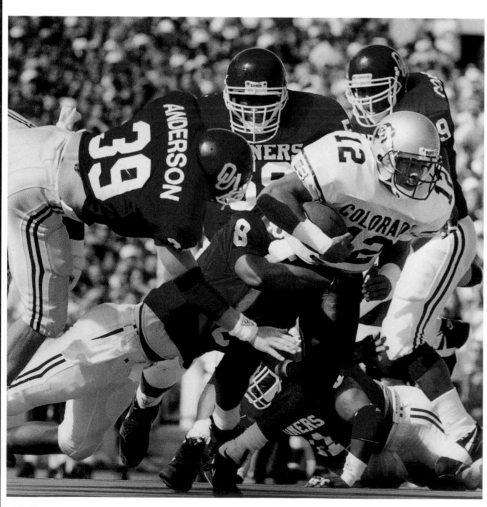

All-Conference
(first team selection only)

MISSOURI VALLEY

- 1907 **Owen Acton,** Back

SOUTHWEST CONFERENCE

- 1915 **Homer Montgomery,** End
  Oliver Hott, Tackle
  Willis Hott, Guard
  Hap Johnson, Back
  Elmer Capshaw, Back
  Forest Geyer, Back

- 1916 **Willis Hott,** Guard

- 1917 **W.E. Durant,** End
  Walt Abbott, Back

- 1919 **Paul Johnston,** Tackle
  Claude Tyler, Guard
  Sol Swatek, Back
  Hugh McDermott, Back

MISSSOURI VALLEY CONFERENCE

- 1920 **Howard Marsh,** End
  Roy Smoot, Tackle
  Bill McKinley, Guard
  Harry Hill, Back
  Sol Swatek, Back

- 1921 **Howard Marsh,** End

- 1922 **Howard Marsh,** End

- 1923 **King Price,** End

- 1924 **Obie Briston,** Back

- 1926 **Roy LeCrone,** End
  Pollack Wallace, Center
  Frank Potts, Back

- 1927 **Roy LeCrone,** End

BIG SIX CONFERENCE

- 1928 **Tom Churchill,** End

- 1929 **Frank Crider,** Back

- 1930 **Hilary Lee,** Guard
  Buster Mills, Back

- 1931 **Charles Teel,** Guard

- 1932 **Ellis Bashara,** Guard
  Bob Dunlap, Back

- 1933 **Cassius Gentry,** Tackle
  Ellis Bashara, Guard
  James Stacy, Guard
  Robert Dunlap, Back

- 1934 **Dub Wheeler,** Tackle
  Cassius Gentry, Tackle
  James Stacy, Guard
  Ben Poyner, Back

- 1935 **Dub Wheeler,** Tackle
  Ralph Brown, Tackle
  Nick Robertson, Back
  Bill Breedon, Back

- 1936 **Ralph Brown,** Tackle
  Red Conkwright, Center

- 1937 **Pete Smith,** End
  Waddy Young, End
  Mickey Parks, Center
  Jack Baer, Back

- 1938 **Waddy Young,** End
  Gilford Duggan, Tackle
  Hugh McCullough, Back
  Earl Crowder, Back

- 1939 **Frank Ivy,** End
  Gilford Duggan, Tackle
  Justin Bowers, Tackle
  Bcryl Clark, Back
  Robert Seymour, Back

- 1940 **Bill Jennings,** End
  Roger Eason, Tackle
  Harold Lahar, Guard
  John Martin, Back

- 1941 **Roger Eason,** Tackle
  Jack Jacobs, Back

- 1942 **W.G. Lamb,** End
  Homer Simmons, Tackle
  Clare Morford, Guard
  Jack Marsee, Center
  William Campbell, Back
  Huel Hamm, Back

- 1943 **W.G. Lamb,** End
  Lee Kennon, Tackle
  Gale Fulgham, Guard
  Bob Mayfield, Center
  Bob Brumley, Back
  Derald Lebow, Back

- 1944 **W.G. Wooten,** End
  John Harley, Tackle
  Bob Mayfield, Center
  Merle Dinkins, End

- 1945 **Omer Burgert,** End
  Thomas Tallchief, Tackle
  Lester Jensen, Guard
  John West, Back
  Jack Venable, Back

- 1946 **Warren Geise,** End
  Homer Paine, Tackle
  Wade Walker, Tackle
  Buddy Burris, Guard
  Plato Andros, Guard
  John Rapacz, Center
  Joe Golding, Back

- 1947 **Jim Tyree,** End
  Wade Walker, Tackle
  Buddy Burris, Guard
  John Rapacz, Center
  Jack Mitchell, Back

BIG SEVEN CONFERENCE

- 1948 **Jim Owens,** End
  Wade Walker, Tackle
  Homer Paine, Tackle
  Buddy Burris, Guard
  Jack Mitchell, Back
  George Thomas, Back

- 1949 **Jim Owens,** End
  Wade Walker, Tackle
  Stan West, Guard
  Darrell Royal, Back
  George Thomas, Back

- 1950 **Frankie Anderson,** End
  Jim Weatherall, Tackle
  Norman McNabb, Guard
  Harry Moore, Center
  Tom Catlin, Center
  Claude Arnold, Back
  Billy Vessels, Back
  Leon Heath, Back

- 1951 **Art Janes,** Tackle
  Jim Weatherall, Tackle
  Roger Nelson, Guard
  Bert Clark, Guard
  Fred Smith, Guard
  Tom Catlin, Center
  Eddie Crowder, Back
  Larry Grigg, Back
  Buck McPhail, Back

- 1952 **Max Boydston,** End
  Ed Rowland, Tackle
  Jim Davis, Tackle
  J.D. Roberts, Guard
  Tom Catlin, Center
  Eddie Crowder, Back
  Billy Vessels, Back
  Buck McPhail, Back

- 1953 **Max Boydston,** End
  Roger Nelson, Tackle
  J.D. Roberts, Guard
  Kurt Burris, Center
  Gene Calame, Back
  Larry Grigg, Back

- 1954 **Max Boydston,** End
  Carl Allison, End
  Bo Bolinger, Guard
  Kurt Burris, Center
  Buddy Leake, Back
  Gene Calame, Back

- 1955 **Ed Gray,** Tackle
  Cal Woodworth, Tackle
  Bo Bolinger, Guard
  Cecil Morris, Guard
  Jerry Tubbs, Center
  Tommy McDonald, Back
  Bob Burris, Back

- 1956 **John Bell,** End
  Ed Gray, Tackle
  Tom Emerson, Tackle
  Bill Krisher, Guard
  Jerry Tubbs, Center
  Tommy McDonald, Back
  Clendon Thomas, Back

- 1957 **Don Stiller,** End
  Ross Coyle, End
  Bill Krisher, Guard
  Clendon Thomas, Back

BIG EIGHT CONFERENCE

- 1958 **Ross Coyle,** End
  Steve Jennings, Tackle
  Gilmer Lewis, Tackle
  Dick Corbitt, Guard
  Bob Harrison, Center
  Prentice Gautt, Back

- 1959 **Jerry Thompson,** Guard
  Bobby Boyd, Back
  Prentice Gautt, Back

- 1960 **Billy White,** Tackle

- 1961 **Billy White,** Tackle

- 1962 **Dennis Ward,** Tackle
  Wayne Lee, Center
  Jim Grisham, Back
  Joe Don Looney, Back

- 1963 **John Flynn,** End
  Ralph Neely, Tackle
  Newt Burton, Guard
  Jim Grisham, Back

- 1964 **Ralph Neely,** Tackle
  Newt Burton, Guard
  Jim Grisham, Back
  Carl McAdams, Linebacker

- 1965 **Carl McAdams,** Linebacker

- 1966 **Ben Hart,** Split End
  Ed Hall, Offensive Tackle
  Eugene Ross, Linebacker

- 1967 **Bob Kalsu,** Offensive Tackle
  Steve Owens, Running Back
  Bob Warmack, Quarterback
  John Koller, Defensive End
  Granville Liggins, Noseguard

- 1968 **Steve Zabel,** Tight End
  Ken Mendenhall,
    Offensive Guard
  Eddie Hinton, Wingback
  Steve Barrett, Defensive Back

- 1969 **Steve Zabel,** Tight End
  Ken Mendenhall,
    Offensive Guard
  Bill Elfstrom, Offensive Guard
  Steve Owens, Running Back

- 1970 **Joe Wylie,** Running Back
  Steve Aycock, Linebacker
  Monty Johnson,
    Defensive Back

- 1971 **Albert Chandler,** Tight End
  Ken Jones, Offensive Guard
  Tom Brahaney, Center
  Jack Mildren, Quarterback
  Greg Pruitt, Running Back
  Raymond Hamilton,
    Defensive End
  Derland Moore,
    Defensive Tackle
  Steve Aycock, Linebacker
  John Shelley, Defensive Back

- 1972 **Dean Unruh,** Offensive Tackle
  Tom Brahaney, Center
  Greg Pruitt, Running Back
  Leon Crosswhite, Fullback
  Derland Moore,
    Defensive Tackle
  Lucious Selmon,
    Defensive Tackle
  Raymond Hamilton,
    Defensive Tackle
  Rod Shoate, Linebacker

- 1973 **John Roush,** Offensive Guard
  Joe Washington,
    Running Back
  Gary Baccus, Defensive End
  Lucious Selmon,
    Defensive Tackle
  Rod Shoate, Linebacker
  Randy Hughes,
    Defensive Back

- 1974 **Wayne Hoffman,** Tight End
  Tinker Owens, Split End
  Jerry Arnold, Offensive Tackle
  John Roush, Offensive Guard
  Terry Webb, Offensive Guard
  Joe Washington,
    Running Back
  Jimbo Elrod, Defensive End
  Dewey Selmon,
    Defensive Tackle
  Lee Roy Selmon,
    Defensive Tackle
  Rod Shoate, Linebacker
  Randy Hughes,
    Defensive Back

- 1975 **Mike Vaughan,**
    Offensive Tackle
  Terry Webb, Offensive Guard
  Joe Washington,
    Running Back
  Tony DiRienzo, Kicker
  Jimbo Elrod, Defensive End
  Dewey Selmon, Middle Guard
  Zac Henderson,
    Defensive Back

- 1976 **Mike Vaughan,**
    Offensive Tackle
  Daryl Hunt, Linebacker
  Zac Henderson,
    Defensive Back
  Scott Hill, Defensive Back

- 1977 **Karl Baldischwiler,**
    Offensive Tackle
  Greg Roberts,
    Offensive Guard
  Thomas Lott, Quarterback
  Reggie Kinlaw, Noseguard
  George Cumby, Linebacker
  Daryl Hunt, Linebacker
  Zac Henderson,
    Defensive Back

- 1978 **Greg Roberts,**
    Offensive Guard
  Thomas Lott, Quarterback
  Billy Sims, Running Back
  Uwe von Schamann, Kicker
  Reggie Mathis, Defensive End
  Phil Tabor, Defensive Tackle
  Reggie Kinlaw, Noseguard
  Daryl Hunt, Linebacker
  George Cumby, Linebacker
  Darrol Ray, Defensive Tackle

- 1979 **Louis Oubre,** Offensive Tackle
  Paul Tabor, Center
  Billy Sims, Running Back
  John Goodman,
    Defensive Tackle
  George Cumby, Linebacker
  Darrol Ray, Defensive Back

- 1980 **Forrest Valora,** Tight End
  Louis Oubre, Offensive Tackle
  Terry Crouch,
    Offensive Guard
  Richard Turner,
    Defensive Tackle

- 1981 **Lyndle Byford,**
    Offensive Tackle
  Terry Crouch,
    Offensive Guard
  Don Key, Offensive Guard
  Stanley Wilson,
    Running Back
  Rick Bryan, Defensive Tackle

- 1982 **Steve Williams,**
    Offensive Guard
  Paul Parker, Offensive Guard
  Marcus Dupree,
    Running Back
  Kevin Murphy, Defensive End
  Rick Bryan, Defensive Tackle
  Jackie Shipp, Linebacker

- 1983 **Chuck Thomas,** Center
  Kevin Murphy, Defensive End

Rick Bryan, Defensive Tackle
Jackie Shipp, Linebacker
Scott Case, Defensive Back

• 1984 **Danny Bradley,** Quarterback
Darrell Reed, Defensive End
Tony Casillas, Noseguard
Brian Bosworth, Linebacker

• 1985 **Jamelle Holieway,**
Quarterback
Anthony Phillips,
Offensive Tackle
Mark Hutson, Offensive Guard
Keith Jackson, Tight End
Darrell Reed, Defensive End
Kevin Murphy, Defensive End
Tony Casillas, Noseguard
Brian Bosworth, Linebacker

• 1986 **Jamelle Holieway,**
Quarterback
Anthony Phillips,
Offensive Tackle
Mark Hutson, Offensive Guard
Keith Jackson, Tight End
Tim Lashar, Kicker
Brian Bosworth, Linebacker
Darrell Reed, Defensive End
David Vickers, Defensive Back
Steve Bryan, Defensive Tackle
Rickey Dixon, Defensive Back

• 1987 **Mark Hutson,** Offensive Guard
Keith Jackson, Tight End
Greg Johnson,
Offensive Tackle
Bob Latham, Center
Anthony Phillips,
Offensive Guard

Rickey Dixon, Defensive Back
Danté Jones, Linebacker
Darrell Reed, Defensive End
David Vickers, Defensive Back

• 1988 **Anthony Phillips,**
Offensive Guard
Charles Thompson,
Quarterback
Scott Evans, Defensive Tackle
Scott Garl, Defensive Back
Curtice Williams,
Defensive Tackle
Tony Woods, Noseguard

• 1989 **Frank Blevins,** Linebacker
Scott Evans, Defensive Tackle
Dante Williams, Noseguard

• 1990 **Adrian Cooper,** Tight End
Mike Sawatzky,
Offensive Guard
Scott Evans, Defensive Tackle
Joe Bowden, Linebacker
Jason Belser, Defensive Back

• 1991 **Reggie Barnes,** Defensive End
Jason Belser, Defensive Back
Joe Bowden, Linebacker
Brian Brauninger,
Offensive Tackle
Mike Gaddis, Running Back

• 1992 **Darnell Walker,**
Defensive Back

• 1993 **Aubrey Beavers,** Linebacker
Rickey Brady, Tight End
Mario Freeman, Linebacker
Cale Gundy, Quarterback

• 1994 **Cedric Jones,** Defensive End
Darrius Johnson,
Defensive Back
Scott Blanton, Kicker

FOUR-TIME ALL CONFERENCE

1946-49	Wade Walker
1984-87	Darrell Reed
1985-88	Anthony Phillips

THREE-TIME ALL-CONFERENCE

1920-22	Howard Marsh
1946-48	Buddy Burris
1950-52	Tom Catlin
1952-54	Max Boydston
1962-64	Jim Grisham
1967-69	Steve Owens
1972-74	Rod Shoate
1973-75	Joe Washington
1975-77	Zac Henderson
1976-78	Daryl Hunt
1977-79	George Cumby
1981-83	Rick Bryan
1982, 83, 85	Kevin Murphy
1984-86	Brian Bosworth
1985-87	Mark Hutson
1985-87	Keith Jackson
1988-90	Scott Evans

NOTE: 75 other Sooners have been named All-Conference twice

Individual Honors
(1895-1994)

HEISMAN MEMORIAL TROPHY
(Player of the Year)

1952	**Billy Vessels**, Halfback, Cleveland, Oklahoma
1969	**Steve Owens**, Tailback, Miami, Oklahoma
1978	**Billy Sims**, Halfback, Hooks, Texas

MAXWELL MEMORIAL AWARD
(Player of the Year)

1956   **Tommy McDonald,** Halfback, Albuquerque, N.M.

WALTER CAMP TROPHY
(Player of the Year)

1956   **Jerry Tubbs**, Center, Breckenridge, Texas
1969   **Steve Owens**, Tailback, Miami, Oklahoma
1978   **Billy Sims**, Halfback, Hooks, Texas

DICK BUTKUS AWARD
(Outstanding Linebacker)

1985   **Brian Bosworth**, Linebacker, Irving, Texas
1986   **Brian Bosworth**, Linebacker, Irving, Texas

VINCE LOMBARDI AWARD
(Outstanding Lineman)

1975   **Lee Roy Selmon**, Tackle, Eufaula, Oklahoma
1985   **Tony Casillas**, Noseguard, Tulsa, Oklahoma

HELMS AND CITIZENS SAVINGS ATHLETIC FOUNDATION
(Player of the Year)

1954   **Kurt Burris**, Center, Muskogee, Oklahoma
1969   **Steve Owens**. Tailback, Miami, Oklahoma
1978   **Billy Sims**, Halfback, Hooks, Texas

SPORTING NEWS AWARD
(Player of the Year)

1956   **Tommy McDonald**, Halfback, Albuquerque, N.M.

FOOTBALL NEWS
(Freshman of the Year)

1982   **Marcus Dupree**, Tailback, Philadelphia, Miss.

JIM THORPE AWARD
(Outstanding Defensive Back)

1987   **Rickey Dixon**, Safety, Dallas, Texas

OUTLAND TROPHY
(Outstanding Lineman)

1951   **Jim Weatherall**, Tackle, White Deer, Texas

1953	**J.D. Roberts**, Guard, Dallas, Texas
1975	**Lee Roy Selmon**, Tackle, Eufaula, Oklahoma
1978	**Greg Roberts**, Offensive Guard Nacogdoches, Texas

WASHINGTON, D.C., PLAYER OF THE YEAR

| 1972 | **Greg Pruitt**, Halfback, Houston, Texas |
| 1974 | **Joe Washington**, Halfback, Port Arthur, Texas |

CHEVROLET ABC OFFENSIVE PLAYER OF THE YEAR

| 1971 | **Jack Mildren**, Quarterback, Abilene, Texas |

CHEVEROLET ABC DEFENSIVE PLAYER OF THE YEAR

| 1973 | **Lucious Selmon**, Noseguard, Eufaula, Oklahoma |

LINEMAN OF THE YEAR

1953	**J.D. Roberts,** Guard, Dallas, Texas (AP, UPI, Fox Movietime News)
1954	**Kurt Burris,** Center, Muskogee, Oklahoma (Philadelphia Sports Writers)
1954	**Max Boydston**, End, Muskogee, Oklahoma (Washington Touchdown Club)
1956	**Jerry Tubbs,** Center, Breckenridge, Texas (UPI)

1958	**Bob Harrison,** Center, Samford, Texas (UPI)
1967	**Granville Liggins**, Noseguard Tulsa, Oklahoma (UPI)
1985	**Tony Casillas**. Noseguard, Tulsa, Oklahoma (UPI)

NATIONAL FOOTBALL HALL OF FAME

1961	**Claude Reeds**, Fullback, Norman, Oklahoma
1973	**Forrest "Spot" Geyer** Fullback Norman, Oklahoma
1974	**Billy Vessels,** Halfback, Cleveland, Oklahoma
1982	**Jim Owens**, End, Oklahoma City, Okla.
1985	**Tommy McDonald**, Halfback Albuquerque, N.M.
1986	**Walter Young**, End, Ponca City, Oklahoma
1988	**Lee Roy Selmon,** Defensive Tackle, Eufaula, Oklahoma
1991	**Steve Owens**, Halfback, Miami, Oklahoma
1992	**Jim Weatherall,** Tackle, White Deer, Texas
1993	**J.D. Roberts**, Guard, Dallas, Texas

NATIONAL FOOTBAL COACHES HALL OF FAME

| 1951 | **Bennie Owen**, 1905-26 |
| 1969 | **Bud Wilkinson**, 1947-63 |

HELMS AND CITIZENS SAVINGS ATHLETIC FOUNDATION HALL OF FAME

1969	**Buddy Burris**, Guard 1946-48
1975	**Jim Weatherall**, Tackle 1949-51
1975	**Greg Pruitt**, Halfback 1970-72

HELMS AND CITIZENS SAVINGS ATHLETIC COACHES HALL OF FAME

| 1969 | **Bennie Owen,** 1905-26 |
| 1969 | **Bud Wilkinson,** 1947-63 |

NCAA FOOTBALL PLAYER OF THE YEAR
(Selected by Washington, D.C., Pigskin Club)

| 1972 | **Greg Pruitt,** Halfback, Houston, Texas |
| 1974 | **Joe Washington**, Halfback, Port Arthur, Texas |

NEW YORK ATHLETIC CLUB DEFENSIVE BACK OF THE YEAR

| 1977 | **Zac Henderson,** Free Safety, Burkburnett, Texas |

DAVEY O'BRIEN AWARD

| 1978 | **Billy Sims,** Halfback, Hooks, Texas |

NCAA TOP SIX AWARD

| 1987 | **Keith Jackson,** Tight End, Little Rock, Ark. |
| 1988 | **Anthony Phillips**, Offensive Guard, Tulsa, Okla. |

Individual Records
(1895-1994)

RUSHING

MOST RUSHES
Game: 55, Steve Owens vs. Oklahoma State, 1969
Season: 358, Steve Owens, 1969
Career: 905, Steve Owens, 1967-69

RUSHING YARDAGE
Game: 294, Greg Pruitt vs. Kansas State, 1971
Season: 1762, Billy Sims, 1978
Career: 3995, Joe Washington, 1972-75

YARDS PER ATTEMPT
Game: 26.8 (6-161), Eric Mitchel vs. Kansas State, 1988
Season: 9.41, Greg Pruitt, 1971 (NCAA Record)

200-YARD GAMES
Season: 4, Billy Sims, 1978
Career: 6, Billy Sims, 1975-79

RUSHING YARDS BY A FRESHMAN
Game: 259, Earl Johnson vs. Colorado, 1983
Season: 1047, Spencer Tillman, 1983 (redshirt)
        905, Marcus Dupree, 1982 (true)

YARDS RUSHING BY A QUARTERBACK
Game: 162, Jamelle Holieway vs. Kansas, 1985
Season: 1140, Jack Mildren, 1971
Career: 2699, Jamelle Holieway, 1985-88

RUSHING TOUCHDOWNS
Game: 5, Steve Owens vs. Nebraska, 1969
        5, Jerald Moore vs. Oklahoma State, 1994
Season: 23, Steve Owens, 1969
Career: 56, Steve Owens, 1967-69

ALL-PURPOSE RUNNING YARDS
Game: 374, Greg Pruitt vs. Kansas State, 1971 (294 Rushing, 34 Receiving, 46 Return Yards)
Season: 1940, Greg Pruitt, 1971 (1665 Rushing, 103 Receiving, 172 Return Yards)
Career: 5784, Joe Washington, 1972-75 (3995 Rushing, 254 Receiving, 1535 Return Yards)

PASSING

MOST PASS ATTEMPTS
Game: 45, Garrick McGee vs. Kansas State, 1994
Season: 284, Garrick McGee, 1994

Career: 751, Cale Gundy, 1990-93

PASS COMPLETIONS
Game: 25, Cale Gundy vs. Virginia, 1991
Season: 149, Garrick McGee, 1994
Career: 420, Cale Gundy, 1990-93

COMPLETION PERCENTAGE
Game: 1.000 (9-9), Jack Jacobs vs. Kansas, 1941
Season: .708, (17-24), Tommy McDonald, 1955

Career: .559, (420-751), Cale Gundy, 1990-93

PASSES HAD INTERCEPTED
Game: 5, Jack Jacobs vs. Kansas State, 1940
Season: 15, Cale Gundy, 1992
Career: 31, Cale Gundy, 1990-93

LOWEST INTERCEPTION PERCENTAGE
Season: .000, Monte Deere, 1960
Career: .036, Bob Warmack, 1966-68

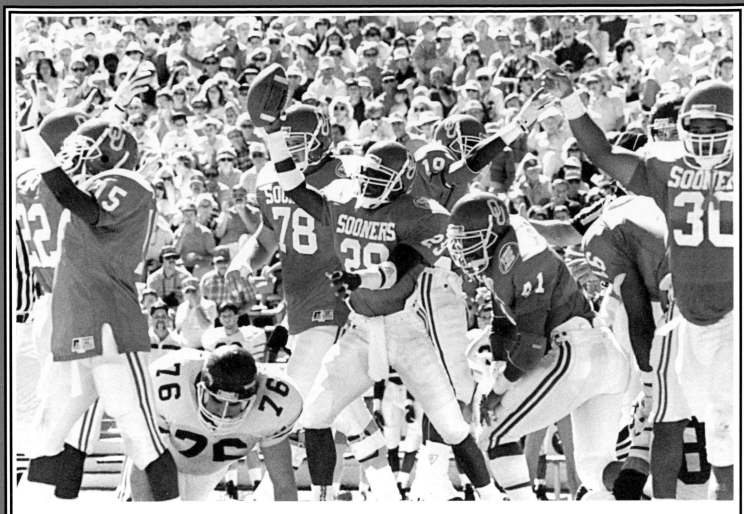

MOST YARDS PASSING
Game: 341, Cale Gundy vs. Texas
        Tech, 1992
Season: 2096, Cale Gundy, 1993
Career: 6142, Cale Gundy, 1990-93

300-YARD GAMES
Season: 2, Cale Gundy, 1992 & 1993
Career: 5, Cale Gundy, 1990-93

TOUCHDOWN PASSES
Game: 4, Claude Arnold vs. Kansas,
        1950
        4, Eddie Crowder vs. Colorado,
        1951
Season: 14, Cale Gundy, 1993
Career: 35, Cale Gundy, 1990-93

TOTAL OFFENSE

MOST TOTAL OFFENSE YARDS
Game: 351, Cale Gundy vs. Iowa State,
        1992 (333 Passing, 18 Rushing)
Season: 2291, Cale Gundy, 1993 (2096
        Passing, 195 Rushing)
Career: 6389, Cale Gundy, 1990-93 (6142
        Passing, 247 Rushing)

PASS RECEIVING

MOST PASSES CAUGHT
Game: 10, Gordon Brown vs.
        Oklahoma State, 1965

10, Eddie Hinton vs. Oklahoma
State, 1968
Season: 60, Eddie Hinton, 1968
Career: 114, Eddie Hinton, 1966-68

MOST YARDS GAINED
Game: 187, Corey Warren vs. Texas,
        1992
Season: 967, Eddie Hinton, 1968
Career: 1735, Eddie Hinton, 1966-68

YARDS PER RECEPTION
Season: 29.1, Jon Harrison, 1971
Career: 27.4, Jon Harrison, 1970-71

MOST TOUCHDOWN PASSES CAUGHT
Season: 6, Eddie Hinton, 1968
Career: 13, Keith Jackson, 1984-87

PUNTING

MOST PUNTS
Game: 18, Jack Jacobs vs. Santa Clara,
        1941
Season: 49, Michael Keeling, 1982
        49, Brad Reddell, 1992
Career: 185, Brad Reddell, 1989-92

BEST PUNTING AVERAGE
Game: 56.3, Michael Keeling vs.
        Kansas, 1981
Season: 50.2, Joe Washington, 1975
Career: 42.3, Jack Jacobs, 1939-41

PUNT RETURNS

MOST PUNT RETURNS
Game: 8, Jack Jacobs vs. Santa Clara,
        1941
Season: 34, Darrius Johnson, 1994
Career: 88, Joe Washington, 1972-75

MOST PUNT RETURN YARDS
Season: 515, Jack Mitchell, 1948
Career: 922, Jack Mitchell, 1946-48

BEST PUNT RETURN AVERAGE
Season: 45.0, Merrill Green, 1953
Career: 23.4, Jack Mitchell, 1946-48

KICKOFF RETURNS

MOST KICKOFF RETURNS
Game: 6, Basil Banks vs. Colorado,
        1980
Season: 18, Everette Marshall, 1969
Career: 48, Buster Rhymes, 1980-84

MOST KICKOFF RETURN YARDS
Season: 386, Everette Marshall, 1969
Career: 1037, Buster Rhymes, 1980-84

BEST KICKOFF RETURN AVERAGE
Season: 35.5, Buster Rhymes, 1980
Career: 25.9, Lance Rentzel, 1962-64

SCORING

MOST POINTS
Game: 30, Steve Owens vs. Nebraska, 1968
30, Jerald Moore vs. Oklahoma State, 1994
Season: 138, Steve Owens, 1969
Career: 336, Steve Owens, 1967-69

MOST TOUCHDOWNS
Game: 5, Steve Owens vs. Nebraska, 1968
5, Jerald Moore, vs. Oklahoma State, 1994
Season: 23, Steve Owens, 1969
Career: 56, Steve Owens, 1967-69

MOST EXTRA POINTS MADE
Game: 11, Tim Lashar vs. Missouri, 1986
Season: 60, Tim Lashar, 1986
Career: 194, R.D. Lashar, 1987-90

MOST EXTRA POINTS ATTEMPTED
Game: 11, Tim Lashar vs. Missouri, 1986
Season: 62, John Carroll, 1971
Career: 213, R.D. Lashar, 1987-90

MOST CONSECUTIVE EXTRA POINTS
Season: 60, Tim Lashar, 1985
Career: 135, Tim Lashar, 1983-86

MOST FIELD GOALS
Game: 4, Mike Vachon vs. Texas, 1966
4, Tim Lashar vs. Penn State, 1985 Orange Bowl and vs. Oklahoma State, 1986
Season: 16, Scott Blanton, 1992
Career: 43, Tim Lashar, 1983-86

MOST POINTS BY A KICKER
Season: 96, Tim Lashar, 1986
Career: 320, R.D. Lashar, 1987-90

DEFENSE

TOTAL TACKLES
Game: 22, Brian Bosworth vs. Miami, 1986
Season: 182, Jackie Shipp, 1981
Career: 506, Daryl Hunt, 1975-78

TACKLES BY A LINEMAN
Game: 17, Dewey Selmon vs. Texas, 1974
Season: 144, Kevin Murphy, 1983
Career: 352, Rick Bryan, 1980-83

TACKLES BY A DEFENSIVE BACK
Game: 21, John Anderson vs. Missouri, 1993
Season: 97, Monty Johnson, 1970
Career: 291, Zac Henderson, 1974-77

TACKLES FOR LOSS
Game: 4, Lucious Selmon vs. Kansas, 1973
Season: 20, Jimbo Elrod, 1975
Career: 44, Jimbo Elrod, 1973-75

INTERCEPTIONS
Season: 8, Rickey Dixon, 1987
8, Scott Case, 1983
Career: 17, Darrell Royal, 1946-49

SACKS
Season: 14, Cedric Jones, 1994
Career: 24, Scott Evans, 1987-90

Team Records
(1895-1994)

RUSHING

MOST RUSHES
Game: 88 vs. Oklahoma State, 1972
Season: 813 in 1974
Per Game: 73.9 in 1974

MOST RUSHING YARDS
Game: 768 vs. Kansas Stae, 1988
Season: 5196 in 1971

RUSHING YARDS PER ATTEMPT
Game: 10.6 (72-768) vs. Kansas State, 1988
Season: 7.3 (710-5196) in 1971

PASSING

MOST ATTEMPTS
Game: 45 vs. Kansas State, 1994
Season: 288 in 1994
Per Game: 26.2 in 1994

MOST COMPLETIONS
Game: 27 vs. Virginia, 1991 (Gator Bowl)
Season: 158 in 1992
Per Game: 14.3 in 1992

FEWEST ATTEMPTS
Season: 58, 1976
Per Game: 5.3, 1976

FEWEST COMPLETIONS
Game: 0, Several Times (last vs. Arizona, 1989)
Season: 21, 1976
Per Game: 1.9, 1976

MOST YARDS PASSING
Game: 357 vs. Virginia, 1992 (Gator Bowl)
Season: 2214 in 1992
Per Game: 201.3 in 1992

COMPLETION PERCENTAGE
Game: 1.000, several times
Season: 58.4 in 1993

MOST YARDS PER ATTEMPT
(Minimum 5 attempts)
Game: 25.7 vs. Colorado, 1962
Season: 13.2 in 1971

MOST YARDS PER COMPLETION
Game: 36.1 vs. Colorado, 1962
Season: 27.3 in 1971

MOST PASSES INTERCEPTED
Game: 5 vs. Kansas State, 1969
Season: 17 in 1992

OFFENSE

TOTAL OFFENSE
Game: 875 vs. Colorado, 1980
Season: 6232 in 1971
Per Game: 566.5 in 1971

MOST PLAYS
Season: 953 in1972
Per Game: 86.6 in 1972

YARDS PER PLAY
Game: 10.9 vs. Colorado, 1980
Season: 7.9, 1971

FEWEST TURNOVERS
Game: 0, several times (last vs. Oklahoma State, 1994)
Season: 16 in 1993
Per Game: 1.5 in 1993

SCORING
Game: 82 vs. Colorado, 1980
Season: 494 in 1971
Per Game: 44.9 in 1971

MOST TOUCHDOWNS
Game: 12 vs. Colorado, 1980
Season: 66 in 1971
Per Game: 6.0 in 1971

MOST RUSHING TOUCHDOWNS
Game: 12 vs. Colorado, 1980
Season: 58 in 1957
Per Game: 5.8 in1957

MOST PASSING TOUCHDOWNS
Game: 4 vs. Colorado 1951, vs. Kansas, 1950
Season: 14 in 1993
Per Game: 1.3 in 1993

FIELD GOALS
Game: 4 vs. Texas, 1966; vs. Penn State, 1986; vs. Oklahoma State, 1986
Season: 16 in 1992
Per Game: 1.45 in 1992

FIELD GOAL PERCENTAGE
Game: 1.000, several times
Season: 88.9 in 1992

MOST EXTRA POINTS
Game: 11 vs. Missouri, 1986
Season: 60 in 1986

EXTRA POINT PERCENTAGE
Game: 1.000, several times (last vs. Kansas, 1994, 2-2)
Season: 1.000, several times (last in 1990, 45-45)

SPECIAL TEAMS

MOST PUNTS
Game: 18 vs. Santa Clara, 1941
Season: 58 in 1994

PUNTING AVERAGE
Game: 56.3 vs. Kansas State, 1981
Season: 43.0 in 1982

MOST PUNT RETURN YARDS
Game: 227 vs. Kansas State, 1948
Season: 963 in 1948
Per Game: 57.1 in 1971

MOST KICKOFF RETURN YARDS
Game: 207 vs. Santa Clara, 1941
Season: 629 in 1971
Per Game: 57.1 in 1971

RUSHING DEFENSE

FEWEST RUSHING YARDS ALLOWED
Game: -52 vs. Kansas State, 1986
Season: 668 in 1986
Per Game: 60.7 in 1986

FEWEST RUSHING ATTEMPTS
Season: 387, 1984
Per Game: 35.1, 1984

FEWEST RUSHING YARDS PER ATTEMPT
Season: 1.6, 1986

PASSING DEFENSE

FEWEST PASSING YARDS ALLOWED
Game: -2 vs. Oklahoma State, 1993
Season: 555 in 1956
Per Game: 55.5 in 1956

FEWEST PASSING ATTEMPTS
Season: 47 in 1960
Per Game: 4.7 in 1960

MOST SACKS
Game: 7 vs. Texas, 1989
Season: 40 in 1989
Per Game: 3.6 in 1989

SCORING DEFENSE

FEWEST POINTS ALLOWED
Game: 0, several times (last vs. Oklahoma State, 1993)
Season: 29 in 1938
Per Game: 2.6 in 1938

FEWEST TOUCHDOWNS ALLOWED
Game: 0, several times (last vs. Oklahoma State, 1993)
Season: 29 in 1938
Per Game: 2.6 in 1938

FEWEST TOUCDOWNS ALLOWED
Game: 0, several times (last vs. Oklahoma State, 1993)
Season: 2 in 1938
Per Game: 0.5 in 1938

Longest Plays in Sooner History

FROM SCRIMMAGE – ALL PLAYS

Yds	Player	Type Play	Opponent
100	Al Needs	Int. Return	Kansas State, 1945
100	Buster Rhymes	Kickoff Return	Kansas State, 1980
99	Jerome Ledbetter	Kickoff Return	Colorado, 1980
99	Joe Golding	Int. Return	Texas, 1946
96	Buck McPhail	Run	Kansas State, 1951
96	Darrell Royal	Punt Return	Kansas State, 1948
95	Jerome Ledbetter	Kickoff Return	Oklahoma State, 1980
95	Randy Hughes	Int. Return	Colorado, 1973
95	Rickey Dixon	Int. Return	Oklahoma State, 1987
95	Ben Hart from Ronnie Fletcher	Pass	Florida State, 1965
94	Eddie Johnson	Int. Return	Oklahoma State, 1923
94	David Baker	Int. Return	Duke, 1958
93	Eddie Hinton	Punt Return	Colorado, 1966
91	Jimmy Harris	Run	Kansas, 1954
91	Tommy McDonald	Punt Return	Iowa State, 1955
90	George Thomas	Run	Oklahoma State, 1949
90	Mike Thomas	Run	Oregon, 1972
90	Lance Rentzel from John Hammond	Pass	Maryland, 1964
90	Obie Bristow	Int. Return	Kansas State, 1923
89	Darrell Shepard	Run	Colorado, 1980
88	Keith Jackson	Run	Nebraska, 1985
87	Darrius Johnson	Punt Return	Missouri, 1994
87	Max Boydston from Buddy Leake	Pass	California, 1954
86	Wahoo McDaniel from Bobby Boyd	Pass	West Virginia, 1958
86	Leon Heath	Run	Louisiana State, 1950
86	Marcus Dupree	Run	Nebraska, 1982
86	Anthony Stafford	Run	Texas, 1988
85	Eric Mitchell	Run	Kansas State, 1988
85	George Thomas	Run	Iowa State, 1947
85	Ed Kreick	Run	Iowa State, 1947
85	Freddie Nixon	Punt Return	Iowa State, 1977
84	David Overstreet	Run	Colorado, 1980
84	Elvis Peacock	Run	Oklahoma State, 1976
84	Joe Don Looney	Run	Colorado, 1962

FROM SCRIMMAGE – RUNS

Yds	Player	Opponent
96	Buck McPhail	Kansas State, 1951
91	Jimmy Harris	Kansas, 1954
90	George Thomas	Oklahoma State, 1949
90	Mike Thomas	Oregon, 1972
89	Darrell Shepard	Colorado, 1980
88	Keith Jackson	Nebraska, 1985
86	Leon Heath	Louisiana State, 1950
86	Marcus Dupree	Nebraska, 1982
86	Anthony Stafford	Texas, 1988
85	Eric Mitchell	Kansas State, 1988
85	George Thomas	Iowa State, 1947
85	Ed Kreick	Iowa State, 1947
84	David Overstreet	Colorado, 1980
84	Elvis Peacock	Oklahoma State, 1976
84	Joe Don Looney	Colorado, 1962
82	George Thomas	Santa Clara, 1948
82	Anthony Stafford	Missouri, 1986
82	Eric Mitchell	Kansas State, 1987

FROM SCRIMMAGE – PASS

Yds	Player	Opponent
95	Ben Hart from Ronnie Fletcher	Florida State, 1965
90	Lance Rentzel from John Hammond	Maryland, 1964
87	Max Boydston from Buddy Leake	California, 1954
86	Wahoo McDaniel from Bobby Boyd	West Virginia, 1958
83	Virgil Boll from Monte Deere	Colorado, 1962
82	Arthur Guess from Steve Collins	Nebraska, 1989
80	Larry Grigg from Buddy Leake	Pittsburgh, 1953
80	Ted Long from Cale Gundy	Colorado, 1990
79	Ross Coyle from B. Hobby	Syracuse, 1959
77	Joe Killingsworth from Jack Mildren	Kansas State, 1969
77	Derrick Shepard from J. Holieway	Iowa State, 1985
75	Steve Zabel from Bob Warmack	Iowa State, 1967
75	Willie Franklin from Jack Mildren	Iowa State, 1970

FIELD GOALS

Yds	Player	Opponent
60	Tony DiRienzo	Kansas, 1973
58	Uwe von Schamann	Oklahoma State, 1977
54	R.D. Lashar	Missouri, 1990
54	Uwe von Schamann	Colorado, 1976
54	Uwe von Schamann	Missouri, 1978
53	R.D. Lashar	Tulsa, 1987
52	Scott Blanton	Texas, 1992
52	Scott Blanton	Iowa State, 1993
51	Bruce Derr	Oklahoma State, 1970
49	R.D. Lashar	Tulsa, 1990
49	R.D. Lashar	Oklahoma State, 1989
49	Michael Keeling	Houston, 1981
49	Bruce Derr	Oklahoma State, 1970

PUNTS

Yds	Player	Opponent
91	Wahoo McDaniel	Iowa State, 1958
87	Joe Wylie	Kansas State, 1970
78	Michael Keeling	Kansas, 1981
78	Scott Blanton	Texas Tech, 1993
78	Todd Thomsen	Iowa State, 1987
76	Joe Washington	Texas, 1975
74	John Carroll	Oklahoma State, 1974
72	Michael Keeling	Kentucky, 1982
72	Michael Keeling	Iowa State, 1980
70	Michael Keeling	Kansas, 1980
69	Todd Thomsen	Oklahoma State, 1988
69	Clendon Thomas	Duke, 1958
107	Claude Reeds	1910 (NOTE: Field was 110 yards at that time)

OPPONENTS' LONGEST PLAYS

Yds	Player	Type of Play	Team
100	Mack Heron	Kickoff Return	Kansas State, 1968
95	Willie Jones	Kickoff Return	Iowa State, 1971
93	Gale Sayers	Kickoff Return	Kansas, 1964
92	Charles Johnson from Koy Detmer	Pass	Colorado, 1992
89	Greg Washington from Carl Straw	Pass	Kansas State, 1988
89	Jarvis Redwine	Run	Nebraska, 1980
85	Sam Smith from Darian Hagan	Pass	Colorado, 1990
84	Ben Kirkpatrick	PAT Return	Texas Tech, 1992
82	Mike Clark	Punt Return	Oklahoma State, 1989
82	Tom Busch from Tim Van Galder	Pass	Iowa State, 1965
80	Willie Vaughn from Kelly Donohoe	Pass	Kansas, 1988
79	Ryan Mitchell	Run	Miami, 1973
78	Marvin Harrison from Kevin Mason	Pass	Syracuse, 1994
78	Kelly Culpepper	Int. Return	Texas, 1960
77	Malcom McAlister from Rusty Hilger	Pass	Oklahoma State, 1984
76	Chris Spachman	Fumble Return	Nebraska, 1985
75	George McGown from Bob Douglas	Pass	Kansas, 1968
74	Keith Burns	PAT Return	Oklahoma State, 1992
72	Terry Miller	Run	Oklahoma State, 1976
72	Bill Matan	Blocked FG	Kansas State, 1962
71	Steve Lester from Bret Oberg	Pass	Iowa State, 1989
70	Keith Wilkerson	PAT Return	North Texas, 1991
70	Ken Cooper	Run	Rice, 1979
70	Tom Waddy from Jeff Knapple	Pass	Colorado, 1960
70	Rodney Guggenheim	Run	Iowa State,

All-Time Scores
(1895-1994)

1895 (0-1)
Nov. 7 Oklahoma City   L   34-0

1896 (2-0)
Oct. 28 Norman High*   W   12-0
Nov. 11 Norman High*   W   16-4

1897 (2-0)
Dec. 1 Oklahoma City   W   16-0
Dec. 31 Kingfisher College#   W   17-8

1898 (2-0)
Nov. 17 Arkansas City*   W   5-0
Nov. 28 at Fort Worth   W   24-0

1899 (2-1)
Oct. 12 KINGFISHER COLLEGE   W   39-6
Oct. 24 at Arkansas   W   11-5
Nov. 2 at Arkansas City   L   17-11

1900 (3-1-1)
Oct. 10 at Texas   L   28-2
Oct. 17 CHILOCCO   W   27-0
Oct. 24 FORT RENO   W   79-0
Nov. 6 at Kingfisher College   T   0-0
Nov. 20 ARKANSAS CITY   W   10-0

1901 (3-2)
Oct. 19 at Texas   L   12-6
Oct. 26 BAYLOR   W   17-0
Nov. 6 at Fairmont   W   42-0
Nov. 13 KINGFISHER COLLEGE   W   28-6
Nov. 25 TEXAS   L   11-0

1902 (6-3)
Oct. 1 GUTHRIE   W   62-0
Oct. 8 at Texas   L   22-6
Oct. 15 at Dallas Athletic Club   L   11-6
Oct. 22 at Arkansas   W   28-0
Oct. 29 OKLAHOMA CITY   W   30-0
Nov. 5 KINGFISHER COLLEGE   W   15-0
Nov. 12 at Missouri   L   22-5
Nov. 19 EMPORIA STATE   W   6-5
Nov. 24 KINGFISHER COLLEGE   W   17-0

1903 (5-4-3)
Oct. 3 at Chilocco Indian   W   38-5
Oct. 10 KINGFISHER COLLEGE   T   0-0
Oct. 17 at Texas   T   6-6
Oct. 24 at Texas A&M   W   6-0
Oct. 31 FAIRMONT   W   11-5
Nov. 6 EMPORIA STATE   T   6-6
Nov. 13 at Kansas   L   17-5
Nov. 20 TEXAS   L   11-5
Nov. 25 ARKANSAS   L   12-0
Nov. 30 at Missouri Mines   W   12-6
Dec. 3 at Bethany   L   12-10
Dec. 10 LAWTON   W   27-5

1904 (4-3-1)
Oct. 10 KINGFISHER COLLEGE   T   0-0
Oct. 17 at Pauls Valley   W   33-0
Oct. 24 KANSAS   L   16-0
Oct. 31 at Lawton   W   6-0
Nov. 6 Oklahoma State#   W   75-0
Nov. 13 at Texas   L   40-10
Nov. 20 O.C. MILITARY   W   71-4
Nov. 25 BETHANY   L   36-9

1905 (7-2)
Oct. 9 at Central Oklahoma   W   28-0
Oct. 13 HASKELL   W   18-12
Oct. 16 at Kansas   L   34-0
Oct. 23 KANSAS CITY MEDICS   W   33-0
Oct. 30 WASHBURN   L   9-6
Nov. 5 Texas*   W   2-0
Nov. 12 at Kingfisher College   W   55-0
Nov. 19 CENTRAL OKLAHOMA   W   58-0
Nov. 24 BETHANY   W   29-0

1906 (5-2-2)
Oct. 6 CENTRAL OKLAHOMA   W   12-0
Oct. 13 KINGFISHER COLLEGE   W   11-6
Oct. 19 at Oklahoma State   W   23-0
Oct. 26 at Kansas   L   20-4
Nov. 2 Texas*   L   10-9
Nov. 9 at Central Oklahoma   W   17-0
Nov. 16 PAWHUSKA   T   0-0
Nov. 23 SULPHUR   W   48-0
Nov. 28 at Washburn   T   0-0

1907 (4-4)
Oct. 4 at Kingfisher College   W   32-0
Oct. 11 CHILOCCO   W   43-0
Oct. 19 KANSAS   L   15-0
Oct. 25 EPWORTH   W   29-0
Nov. 9 OKLAHOMA STATE   W   67-0
Nov. 12 at Texas A&M   L   19-0
Nov. 15 at Texas   L   29-10
Nov. 28 WASHBURN   L   12-0

1908 (8-1-1)
Sept. 25 at Central Oklahoma   W   51-5
Oct. 3 at Oklahoma State   W   18-0
Oct. 10 KINGFISHER COLLEGE   W   51-0
Oct. 17 at Kansas   L   11-0
Oct. 23 at Kansas State   W   33-4
Oct. 30 ARKANSAS   W   27-5
Nov. 5 EPWORTH   W   24-0
Nov. 13 TEXAS   W   50-0
Nov. 19 FAIRMONT   W   12-4
Nov. 24 at Washburn   T   6-6

1909 (6-4)
Sept. 23 CENTRAL OKLAHOMA   W   55-0
Oct. 2 KINGFISHER COLLEGE   W   46-5
Oct. 9 at Kansas   L   11-0
Oct. 13 NW OKLAHOMA   W   23-2
Oct. 20 at Arkansas   L   21-5
Nov. 5 WASHBURN   W   42-8
Nov. 12 at Washington Univ.   W   11-5
Nov. 17 Texas A&M at Dallas   L   14-8
Nov. 19 at Texas   L   30-0
Nov. 29 Epworth*   W   12-11

1910 (4-2-1)
Oct. 7 at Kingfisher College   W   66-0
Oct. 17 at Central Oklahoma   W   79-0
Oct. 21 OKLAHOMA STATE   W   12-0
Oct. 28 MISSOURI   L   26-0
Nov. 12 KANSAS   L   2-0
Nov. 28 at Texas   W   3-0
Dec. 2 EPWORTH   T   3-3

1911 (8-0)
Oct. 7 KINGFISHER COLLEGE   W   104-0
Oct. 14 OKLAHOMA CHRISTIAN   W   62-0
Oct. 20 at Oklahoma State   W   22-0

Oct. 27 WASHBURN   W   37-0
Nov. 4 at Missouri   W   14-6
Nov. 11 at Kansas   W   3-0
Nov. 22 NW OKLAHOMA   W   34-6
Nov. 30 at Texas   W   6-3

1912 (5-4)
Oct. 5 at Kingfisher College   W   40-0
Oct. 11 CENTRAL OKLAHOMA   W   87-0
Oct. 19 Texas at Dallas   W   21-6
Oct. 26 MISSOURI   L   14-0
Nov. 2 at Kansas   W   6-5
Nov. 9 Texas A&M at Houston   L   28-6
Nov. 16 OKLAHOMA STATE   W   16-0
Nov. 23 at Nebraska   L   13-9
Nov. 28 COLORADO   L   14-12

1913 (6-2)
Sept. 27 KINGFISHER COLLEGE   W   74-0
Oct. 4 at Central Oklahoma   W   83-0
Oct. 11 NW OKLAHOMA   W   101-0
Oct. 18 at Missouri   L   20-17
Oct. 31 KANSAS   W   21-7
Nov. 10 Texas at Houston   L   14-6
Nov. 21 at Oklahoma State   W   7-0
Nov. 27 COLORADO   W   14-3

1914 (9-1-1)
Sept. 26 CENTRAL OKLAHOMA   W   67-0
Oct. 3 at Kingfisher College   W   67-0
Oct. 9 EAST CENTRAL   W   96-6
Oct. 17 MISSOURI   W   13-0
Oct. 24 Texas at Dallas   L   32-7
Oct. 31 at Kansas   T   16-16
Nov. 6 OKLAHOMA STATE   W   23-6
Nov. 13 at Kansas State   W   52-10
Nov. 20 at Arkansas   W   35-7
Nov. 26 HASKELL   W   33-12
Nov. 30 at Tulsa   W   26-7

1915 (10-0)
Sept. 25 KINGFISHER COLLEGE   W   67-0
Oct. 2 at SW Oklahoma   W   55-0
Oct. 9 NW OKLAHOMA   W   102-0
Oct. 16 at Missouri   W   24-0
Oct. 23 Texas at Dallas   W   14-13
Oct. 30 KANSAS   W   23-14
Nov. 6 at Tulsa   W   14-13
Nov. 13 ARKANSAS   W   24-0
Nov. 20 at Kansas State   W   21-7
Nov. 25 Oklahoma State*   W   26-7

1916 (6-5)
Sept. 23 CENTRAL OKLAHOMA   W   27-0
Sept. 30 at Shawnee   W   107-0
Oct. 7 SW OKLAHOMA   W   140-0
Oct. 14 TULSA   L   16-0
Oct. 21 Texas at Dallas   L   21-7
Oct. 28 MISSOURI   L   23-14
Nov. 4 at Kansas   L   21-13
Nov. 11 at Kingfisher College   W   96-0
Nov. 18 KANSAS STATE   L   14-13
Nov. 25 at Arkansas   W   14-13
Nov. 30 Oklahoma State*   W   41-7

1917 (6-4-1)
Sept. 22 at Central Oklahoma   W   99-0
Sept. 29 KINGFISHER COLLEGE   W   179-0
Oct. 6 Phillips*   W   52-9

Oct. 13	at Illinois	L 44-0
Oct. 20	Texas at Dallas	W 14-0
Nov. 3	at Missouri	W 14-7
Nov. 10	KANSAS	L 13-6
Nov. 17	ARKANSAS	T 0-0
Nov. 24	TULSA	W 80-0
Nov. 29	Oklahoma State*	L 9-0
Dec. 15	at Camp Doniphan	L 21-7

1918 (6-0)

Oct. 26	CENTRAL OKLAHOMA	W 44-0
Nov. 2	POST FIELD	W 58-0
Nov. 9	at Kansas	W 33-0
Nov. 16	at Arkansas	W 103-0
Nov. 23	Phillips*	W 13-7
Nov. 28	Oklahoma State*	W 27-0

1919 (5-2-3)

Sept. 27	at Central Oklahoma	W 40-0
Oct. 4	KINGFISHER COLLEGE	W 157-0
Oct. 11	TULSA	L 27-0
Oct. 18	Texas at Dallas	W 12-7
Oct. 25	at Nebraska	T 7-7
Nov. 1	MISSOURI	T 6-6
Nov. 8	at Kansas	T 0-0
Nov. 15	ARKANSAS	L 7-6
Nov. 22	at Kansas State	W 14-3
Nov. 27	Oklahoma State*	W 33-6

1920 (6-0-1)

Oct. 9	CENTRAL OKLAHOMA	W 16-7
Oct. 23	WASHINGTON	W 24-14
Oct. 30	at Missouri	W 28-7
Nov. 6	KANSAS	W 21-9
Nov. 13	at Oklahoma State	W 36-0
Nov. 20	at Kansas State	T 7-7
Nov. 25	DRAKE	W 44-7

1921 (5-3)

Oct. 8	at Central Oklahoma	W 21-0
Oct. 15	OKLAHOMA STATE	W 6-0
Oct. 22	WASHINGTON	W 28-13
Oct. 29	at Nebraska	L 44-0
Nov. 5	KANSAS	W 24-7
Nov. 12	at Missouri	L 24-14
Nov. 19	at Kansas State	L 14-7
Nov. 24	RICE	W 27-0

1922 (2-3-3)

Oct. 14	CENTRAL OKLAHOMA	W 21-0
Oct. 21	KANSAS STATE	T 7-7
Oct. 28	NEBRASKA	L 39-7
Nov. 4	at Kansas	L 19-3
Nov. 11	MISSOURI	W 18-14
Nov. 18	TEXAS	L 32-7
Nov. 25	at Oklahoma State	T 3-3
Dec. 2	at Washington	T 0-0

1923 (3-5)

Oct. 13	at Nebraska	L 24-0
Oct. 20	WASHINGTON	W 62-7
Oct. 27	OKLAHOMA STATE	W 12-0
Nov. 3	KANSAS	L 7-3
Nov. 10	at Missouri	W 13-0
Nov. 17	at Texas	L 26-14
Nov. 24	at Kansas State	L 21-20
Nov. 29	DRAKE	L 26-20

1924 (2-5-1)

Oct. 4	CENTRAL OKLAHOMA	L 2-0
Oct. 11	NEBRASKA	W 14-7
Oct. 25	at Drake	L 28-0
Nov. 1	at Oklahoma State	L 6-0
Nov. 8	MISSOURI	L 10-0
Nov. 15	at Kansas	L 20-0
Nov. 22	at Washington	W 7-0
Nov. 27	KANSAS STATE	T 7-7

1925 (4-3-1)

Oct. 3	at Kansas State	L 16-0
Oct. 17	DRAKE	W 7-0
Oct. 24	at Southern Methodist	W 9-0
Oct. 31	at Nebraska	L 12-0
Nov. 7	KANSAS	T 0-0
Nov. 14	at Missouri	L 16-14
Nov. 21	WASHINGTON	W 28-0
Nov. 26	OKLAHOMA STATE	W 35-0

1926 (5-2-1)

Oct. 9	ARKANSAS	W 13-6
Oct. 16	at Drake	W 11-0
Oct. 23	KANSAS STATE	L 15-12
Oct. 30	at Washington	W 21-0
Nov. 6	MISSOURI	W 10-7
Nov. 13	at Kansas	L 10-9
Nov. 20	ST. LOUIS	W 47-0
Nov. 25	at Oklahoma State	T 14-14

1927 (3-3-2)

Oct. 8	at Chicago	W 13-7
Oct. 15	CREIGHTON	T 13-13
Oct. 22	at Kansas State	L 20-14
Oct. 29	at Central Oklahoma	T 14-14
Nov. 5	WASHINGTON	W 23-7
Nov. 12	KANSAS	W 26-7
Nov. 19	OKLAHOMA STATE	L 13-7
Nov. 24	at Missouri	L 20-7

1928 (5-3)

Oct. 6	at Indiana	L 10-7
Oct. 13	CREIGHTON	W 7-0
Oct. 27	KANSAS STATE	W 33-21
Nov. 3	at Iowa State	L 13-0
Nov. 10	NEBRASKA	L 44-6
Nov. 17	at Kansas	W 7-0
Nov. 24	at Oklahoma State	W 46-0
Nov. 29	MISSOURI	W 14-0

1929 (3-3-2)

Oct. 12	at Creighton	W 26-0
Oct. 19	Texas at Dallas	L 21-0
Oct. 26	KANSAS STATE	W 14-13
Nov. 2	IOWA STATE	W 21-7
Nov. 9	KANSAS	L 7-0
Nov. 16	at Nebraska	T 13-13
Nov. 23	OKLAHOMA STATE	T 7-7
Nov. 28	at Missouri	L 13-0

1930 (4-3-1)

Oct. 4	NEW MEXICO	W 47-0
Oct. 11	NEBRASKA	W 20-7
Oct. 18	Texas at Dallas	L 17-7
Oct. 25	KANSAS STATE	W 7-0
Nov. 1	at Iowa State	W 19-13
Nov. 15	at Kansas	L 13-0
Nov. 22	at Oklahoma State	L 7-0
Nov. 27	MISSOURI	T 0-0

1931 (4-7-1)

Oct. 3	RICE	W 19-6
Oct. 10	at Nebraska	L 13-0
Oct. 17	Texas at Dallas	L 3-0
Oct. 24	at Kansas State	L 14-0
Oct. 31	IOWA STATE	L 13-12
Nov. 7	KANSAS	W 10-0
Nov. 14	at Missouri	L 7-0
Nov. 26	OKLAHOMA STATE	T 0-0
Dec. 5	at Oklahoma City	L 6-0
Dec. 12	at Tulsa	W 20-7
Dec. 19	at Honolulu	L 39-20
Dec. 26	at Hawaii	W 7-0

1932 (4-4-1)

Oct. 1	TULSA	W 7-0
Oct. 8	at Kansas	W 21-6
Oct. 15	Texas at Dallas	L 17-10
Oct. 22	KANSAS STATE	W 20-13
Oct. 29	at Oklahoma State	L 7-0
Nov. 5	MISSOURI	L 14-6
Nov. 12	at Iowa State	W 19-12
Nov. 19	NEBRASKA	L 5-0
Nov. 24	at George Washington	T 7-7

1933 (4-4-1)

Sept. 30	VANDERBILT	T 0-0
Oct. 7	at Tulsa	L 20-6
Oct. 14	Texas at Dallas	W 9-0
Oct. 21	IOWA STATE	W 19-7
Oct. 28	at Nebraska	L 16-7
Nov. 4	KANSAS	W 20-0
Nov. 11	at Missouri	W 21-0
Nov. 18	at Kansas State	L 14-0
Nov. 23	OKLAHOMA STATE	L 13-0

1934 (3-4-2)

Oct. 6	CENTENARY	W 7-0
Oct. 13	Texas at Dallas	L 19-0
Oct. 20	NEBRASKA	L 6-0
Oct. 27	at Kansas	T 7-7
Nov. 3	MISSOURI	W 31-0
Nov. 10	IOWA STATE	W 12-0
Nov. 17	KANSAS STATE	L 8-7
Nov. 22	at Oklahoma State	T 0-0
Dec. 1	at George Washington	L 3-0

1935 (6-3)

Sept. 28	COLORADO	W 3-0
Oct. 5	NEW MEXICO	W 25-0
Oct. 12	Texas at Dallas	L 12-7
Oct. 19	IOWA STATE	W 16-0
Oct. 26	at Nebraska	L 19-0
Nov. 2	KANSAS	L 7-0
Nov. 9	at Missouri	W 20-6
Nov. 16	at Kansas State	W 3-0
Nov. 28	OKLAHOMA STATE	W 25-0

1936 (3-3-3)

Sept. 26	TULSA	T 0-0
Oct. 3	at Colorado	W 8-0
Oct. 10	Texas at Dallas	L 6-0
Oct. 17	at Kansas	W 14-0
Oct. 24	NEBRASKA	L 14-0
Oct. 31	at Iowa State	T 7-7
Nov. 7	KANSAS STATE	T 6-6
Nov. 14	MISSOURI	L 21-14
Nov. 26	at Oklahoma State	W 35-3

1937 (5-2-2)

Sept. 25	at Tulsa	L 19-7
Oct. 2	RICE	W 6-0
Oct. 9	Texas at Dallas	T 7-7
Oct. 16	at Nebraska	T 0-0
Oct. 23	KANSAS	L 6-3
Oct. 30	at Kansas State	W 19-0
Nov. 6	IOWA STATE	W 33-7
Nov. 13	at Missouri	W 7-0
Nov. 25	OKLAHOMA STATE	W 16-0

1938 (10-1)

Oct. 1	at Rice	W 7-6
Oct. 8	Texas at Dallas	W 13-0
Oct. 15	at Kansas	W 19-0
Oct. 22	NEBRASKA	W 14-0
Oct. 29	TULSA	W 28-6
Nov. 5	KANSAS STATE	W 26-0
Nov. 12	MISSOURI	W 21-0
Nov. 19	at Iowa State	W 10-0
Nov. 24	at Oklahoma State	W 19-0
Dec. 3	WASHINGTON STATE	W 28-0

ORANGE BOWL AT MIAMI, FLA.

Jan. 2	Tennessee	L 17-0

1939 (6-2-1)
Sept. 30	SOUTHERN METHODIST†		7-7
Oct. 7	at Northwestern	W	23-0
Oct. 14	Texas at Dallas	W	24-12
Oct. 21	KANSAS	W	27-7
Oct. 28	OKLAHOMA STATE	W	41-0
Nov. 4	IOWA STATE	W	38-6
Nov. 11	at Kansas State	W	13-10
Nov. 18	at Missouri	L	7-6
Nov. 23	at Nebraska	L	13-7

1940 (6-3)
Oct. 5	OKLAHOMA STATE	W	29-27
Oct. 12	Texas at Dallas	L	19-16
Oct. 19	KANSAS STATE	W	14-0
Oct. 26	at Iowa State	W	20-7
Nov. 2	NEBRASKA	L	13-0
Nov. 9	at Kansas	W	13-0
Nov. 16	MISSOURI	W	7-0
Nov. 23	TEMPLE	W	9-6
Nov. 30	at Santa Clara	L	33-13

1941 (6-3)
Oct. 4	OKLAHOMA STATE	W	19-0
Oct. 11	Texas at Dallas	L	40-7
Oct. 18	at Kansas State	W	16-0
Oct. 25	SANTA CLARA	W	16-6
Nov. 1	KANSAS	W	38-0
Nov. 8	IOWA STATE	W	55-0
Nov. 15	at Missouri	L	28-0
Nov. 22	MARQUETTE	W	61-14
Nov. 29	at Nebraska	L	7-6

1942 (3-5-2)
Sept. 26	at Oklahoma State	T	0-0
Oct. 3	at Tulsa	L	23-0
Oct. 10	Texas at Dallas	L	7-0
Oct. 17	at Kansas	W	25-0
Oct. 24	NEBRASKA	L	7-0
Oct. 31	at Iowa State	W	14-7
Nov. 7	KANSAS STATE	W	76-0
Nov. 14	MISSOURI	T	6-6
Nov. 21	at Temple	L	14-7
Nov. 28	WILLIAM & MARY	L	14-7

1943 (7-2)
Sept. 25	NORMAN NAS	W	22-6
Oct. 2	Oklahoma State*	W	22-13
Oct. 9	Texas at Dallas	L	13-7
Oct. 16	Tulsa*	L	20-6
Oct. 23	KANSAS STATE	W	37-0
Oct. 30	IOWA STATE	W	21-7
Nov. 6	KANSAS	W	26-13
Nov. 13	at Missouri	W	20-13
Nov. 20	at Nebraska	W	26-7

1944 (6-3-1)
Sept. 30	NORMAN NAS	L	28-14
Oct. 7	Texas A&M*	W	21-14
Oct. 14	Texas at Dallas	L	20-0
Oct. 21	KANSAS STATE	W	68-0
Oct. 28	Texas Christian*	W	34-19
Nov. 4	at Iowa State	W	12-7
Nov. 11	MISSOURI	T	21-21
Nov. 18	at Kansas	W	20-0
Nov. 25	Oklahoma State*	L	28-6
Dec. 2	Nebraska*	W	31-12

1945 (5-5)
Sept. 22	at Hondo, Texas, AAF	W	21-6
Sept. 29	at Nebraska	W	20-0
Oct. 6	TEXAS A&M	L	19-14
Oct. 13	Texas at Dallas	L	12-7
Oct. 20	KANSAS	W	39-7
Oct. 27	at Kansas State	W	41-13
Nov. 3	TEXAS CHRISTIAN	L	13-7
Nov. 10	IOWA STATE	W	14-7
Nov. 17	at Missouri	L	14-6
Nov. 24	OKLAHOMA STATE	L	47-0

1946 (8-3)
Sept. 28	Army (Yankee Stadium)	L	21-7
Oct. 5	TEXAS A&M	W	10-7
Oct. 12	Texas at Dallas	L	20-13
Oct. 19	KANSAS STATE	W	28-7
Oct. 26	at Iowa State	W	63-0
Nov. 2	at Texas Christian	W	14-12
Nov. 9	at Kansas	L	16-13
Nov. 16	MISSOURI	W	27-6
Nov. 23	NEBRASKA	W	27-6
Nov. 30	at Oklahoma State	W	73-12

GATOR BOWL AT JACKSONVILLE
Jan. 1	North Carolina State	W	34-13

1947 (7-2-1)
Sept. 27	at Detroit	W	24-20
Oct. 4	TEXAS A&M	W	26-14
Oct. 11	Texas at Dallas	L	34-14
Oct. 18	KANSAS	T	13-13
Oct. 25	TEXAS CHRISTIAN	L	20-7
Nov. 1	IOWA STATE	W	27-9
Nov. 8	at Kansas State	W	27-13
Nov. 15	at Missouri	W	21-12
Nov. 22	at Nebraska	W	14-13
Nov. 29	OKLAHOMA STATE	W	21-13

1948 (10-1)
Sept. 25	at Santa Clara	L	20-17
Oct. 2	TEXAS A&M	W	42-14
Oct. 9	Texas at Dallas	W	20-14
Oct. 16	KANSAS STATE	W	42-0
Oct. 23	at Texas Christian	W	21-18
Oct. 30	at Iowa State	W	33-6
Nov. 6	MISSOURI	W	41-7
Nov. 13	NEBRASKA	W	41-14
Nov. 20	at Kansas	W	60-7
Nov. 27	at Oklahoma State	W	19-15

SUGAR BOWL AT NEW ORLEANS
Jan. 1	North Carolina	W	14-6

1949 (11-0)
Sept. 23	at Boston College	W	46-0
Oct. 1	TEXAS A&M	W	33-13
Oct. 8	Texas at Dallas	W	20-14
Oct. 15	KANSAS	W	48-26
Oct. 22	at Nebraska	W	48-0
Oct. 29	IOWA STATE	W	34-7
Nov. 5	at Kansas State	W	39-0
Nov. 12	at Missouri	W	27-7
Nov. 19	SANTA CLARA	W	28-21
Nov. 26	OKLAHOMA STATE	W	41-0

SUGAR BOWL AT NEW ORLEANS
Jan. 1	Louisiana State	W	35-0

1951 (8-2)
Sept. 29	WILLIAM & MARY	W	49-7
Oct. 6	at Texas A&M	L	14-7
Oct. 13	Texas at Dallas	L	9-7
Oct. 20	KANSAS	W	33-21
Oct. 27	COLORADO	W	55-14
Nov. 3	at Kansas State	W	33-0
Nov. 10	at Missouri	W	34-20
Nov. 17	IOWA STATE	W	35-6
Nov. 24	at Nebraska	W	27-0
Dec. 1	OKLAHOMA STATE	W	41-6

1952 (8-1-1)
Sept. 27	at Colorado	T	21-21
Oct. 4	PITTSBURGH	W	49-20
Oct. 11	Texas at Dallas	W	49-20
Oct. 18	at Kansas	W	42-20
Oct. 25	KANSAS STATE	W	49-6
Nov. 1	at Iowa State	W	41-0
Nov. 8	at Notre Dame	L	27-21
Nov. 15	MISSOURI	W	47-7
Nov. 22	NEBRASKA	W	34-13
Nov. 29	at Oklahoma State	W	54-7

1953 (9-1-1)
Sept. 26	NOTRE DAME	L	28-21
Oct. 3	at Pittsburgh	T	7-7
Oct. 10	Texas at Dallas	W	19-14
Oct. 17	KANSAS	W	45-0
Oct. 24	COLORADO	W	27-20
Oct. 31	KANSAS STATE	W	34-0
Nov. 7	at Missouri	W	14-0
Nov. 14	IOWA STATE	W	47-0
Nov. 21	at Nebraska	W	30-7
Nov. 28	OKLAHOMA STATE	W	42-7

ORANGE BOWL AT MIAMI
Jan. 1	Maryland	W	7-0

1954 (10-0)
Sept. 18	at California	W	27-13
Sept. 25	TEXAS CHRISTIAN	W	21-16
Oct. 9	Texas at Dallas	W	14-7
Oct. 16	at Kansas	W	65-0
Oct. 23	KANSAS STATE	W	21-0
Oct. 30	at Colorado	W	13-6
Nov. 6	at Iowa State	W	40-0
Nov. 13	MISSOURI	W	34-13
Nov. 20	NEBRASKA	W	55-7
Nov. 27	at Oklahoma State	W	14-0

1957 (10-1)
Sept. 21	at Pittsburgh	W	26-0
Oct. 5	IOWA STATE	W	40-14
Oct. 12	Texas at Dallas	W	21-7
Oct. 19	KANSAS	W	34-12
Oct. 26	COLORADO	W	14-13
Nov. 2	at Kansas State	W	13-0
Nov. 9	at Missouri	W	39-14
Nov. 16	NOTRE DAME	L	7-0
Nov. 23	at Nebraska	W	32-7
Nov. 30	OKLAHOMA STATE	W	53-6

ORANGE BOWL AT MIAMI
Jan. 1	Duke	W	48-21

1958 (10-1)
Sept. 27	WEST VIRGINIA	W	47-14
Oct. 4	OREGON	W	6-0
Oct. 11	Texas at Dallas	L	15-14
Oct. 18	at Kansas	W	43-0
Oct. 25	KANSAS STATE	W	40-6
Nov. 1	at Colorado	W	23-7
Nov. 8	at Iowa State	W	20-0
Nov. 15	MISSOURI	W	39-0
Nov. 22	NEBRASKA	W	40-7
Nov. 29	at Oklahoma State	W	7-0

ORANGE BOWL AT MIAMI
Jan. 1	Syracuse	W	21-6

1959 (7-3)
Sept. 26	at Northwestern	L	45-13
Oct. 3	COLORADO	W	42-12
Oct. 10	Texas at Dallas	L	19-12
Oct. 17	at Missouri	W	23-0
Oct. 24	KANSAS	W	7-6
Oct. 31	at Nebraska	L	25-21
Nov. 7	at Kansas State	W	36-0
Nov. 14	ARMY	W	28-20
Nov. 21	IOWA STATE	W	35-12
Nov. 28	OKLAHOMA STATE	W	17-7

1960 (3-6-1)
Sept. 24	NORTHWESTERN	L	19-3
Oct. 1	PITTSBURGH	W	15-14
Oct. 8	Texas at Dallas	L	24-0
Oct. 15	at Kansas	T	13-13
Oct. 22	KANSAS STATE	W	49-7
Oct. 29	at Colorado	L	7-0
Nov. 5	at Iowa State	L	10-6
Nov. 12	MISSOURI	L	41-19
Nov. 19	NEBRASKA	L	17-14
Nov. 26	at Oklahoma State	W	17-6

1961 (5-5)
Sept. 30	at Notre Dame	L	19-6
Oct. 7	IOWA STATE	L	21-15
Oct. 14	Texas at Dallas	L	28-7
Oct. 21	KANSAS	L	10-0
Oct. 28	COLORADO	L	22-14
Nov. 4	at Kansas State	W	17-6
Nov. 11	at Missouri	W	7-0
Nov. 18	Army (Yankee Stadium)	W	14-8
Nov. 25	at Nebraska	W	21-14
Dec. 2	OKLAHOMA STATE	W	21-13

1962 (8-3)
Sept. 22	SYRACUSE	W	7-3
Sept. 29	NOTRE DAME	L	13-7
Oct. 13	Texas at Dallas	L	9-6
Oct. 20	at Kansas	W	13-7
Oct. 27	KANSAS STATE	W	47-0
Nov. 3	at Colorado	W	62-0
Nov. 10	at Iowa State	W	41-0
Nov. 17	MISSOURI	W	13-0
Nov. 24	NEBRASKA	W	34-6
Dec. 1	at Oklahoma State	W	37-6

ORANGE BOWL AT MIAMI
Jan. 1	Alabama	L	17-0

1963 (8-2)
Sept. 21	CLEMSON	W	31-14
Sept. 28	at Southern Cal	W	17-12
Oct. 12	Texas at Dallas	L	28-7
Oct. 19	KANSAS	W	21-18
Oct. 26	at Kansas State	W	34-9
Nov. 2	COLORADO	W	35-0
Nov. 9	IOWA STATE	W	24-14
Nov. 16	at Missouri	W	13-3
Nov. 23	at Nebraska	L	29-20
Nov. 30	OKLAHOMA STATE	W	34-10

1964 (6-4-1)
Sept. 19	at Maryland	W	13-3
Sept. 26	SOUTHERN CAL	L	40-14
Oct. 10	Texas at Dallas	L	28-7
Oct. 17	at Kansas	L	15-14
Oct. 24	KANSAS STATE	W	44-0
Oct. 31	at Colorado	W	14-11
Nov. 7	IOWA STATE	W	30-0
Nov. 14	MISSOURI	T	14-14
Nov. 21	NEBRASKA	W	17-7
Nov. 28	at Oklahoma State	W	21-16

GATOR BOWL AT JACKSONVILLE
Jan. 2	Florida State	L	36-19

1965 (3-7)
Sept. 25	at Pittsburgh	L	13-9
Oct. 2	NAVY	L	10-0
Oct. 9	Texas at Dallas	L	19-0
Oct. 16	KANSAS	W	21-7
Oct. 23	at Kansas State	W	27-0
Oct. 30	COLORADO	L	13-0
Nov. 6	IOWA STATE	W	24-20
Nov. 13	at Missouri	L	30-0
Nov. 25	at Nebraska	L	21-9
Dec. 4	OKLAHOMA STATE	L	17-16

1966 (6-4)
Sept. 17	OREGON	W	17-0
Sept. 24	at Iowa State	W	33-11
Oct. 8	Texas at Dallas	W	18-9
Oct. 15	at Kansas	W	35-0
Oct. 22	NOTRE DAME	L	38-0
Oct. 29	at Colorado	L	24-21
Nov. 5	KANSAS STATE	W	37-6
Nov. 12	MISSOURI	L	10-7
Nov. 24	NEBRASKA	W	10-9
Dec. 3	at Oklahoma State	L	15-14

1967 (10-1)
Sept. 23	WASHINGTON STATE	W	21-0
Sept. 30	MARYLAND	W	35-0
Oct. 14	Texas at Dallas	L	9-7
Oct. 21	at Kansas State	W	46-7
Oct. 28	at Missouri	W	7-0
Nov. 4	COLORADO	W	23-0
Nov. 11	at Iowa State	W	52-14
Nov. 18	KANSAS	W	14-10
Nov. 23	at Nebraska	W	21-14
Dec. 2	OKLAHOMA STATE	W	38-14

ORANGE BOWL AT MIAMI
Jan. 1	Tennessee	W	26-24

1968 (7-4)
Sept. 21	at Notre Dame	L	45-21
Sept. 28	NORTH CAROLINA ST.	W	28-14
Oct. 12	Texas at Dallas	L	26-20
Oct. 19	IOWA STATE	W	42-7
Oct. 26	at Colorado	L	41-27
Nov. 2	KANSAS STATE	W	35-20
Nov. 9	at Kansas	W	27-23
Nov. 16	MISSOURI	W	28-14
Nov. 23	NEBRASKA	W	47-0
Nov. 30	at Oklahoma State	W	41-7

ASTRO-BLUEBONNET BOWL AT HOUSTON, TEXAS
Dec. 31	Southern Methodist	L	28-27

1969 (6-4)
Sept. 20	at Wisconsin	W	48-21
Sept. 27	PITTSBURGH	W	37-8
Oct. 11	Texas at Dallas	L	27-17
Oct. 18	COLORADO	W	42-30
Oct. 25	at Kansas State	L	59-21
Nov. 1	IOWA STATE	W	37-14
Nov. 8	at Missouri	L	44-10
Nov. 15	KANSAS	W	31-15
Nov. 22	NEBRASKA	L	44-14
Nov. 29	at Oklahoma State	W	28-27

1970 (7-4-1)
Sept. 12	at Southern Methodist	W	28-11
Sept. 19	WISCONSIN	W	21-7
Sept. 26	OREGON STATE	L	23-14
Oct. 10	Texas at Dallas	L	41-9
Oct. 17	at Colorado	W	23-15
Oct. 24	KANSAS STATE	L	19-14
Oct. 31	at Iowa State	W	29-28
Nov. 7	MISSOURI	W	28-13
Nov. 14	at Kansas	W	28-24
Nov. 21	at Nebraska	L	28-21
Nov. 28	OKLAHOMA STATE	W	66-6

ASTRO-BLUEBONNET BOWL AT HOUSTON, TEXAS
Dec. 31	Alabama	T	24-24

1971 (11-1)
Sept. 18	SOUTHERN METHODIST	W	30-0
Sept. 25	at Pittsburgh	W	55-29
Oct. 2	SOUTHERN CAL	W	33-20
Oct. 9	Texas at Dallas	W	48-27
Oct. 16	COLORADO	W	45-17
Oct. 23	at Kansas State	W	75-28
Oct. 30	IOWA STATE	W	43-12
Nov. 6	at Missouri	W	20-3
Nov. 13	KANSAS	W	56-10
Nov. 25	NEBRASKA	L	35-31
Dec. 4	at Oklahoma State	W	58-14

SUGAR BOWL AT NEW ORLEANS
Jan. 1	Auburn	W	40-22

1972 (8-4)
Sept. 16	UTAH STATE	W	49-0
Sept. 23	OREGON	W	68-3
Sept. 30	CLEMSON	W	52-3

Oct. 14	Texas at Dallas	W	27-0
Oct. 21	at Colorado	L	20-14
Oct. 28	KANSAS STATE	W	52-0
Nov. 4	at Iowa State	W	20-6
Nov. 11	MISSOURI*	W	17-6
Nov. 18	at Kansas*	W	31-7
Nov. 23	at Nebraska	W	17-14
Dec. 2	OKLAHOMA STATE*	W	38-15

SUGAR BOWL AT NEW ORLEANS
Dec. 31	Penn State	W	14-0

*Oklahoma forfeited ineligible player

1973 (10-0-1)
Sept. 15	at Baylor	W	42-14
Sept. 29	at Southern Cal	T	7-7
Oct. 6	MIAMI, FLA.	W	24-20
Oct. 13	Texas at Dallas	W	52-13
Oct. 20	COLORADO	W	34-7
Oct. 27	at Kansas State	W	56-14
Nov. 3	IOWA STATE	W	34-17
Nov. 10	at Missouri	W	31-3
Nov. 17	KANSAS	W	48-20
Nov. 23	NEBRASKA	W	27-0
Dec. 1	at Oklahoma State	W	45-18

1976 (9-2-1)
Sept. 11	at Vanderbilt	W	24-3
Sept. 18	CALIFORNIA	W	28-17
Sept. 25	FLORIDA STATE	W	24-19
Oct. 2	at Iowa State	W	24-10
Oct. 9	Texas at Dallas	T	6-6
Oct. 16	at Kansas	W	28-10
Oct. 23	OKLAHOMA STATE	L	31-24
Oct. 30	at Colorado	L	41-31
Nov. 6	KANSAS STATE	W	49-20
Nov. 13	MISSOURI	W	27-20
Nov. 26	at Nebraska	W	20-17

FIESTA BOWL AT TEMPE
Dec. 25	Wyoming	W	41-7

1977 (10-2)
Sept. 10	VANDERBILT	W	25-23
Sept. 17	UTAH	W	62-24
Sept. 24	at Ohio State	W	29-28
Oct. 1	KANSAS	W	24-9
Oct. 8	Texas at Dallas	L	13-6
Oct. 15	at Missouri	W	21-17
Oct. 22	IOWA STATE	W	35-16
Oct. 29	at Kansas State	W	42-7
Nov. 5	at Oklahoma State	W	61-28
Nov. 12	COLORADO	W	52-14
Nov. 25	NEBRASKA	W	38-7

ORANGE BOWL AT MIAMI
Jan. 1	Arkansas	L	34-6

1978 (11-1)
Sept. 9	at Stanford	W	35-29
Sept. 16	WEST VIRGINIA	W	52-10
Sept. 23	RICE	W	66-7
Sept. 30	MISSOURI	W	45-23
Oct. 7	Texas at Dallas	W	31-10
Oct. 14	at Kansas	W	17-16
Oct. 21	at Iowa State	W	34-6
Oct. 28	KANSAS STATE	W	56-19
Nov. 4	at Colorado	W	28-7
Nov. 11	at Nebraska	L	17-14
Nov. 18	OKLAHOMA STATE	W	62-7

ORANGE BOWL AT MIAMI
Jan. 1	Nebraska	W	31-24

1979 (11-1)
Sept. 15	IOWA	W	21-6
Sept. 22	TULSA	W	49-13
Sept. 29	at Rice	W	63-21
Oct. 6	COLORADO	W	49-24

Oct. 13 Texas at Dallas   L 16-7
Oct. 20 at Kansas State   W 38-6
Oct. 27 IOWA STATE   W 38-9
Nov. 3   at Oklahoma State   W 38-7
Nov. 10 KANSAS   W 38-0
Nov. 17 at Missouri   W 24-22
Nov. 24 NEBRASKA   W 17-14
         ORANGE BOWL AT MIAMI
Jan. 1   Florida State   W 24-7

1980 (10-2)
Sept. 13 KENTUCKY   W 29-7
Sept. 27 STANFORD   L 31-14
Oct. 4   at Colorado   W 82-42
Oct. 11   Texas at Dallas   L 20-13
Oct. 18   KANSAS STATE   W 35-21
Oct. 25   at Iowa State   W 42-7
Nov. 1   NORTH CAROLINA   W 41-7
Nov. 8   at Kansas   W 21-19
Nov. 15   MISSOURI   W 17-7
Nov. 22   at Nebraska   W 21-17
Nov. 29   OKLAHOMA STATE   W 63-7
          ORANGE BOWL AT MIAMI
Jan. 1   Florida State   W 18-17

1981 (7-4-1)
Sept. 12 WYOMING   W 37-20
Sept. 26 at Southern Cal   L 28-24
Oct. 3   IOWA STATE   T 7-7
Oct. 10   Texas at Dallas   L 34-14
Oct. 17   KANSAS   W 45-7
Oct. 24   OREGON STATE   W 42-3
Oct. 31   COLORADO   W 49-0
Nov. 7   at Kansas State   W 28-21
Nov. 14   at Missouri   L 19-14
Nov. 21   NEBRASKA   L 37-14
Nov. 28   at Oklahoma State   W 27-3
          SUN BOWL AT EL PASO
Dec. 26   Houston   W 40-14

1982 (8-4)
Sept. 11 WEST VIRGINIA   L 41-27
Sept. 18 at Kentucky   W 29-8
Sept. 25 SOUTHERN CAL   L 12-0
Oct. 2   at Iowa State   W 13-3
Oct. 9   Texas at Dallas   W 28-22
Oct. 16   at Kansas   W 38-14
Oct. 23   OKLAHOMA STATE   W 27-9
Oct. 30   at Colorado   W 45-10
Nov. 6   KANSAS STATE   W 24-10
Nov. 13   MISSOURI   W 41-14
Nov. 26   at Nebraska   L 28-24
          FIESTA BOWL AT TEMPE
Jan. 1   Arizona State   L 32-21

1983 (8-4)
Sept. 10 at Stanford   W 27-14
Sept. 17 OHIO STATE   L 24-14
Sept. 24 TULSA   W 28-18
Oct. 1   at Kansas State   W 29-10
Oct. 8   Texas at Dallas   L 28-16
Oct. 15   at Oklahoma State   W 21-20
Oct. 22   IOWA STATE   W 49-11
Oct. 29   KANSAS   W 45-14
Nov. 5   at Missouri   L 10-0
Nov. 12   COLORADO   W 41-28
Nov. 26   NEBRASKA   L 28-21
Dec. 3   at Hawaii   W 21-17

1984 (9-2-1)
Sept. 8   STANFORD   W 19-7
Sept. 15 at Pittsburgh   W 42-10
Sept. 22 BAYLOR   W 34-15
Sept. 29 KANSAS STATE   W 24-6
Oct. 13   Texas at Dallas   T 15-15
Oct. 20   at Iowa State   W 12-10

Oct. 27   at Kansas   L 28-11
Nov. 3   MISSOURI   W 49-7
Nov. 10   at Colorado   W 42-17
Nov. 17   at Nebraska   W 17-7
Nov. 24   OKLAHOMA STATE   W 24-14
          ORANGE BOWL AT MIAMI
Jan. 1   Washington   L 28-17

1986 (11-1)
Sept. 6   UCLA   W 38-3
Sept. 20 MINNESOTA   W 63-0
Sept. 27 at Miami, Fla.   L 28-16
Oct. 4   KANSAS STATE   W 56-10
Oct. 11   Texas at Dallas   W 47-12
Oct. 18   OKLAHOMA STATE   W 19-0
Oct. 25   at Iowa State   W 38-0
Nov. 1   at Kansas   W 64-3
Nov. 8   MISSOURI   W 77-0
Nov. 15   at Colorado   W 28-0
Nov. 22   at Nebraska   W 20-17
          ORANGE BOWL AT MIAMI
Jan. 1   Arkansas   W 42-8

1987 (11-1)
Sept. 5   NORTH TEXAS   W 69-14
Sept. 12 NORTH CAROLINA   W 28-0
Sept. 26 at Tulsa   W 65-0
Oct. 3   at Iowa State   W 56-3
Oct. 10   Texas at Dallas   W 44-9
Oct. 17   at Kansas State   W 59-10
Oct. 24   COLORADO   W 24-6
Oct. 31   at Kansas   W 71-10
Nov. 7   OKLAHOMA STATE   W 29-10
Nov. 14   MISSOURI   W 17-13
Nov. 21   at Nebraska   W 17-7
          ORANGE BOWL AT MIAMI
Jan. 1   Miami, Fla.   L 20-14

1988 (9-3)
Sept. 10 at North Carolina   W 28-0
Sept. 17 ARIZONA   W 28-10
Sept. 24 at Southern Cal   L 23-7
Oct. 1   IOWA STATE   W 35-7
Oct. 8   Texas at Dallas   W 28-10
Oct. 15   KANSAS STATE   W 70-24
Oct. 22   at Colorado   W 17-14
Oct. 29   KANSAS   W 63-14
Nov. 5   at Oklahoma State   W 31-28
Nov. 12   at Missouri   W 16-7
Nov. 19   NEBRASKA   L 7-3
          CITRUS BOWL AT ORLANDO
Jan. 1   Clemson   L 13-6

1989 (7-4)
Sept. 2   NEW MEXICO STATE   W 73-3
Sept. 9   BAYLOR   W 33-7
Sept. 16 at Arizona   L 6-3
Sept. 30 at Kansas   W 45-6
Oct. 7   OKLAHOMA STATE   W 37-15
Oct. 14   Texas at Dallas   L 28-24
Oct. 21   at Iowa State   W 43-40
Oct. 28   COLORADO   L 20-3
Nov. 4   MISSOURI   W 52-14
Nov. 11   KANSAS STATE   W 42-19
Nov. 18   at Nebraska   L 42-25

1990 (8-3)
Sept. 8   at UCLA   W 34-14
Sept. 15 PITTSBURGH   W 52-10
Sept. 22 TULSA   W 52-10
Sept. 29 KANSAS   W 31-17
Oct. 6   at Oklahoma State   W 31-17
Oct. 13   Texas at Dallas   L 14-13
Oct. 20   IOWA STATE   L 33-31
Oct. 27   at Colorado   L 32-23
Nov. 3   at Missouri   W 55-10

Nov. 10   KANSAS STATE   W 34-7
Nov. 23   NEBRASKA   W 45-10

1991 (9-3)
Sept. 14 NORTH TEXAS   W 40-2
Sept. 21 UTAH STATE   W 55-21
Sept. 28 VIRGINIA TECH   W 27-17
Oct. 5   at Iowa State   W 29-8
Oct. 12   Texas at Dallas   L 10-7
Oct. 19   COLORADO   L 34-17
Oct. 26   KANSAS   W 41-3
Nov. 2   KANSAS STATE   W 28-7
Nov. 9   at Missouri   W 56-16
Nov. 16   OKLAHOMA STATE   W 21-6
Nov. 29   at Nebraska   L 19-14
          GATOR BOWL AT JACKSONVILLE
Dec. 29   Virginia   W 48-14

1992 (5-4-2)
Sept. 3   at Texas Tech   W 34-9
Sept. 12 ARKANSAS STATE   W 61-0
Sept. 19 SOUTHERN CAL   L 20-10
Oct. 3   IOWA STATE   W 14-3
Oct. 10   Texas at Dallas   L 34-24
Oct. 17   at Colorado   T 24-24
Oct. 24   at Kansas   L 27-10
Oct. 31   KANSAS STATE   W 16-14
Nov. 7   MISSOURI   W 55-17
Nov. 14   at Oklahoma State   T 15-15
Nov. 27   NEBRASKA   L 33-9

1993 (9-3)
Sept. 4   at Texas Christian   W 35-3
Sept. 11 TEXAS A&M   W 44-14
Sept. 25 TULSA   W 41-20
Oct. 2   at Iowa State   W 24-7
Oct. 9   Texas at Dallas   W 38-17
Oct. 16   COLORADO   L 27-10
Oct. 23   KANSAS   W 38-21
Oct. 30   at Kansas State   L 21-7
Nov. 6   at Missouri   W 42-23
Nov. 13   OKLAHOMA STATE   W 31-0
Nov. 26   at Nebraska   L 21-7
          JOHN HANCOCK BOWL AT EL PASO
Dec. 24   Texas Tech   W 41-10

1994 (6-6)
Sept. 3   Syracuse   W 30-29
Sept. 11 Texas A&M   L 36-14
Sept. 17 TEXAS TECH   W 17-11
Oct. 1   IOWA STATE   W 34-6
Oct. 8   Texas at Dallas   L 17-10
Oct. 15   Colorado   L 45-7
Oct. 22   Kansas   W 20-17
Oct. 29   KANSAS STATE   L 37-20
Nov. 5   MISSOURI   W 30-13
Nov. 13   at OSU   W 33-14
Nov. 25   NEBRASKA   L 13-3
          COPPER BOWL AT TUCSON
Dec. 29   BYU   L 31-6

ALL CAPS INDICATES GAME PLAYED IN
NORMAN, (except Bowl Games)
(*) at Oklahoma City
(#) at Guthrie

Coaching Records
(ranked by winning percentage)
1895-1994

1. BARRY SWITZER, 1973-1988

Alma Mater	Years Coached	W	L	T	Pct.	Pts.	Avg.	Opp. Pts.	Opp. Avg.
Arkansas	16	157	29	4	.837	6093	32.1	2425	12.8

Oklahoma's all-time winningest coach, Barry Switzer, led his Sooner team to three national championships, 12 Big Eight Conference championships and eight bowl games in 13 appearances. Switzer led the Sooners on a 28-game win streak from 1973 (his first season as head coach) to 1975. When the Sooners won the national championship in 1975, it marked the first time in history a team had won back-to-back titles more than once. Switzer, the current head coach of the Dallas Cowboys, overcame meager beginnings in a rickety house in the Arkansas woods to gain his many successes. He graduated from Crosset High with honors and played center and linebacker for the Unversity of Arkansas. Before coming to Oklahoma as an offensive line coach in 1966, Switzer was a B team coach and scout for the Razorbacks. In 1967, he was named offensive coordinator for the Sooners. In 1970, he convinced Chuch Fairbanks, then OU head coach, to make the most significant and gutsy move in OU's football history, a switch to the wishbone offense. The only vehicles for learning this novel offense were films of 1968-69 OU/Texas games, since Texas was the only school that used the wishbone. This offense saved the career of Fairbanks and his seven assistants and made possible Oklahoma's second football dynasty. Switzer resigned as Sooner coach in June of 1989, saying that "coaching was no longer fun." He stayed out of coaching, despite many offers, until Jerry Jones, the owner of the Dallas Cowboys, offered him the head coaching position in April of 1994. During the 1994 season, Switer led the Cowboys to a 13-5 record and the NFC Championship game.

YEAR-BY-YEAR RECORD

Year	W	L	T	Pct	Pts	Pts	Captains
1973	10	0	1	.952	400	133	Eddie Foster, Monahans, Texas / Gary Baccus, Brownsfield, Texas / Tim Welch, Bowie, Texas / Lucious Selmon, Eufaula, Okla.
1974	11	0	0	1.000	473	92	Steve Davis, Sallisaw, Okla. / Kyle Davis, Altus, Okla. / Rod Shoate, Spiro, Okla. / Randy Hughes, Tulsa, Okla.
1975	11	1	0	.917	344	154	Lee Roy Selmon, Eufaula, Okla. / Dewey Selmon, Eufaula, Okla. / Joe Washington, Port Arthur, Texas / Steve Davis, Sallisaw, Okla.
1976	9	2	1	.826	326	192	Mike Vaughan, Ada, Okla. / Scott Hill, Hurst, Texas / Jerry Anderson, Murfreesboro, Tenn.
1977	10	2	0	.833	411	217	Karl Baldischwiler, Okmulgee, Okla. / Zac Henderson, Burkburnett, Texas / Elvis Peacock, Miami, Fla.
1978	11	1	0	.917	440	151	Daryl Hunt, Odessa, Texas / Greg Roberts, Nacogdoches, Texas / Phil Tabor, Houston, Texas / Thomas Lott, San Antonio, Texas
1979	11	1	0	.917	406	145	Billy Sims, Hooks, Texas / Darrol Ray, Killeen, Texas / Sherwood Taylor, Ada, Okla. / George Cumby, Tyler, Texas / Paul Tabor, Houston, Texas
1980	10	2	0	.933	396	209	J.C. Watts, Eufaula, Okla. / Richard Turner, Edmond, Okla. / Steve Rhodes, Dallas, Texas / David Overstreet, Big Sandy, Texas / Louis Oubre, New Orleans, La.
1981	7	4	1	.625	341	193	Terry Crouch, Dallas, Texas / Ed Culver, Tahlequah, Okla. / Johnny Lewis, Carol City, Fla.
1982	8	4	0	.666	317	203	selected before each game
1983	8	4	0	.666	312	222	Rick Bryan, Coweta, Okla. / Scott Case, Edmond, Okla. / Danny Bradley, Pine Bluff, Ark. / Paul Parker, Tulsa, Okla.
1984	9	2	1	.826	289	136	Danny Bradley, Pine Bluff, Ark. / Chuck Thomas, Houston, Texas / Tony Casillas, Tulsa, Okla. / Kevin Murphy, Richardson, Texas / Keith Stanberry, Mt. Pleasant, Texas
1985	11	1	0	.917	346	93	Tony Casillas, Tulsa, Okla. / Kevin Murphy, Richardson, Texas / Eric Pope, Seminole, Okla.
1986	11	1	0	.917	466	73	Brian Bosworth, Irving, Texas / Steve Bryan, Broken Arrow, Okla. / Sonny Brown, Alice, Texas / Spencer Tillman, Tulsa, Okla.
1987	11	1	0	.917	479	82	Patrick Collins, Tulsa, Okla. / Mark Hutson, Fort Smith, Ark. / Greg Johnson, Moore, Okla. / Danté Jones, Dallas, Texas / Darrell Reed, Cypress, Texas / David Vickers, Tulsa, Okla.
1988	9	3	0	.750	326	147	Scott Garl, Hominy, Okla. / Jamelle Holieway, Carson, Calif. / Anthony Phillips, Tulsa, Okla. / Anthony Stafford, St. Louis, Mo.

2. BUD WILKINSON, 1947-1963

Alma Mater	Years Coached	W	L	T	Pct.	Pts. Avg.	Opp. Pts.	Opp. Avg.
Minnesota	17	145	29	4	.833	5092 28.6	1973	10.0

While confining OU's recruiting to a 150-mile radius of the Norman campus, Oklahoma's 13th football coach produced teams that were 6-2 in postseason play, won the national championship in 1950, 1955 and 1956 and didn't lose an astounding 74 straight conference games from 1946-59 (72 wins, 2 ties). He still holds the modern record for 47 straight wins from 1953 to 1957, a streak that stopped when the Sooners lost to Notre Dame, 7-0. After the 1947 season, the Sooners won 12 straight conference championships. In 17 seasons at Oklahoma, Wilkinson fostered racial integration and graduated players at an 87.2 percentage rate while becoming the eighth-winningest coach in Division I-A history. His career began as a player at Minnesota, where he helped the Golden Gophers win two national championships in football, captained the golf team and was a goaltender in hockey. Wilkinson won the Big Ten Medal of Honor as the outstanding scholar-athlete in 1937. After serving as an assistant at Syracuse where he received his master's in English Education, Wilkinson coached at Minnesota and with the Navy's Pre-Flight School Seahawks. He also served in the Navy during World War II. Upon his arrival back in the states, Wilkinson decided to give up football and work in his father's Minneapolis mortgage business. Not long after his decision, Wilkinson's Navy buddy, Jim Tatum, Oklahoma's new head coach, asked him to come to Norman as an assistant coach. Wilkinson accepted and in one year, he was the Oklahoma head coach and athletic director. In 1964, he resigned from OU and ran for the U.S. Senate as a Republican, but fell short. Wilkinson was an ABC sports analyst from 1965-77 and from 1979-80, he coached the St. Louis Cardinals. He also served as a consultant to President Nixon and was a member of the White House Staff from 1969-71. Wilkinson died in 1994 of congestive heart failure at age 77.

YEAR-BY-YEAR RECORD

Year	W	L	T	Pct.	Pts.	Pts.	Captains
1947	7	2	1	.750	194	161	Jim Tyree, Oklahoma City, Okla. / Wade Walker, Gastonia, N.C.
1948	10	1	0	.909	350	121	Wade Walker, Gastonia, N.C. / Homer Paine, Enid, Okla.
1949	11	0	0	1.000	399	88	Stanley West, Enid, Okla. / Jim Owens, Oklahoma City, Okla.
1950	10	1	0	.909	352	148	Harry Moore, Blackwell, Okla. / Norman McNabb, Norman, Okla.
1951	8	2	0	.800	321	97	Bert Clark, Wichita Falls, Texas / Jim Weatherall, White Deer, Texas
1952	8	1	1	.888	407	141	Eddie Crowder, Muskogee, Okla. / Tom Catlin, Ponca City, Okla.
1953	9	1	1	.900	293	90	Larry Grigg, Sherman, Texas / Roger Nelson, Wynnewood, Okla.
1954	10	0	0	1.000	304	62	Gene Mears, Seminole, Okla. / Gene Calame, Sulphur, Okla.
1955	11	0	0	1.000	385	60	Bo Bolinger, Muskogee, Okla. / Cecil Morris, Lawton, Okla. / Bob Loughridge, Poteau, Okla.
1956	10	0	0	1.000	466	51	Ed Gray, Odessa, Texas / Jerry Tubbs, Breckenridge, Texas
1957	10	1	0	.909	333	89	Don Stiller, Shawnee, Okla. / Clendon Thomas, Oklahoma City, Okla.
1958	10	1	0	.909	300	55	Joe Rector, Muskogee, Okla. / Bob Harrison, Stamford, Texas
1959	7	3	0	.700	234	146	Gilmer Lewis, Wichita Falls, Texas / Bobby Boyd, Garland, Texas
1960	3	6	1	.350	136	158	Ronnie Hartline, Lawton, Okla. / Marshall York, Amarillo, Texas
1961	5	5	0	.500	122	141	Billy White, Amarillo, Texas
1962	8	3	0	.727	267	61	Wayne Lee, Ada, Okla. / Leon Cross, Hobbs, N.M.
1963	8	2	0	.800	236	137	John Garrett, Stilwell, Okla. / Larry Vermillion, Chickasha, Okla.

3. VERNON PARRINGTON, 1897-1900

Alma Mater	Years Coached	W	L	T	Pct	Pts	Avg	Opp Pts	Opp Avg
Harvard	4	9	2	1	.818	241	20.0	64	5.3

Vernon Parrington came to Oklahoma in 1897 after running for office as a member of the Populist political party. After leaving OU, he won the Pulitzer Prize in 1928 while teaching at the University of Washington with his book, Main Currents of Political Thought. He was the first full-time football coach at OU. He played football at both Emporia College in Kansas and Harvard. He coached primarily the "tackle back" style which he learned from his Harvard coach, Bernard W. Trafford. Parrington gave up his coaching position in 1901 because it interfered with his teaching, but he remained as athletic director. He taught English, French and German for the next seven years at OU until he was fired along with other faculty members, including OU pioneer president, Dr. David Ross Boyd, when the party in control of state government changed. Parrington then went to Washington. He died suddenly in 1929 in Gloucestershire, England, while taking the first vacation of his life.

YEAR-BY-YEAR RECORD

Year	W	L	T	Pct.	Pts.	Pts.	Captains
1897	2	0	0	1.000	33	8	C.C. Roberts, Medford, Okla.
1898	2	0	0	1.000	29	0	C.C. Roberts, Medford, Okla.
1899	2	1	0	.667	61	28	C.C. Roberts, Medford, Okla.
1900	3	1	1	.750	118	28	C.C. Roberts, Medford, Okla.

4. CHUCK FAIRBANKS, 1967-1972

Alma Mater	Years Coached	W	L	T	Pct.	Pts.	Avg.	Opp. Pts.	Opp. Avg.
Michigan State	6	*49	18	1	.772	2142	31.5	1136	16.7

As Oklahoma's 16th head coach, Chuck Fairbanks won three Big Eight Conference titles (1967, 1972 and a shared title in 1968). He had 24 players earn all-league honors while nine received All-America accolades. Fairbanks also coached the 1969 Heisman Trophy winner, running back Steve Owens. In bowl games at OU, he posted a 3-1-1 record with the Sooners playing in a pair of Sugar and Astro-Bluebonnet bowls, and one Orange Bowl. Fairbanks was the first OU coach to use the wishbone formation, a triple option offensive attack that Texas used on its way to the 1969 national title. The wishbone became the backbone of OU's offensive dynasty for the next 20 years. In 1973, Fairbanks left OU to coach in the NFL for the New England Patriots. During his six-year tenure as the Patriots' head coach, Fairbanks set a club record with 46 wins. The Patriots also won two division titles in the American Football Conference's East division (1978 and shared in 1976). In 1978, Colorado began its battle to get Fairbanks as head coach, despite his four remaining years with the Patriots. After more than three months of legal battles between the Patriots and Buffaloes, the two factions agreed on a settlement that released Fairbanks from his NFL contract and allowed him to take over the helm at Colorado. He remained with the Buffaloes for three years. Fairbanks began his coaching career at Ishpeming High School in Michigan. From there, he went to Arizona State and Houston before coming to OU as a defensive backfield coach in 1966. As a player at Michigan State, Fairbanks played offensive end on the Spartans' 1952 national championship team. In 1954, he concluded his playing career by earning a berth in the Blue-Gray All-Star game.

YEAR-BY-YEAR RECORD

Year	W	L	T	Pct.	Pts.	Pts.	Captains
1967	10	1	0	.909	290	92	Bob Kalsu, Del City, Okla.
1968	7	4	0	.636	343	225	Bob Warmack, Ada, Okla. / John Titsworth, Heavener, Okla.
1969	6	4	0	.600	285	289	Steve Zabel, Thornton, Colo. / Steve Owens, Miami, Okla. / Jim Files, Fort Smith, Ark. / Ken Mendenhall, Enid, Okla.
1970	7	4	1	.636	305	239	Monty Johnson, Amarillo, Texas / Steve Casteel, Garland, Texas
1971	11	1	0	.917	534	217	Jack Mildren, Abilene, Texas / Glenn King, Jacksboro, Texas / Steve Aycock, Midland, Texas
1972	8	4	0	.667	385	74	Tom Brahaney, Midland, Texas / Greg Pruitt, Houston, Texas

5. TOM STIDHAM, 1937-1940

Alma Mater	Years Coached	W	L	T	Pct.	Pts.	Avg.	Opp. Pts.	Opp. Avg.
Haskell	4	27	8	3	.771	590	15.5	218	5.8

Oklahoma's 10th football coach, Tom Stidham posted OU's most successful record of all time against Texas with only one loss in four years. His greatest triumph while at OU was his 23-0 demolition in 1939 of Coach Lynn Waldorf's Northwestern team that was picked to win the national championship. Stidham was the first Oklahoma coach to defeat Waldorf (both Adrian "Ad" Lindsey and Lewie Hardage had also tried). Stidham's 1938 Sooners were undefeated in the regular season and were ranked No. 4 in the AP poll, but lost in the Sooners' first bowl appearance, the Orange Bowl, to Tennessee. After OU's hard-fought loss to the Volunteers, Stidham went back to his hotel room, took off the gray suit he had worn triumphantly in the 10 games Oklahoma had won and dropped it out the fifth-floor window. He was a native Oklahoman who grew up in Checotah. Stidham was one-sixteenth Creek Indian. He went to Haskell Indian Institute of Lawrence, Kan., and played football from 1925-26 under Coach Dick Hanley. In 1927, Stidham went to the University of Iowa, but before he gained eligibility, Hanley, who had accepted the coaching position at Northwestern, asked him to be an assistant coach. He was Northwestern line coach from 1933-34. Captain "Biff" Jones hired Stidham to coach the Oklahoma line in 1935. When Jones left in 1937, Stidham became the head coach. In his time, Stidham placed more of his Oklahoma players with professional teams than any other coach. In 1940, 17 Sooners started in pro football and 10 stayed all season.

YEAR-BY-YEAR RECORD

Year	W	L	T	Pct.	Pts.	Pts.	Captains
1937	5	2	2	.714	98	39	Al Corrotto, Fort Smith, Ark.
1938	10	1	0	.909	185	29	Gene Corrotto, Fort Smith, Ark. / Earl Crowder, Cherokee, Okla.
1939	6	2	1	.750	186	62	Norval Locke, Ardmore, Okla.
1940	6	3	0	.667	121	105	Gus Kitchens, Purcell, Okla.

6. JIM TATUM, 1946

Alma Mater	Years Coached	W	L	T	Pct.	Pts.	Avg.	Opp. Pts.	Opp. Avg.
North Carolina	1	8	3	0	.727	309	28.0	120	10.9

In his only year as OU coach, Jim Tatum devised a massive recruiting scheme that took the Sooners to prominence. His venture in the first year after World War II had never happened before or since because NCAA rules would not permit it and no school could afford it. The process almost bankrupted OU. Tatum had tryouts, winter practices, spring practices and summer practices. The few rules the NCAA had in those days were largely ignored by Tatum. In pursuit of building a national powerhouse, he snared many discharged servicemen who had played at other colleges before the war. Tatum also raided rival campuses, recruited a conventional number of high school seniors and ran off most of the 1945 players. Estimates on the number of players who tried out ran as high as 600. Oklahoma's 1946 recruiting class produced nine All-Americans. In the 1945 coaching search, Oklahoma opted to hire Tatum over Bear Bryant. A 32-year-old North Carolina native, Tatum had served with Jap Haskell, OU athletic director, in the Navy. Tatum was head coach one year at North Carolina before the war and led a Navy team at Jacksonville. He also was line coach at Iowa Pre-Flight under Missouri's Don Faurot, inventor of the Split-T offense. Some of the regents were more impressed with Charles (Bud) Wilkinson, Tatum's friend who accompanied him on the interview, than Tatum. After the Sooner victory over North Carolina State in the Gator Bowl, Maryland contacted Tatum and offered a coaching position. OU President Dr. George Cross privately hoped Tatum would leave so he could elevate Wilkinson. Tatum had become "very difficult to work with," said Cross. Tatum had also spent the athletic department's entire surplus of $125,000 before the first game and run up a deficit of $113,000. Tatum did accept the contract with Maryland. From there, he accepted the head coaching position at the University of North Carolina. Tatum died suddenly in 1958 of a mysterious viral infection despite appearing to be in excellent health.

YEAR-BY-YEAR RECORD

Year	W	L	T	Pct.	Pts.	Pts.	Captain
1946	8	3	0	.727	309	120	Jim Tyree, Oklahoma City, Okla.

7. BENNIE OWEN, 1905-1926

Alma Mater	Years Coached	W	L	T	Pct.	Pts.	Avg.	Opp. Pts.	Opp. Avg.
Kansas	22	122	54	16	.693	5132	26.5	1426	7.3

At 17, Oklahoma's sixth football coach made part of the famous Cherokee Strip run from the south Kansas border into Oklahoma Indian territory, making him a true Boomer Sooner. His age prevented acquisition of any land, but his sense of adventure took him four miles into the territory before turning back, making him a true Okie. Bennie Owen coached Oklahoma for 22 seasons, longer than anyone else in school history. He began a tradition and a stadium that have endured for almost a century. Before coming to the university, Owen played and coached under Fielding Yost at Kansas and Michigan, and helped develop Yost's feared hurry-up offense. In it, Owen, the quarterback, would yell out signals for the next play on the bottom of the pile up of the preceding play. Although Owen only weighed 126 pounds, he was respected by all as a fierce competitor. Before coming to OU in 1905, Owen coached and taught chemistry at Bethany, Kan., an early football power. Four of Owen's Oklahoma teams—1911, 1915, 1918 and 1920—were undefeated. Owen's first football star at OU was Owen Acton in 1907, a halfback, who the university recognizes as its first all-conference player. Despite this, the 1907 season was misfortunate for both Owen and Oklahoma athletics. Owen lost his arm in an October hunting accident which left him out of coaching for the remainder of the season, and the athletic director, Vernon Parrington, was discharged by the new governor, Charles Haskell, along with all other Republicans at the university. It was not until 1911 that Owen and his players began to get national attention. In 1913, OU's Claude Reeds was recognized as an All-American. About this time, Owen began to seriously play around with the forward pass, which had been introduced on a highly restricted basis in 1907, to open up the game. Reeds was the first to make good use of the pass, but another Sooner All-American, Forrest "Spot" Geyer, built a legend with it. At the end of the 1920 season, Owen announced that he intended to raise $340,000 to build a 30,000-seat stadium, with an eventual expansion to 52,000 seats, and a 5,000-seat gymnasium. By 1928, Owen's vision resulted in Memorial Stadium circling Owen Field, as well as the OU Field House. Owen coached six more years after 1920 before becoming solely athletic director. In 1950, Owen was one of the 21 coaches to be elected to football's first National Hall of Fame.

YEAR-BY-YEAR RECORD

Year	W	L	T	Pct.	Pts.	Pts.	Captains	Year	W	L	T	Pct.	Pts.	Pts.	Captains
1905	7	2	0	.777	229	55	Byron McCreary, Norman, OK	1916	6	5	0	.545	472	115	Homer Montgomery, Muskogee, OK
1906	5	2	2	.714	124	36	James Monnett, Yale, OK	1917	6	4	1	.600	451	103	Frank McCain, Ada, OK
1907	4	4	0	.500	181	75	Bill Cross, Kingfished, OK	1918	6	0	0	1.000	278	7	Hugh McDermott, Duncan, OK
1908	8	1	1	.888	272	35	Key Wolf, Davis, OK	1919	5	2	3	.714	275	63	Erl Deacon, Tecumseh, OK
1909	6	4	0	.600	202	110	Charlie Armstrong, Kingfisher, OK	1920	6	0	1	1.000	176	51	Dewey Luster, Chickasha, OK
1910	4	2	1	.667	163	31	Cleve Thompson, Erick, OK	1921	5	3	0	.625	127	102	Lawrence Haskell, Anadarko, OK
1911	8	0	0	1.000	282	15	Fred Capshaw, Norman, OK	1922	2	3	3	.400	64	114	Howard Marsh, Madill, OK
1912	5	4	0	.555	197	80	Glenn Clark, Comanche, OK	1923	3	5	0	.375	144	111	Pete Hammert, Anadarko,OK
1913	6	2	0	.750	323	44	Hubert Ambrister, Norman, OK	1924	2	5	1	.285	28	80	Obie Bristow, Ardmore, OK
1914	9	1	1	.900	440	96	Billy Clark, Comanche, OK	1925	4	3	1	.571	93	44	Eddie Brockman, Tulsa, OK
1915	10	0	0	1.000	370	54	Forest Geyer, Norman, OK	1926	5	2	1	.714	137	52	Pollack Wallace, Oklahoma City,

8. GARY GIBBS, 1989-1994

Alma Mater	Years Coached	W	L	T	Pct.	Pts.	Avg.	Opp. Pts.	Opp. Avg.
Oklahoma	6	44	23	2	.657	2018	30.1	1096	16.4

During his six seasons as the Sooners' head coach, Gary Gibbs led the football program through some of the toughest times in recent history. He took the helm in the summer of 1989 after Barry Switzer resigned. The Sooners began a probation period during that same period. In his first three seasons, the Sooners continued their pattern of success with the team making its first trip to a bowl game in two years. Oklahoma defeated Virginia at the 1991 Gator Bowl, 48-14. The full effects of probation finally caught up with the Sooners in 1992 as they compiled a 5-4-2 record. In 1993, Oklahoma defeated Texas for the first time in the Gibbs era, 38-17, as well as Texas A&M. The Sooners faced Texas Tech in the John Hancock Bowl, beating the Red Raiders 41-10. Gibbs started as a linebacker on Oklahoma's 1974 national championship squad and graduated from OU in 1975. Before deciding to join the OU coaching staff in 1975, Gibbs signed with the New England Patriots as a free agent. In 1981, Gibbs was named the Oklahoma defensive coordinator. Under his direction, OU defenders led the nation in total defense three straight years (1985-87) and twice finished first in rushing defense (1986 and 1987). Gibbs also helped the Sooners win a national championship in 1985.

YEAR-BY-YEAR RECORD

Year	W	L	T	Pct.	Pts.	Pts.	Captains
1989	7	4	0	.636	380	200	Scott Evans, Edmond, Okla. / Ken McMichael, Indianapolis, Ind. / Leon Perry, Miami, Fla. / Kevin Thompson, Houston, Texas / Mark VanKeirsbilck, Shawnee, Okla.
1990	8	3	0	.727	401	174	Scott Evans, Edmond, Okla. / Larry Medice, Gretna, La. / Mike Sawatzky, Weatherford, Okla. / Chris Wilson, Richardson, Texas
1991	9	3	0	.750	335	143	Jason Belser, Kansas City, Mo. / Joe Bowden, Mesquite, Texas / Brandon Houston, Abernathy, Texas / Mike McKinley, Perryton, Texas / Randy Wilson, Midwest City, Okla. / Chris Wilson, Richardson, Texas
1992	5	4	2	.545	271	196	Reggie Barnes, Grand Prairie, Texas / Cale Gundy, Midwest City, Okla. / Kenyon Rasheed, Kansas City, Mo. / Darnell Walker, St. Louis, Mo.
1993	9	3	0	.750	406	145	Cale Gundy, Midwest City, Okla. / Aubrey Beavers, Houston, Texas / Corey Warren, Houston, Texas / Mike Coats, Oklahoma City, Okla.
1994	6	6	0	.500	225	238	Garrick McGee, Tulsa, Okla. / Albert Hall, Bay City, Texas / John Anderson, Sugarland, Texas / Darrius Johnson, Terrell, Texas

9. FRED ROBERTS, 1901

Alma Mater	Years Coached	W	L	T	Pct.	Pts.	Avg.	Opp. Pts.	Opp. Avg.
Oklahoma	1	3	2	0	.600	93	18.6	29	5.8

Fred Roberts first came to Norman in 1899 at the insistence of C.C. "Lum" Roberts, his cousin, who was then captain of the Sooner football team. Oklahoma's third football coach was a halfback who could both dodge and smash dangerously. When the 1899 OU team beat Arkansas, Roberts scored both Oklahoma touchdowns. In the final game of the that same season against the Arkansas City, Kan., Town Team, Roberts ran 70 yards off tackle for a touchdown. In 1900, Roberts left OU to play halfback for Bennie Owen at Washburn College of Topeka. When Vernon Parrington relinquished his coaching duties in 1901, Roberts was persuaded to return to Oklahoma to coach the team as well as play on it. In the Texas game at Austin, Roberts played so well that *The Dallas Morning News* said, "Roberts of OU played one of the prettiest individual games ever seen in this city." Against Fairmont, Roberts kicked seven field goals out of seven tries. He gained the reputation of being the outstanding halfback of the southwest. Roberts had to refuse the coaching job in 1902 because of increasing duties on his farm. He still returned from his farm to play for Oklahoma occasionally under Coach McMahon when the team needed him. In OU's final game of the 1903 season versus the previously undefeated Lawton Town Team, Roberts led Oklahoma over its opponent, 27-5.

YEAR-BY-YEAR RECORD

Year	W	L	T	Pct.	Pts.	Pts.	Captain
1901	3	2	0	.600	93	29	Ray Crowe, Deer Creek, Okla.

10. LAWRENCE "BIFF" JONES, 1935-1936

Alma Mater	Years Coached	W	L	T	Pct.	Pts.	Avg.	Opp. Pts.	Opp. Avg.
Army	2	9	6	3	.600	183	10.1	111	6.1

Oklahoma's ninth football coach, Lawrence "Biff" Jones had also served as head coach at Army for four years (1926-29) and at Louisiana State for three years (1932-35). He left Oklahoma originally because the Army decided to transfer him to Fort Leavenworth, Kan., but an offer to head the Nebraska football team prompted Jones to resign from the Army and travel to Lincoln. During his 19-month tenure at OU, he rebuilt the athletic training department by adding whirlpool baths and needle showers and organized the equipment department to save thousands of dollars. He installed the Warner system of single and double wingbacking, a 1-9-1 shift, and strengthened the faulty Sooner running game. At the end of Jones' first season, the Sooners rushed 1,748 yards, nearly 200 yards per game, while permitting the opponents only 873 yards. At Nebraska, Jones led the team to two Big Six titles in four years. He coached the 'Huskers from 1937-40. In 1937, Nebraska was ranked 11th in the country and in 1940, NU was ranked seventh in the country.

YEAR-BY-YEAR RECORD

Year	W	L	T	Pct.	Pts.	Pts.	Captains
1935	6	3	0	.667	99	44	Morris McDannald, Electra, Texas
1936	3	3	3	.500	84	67	Connie Ahrens, Oklahoma City, Okla.

11. DEWEY "SNORTER" LUSTER, 1941-1945

Alma Mater	Years Coached	W	L	T	Pct.	Pts.	Avg.	Opp. Pts.	Opp. Avg.
Oklahoma	5	27	18	3	.600	936	19.5	552	11.5

At 5-foot-4, 135 pounds, Dewey "Snorter" Luster made a mark at his alma mater as the football and boxing coach. He piloted Oklahoma football to Big Six Conference titles in 1943 and 1944, and his team never finished below second place in the Big Six. Because of ill health, Luster missed several practices and the final game of the season against Oklahoma A&M in 1945. He resigned after that season. Luster lettered four years as a football player at OU. He was a starting end his last two years and team captain of the undefeated 1920 team (6-0-1) his senior year. Luster organized the Sooners' first wrestling team in 1920 while he was still an undergraduate. At that time, he also installed a boxing program at the university, which was winless in two meets. Thirty-six years later in 1956, Luster's boxing team placed sixth in the NCAA Championships. The sport was discontinued after that season. Luster got his nickname because he snorted so much as an amateur boxer. He decided he did not want a boxing career after fighting professional Mutt McGee for 10 rounds when Luster was only 15 years old. Before coaching at OU, Luster coached football at Norman High School. In 1922, he received his law degree from Oklahoma. Luster died at age 81 in his Norman home.

YEAR-BY-YEAR RECORD

Year	W	L	T	Pct.	Pts.	Pts.	Captains
1941	6	3	0	.667	218	95	Orville Mathews, Chickasha, Okla. / Rogers Eason, Oklahoma City, Okla.
1942	3	5	2	.375	135	78	Bill Campbell, Pawhuska, Okla. / W.G. "Dub" Lamb, Ardmore, Okla.
1943	7	2	0	.778	187	92	W.C. "Dub" Wooten, Amarillo, Texas / Bob Brumley, Edinburg, Texas
1944	6	3	1	.667	227	149	W.C. "Dub" Wooten, Amarillo, Texas / Bob Mayfield, Norman, Okla.
1945	5	5	0	.500	169	138	Omer Burgert, Enid, Okla.

12. JIM MACKENZIE, 1966

Alma Mater	Years Coached	W	L	T	Pct.	Pts.	Avg.	Opp. Pts.	Opp. Avg.
Kentucky	1	6	4	0	.600	192	19.2	122	12.2

After finishing his first season as the head coach at Oklahoma, 37-year-old Jim Mackenzie died from a massive heart attack. In his only season at OU, his Sooners finished 6-4, but missed being 9-1 by only 10 points. Mackenzie's team upset two bowl teams, Texas and Nebraska, and he was named the 1966 Big Eight coach of the year by both AP and UPI. Mackenzie came to Oklahoma in December, 1965, after spending nine years as assistant to Frank Broyles. Mackenzie was with Broyles for one year at Missouri as well as eight years at Arkansas. Mackenzie built great defenses for the Razorbacks, and in 1964, Broyles named Mackenzie assistant head coach. Oklahoma's 15th head coach was an All-Southeastern Conference tackle under Coach Bear Bryant at Kentucky. Kentucky compiled a 28-3 record and went to a bowl every season Mackenzie played. The Wildcats also upset Oklahoma's 1950 national champions, 13-7, in the 1951 Sugar Bowl. Mackenzie left an outline for Oklahoma's success in "The Winning Edge," a list of 20 principles Mackenzie believed held the keys to success in both football and life.

YEAR-BY-YEAR RECORD

Year	W	L	T	Pct.	Pts.	Pts.	Captains
1966	6	4	0	.600	192	122	Ed Hall, Eden, Texas / Jim Riley, Enid, Okla.

13. FRED EWING, 1904

Alma Mater	Years Coached	W	L	T	Pct.	Pts.	Avg.	Opp. Pts.	Opp. Avg.
Knox	1	4	3	1	.571	204	25.5	90	11.2

Oklahoma's fifth football coach, Fred Ewing was hired to coach the Sooners for the 1904 season, through Thanksgiving Day. To coach, Ewing took an extended vacation from the University of Chicago Medical School. At Knox College in Galesburg, Illinois, Ewing had been rated as the greatest Knox tackle of all time. He became the first Oklahoma coach to insist on using only scholastically eligible varsity players. Despite the fact that Ewing was only one year removed from his collegiate football career and that Roberts and McMahon, the two Oklahoma coaches before him had played, he never participated in any of Oklahoma's varsity games. Ewing regularly used the Minnesota Shift, a formation in which on nearly every play, one offensive tackle was set behind the other offensive tackle and carried the ball or blocked. The 1904 season marked the first meeting between Oklahoma and Oklahoma A&M. Ewing's team defeated the Aggies, 75-0. One week later, Oklahoma faced Texas for the first game of the long series at the Texas State Fair in Dallas. Texas won, 50-10. Ewing devised a system of strapping strained ankles with adhesive tape that was years ahead of the time. The system got varsity players with injured ankles back into action quickly. The day after the Thanksgiving game, Ewing returned to medical school in Chicago.

YEAR-BY-YEAR RECORD

Year	W	L	T	Pct.	Pts.	Pts.	Captain
1904	4	3	1	.571	204	96	Byron McCreary, Norman, Okla.

14. MARK McMAHAN, 1902-1903

Alma Mater	Years Coached	W	L	T	Pct.	Pts.	Avg.	Opp. Pts.	Opp. Avg.
Texas	2	11	7	3	.555	301	14.3	14.5	6.9

Captain and left tackle of the 1901 University of Texas team, Mark McMahan heard of Oklahoma's head coaching vacancy after the Texas and Pacific Railroad team of Dallas, composed of ex-college players like himself, defeated Oklahoma 11-5. That game marked the first time an Oklahoma football team ever played at the Texas State Fair. McMahan, who just graduated from UT Law School, asked for the coaching job to pay back his school expenses. He was hired under the condition that he would teach the OU team the wing shift, the trick play the Dallas team used to defeat the Sooners. McMahan's style was a mixture of the popular Princeton vogue he had learned at Austin combined with some moves he learned from the coach of the Dallas team, Charley Moran. He stressed line play and introduced the first tackling dummy in Norman. McMahan was known to suit up and throw some tackles if the team needed him. He liked long, hard schedules and because of that, the 1903 team played more games on the road than any OU team before or since. Of the 12 games in two months, only two were played in Norman. After repaying his law school debts, McMahan moved to Durant in the winter of 1903 to practice law.

YEAR-BY-YEAR RECORD

Year	W	L	T	Pct.	Pts.	Pts.	Captains
1902	6	3	0	.667	175	60	Clyde Bogle, Norman, Okla.
1903	5	4	3	.555	126	85	Clyde Bogle, Norman, Okla.

15. ADRIAN "AD" LINDSEY, 1927-1931

Alma Mater	Years Coached	W	L	T	Pct.	Pts.	Avg.	Opp. Pts.	Opp. Avg.
Kansas	5	19	19	6	.500	511	12.1	435	10.3

Oklahoma's seventh football coach, Adrian "Ad" Lindsey is remembered as the coach who resigned quietly after failing to produce a winning team. Lindsey's record (19-19-6) was not that bad, however. His players were small in size and number and the schedules they faced were too difficult for such a small squad. Lindsey's 1929 team defeated Nebraska, 20-7, marking the worst defeat the Cornhuskers saw from a Big Six team in two decades. In 1931, he took his team and defeated the University of Hawaii in Hawaii 7-0. This game marked the first time a university from the midwest was asked to play in the islands. Before coming to Oklahoma, Lindsey was an assistant football coach at Kansas, his alma mater. After his coaching tenure with the Sooners, Lindsey returned to KU as the head football coach until 1938. He also played professional baseball for the Pittsburgh Pirates from 1921 to 1925 and in Montreal for the Canadian League from 1925 to 1927. Lindsey fought with the Army in World War II and retired as a colonel in 1954. He died at age 85 in 1980.

YEAR-BY-YEAR RECORD

Year	W	L	T	Pct.	Pts.	Pts.	Captains
1927	3	3	2	.500	122	101	Granville Norris, Laverne, Okla.
1928	5	3	0	.625	120	88	Bill Hamilton, Ardmore, Okla.
1929	3	3	2	.500	81	81	Frank Crider, Durant, Okla.
Year	W	L	T	Pct.	Pts.	Pts.	Captains
1930	4	3	1	.571	100	57	Bob Fields, Ponca City, Okla.
1931	4	7	1	.363	88	108	Guy Warren, Norman, Okla.